The First American
Declaration
of Independence?

The First American Declaration of Independence?

The Disputed History of the Mecklenburg Declaration of May 20, 1775

SCOTT SYFERT

McFarland & Company, Inc., Publishers
Jefferson, North Carolina

LIBRARY OF CONGRESS CATALOGUING-IN-PUBLICATION DATA

Syfert, Scott.
The First American Declaration of Independence? : the disputed history
of the Mecklenburg Declaration of May 20, 1775 / Scott Syfert.
p.   cm.
Includes bibliographical references and index.

ISBN 978-0-7864-7559-9
softcover : acid free paper ∞

1. Mecklenburg Declaration of Independence.   2. Mecklenburg County (N.C.)—
Politics and government—18th century.   3. North Carolina—Politics and
government—To 1775.   4. United States—Politics and government.   I. Title.

E215.9.S94 2014   975.6'76—dc23   2013046128

BRITISH LIBRARY CATALOGUING DATA ARE AVAILABLE

On the cover: *Colonel Thomas Polk Reading the
Mecklenburg Declaration of Independence,
May 20, 1775* (courtesy artist Dan Nance)

Manufactured in the United States of America

*McFarland & Company, Inc., Publishers
Box 611, Jefferson, North Carolina 28640
www.mcfarlandpub.com*

To Harrison and Madison,
future lovers of history

Table of Contents

Acknowledgments

In writing this book I am indebted to many, many people for inspiration, encouragement and assistance. But let me mention just a few who are foremost. Jim Williams of the Mecklenburg Historical Association and his wife, Ann, read countless drafts of the book and provided invaluable insights on the lives and characters of the early Scots-Irish settlers. Jim spent many hours over more than a few pints helping me to understand Thomas Polk, Ephraim Brevard and the other central characters, and the spirit of the times. He was always in good spirits and frequently pointed out that "history should be fun." Amen. He is a true historical amateur, in its classical sense, meaning one who acts out of love.

Jane Johnson of the Carolina Room of the Charlotte Public Library is without question the most tireless promoter of MecDec in Charlotte. For the last six years, every week or so a bundle of papers would arrive from Jane with different clues. She ran down numerous leads and challenged my assumptions throughout. Without her indefatigable research and commitment, this book would have been impossible. Thanks, Jane.

Mary Boyer, a descendent of one of the main characters in the story (Hezekiah Alexander), provided archival material she had collected over the course of a lifetime and pushed me to get the facts right. Early in the process, I gulped with apprehension when Mary showed me her vast archival collection. I remember thinking, *This is going to be a lot harder than I thought* and *What have I gotten myself into?* Her research brought the characters, in particular the main man, John McKnitt Alexander, to life for me. She is a patriot.

Jim, Ann, Jane and Mary showed me the story was vital and important and set a high bar for getting the details correct.

Dr. Tony Zeiss of Central Piedmont Community College provided boundless enthusiasm and energy, which I often needed and sought to emulate. Jim Puckett spent a rainy morning in February driving me around the Revolutionary War sites in the area, including Hopewell Presbyterian Church and Cowan's Ford. Thanks, Jim, it made the story real — which I have attempted to do here.

I have been lucky to have smart, dedicated and relentless assistants at many steps in the process. In particular, Julie Lentz, Megan Brooks, Collins Bailey, and Danny Moyer undertook countless thankless research and editing tasks, so I am thanking them each now. Ann Wicker read and gave me great editorial suggestions. Special thanks go to my agent, Sally McMillan.

Thanks to Joe Epley for reading the manuscript and making helpful suggestions. His novel *Passel of Hate* brings to life much of the history of the period, and I highly recommend it.

Noted historians Andrew Roberts and Ken Burns took the time to read this work as well, for which I am most grateful and humbled.

Gary Ritter and Hugh Dussek, professors at Central Piedmont Community College, were gracious enough to read this manuscript.

Dozens of other individuals helped me find missing documents or images, gave suggestions or assisted in other ways. These include the staff of the Carolina Room of the Charlotte Public Library (thanks Tom Cole); Kim Andersen, William Brown, Christopher Meekins and Matt Waehner of the North Carolina State Archives; Matt Turi and Keith Longiotti of Wilson Library at the University of North Carolina at Chapel Hill; Barbara Taylor; Kyna Herzinger of Tryon Palace in New Bern; Carol Jones of the Charleston Library Society (who found and allowed me to see firsthand the Mecklenburg Resolves); Richard Starbuck of the Moravian Archives in Winston-Salem; Bill Pfitzer of the *Charlotte Observer*, who edited the map of Captain Jack's ride to Philadelphia; Liam Fox for challenging me; Lauren Robinson, my graphic artist, who has always done great work; Dan Nance, a superb artist and friend who permitted me to use his unique images of the Battle of Charlotte, Queen's College and the Reading of the Mecklenburg Declaration in this work; Will Puckett, whose unique artistic vision I was proud and privileged to watch unfold when he painted the Matheson Street Bridge (and his fab wife, Lauren) and who permitted me to use the sketches of the arrest of Booth and Dunn and Alexander Craighead; Chas Fagan, whose artistic excellence is a constant inspiration and who has devoted untold hours to keeping the MecDec flame burning (thanks for the use of the image of Captain Jack riding north); the boards of the Trail of History, the May 20th Society, Bob Morgan and Mike Smith for their time and energy; and of course Charles Jonas, who sucked me into this whole project a decade ago over too many glasses of wine. To all of them (and others unnamed) I owe a great debt of gratitude, respect and humility. But, as is said, any errors in the book remain solely mine.

Most important, the kids deserve my thanks. Maddie, my daughter, endured a few Revolutionary War reenactments with patience. My challenge was always how to make history interesting for Maddie. Thanks for keeping me centered.

And for every Sherlock Holmes there is a Dr. Watson. My own Watson was my son, Harrison. For five years Harrison rode around with me on Saturday or Sunday afternoon field trips. We visited McKnitt's grave at Hopewell; the ruins of Davidson's home at Rural Hill in northern Mecklenburg; the forgotten headstones in the woods of Clear Creek Burying Ground; the cemetery at Steele Creek Presbyterian Church, where Humphrey and other signers lie buried; and the battlefields of Cowan's Ford, Kings Mountain, Guilford Courthouse and the Cowpens. Harrison endured having his picture taken at more obscure historical cemeteries than any other 12-year-old in America. He didn't know it at the time, but he was my investigative partner in this process and I couldn't have done it without him. Thanks, MLHB.

Finally, thanks to my parents, whose lives of education and public service remain a beacon, and my wife, Gail, for putting up with this private obsession for over a decade and who was my devoted proofreader.

To everyone who touched this process, visited a graveyard, stood in the cold at a reenactment, or gave me their thoughts I say thank you and — *huzzah!*

Preface

Even 239 years later the story of whether Mecklenburg County, North Carolina, made the first declaration of independence in the American colonies (known as the Mecklenburg Declaration of Independence, or more colloquially the "MecDec") continues to arouse strong passions. Most of the academic historical community dismisses the story as (at best) a myth or (at worst) a ridiculous hoax. The widely held view is that the Mecklenburg Declaration is a fairy tale, but an irritating one that refuses to go away. Even in Charlotte, where the story begins, raising the topic can elicit a visceral, negative response.

Supporters of MecDec are fewer, but no less passionate in their views. For over two centuries, die-hard enthusiasts in Mecklenburg have refused to let the story die. Some are local historians; others advocate the story out of civic pride; while still others (at last count, more than 1,400 nationally) are direct descendants of key participants in the tale. To say these people *believe* the story of the Mecklenburg Declaration of Independence is an understatement. They are zealous, committed advocates to the cause. Between MecDec supporters and MecDec doubters, there is little common ground.

At the outset I should declare an interest: I believe the story of the Mecklenburg Declaration of Independence, and this preference (or bias, if you prefer) may come through in this book. That being said, however, this work is not intended as a polemical work "proving" the story is true. I have attempted to remain objective and faithful to the facts and the arguments, even where they lead to a conclusion perhaps contrary to my own beliefs. This book is an attempt to tell the tale in its entirety, warts and all.

As an attorney, I see both sides of the argument for and against the MecDec; and make no mistake, there is a considerable body of evidence in favor of both sides. Believers point to the existing written records, the testimony of numerous and highly credible eyewitnesses and the enduring local legend — in particular, the Moravian chronicles which record that the county declared itself "free and independent" in the summer of 1775. None of this is definitive proof, but as circumstantial evidence, it is very good, and there is a lot of it.

On the other hand, the skeptics, particularly the historians William Hoyt and A.S. Salley, Jr., provided compelling arguments that the story is false. They argued that the existing written evidence, such as John McKnitt Alexander's "rough notes" and the "copy in an unknown hand" (both found after Alexander's death and in questionable condition) simply suffer too many evidentiary failings to prove anything. They believe that the story of a (fictitious) Mecklenburg Declaration was confused with a (true) historical document called

1

the Mecklenburg Resolves. In short, they think the entire saga is a case of mistaken identity. They make some excellent arguments in support of this theory. But even their best arguments remain simply that — arguments.

To a legal mind, the evidence, to the frustration of both camps, is simply inconclusive. The skeptics are no closer to "proving" the story is false than the supporters are in "proving" it is real. We have a hung jury. This is what makes the controversy fresh and alive, just as it was nearly two hundred years ago, when President John Adams declared that the Mecklenburg Declaration represented the "genuine sense of America" while Thomas Jefferson deemed the tale "spurious."

My own belief, after exhaustive research, discussion and thought on the subject over more than a decade, is that the "truth" of whether the Mecklenburg Declaration of Independence existed cannot, on the existing evidence, be definitively proven or disproven, at least not to the satisfaction of everyone. Whether one believes the story comes down to personal preference, and, in particular, whether one believes the testimony of the eyewitnesses. As the historian Andrew Roberts well put it, "if twenty-six North Carolinians say that something took place, my inclination as a historian is to believe them." I stand with Roberts.

Nor in my view does the existence of the Mecklenburg Resolves (which are dated May 31, 1775, and which are argued to represent the only "true" resolutions adopted in Charlotte) "disprove" the story of the Mecklenburg Declaration of May 20, as many seem to believe. On the contrary, the Resolves can quite easily be interpreted as validating the overall story. Again, the evidence can be read two ways.

Is the story of the Mecklenburg Declaration "genuine" or "spurious"?

You be the judge.

Prologue
"One of the deepest mysteries"

The genuine sense of America at that moment was never expressed so well before, nor since.

—Letter from John Adams to Thomas Jefferson, June 22, 1819

Early on the morning of Friday, May 19, 1775, John McKnitt Alexander of Mecklenburg County, in the Royal Province of North Carolina, rode his horse slowly south along a narrow dirt path. His destination was the county courthouse in the village of Charlotte, a small hamlet of less than a hundred people. A meeting of local militia leaders, of which McKnitt was one, had been scheduled for later that day. Two representatives from each of the county's nine militia companies had been summoned to attend.

McKnitt lived in the northern part of Mecklenburg, on a sprawling tract of land that he called "Alexandriana." Alexandriana was a plantation with gently rolling hills, oaks, maples, and other hardwoods, a handful of modest sandy creeks, and at least one natural spring, not far from McKnitt's hewn-log cabin. In order to reach the meeting in Charlotte in good time, McKnitt left early on the morning of May 19, not long after sunrise. Although McKnitt was his middle name, he signed his name "J. McKnitt" and McKnitt was the name his friends and neighbors knew him by. His name pronounced "M'Nitt" or "McKnight," he was a well-known and respected figure in the county.

Friday was a day of fasting among the devout Presbyterians in Mecklenburg. It was a preparation day for religious services on Saturday and Sunday, the latter being so holy that, it was said, not even cracking walnuts was permitted. On Friday services the minister pointed out the duties of self-examination and personal commitment to God. These services were mandatory for believers like McKnitt, who was also a church elder, so he probably attended service at Hopewell Presbyterian Church before his ride into Charlotte. For McKnitt and his fellow Presbyterians in Mecklenburg, the Word of God took precedence over earthly worries or obligations.

The weather on the ride into town was warm and humid, as it invariably is in late May in the Carolinas. The forest path was overhung with lime-green boughs full of spring leaves. Although it was only mid–morning, a bright, arcing sun shone through the forest canopy, causing shadows and fragments of green light to bounce as if underwater. It was silent. The only sounds other than the clop-clop of his horse were the energetic, saw-mill-like buzz of insects and the tinny caw of crows high in the trees. Squirrels and white-tailed deer moved in the underbrush on the periphery of McKnitt's vision. Otherwise the forest was still.

Men on horseback were rare here on the western frontier of Britain's North American colonies. Indeed, there was scant evidence of human existence in 99 percent of Mecklenburg County at all. The county had no cobblestoned roads nor any industry. The cotton gin would not be invented for another twenty-three years; the steam-powered locomotive for twenty-eight; and the lightbulb for more than a century. The most complicated machines within a hundred miles of McKnitt that morning were a few primitive open-hearth blast furnaces for smelting iron and tin and a dozen or so water-turned saw and grist mills along a few rocky creeks. Only three homes in the county were made of stone; the rest were log or wooden cabins, and of these only one was even painted. Mecklenburg was virtually uninhabited, pristine, primitive and quiet. This was the *back*country, both geographically and metaphorically. *Back* because the colonists, intellectually and spiritually, faced East towards the mother country and home.

The Indian trading path on which McKnitt rode was known by many names. To some it was the *Iroquois Path* or the *Great Warriors Path*, so-called because it ran north from the Carolinas to the Iroquois tribes of New York. South of the county it was called the *Path to*

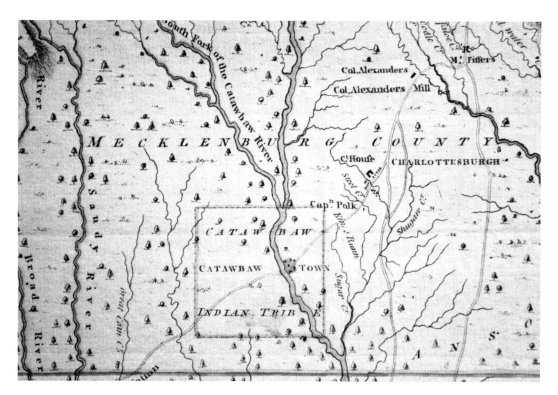

The town is named "Charlottesburgh" in John Collet's *Compleat Map of North Carolina* (1770). Thomas Polk's house and the county courthouse can both be seen (courtesy Tryon Palace, New Bern, North Carolina).

the Cherokee Nation (as shown on the *Compleat Map of North Carolina from an Actual Survey* by Swiss cartographer John Collet in 1770). On *A Map of the Most Inhabited Part of Virginia* (1751), surveyed in part by Thomas Jefferson's father, Peter, it was called the *Trading Path Leading to the Catawban and Cherokee Indian Nations*.[1]

North of Mecklenburg County it was called the Salisbury Road, for the road passed through Salisbury, where the district court was held, forty-odd miles north of Charlotte, and the nearest, and largest, neighboring settlement. Salisbury at the time consisted of "forty or fifty straggling houses in an open pretty plain," one observer wrote in 1781, and was "a poor place and has but little business," with only "300 inhabitants among them a great number of children."[2] Past Salisbury, after crossing the Yadkin River it was called the Great Wagon Road or the Philadelphia Road, and was among the most heavily trafficked arteries of commerce in the American colonies.[3]

By whatever name the road was known, travel on it was difficult, dangerous and slow. One traveler riding through the region in May 1791 recalled "[f]or twelve or fourteen miles the road is very disagreeable, being hilly, and broken by deep gullies, and passes through several creeks, which in wet weather must be extremely bad." Further along the road to Charlotte it was "abominable, a succession of steep hills, full of deep gullies and large rocks, intermixed with root stumps and ruts."[4]

Regardless of the travel conditions, McKnitt rode with a purpose. The agenda for that day's meeting was to discuss the unsettled, volatile and increasingly alarming state of affairs in the American colonies. By the spring of 1775, the American colonies were in turmoil, or, as Lord Dartmouth put it in a letter to North Carolina Royal Governor Josiah Martin, a "state of general frenzy."[5] The principal issue was Parliament's continued insistence on taxing tea imported from India. Taxation had long been a contentious subject in America. The Americans were not represented by elected officials in Parliament, and thus taxation was regarded by the American colonists as illegal and arbitrary — little more than government sanctioned theft. Earlier protests in the colonies had led to the repeal of the despised Stamp Act, but in May 1775 the tea tax remained. Attempts by the British to enforce the tax only exacerbated tensions.

Two years earlier, on the night of December 16, 1773, a handful of New England citizens, some disguised as Mohawk Indians, boarded three merchant ships owned by the East India Company tied up at Griffin's Wharf and dumped 342 chests of tea, worth more than £90,000 sterling, into Boston harbor. "The Parliament of Great Britain, transported with indignation against the people of Boston," in the words of *A History of the American Revolution* (1789), "in a fit of rage resolved to take legislative vengeance, on that devoted town."[6] The port of Boston was ordered shut by Parliament. British warships patrolled the harbor, enforcing the blockade. British redcoats (or "lobster backs," as they were called by the townspeople) were garrisoned in the city to enforce martial law. The harbor blockaded and the place occupied, disease and starvation appeared to doom the city.

Throughout the American colonies, alarmist stories of the starving and suffering city quickly spread. Boston became a symbol for British oppression. "The cause of Boston was the cause of all" captured the sentiment of the time.[7] "Pamphlets, essays, addresses and newspaper dissertations were daily presented to the public," said one history of the time, "proving that Massachusetts was suffering in the common cause, and that interest and policy, as well as good neighborhood, required the united exertions of all the colonies, in support of that much injured province."[8] Meetings were held throughout America and various resolutions proclaimed. "The Cause of the Town of Boston is the common Cause of the American Colonies," declared the "freeholders" of Rowan County on August 8, 1774.[9] Rowan County was adjacent to Mecklenburg.

Meanwhile, in Mecklenburg, neighbors met in the two local taverns, Cook's Inn or Pat Jack's, or drank peach brandy near the spring at McKnitt's home and asked one another *what is to be done?* Hard choices faced them on every side. The sentiment was that "their destinies were indissolubly connected with those of their Eastern fellow-citizens — and that they must either submit to all the impositions which an unprincipled, and to them an unrepresentative, Parliament might impose — or support their brethren who were doomed to sustain the first shock of that power, which, if successful there, would ultimately overwhelm all in the common calamity."[10]

It was in this alarming and troubled atmosphere that Colonel Thomas Polk, the commander of the county militia, requested a meeting of the militia leaders of the county. A summons was sent forth, McKnitt would later write, "to each Captain of Militia in his regiment of Mecklenburg County, to elect, nominate and appoint 2 persons of their militia company, clothed with ample powers to devise ways & means to extricate themselves and ward off the dreadful impending storm bursting on them by the British Nation."[11] The location of the meeting was the Mecklenburg County courthouse, a rustic, unpainted log cabin which stood atop six red brick pillars, each ten feet high, in the middle of Charlotte. Word of the meeting spread from church to church and from farm to farm. By May 19, concerned citizens from throughout the region converged on the courthouse.

The hamlet of Charlotte — like the county of Mecklenburg — had been named in honor of Queen Charlotte of Mecklenburg-Strelitz, the wife of King George III. Seven years after her marriage to the king of England in the Royal Chapel at St. James Palace, the faraway North Carolina general assembly passed "An Act for Establishing a Town in Mecklenburg County." In those days it was customary to name towns and counties after prominent personages and since the county had been named after her birthplace, it was only logical to name the city after her as well. And thus the 1768 act provided that "a Town and Town Common" be "hereby constituted, erected, and established ... called by the Name of Charlotte."[12] And in a bizarre coincidence, May 19 — the day scheduled for the meeting — happened to be the queen's thirty-first birthday

The name of Charlotte was a fitting choice, although not in the way anyone intended. By most accounts, the queen was not very attractive. While the writer Horace Walpole wrote that she "looks very sensible," Charles Dickens described Queen Charlotte as a "queen with a plain face" in the opening of *A Tale of Two Cities*. In her official portrait (which hangs in a massive wood-paneled reception room in the House of Lords in London), she appears thin and pale, with a long bird-like neck and a collapsing chin. "She was famously ugly," according to Desmond Shawe-Taylor, surveyor of the queen's pictures. "A courtier once said of Charlotte late in life, 'Her Majesty's ugliness has quite faded.'"[13]

Like the queen for which the new town was named, the newly chartered settlement was squat, dour and unappealing. In fact it consisted of nothing more than a dozen or so unpainted log cabins huddled around a muddy intersection. William Moultrie, a survey commissioner passing through Charlotte in May 1772 wrote, "The town has a tolerable Court-House of wood about 80 by 40 feet, and a Gaol [jail], a store, a tavern, and several other houses say 5 or 6, but very ordinary build of logs."[14] By 1775 there were two or three taverns, likely built in the style common to colonial Pennsylvania, from where many of the town residents had come. Just north up Tryon Street stood the county jail and nearby were a pillory, stocks and a whipping post.

In the summer the town stank of wood-smoke, manure and hogs, while in the rainy

Sir Allan Ramsay's 1762 portrait of Queen Charlotte. Both Mecklenburg County and the village of Charlotte were named for her (collection of the Mint Museum, Charlotte, North Carolina. Gift of Mr. Frank Ryan Harty. 1970.56).

spring it was a mud pit. Nor was it very civilized. There was sufficient gunplay in the town that in 1774 a royal act decreed that "no Person whatsoever shall shoot with a Gun except it be to kill Cattle or Hogs."[15] All around these primitive buildings stood a vast and dark forest of scrub pine, brush, and hardwoods. "[T]he plantations in the neighborhood were small and uncultivated," British lieutenant-colonel Banastre Tarleton would later write, while the roads "were narrow, and crossed in every direction."[16]

One visitor summed the place up perfectly. "This place does not deserve the name of a town," William Loughton Smith, a thirty-three-year-old lawyer from Charleston, recorded in his journal of May 1791. Charlotte he wrote "consists only of a wretched courthouse, and a few dwellings falling to decay." (Smith was further nonplussed that at Mason's Tavern in Charlotte he "paid the dearest bill on the road."[17]) It was, as General Washington accurately said upon visiting in 1791, "a trifling place."[18] Indeed, Charlotte was so small and rustic that it was not even clear what its proper name was. While Tarleton called it "Charlotte Towne" in his memoirs, the most accurate map of the time (Collet's *A Compleat Map of North Carolina*) gives the village as "Charlottesburgh." In *A New and Accurate Map of North Carolina in America* published in 1779 the town does not even appear at all.[19] This makes it all the more remarkable that this nondescript backwoods cross-roads would become the setting for one of the greatest American historical controversies of all time. Was this the location of the first declaration of independence in America?

As the story was later told, on the afternoon of May 19 — at the meeting to which McKnitt was riding — following a furious debate in the log courthouse in Charlotte, the citizens of Mecklenburg resolved to declare themselves "free and independent" from Great Britain. They drafted, debated and unanimously adopted the first declaration of independence in the American colonies. It was called the Mecklenburg Declaration of Independence. And it was written in language that was magisterial, succinct and timeless. As President John Adams would later write, "The genuine sense of America at that moment was never expressed so well before, nor since."[20]

The Mecklenburg Declaration was less than a page long and consisted of only five, brief resolutions, the third of which read, "We do hereby declare ourselves a free and independent people ... to the maintenance of which independence, we solemnly pledge to each other, our mutual co-operation, our lives, our fortunes and our most sacred honor."[21]

As the story went, the people of Mecklenburg then tasked a local tavern owner and militia Captain named James Jack to deliver the resolutions to North Carolina's three elected delegates at the Second Continental Congress in Philadelphia. Captain Jack completed his mission, delivering the Mecklenburg Declaration in June 1775, but the delegates deemed it "premature." And all this had taken place almost fifteen months before July 4, 1776, while national figures such as George Washington, Benjamin Franklin and Thomas Jefferson were still contemplating reconciliation with Great Britain, not independence. It was the first American declaration of independence, a document that many argued deserved to be ranked with the Magna Carta and the French Rights of Man.

However, not everyone believed that the document existed. There were a number of problems with this so-called Mecklenburg Declaration of Independence, which Jefferson, among others, was quick to point out. Why had no one ever heard of it? The three congressional delegates to whom Captain Jack delivered the Mecklenburg Declaration never mentioned it, nor do the records of the Continental Congress. Nor apparently was it ever published. "How is it possible that this paper should have been concealed from me to this day?" John Adams would ask many years later.[22]

Then there was the question of the language of the Mecklenburg Declaration itself. Elegant, perhaps, but also strangely familiar: *Our lives, our fortunes & our sacred honor; inalienable rights; dissolve the political bands.* The phrases sounded much — perhaps too much — like the Declaration of Independence of July 4, 1776, the famous document written in Philadelphia over a year later.

Was this a coincidence? Was the Mecklenburg Declaration a loose copy, after the fact, of Jefferson's Declaration of July 4? Or perhaps the opposite was true. Perhaps Jefferson had plagiarized from the Mecklenburg Declaration. As bizarre and conspiratorial as this sounded, no less than an authority as Adams believed this might be the case. "Either these resolutions are a plagiarism from Mr. Jefferson's Declaration of Independence," Adams would privately write to a friend, "or Mr. Jefferson's Declaration of Independence is a plagiarism from those resolutions."[23] And as it happened, one of the North Carolina delegates to whom Captain Jack delivered a copy of the Mecklenburg Declaration was William Hooper, later a member of the committee charged with drafting the National Declaration, and a friend of Jefferson. Had Hooper (or even Jefferson) copied the Mecklenburg Declaration and then covered it up? Was this the original government conspiracy? Finally, and the biggest mystery of all, if the Mecklenburg Declaration did exist, *where was it?*

The man with all of these answers was John McKnitt Alexander. It was McKnitt who acted as secretary of the convention of May 19–20, 1775. He was the chief eyewitness. He retained all of the original records of the convention. Unfortunately, by the time these questions were asked, McKnitt was dead, and with him the secrets that he alone held. As to the most important question — *Where was the Mecklenburg Declaration?*—that was the easiest to answer. The original was gone, destroyed. On April 6, 1800, a fire at McKnitt's home at Alexandriana destroyed the original minute book and any surviving originals of the Mecklenburg Declaration of Independence.

Later a myth arose that all the papers associated with the Mecklenburg Declaration were lost. This is not true. Several of McKnitt's papers survived the fire, including his handwritten notes. But these records only deepened the mystery. The surviving papers were fragmentary, torn, undated and — in a critical instance — not in McKnitt's handwriting. And the only man who could make sense of them, who could explain what they meant, and who wrote them — McKnitt himself — was long dead. These ambiguous writings would confuse and confound a century of historians, leading to what became known as the "Mecklenburg Controversy." It was — and remains — a controversy over whether the Mecklenburg Declaration ever existed at all.

And so the story of the Mecklenburg Declaration would in many ways become the story of John McKnitt Alexander. He was bound up in it, and the story was bound up with him. As the "Mecklenburg Controversy" exploded in the early nineteenth century, McKnitt would become a local hero and a national joke — venerated by his fellow citizens in Mecklenburg and denounced as a crazy old man by people in Boston and New York. McKnitt himself became the controversy. Because if you believed his written testimony, the Mecklenburg Declaration was real. It all happened just as he said. And *if* the Mecklenburg Declaration existed, as John Adams understood, its importance to American history is profound. If it were authentic, all conceptions and understandings of American history would change.

The stories of Patrick Henry and Nathan Hale would be arguably secondary to those of McKnitt and Polk, the ride of Paul Revere around Boston superseded entirely by the epic ride of Captain Jack to Philadelphia (over 1,100 miles). The focus of the American Revolution would shift from New England to the thinly settled backwoods of North Carolina. Possibly, an entire new founding legend would be born, new heroes and icons made, and the settled versions of the American Revolution recast in a new light. In short, everything we know or think we know about the founding of America would change.

As Adams instinctively sensed, if the Mecklenburg Declaration had been published in the summer of 1775 in the midst of the national furor over the massacres at Lexington and Concord, it might — *might* — have pushed the Continental Congress to act a year earlier on national independence. It *might* have encouraged larger and more influential towns — Charleston, Philadelphia, New York, Boston — to pass similar resolves for independence. It *might* have started a national debate and put outright independence on the table for discussion in the summer of 1775. It *might* have pushed forward America's independence by more than a year, fundamentally altering the nature of the war that followed and the country that was born as a result of it. It *might* have thrust McKnitt, Polk and others into the national spotlight and turned them into national leaders or even future presidents. (If this seems farfetched consider that a grandnephew of Thomas Polk born just outside Charlotte, James K. Polk, became the eleventh American president and that *another* Polk, Leonidas Lafayette Polk, would have been the People's Party nominee for president in 1892 but for his sudden and unexpected death from stomach cancer.) All of these things *might* have happened directly and logically as a result of the meeting in Charlotte on the afternoon of May 19, 1775.

But these things didn't happen. History was largely silent about the events in Mecklenburg in May 1775, which led many to question whether the Mecklenburg Declaration even happened at all. After all, was it conceivable that these backwoods settlers would have had the gumption, the motivation and the courage to take such an action in the first place? Or was the entire story simply the confused recollections of an old man, John McKnitt Alexander, or worse, a deliberate fabrication? The whole convoluted, entangled and cloudy story was, said Adams, "one of the greatest curiosities and one of the deepest mysteries that ever occurred to me."[24]

PART I. LIFE IN THE CAROLINA BACKCOUNTRY (1663–1775)

1

"Always insolent to their Governors"
The Rule of the Lords Proprietors

The whole Country is a Stage of Debauchery Dissoluteness and Corruption—And how can it be otherwise? The People are compos'd of the Out Casts of all the other Colonies who take Refuge there.

—Diary of Charles Woodmason, 1765

If it were true that the hamlet of Charlotte (or Charlotteburgh or Charlotte Towne, according to taste) "did not deserve the name of a town," as attorney William Loughton Smith sniffed in 1791, one could just as easily conclude that the Royal Province of North Carolina scarcely deserved to be called a *Province*. In 1775, *North Carolina* was a geographic expression—like *Africa* or the *equator*—not a coherent or homogenous political entity. Its territory encompassed a huge cross section of the eastern coast and contained a diverse mix of inhabitants (Englishmen and Englishwomen, highland and lowland Scots, Czech Moravians, Palatinate Germans, Protestant Swiss, both Catholic and Protestant Irish, African slaves and indigenous American Indians) living in small communities which stretched from the pines and scrub land of the coastal plains through the rolling savannahs of central Carolina to the rising foothills and terraced Appalachian Mountains.

In many respects, the *state* of North Carolina—as we understand the term today, with its associated apparatus of laws, courts and democratic institutions—barely existed. There was, in a sense, no state. Royal Governors in theory held supreme executive authority, but often they were absent, corrupt or drunk. The general assembly was regularly at odds with the governor and consequently prorogued or even forbidden to meet. For years at a time, the entire province would degenerate into lawlessness. "The whole colony was in a state of anarchy and confusion," wrote the historian Wheeler in the nineteenth century *Sketches of North Carolina*, describing the year 1771. "The courts were closed; public crime and private injustice had no check."[1]

There were few roads, all of which were largely dirt paths, treacherous and difficult to maintain. On November 10, 1766, Representative Hugh Waddell presented a petition to the Provincial General Assembly from "several of the Inhabitants of Rowan, Anson, and Mecklenburg" counties decrying the "many great hardships they endure for want of roads."[2] There were no bridges over the various rivers and creeks that crosshatched the land. Safe passage could be found only through fording a waterway when the flood was low or paying a ferryman to take one across. There was no census at the time, so we don't know how many residents of the province there were, and the number changed daily as more immigrants arrived in ships or pulled wagons into the interior. Most of the land was entirely unpopulated and therefore up for grabs.

There was no uniform currency, no shared religion, not even a common language. In addition to the English coastal towns, there were small scattered communities of Gaelic-speaking Scots; Celtic-speaking Irishmen; Welsh; German-speaking Swiss; *Hochdeutsch*-speaking Moravians; French Huguenots; West African slaves with various dialects; as well as the multiple languages of the indigenous Indians (the Indians themselves, it is estimated, had possibly as many as 150 individual languages throughout the colonies). The disparate nature of the population was reflected in the names the people gave their settlements: Germantown, Salisbury, Jersey, Ayr, Mackey, New Bern, Dutch Creek, Irish Settlement, New Scotland and so forth.

The province of "Carolina" was born on March 24, 1663, when amidst the flickering of torches in the ancient palace of Westminster along the River Thames, King Charles II signed a Royal Charter (known as the Great Charter) bequeathing eight peers and their "heirs and assigns, all that territory or tract of ground, situate, lying and being within our dominions of America" between 31° and 36° northern latitude, from the Atlantic coast, clear across the continent to the "Great South Seas." To these lucky few (whose names are now given to towns and counties throughout the region) was bequeathed a new province–*Carolina*, a Latin diminutive for the king's name. The eight men who owned Carolina were called the "Lords Proprietors." To them Carolina was first and foremost a business enterprise.

The province would only generate income for its owners if it were populated and its inhabitants engaged in farming or other income-generating activities and, consequently, paying taxes. Although there were a handful of settlers at the time, the vast majority of the province was uninhabited. The few European settlers who had made it to America and survived their first winter clung to wretched outposts on the coast. Even by the early 1700s, no European had been more than a hundred miles inland from the Atlantic seaboard, much less crossed the Appalachians. The Lords Proprietors' first order of business, therefore, was to encourage settlement — or to put it differently, to generate customers.

This was not easy. Convincing a man to abandon his land, country and settled life to embark upon a highly dangerous, largely speculative and one-way trip to an unknown wilderness thousands of miles from home made for an extraordinarily difficult sales pitch. It took a mixture of desperation and recklessness to cause someone to make for the American colonies, much less the remote Carolina territory, and at first few did so. By 1725, the entire population of the province remained at less than 13,000.

In order to induce would-be immigrants to make this long and dangerous trip, the Proprietors offered a variety of incentives. The first was the promise of religious freedom. Although the charter directed that churches in Carolina were to be "dedicated and consecrated according to the ecclesiastical laws," there was a loophole. The Proprietors were permitted to grant "indulgences and dispensations" to those "who really, in their Judgments, and for consciences sake," could not conform to the rituals and beliefs of the Church of England.[3] The Proprietors used this to great advantage. One promotional brochure for Carolina in 1666 promised "[t]here is full and free Liberty of Conscience granted to all, so that no man is to be molested or called in question for matters of Religious Concern; but every one to be obedient to the Civil Government, worshipping God after their own way."[4]

The allure of religious liberty was especially powerful. In Europe in that time, religion was inextricably bound up with the state in a way that is now difficult for us to understand. Every European principality had an officially sanctioned state faith: there was Catholic France and Spain, Orthodox Russia, and of course, the Church of England. Religious minorities — Jews, Huguenots, Moravians, Presbyterians — were everywhere repressed, sometimes violently. From the first wave of Puritan settlers to the northeast coast of America in the 1620s, the freedom to practice a non-state-sanctioned faith was arguably the single greatest motivation to would-be immigrants to the American colonies.

A second incentive was economic — the opportunity for a better life. Europe was rigidly divided into classes: noblemen, a newly emerging mercantile or "middle" class, and the peasantry. Whatever class one was born into, one rarely escaped it. In the New World, however, these class distinctions largely did not exist, and where they did, movement between them was more fluid. Third, and perhaps most important, was the chance of owning land. Where land was even available in Europe it was expensive. Most poor people rented or leased their land and were at the mercy of their landlords.

Whether under compulsion or by free choice, drawn by the lure of religious toleration, economic opportunity, desperation or adventure, settlers began populating North Carolina. Many came as indentured servants, meaning they worked for five to seven years to repay the ship owners who effected their passage. "Let no man be troubled at the thoughts of being a Servant for 4 or 5 year," one promotional circular explained, "so soon as he is out of his time, he hath Land, and Tools, and Clothes given him, and is in a way of advancement."[5]

Where the temptation of cheap land or religious tolerance was insufficient, the Proprietors employed another common sales technique: false advertising. This was widespread. Promotional brochures were distributed in England, Scotland, Ireland, and the various fiefdoms of central Europe calculated to appeal to the lower classes, religious dissenters, adventurers, or the dispossessed. John Lawson, an early explorer and surveyor of North Carolina employed by the Proprietors, wrote in 1707 of "the easy Way of living in that plentiful Country."[6] "The Inhabitants of Carolina, thro' the Richness of the Soil, live an easy and pleasant life," he wrote. "[It is] a Country that, with moderate Industry, will afford all the Necessaries of Life."[7] Not only men but also women were invited to immigrate. "If any Maid or single Woman have a desire to go over," one advertising piece announced, "they will think themselves in the Golden Age, when Men paid a Dowry for their Wives; for if they be but Civil, and under 50 years of Age, some honest Man or other, will purchase them for their Wives."[8]

Other sales promotions described it as a veritable Garden of Eden, overflowing with wildlife. "This country hath Oak, Ash, Beech, Elm," wrote one contemporary account, "and sorts of other useful timber that England hath not, as Cedar, Red and White Locust, Laurel."[9] Carolina, it was said, was overflowing with wild game, fish and birds: "[T]he woods are stored of Deer and Wild Turkey of great Magnitude, weighing many times above fifty pounds apiece and of a more pleasant taste than those found in England."[10]

Later nineteenth-century writers, relying on these false accounts, would describe early Carolina in lurid, gushing and romantic terms. It was, wrote John Logan in 1855 in *A History of Upper Carolina*, "new and beautiful and as remarkable for the luxuriant richness of its landscape as it is still for the striking features of its rolling hills and towering mountains."[11] Another described it as "a region of romance,"[12] of "large and extensive plains and savannas, swarming with deer and buffalo."[13] It was a land of "picturesque beauty and grandeur," of plains "carpeted with grass, and the wild pea vine grew, it is said, as high as a horse's back."[14] The land was "the most fertile in the world."[15] The mountains of Carolina were so high the European Alps were "much inferior."[16]

This was utter nonsense. To a frontiersman in 1730, it was rough and dangerous country and many considered the Carolinas the most unhealthy portion of the colonies. In summer, the heat was intense and inescapable. Sunstroke killed farmers at work in the fields. Diseases spread; wounds suppurated and failed to heal; meat and foodstuffs quickly rotted. Travelers complained of omnipresent snakes, mosquitoes, and horseflies. Fear was constant and life was cheap.

Rather than a peaceful and benign Eden, it was a bleak wilderness: silent, remote, largely unexplored and unseen by white Europeans, and populated with wolves, coyotes, black bears and bobcats, as well as tribes of grim, inscrutable and often violent Indians. One indication of the reality of life was the report of one Swiss émigré, Bachschlij Demuth. Leaving Switzerland in 1734, Demuth succeeded in getting to Carolina with his wife and child, after which he was able to get a letter back to his friends, "the contents of which were, that whoever is at home in his fatherland should remain there; he wished he had done so."[17]

The vastness of the wilderness, the availability of land and the lack of authority in the backcountry appealed to the poor, the dispossessed and others on the fringe of society. Lack of major port harbors and navigable inland rivers meant that settlers moving into the interior had to travel on foot, along dangerous and desolate Indian trading paths. People willing to take on such physical challenges were, almost by definition, tough, tenacious, reckless or slightly crazy — and sometimes a combination of all of the above.

They also had to be self-reliant. Settlers could not look to the government for assistance. But that was fine with them. The types of individuals drawn to life in Carolina were, in any event, deeply suspicious of authority. Many were followers of persecuted minority sects (Moravians, Baptists, Quakers, Presbyterians) or political refugees — in other words, people seeking to escape government. To many, it was the total lack of authority in the province that was appealing.

Not surprisingly, "the region was little more than a refuge for thieves, pirates, fleeing criminals, and runaway servants."[18] Carolina was a lawless backwater filled with wild animals and wilder people. Because there were no major port cities, exports and industry could not develop. And what products the province could produce were considered primitive and shoddy. "The Produce of this colony has been with some justice thought of a worse quality when exported than that of its neighbors," wrote Patrick Gordon in a report for royal governor William Tryon in June 1767. This, he explained, was "entirely occasioned by the slovenly way of coopering, dressing, pickling and filling the commodity for exportation and to the fraud and deceit of those who make the goods."[19] "The Manners of the North Carolinians in General, are Vile and Corrupt," wrote one English observer in 1765. "The whole Country is a Stage of Debauchery Dissoluteness and Corruption — And how can it be otherwise? The People are compos'd of the Out Casts of all the other Colonies who take Refuge there." Nor was he impressed with their morals: "Marriages (thro' want of Clergy) are perform'd by ev'ry ordinary Magistrate. Polygamy is very Common.... Bastardy, no disrepute."[20]

Also not surprisingly, North Carolinians had a reputation for being almost entirely ungovernable. The first rebellion in the American colonies — Culpeper's Rebellion — broke out in eastern North Carolina in 1676. Other revolts (such Cary's Rebellion in 1711) were common. Tax collectors, land agents and judges were frequent victims of assault or murder. Even the governors themselves were not immune. Seth Sothel, who had purchased the interest of Lord Clarendon, arrived to govern the province on behalf of the Proprietors in 1683. "Profligate in his habits, licentious in his tastes, sordid and avaricious in his conduct; his administration is marked by every kind of extortion," as one historian summarized his term as Governor.[21] After six years of misrule, he was imprisoned by the colonists, impeached, and deported. As one writer of that era put it, "it was the common practice of the people in North Carolina to resist and imprison their governors, until they looked upon that as lawful which had been so long tolerated."[22]

"The people of North Carolina are neither to be cajoled or outwitted," reported Governor Burrington in a private report to the Duke of Newcastle in 1731:

> The inhabitants of North Carolina are not industrious, but subtle and crafty; always behaved insolently to their governors; some they have imprisoned, others they have drove out of the country, and at other times set up a governor of their own choice, supported by men under arms.[23]

In the end, the logistical and administrative challenges of running the province — coupled with the outright rebelliousness of its citizens — were simply too much for the proprietors. The Province was too expensive and difficult to govern from afar. In 1729, the Lords Proprietors threw in the towel and tendered their equity in the colony back to the king of England in exchange for £2,500 apiece. (Only one of the original eight peers, John, Lord Carteret, later the Earl of Granville, kept his property, a strip of land sixty miles wide below the border with Virginia. His acres were marked off in 1744, becoming known as the "Granville Grant.") Henceforth, the majority of the province was now a royal — meaning British — colony, governed from London and subject to British laws. To those who thought they had escaped British rule, it had now returned to find them.

Although the governance by the Proprietors was flawed and ultimately failed, it had a profound influence on the political development of the state. First, unlike most other colonies, such as the Commonwealth of Virginia, the Province of North Carolina was initially a private business. As such, the settlers had, in their view, entered into a binding legal contract with the Proprietors when they agreed to come to America. This contract, containing binding warranties, was embodied in the Great Charter.

Rights granted under the charter were "peculiar to them as Carolinians," according to the *Colonial and State Records of North Carolina*, and the people "were so fully vested in them by the charter of Charles, so absolutely their own, that by no process of law could they be either abridged or abrogated without their consent."[24] Consequently, "[u]nder the rule of the Lords Proprietors, the people of North Carolina were confessedly 'the freest of the free,' and their legal status in this respect was due, in their opinion, to the royal Charter under which the Colony had its rise and got its growth," it continues. "To them, Magna Charta, 'the great charter,' was not the one granted by King John to the English Barons at Runnymede, but the one granted by Charles the Second to the Lords Proprietors of the Province of Carolina."[25] As such, the inhabitants enjoyed — and expected, even demanded — a level of freedom and autonomy that was equal to and in some instances greater than that enjoyed by their contemporaries in England. "[T]he liberties, franchises and privileges of Englishmen claimed and enjoyed as a matter of right by our ancestors belonged to them, in their opinion, not because they were Englishmen, indeed for that matter they were not all Englishmen, but because they were inhabitants of Carolina — all of whom were guaranteed the liberties, franchises and privileges of English subjects by the Charter."[26] Nor were these rights abstract, but fundamental, enforceable protections against the acts of government.

Foremost among these enforceable rights was freedom of religion. A 1769 petition by "the inhabitants of Mecklenburg County, of the Presbyterian denomination" to Governor Tryon began as follows: "In the great Charter, his Majesty confirms to his subjects removing from Great Britain into this Province, and their descendants, all the rights, privileges, franchises and immunities to which his Majesty's subjects in Great Britain, to-wit, England and Scotland, are entitled; and instructed the Lords Proprietors to grant other and greater religious privileges to dissenters." They had "settled under these assurances of liberty," they continued, "and the quiet and peaceable enjoyment of religious rites, secured to us by law, by the Charter and by his Majesty's instructions to the Lords Proprietors."[27] In other words, a deal was a deal.

Even after the governance of the province was taken over by the Crown in 1729, the settlers believed that any rights granted to them remained in place, irrespective of what the king might think about them. According to the *Colonial Records*, the people believed that the transfer of ownership of Carolina from the Proprietors back to the Crown "worked no change whatever in their political status, and that the King could no more govern by prerogative after 1728 than the Lords Proprietors could have done so prior to that time."[28] Their rights were inviolable.

The British authorities found this attitude shocking, although there was little they could do about it. In the inaugural session of the general assembly following the reversion to Crown authority, the newly installed royal governor was presented with a resolution, signed by the speaker of the house, putting the governor on notice that, "by the Royal Charter granted by King Charles the Second, to the Lords Proprietors of Carolina, it is granted that the inhabitants of this Province shall have, possess and enjoy all Libert[ie]s, Franchises and Privileges as are held, possest and enjoyed in the Kingdom of England." This was an act of gross lese majeste. The assembly was "showered with abusive epithets" by the governor, prorogued and then dissolved for two years.[29]

Yet so well developed and entrenched was this constitutional mindset that in December 1761 Governor Dobbs wrote to the Board of Trade that the assembly was openly defying the express written instructions of the king on the basis that "their Charter still subsisted."[30] "The Assembly think themselves entitled to all the Privileges of a British House of Commons," he wrote snottily, "and therefore ought not to submit to His Majesty's honorable Privy Council further than do the Commons in England or submit to His Majesty's instruction to His Governor and Council here."[31] Dobbs warned of a "republican spirit of Independency rising in this Colony."[32]

The British authorities had no one to blame but themselves. The rule of the Proprietors had drawn and encouraged people of this mindset. And no one contributed more to this "republican spirit" than a tightly knit, tough and clannish body of settlers known as the Scots-Irish, who were rapidly filling the backcountry.

2

"People of desperate fortune"
The Scots-Irish Settle Mecklenburg County

There are at present 75 families on my Lands.... They are a Colony from Ireland removed from Pennsylvania, or what we call Scotch Irish Presbyterians.
—Letter from Arthur Dobbs to the Board of
Trade of Great Britain, August 24, 1755

Pulled by the twin promises of economic opportunity or religious freedom, or pushed by despotic governments, settlers left Europe for the American colonies. By the early to mid–eighteenth century, the vast majority of North Carolina settlers were settlers from Ireland, Scotland and the border counties of Northern England. They sailed from Liverpool and Blackpool, Portsmouth and Dublin, Rotterdam and Kiel. But mostly, of those who would make their way into the Carolina backcountry, they came from Ireland through five Irish ports, specifically Belfast, Larne, Londonderry, Newry and Portrush.[1] In the Old World they were called Presbyterians, Irish or Ulstermen. In America, however, they were given a new name: Scots-Irish. Often they were called worse. They were "certainly the worst Vermin on Earth," according to Charles Woodmason, an Anglican minister who lived and traveled in the Carolinas in the mid–1760s.[2] "Ignorant, mean, worthless, beggarly Irish Presbyterians," he called them, "the Scum of the Earth, and Refuse of Mankind."[3] "They delight in their present low, lazy, sluttish, heathenish, hellish Life, and seem not desirous of changing it," Woodmason concluded.[4]

As a people, they were professional colonists. As one historian put it, "[t]heir very name is itself witness to the fact that they had known more than one home."[5] In 1607, James Stuart, king of England, confiscated roughly 3.8 million acres of land from the Earls of Tyrone and Tyrconnell, who had fled to France rather than submit to English rule. These lands, in the counties of Armagh, Cavan, Coleraine (later Londonderry), Donegal, Fermanagh and Tyrone, were populated with native islanders, the overwhelming majority of whom were Gaelic-speaking, dirt-poor Roman Catholics. They were a "barbarous and unsubdued people," according to King James, and he intended to introduce them to "civility, order and government" by colonizing Ireland with Scottish settlers. This, he believed, would lead to "the settling of religion" in the disordered province. The lands taken from Earls

Tyrone and Tyrconnell were given to English and Scottish aristocrats, friends of the king, who in turn leased them at favorable rates to Scottish settlers, who began crossing the Irish Sea in large numbers.[6]

By 1619, it is estimated that 8,000 Scottish settlers had settled in Ulster and by 1715 as many as 200,000.[7] They were not welcome. The native Irish hated the English government and its new settlers, who had been sent to displace them from their ancestral homes. The alien Scots were forced to live in fortified towns amidst the hostile natives. They were a minority population, an occupying power forced to rely on their own resources for protection. Surrounded on all sides by enemies, they were twice despised — first by the sullen and resentful Irish and also by the English authorities who governed Ireland. "As a consequence," as one history put it, the Scots-Irish "developed a defensive and intolerant outlook, called by some a 'siege mentality.'"[8]

Over time, as they were no longer truly Scottish nor Irish, they came to be called both — Scots-Irish. By the early 1700s, living conditions, never good, had worsened for them in Ireland. The population increased rapidly in the mid–1700s and land became more and more scarce. Landlords began imposing short, three-year leases, which they then auctioned off to the highest bidder — a practice known as rack renting. When a lease expired, the tenants would be evicted. The result was social dislocation, unrest and anger. A wave of lease terminations in 1717 through 1720 and 1725 through 1727 led in turn to mass migrations from Ireland to the American colonies.[9]

Punitive, even predatory, economic policies imposed from London also drove emigration. Ireland was prohibited from exporting any livestock or wool products to England. It was literally a captive market. These parasitic measures created boom-and-bust cycles in the few commodities Ireland could export (principally linen), created an artificial and low market for wool, and led to poverty and periodic widespread starvation.[10] Edmond Kaine, an estate manager in County Monaghan, in the first quarter of the 18th century wrote: "I know not the meaning of it, but it is believed here that it is occasioned by the hardship England is putting upon us.... We have had the saddest robbing in the country that ever was known and not only robbing but murdering, killing almost everywhere, where they rob. This is all occasioned by the scarceness of money."[11] Like much of contemporary Africa, eighteenth-century Ireland was a violent, destitute, hopeless mess — or to use a modern term, a failed state.

If poverty and oppression weren't reason enough to leave, then there was the issue of religion. Despite the fact that the island was almost entirely populated by native Catholics and (in the north) Presbyterian Scots, the official, state-sponsored church was the Anglican Church — the Church of England. Penal laws prohibited non–Anglicans from holding office or engaging in many lucrative professions. A tax (or tithe) on all citizens went to support the Anglican Church. Presbyterian churches remained open only at the discretion of the English government. Religious oppression went hand in hand with political oppression, and the cause was the same: England.

Presbyterian ministers encouraged and fanned anti–English sentiment. "The Presbyterian ministers have taken their share of pains to seduce their poor ignorant hearers," complained one Irish judge in 1729, "by bellowing from their pulpits against the Landlords and the Clergy, calling them rackers of Rents, and Servers of Tithes, with other reflections of this nature, which they know is pleasing to their people, at the same time telling them that God has appointed a country for them to depart thence, where they will be freed from the bondage of Egypt and go to the land of Canaan."[12] America would be different, they preached. In the New Canaan there were no kings, popish clergy or grasping landlords. In America at least — despite whatever hardships there were — they would be free.

First individuals, then families, and finally whole congregations set sail for the American colonies. Between 1771 and 1775, 17,500 Irishmen and Irishwomen left Ulster; by 1800, a quarter million had gone.[13] It was an exodus, a mass migration on a biblical scale. Entire villages, and sometimes regions, became depopulated. The *Londonderry Journal* in April 1775 reported in alarm that "the North of Ireland has in the last five or six years been drained of one-fourth of its trading class, and the like proportion of the manufacturing people." This early "brain drain," the paper noted, "is sensibly felt in this country. This prevalent humour of industrious Protestants withdrawing from this once flourishing corner of the kingdom, seems to be increasing; and it is thought the number will be considerably larger this year than ever.... Where the evil will end, remains only in the Womb of time to determine."[14]

The Scots-Irish arrived sometimes in a trickle but more often in recurrent waves, vessel after vessel docked on the eastern shores of Maryland and Delaware. In 1727, six ships full of Irish emigrants arrived in Philadelphia in a single week.[15] So many Irish were arriving, wrote James Logan, provincial secretary of Pennsylvania in 1729, "it looks as if Ireland is to send all its inhabitants hither." Indeed, so powerful were the incoming tides of humanity, "[t]he common fear is if they continue to come, they will make themselves proprietors of the province."[16]

They were generally poor, often barefoot and wore the thinnest of clothes. They were also proud, pushy and tough. They had a reputation for making bad servants because of their insolent attitude. The German and English settlers already in America despised them; one contemporary called them "the most lowest vilest Crew breathing."[17] The colonial officials had a tough time dealing with them and were happy to encourage them to move on farther west. It was hoped they would set up a barrier on the flank of the colonies against the French and their Indian allies.

The arriving settlers needed land, and along the increasingly crowded Chesapeake it seemed to be running out. By the mid–1700s many of the best properties in Pennsylvania, Delaware and Maryland had already been claimed. As more and more Scots-Irish pushed into Pennsylvania they found they could not move farther west, lest they run into hostile Indian territory. New lands had to be found. So, like a wave hitting a breakwater, the new settlers were pushed south, first into Virginia and then into the Carolinas.

Travel south meant travel into the interior, and that was difficult. In Maryland and Virginia, the major rivers (the Rappahannock, York, Chesapeake and Potomac) ran roughly east to west and were broad and suitable for travel. That was not true in the Carolinas. There, the main rivers — such as the Yadkin and Catawba — ran obliquely to the sea and were narrow, shallow, irregular and rocky. They had frequent waterfalls and rough passages that made inland travel by boat nearly impossible. Unlike in Virginia, the Carolina rivers were largely barriers and impediments to travel rather than water highways.

As a result, settlement of the interior of Carolina came not from the coastlines of the east, but from the north, along the Great Philadelphia Wagon Road (or to a lesser degree from Charleston, in the southeast). Beginning as its other name — the Philadelphia Road — suggested, it passed south through Lancaster and York to Winchester, Virginia, winding through the Shenandoah Valley. It crossed the Fluvanna River at Looney's Ferry, then the Staunton River, and then the Dan. Leaving the Shenandoah, the Wagon Road bypassed the Moravian townships in central Carolina, then crossed the Yadkin at Trading Ford, near Salisbury, before eventually reaching a place called Reedy Creek in the woods that would become Mecklenburg County. The farther south the Wagon Road went, however, the less it was really a road at all. By the time it reached Carolina it was little more than an unmarked, overgrown forest path.

As settlers left the Virginia valley country, pressing further and further South, they entered a broad plateau characteristic of central North Carolina. This area of forest and grasslands lying between the table-flat, sandy, pine barrens of the coast and the layered, hazy blue ridgeline of the Appalachians, was called the Piedmont. In French the word meant *foot of the mountains* and was taken from the province of *Piemonte* in northwest Italy of the same name. Geologically, the Piedmont was the leveled remains of an ancient and towering mountain range — once higher than the Himalayas — that over the course of millions of years had been eroded by wind and rain until nothing was left but gentle hills sloping from the mountains to the sea. It was a flat and largely featureless landscape. Its topography was ordinary, with vast flat savannahs, interspersed by primeval forests of hardwoods and pines, modest hills, and shallow, rocky creeks. There were no scenic river valleys as in Pennsylvania or Virginia, no great rivers like the Chesapeake or Potomac, and no towering mountain ranges, as in Vermont and New Hampshire.

The land in the Piedmont was appealing in only a few respects. First, it was largely uninhabited. The few indigenous peoples — the Catawbas, for example — were generally nonthreatening. There were no French or Spanish colonists to resist new settlers or attack them. Being uninhabited, it was also ungoverned, which was attractive to anyone seeking to escape governmental or religious authority, such as the Anglican Church, British laws or English taxes. Second, the land was fertile and abounded in natural resources for those tough or industrious enough to exploit them. Early settlers described herds of buffalo and deer roaming fields of indiangrass and switchgrass, which in the spring became carpeted with knee-high waving maroon and magenta petals of pea vine.

In addition to wildlife, the limestone soils were clayey and rich in minerals, which made them excellent for farming. During his tour of the southern states in 1791, George Washington described the area as having "a very rich look" and the woods north of Charlotte as being "very fine, of a reddish cast and well timbered, with but very little underwood." Further south the lands became "Piney & Sandy," he noted, with vast, flat tracks of pine-barrens, which were less suitable for agriculture.[18]

It was a land that responded only to backbreaking, sweaty labor, and therefore only lent itself to a certain type of people. "Piedmont land was red and coarse, often covered with oaks and hickories, which were much more difficult to remove than pines," notes one history of the state. "It was a place far removed from ready markets. The people who took up land here were not often tempted to acquire more than could be tilled by one man and his son. The piedmont, therefore, evolved into a land of small, independent farmers."[19] Trees and brush could be cleared, cattle raised, and crops grown. Agriculture was primitive and difficult. Crude instruments were used as hoes, harrows, forks and spades. Moravian bishop Gottlieb Spangenburg, reconnoitering the area for the site of a settlement in 1752, reported that in his 140-mile journey he saw "not one wagon or plow."[20] Planting and clearing was done with human labor.

Finally, there were rivers and creeks, which if difficult for travel nonetheless provided ample drinking water and were perfect for sawmills or grist mills. Indeed, the region then known as Anson County (some of which would later become Mecklenburg) was defined by two nearby rivers, which enclosed it as if by protecting walls, and which were fed by dozens of crisscrossing creeks and streams. To the west was the Catawba, a slow and winding watercourse which, seen on a map, resembles a fishhook lying on its side from the Appalachian mountains to the Atlantic. The name *Catawba* may have come from the Choctaw words *kat a pa*, meaning to divide, break up, or separate, which could be a physical description of the river itself, which is rather broken.[21] Whether it came from this or some other derivation is not known. The second river delineating Mecklenburg was the Yadkin (on some maps of the time called "Deep River") to the east. Its trajectory was similar to the Catawba, but it originated further north then hooked south below the Moravian Wachovia settlements of central North Carolina. Mecklenburg County would become the geographic center of this area between the Catawba and the Yadkin. The first Scots-Irish settlers, being biblically minded, gave the area a biblical name: *Mesopotamia*, Greek for the "land between two rivers" and the ancient name for the Babylonian kingdom between the Tigris and Euphrates.

The first people to arrive in Mecklenburg along the Wagon Trail, possibly as early as the middle of the seventeenth century, were lone Indian traders. They lived with the Indians in the various tribes, learned their languages and ways of life, and traded beads, cloth, whisky, guns, powder, lead and other goods for deerskins, beaver pelts, antlers, buffalo hides and other pelts. The area was opened to settlement in 1749 and by 1758 hundreds of land grants had been issued to arriving settlers.[22]

In 1755 royal governor Dobbs, inspecting his lands for a report to the London Board of Trade, traveled through the Rocky River settlement in Mecklenburg and noted the following:

> There are at present 75 families on my Lands I viewed betwixt 30 and 40 of them, and except two there was not less than from 5 or 6 to 10 children in each family, each going barefooted in their shifts in the warm weather, no woman wearing more than a shift and one thin petticoat; They are a Colony from Ireland removed from Pennsylvania, of what we call Scotch Irish Presbyterians who with others in the neighbouring Tracts had settled together in order to have a teacher of their own opinion and choice.[23]

The settlers clustered along various creeks where the best land was and they could draw water for cooking and washing and set up mills. These creeks gave their names to the various communities: Mallard Creek, Reedy Creek, Sugar Creek, Rocky River, Steele Creek, Long Creek and so forth. (Some of these creeks themselves were named for their distance along the Wagon Road from the Yadkin [New River; Second Creek; Third Creek] or their appearance [Swift Creek, Flat Rock Creek, Crooked Creek, Difficult Creek] or for the Indian tribes that lived alongside them [the Sugar, the Waxhaw, Waccamaw and Sayapa], but the vast majority were named for the first settlers [Davidson's, McDowell, Torrance, Steele and so forth]).

The settlers established seven Presbyterian churches in the region, sometimes later known as the Pleiades, or "seven sisters." The first, and therefore the oldest, was probably Sugar Creek on the Salisbury road, three miles north of the Charlotte town common. Rocky River was built about the same period (c. 1750). The five others were Steele Creek (1760); Hopewell (1762); Poplar Tent (1764); Centre (1765); Providence (1767); and Clear Creek (later called Philadelphia) (1770).[24] In December 1762 the area was sufficiently populous to make it an independent county. By 1765 there were 1,352 "taxable souls" in Mecklenburg.[25] The community was largely ethnically, linguistically and spiritually homogenous. "[M]ostly Presbyterians," the List of Taxables in North Carolina for the year 1767 succinctly summarized the new county.[26] Other than the few German settlers in the northeast, who actually predated the Scots-Irish Presbyterians by twenty years, Mecklenburg was a one-party state: English-speaking, Scots-Irish and Presbyterian.

Bound together by strong family ties, a common heritage and, of course, their faith, the Scots-Irish settlers were an extremely tight-knit community. They worked together; defended one another's property; buried each other's parents or children; prayed together; farmed together, and intermarried. In fact, so intertwined did the families become that disentangling the many strands of Alexanders, Brevards, Caldwells and Davidsons who had married one another would bedevil generations of later genealogists. They banded together to resist outside authority, whether in the form of English landlords or Anglican priests.

Although "the Settlers on Sugar and Reedy Creeks live in this province," English land agent Henry McCullough reported to Royal Governor Dobbs in 1762, "no officer of Justice from either Province [North or South Carolina] dare meddle with them, their number rendering them formidable, there being near 150 of their Families settled together." He described them as "people of desperate fortune, and without any property or possession but that of the said patentees Lands which they hold by force." The authorities were reluctant to attempt to enforce the law, as the settlers "unite together to repel what they call an injury offered any one of them."[27]

Communication with the outside world existed, but it was slow, sporadic and intermittent. There was no printing press in the colony until 1749. Even by 1775 there were only two newspapers in the province: the *New Bern Gazette* (established in 1749; though discontinued from 1755 to 1768) and the *Wilmington Cape-Fear Mercury* (established in 1767).[28] News was brought along the Wagon Road by express couriers bearing letters from the delegates in larger cities in the east (although this was quite rare), by word of mouth carried by traders or settlers passing through town, or by residents when they returned from the meetings of the assembly, court appearances in the east or buying trips to Charleston or Philadelphia. "With no natural outlet on the east or south, and with the mountains as a barrier on the west," according to one historian, "the people of the Piedmont were virtually cut off from the rest of the state and from the outside world."[29]

Not surprisingly, the settlers had a worldview typical of life on an isolated frontier. They were self-reliant because they had to be. They were able, as one of their descendants would later put it, "to live within themselves."[30] Other than basic foodstuff commodities such as sugar, coffee, salt, and molasses, each farm was largely self-sufficient. "The people made their own hats and shoes, and wove their own cloth ... [and] raised indigo for dyeing. They raised flax and made it into linen."[31] They sold tallow, cheese, butter and hides to Charleston, trading for gunpowder and iron.

They raised horses, cattle and hogs, plus small quantities of sheep and chickens. Deer

The McIntyre farm is representative of log cabins in the Piedmont in the colonial period. A skirmish between British troops and local militia here on October 3, 1780, led to the county's nickname of "hornets' nest" (courtesy of the Robinson-Spangler Carolina Room, Charlotte-Mecklenburg Public Library).

provided meat, plus their skins, which were exported to England. (In 1747, two hundred pounds of beaver and 720 hogsheads of deer hide were exported through the port of Charleston.[32]) Bear meat, because it had a fine, clear odorless fat, was prized (and is still widely eaten by hunters in the eastern parts of North and South Carolina). Bearskins were used for hats, rugs and bedding, claws for ornaments, and fat for cooking and in oil lamps.

Life revolved around the musket and the Bible. Social life revolved around church sermons, hog killings and house raisings plus "court week" four times each year. Church services were held each Saturday and twice on Sunday. Everyone knew each other. Indeed, families were bound together as tightly in marriage, work and self-defense as had been clans from the Old Country, a social arrangement that was not coincidental. Work involved simple and predictable tasks, such as tending to crops or animals, repairing fences and tilling fields.

Simple, rustic and quiet life may have been, but it was also filled with danger, difficulty and privation. Life on the colonial frontier was one of hardship, poverty and disease. The settlers of Mecklenburg were poor, going barefoot in the summer and huddling for warmth in the winter. "Their Cabbins [are] quite open and expos'd," wrote Woodmason. "Little or no Bedding, or anything to cover them — Not a drop of anything, save Cold Water to drink — And all their Cloathing, [but] a Shirt and Trousers[,] Shift and Petticoat ... No Shoes or Stockings — Children run half naked. The Indians are better Cloathed and Lodged. All this arises from their Indolence and Laziness."[33] It was a primitive world without safety, comfort or convenience. According to historian Dan Morrill,

> Drunkenness and fornication were widespread. Modern concepts of hygiene, derived largely from the advent of the germ theory of medicine, had no place in 18th century life. The most common house form was the log cabin, sometimes with three walls. Typically, the only opening in the exterior wall was for an entry door. The floors were dirt. A permanent fire in a large fireplace at the end of the main room billowed smoke into the cramped living quarters, frequently turning the air into an acrid cloud. Privacy, even for the most intimate acts, was virtually unattainable.[34]

Many of the people were illiterate; the vast majority all were poor. Life expectancy, for those who survived childhood, was forty. Life was generally solitary, nasty, brutish and short. Men died from disease, were mauled by wolves, bears or feral dogs; fell from horses or were mangled by plows; or were robbed, beaten or murdered on desolate forest paths by Indians or fellow settlers. Farmers lost limbs in accidents (or as with the young Ephraim Brevard, eyes) or simply fell dead from heart attacks or stroke in the fields. Women died in childbirth or of any one of a dozen then-incurable diseases.

When parents died, orphaned children were sent to live with relations or advertised to work as a housekeepers or servants — in many cases at eight or nine years of age. Many times they were bound to a master as a journeyman, for only by mastering a trade could they bring value to their guardians. Often this meant separating brothers and sisters who had recently lost their parents to accidents, disease or murder. One William McNair was bound at the age of four to James Moore to "Learn the Art and Mistry of a weaver" until he was 21 years old.[35]

When orphans reached the age of 21 for boys and 18 for girls, the law required that their guardians provide them with money and a set of clothes plus the tools of the trade they had mastered. Andrew McMickan was orphaned by the death of his father when he was 15 and sent to learn the art of a blacksmith. When he attained maturity he was to receive "one Bellows, one sledge, one hand hammer, three pair Tongs, Shoeing Tools and some punches, and an Anvle Vise."[36] The county court records are filled with such stories.

Yet despite the hardships, and suffering, the Scots-Irish built a self-contained, self-sufficient, even self-governing community in the lands between the rivers. There, alone in the woods, there were no Anglican bishops, no predatory landlords, and a remote and generally beneficent government. Devout, even fanatical, Presbyterians, they were permitted to practice their religion as they understood it. Outsiders were distrusted, central government perceived as a threat, the world at large viewed as godless and hostile. Mecklenburg was a world apart, and the people living there wanted it that way. The spirit of the community (and later the county motto) was *Leave Us Alone.*

3

"Highly injured and aggrieved"
Alexander Craighead
and the Presbyterians

[T]he Inhabitants of Mecklenburg are entire dissenters of the most rigid kind—[and] have a solemn league and covenant teacher settled among them.
—Letter from Andrew Morton to the
Reverend Daniel Burton, August 25, 1766

By the 1760s, the Carolina backcountry had become a refuge for religious dissidents of many kinds, including Moravians, Quakers and Baptists. But by far the largest and most vocal faction in the Mecklenburg region were the Presbyterians. In the summer of 1768, Woodmason complained of being "Insulted by a Pack of vile, leveling common wealth Presbyterians" full of "Republican Spirit."[1] In this case, even the irascible Woodmason was not exaggerating. The Scots-Irish overrunning Mecklenburg were not only Presbyterians, but followers of a radical splinter group of Presbyterians known as "Covenanters."

Covenanting had ancient roots in Scotland but was something of an anachronism by the mid–1700s. The Covenanters had been on the losing side of the English civil wars, with their leaders murdered or driven out of the British Isles. Followers of this antique doctrine advocated a holy contract (or "covenant") between the people and God, known as the "Solemn League and Covenant." The Covenant superseded all other obligations, even the duty of the people to obey their monarch. Obedience to true, revealed religion, was supreme. As such, Woodmason was correct to label it a "common wealth" (or radical) doctrine. Covenanters viewed Anglicanism as merely a new and degenerate form of hated popery, and the English kings as emissaries of the Anti-Christ. It was a powerful and volatile mix of religion and politics.

The founder of the movement was a Scottish political and religious leader named Richard Cameron. In June 1680, Cameron had led a breakaway movement seeking Scottish independence, declaring war on the English as "enemies to our Lord Jesus Christ, and His cause and covenants."[2] Cameron's rebellion was short-lived. Within a few months he was murdered by English agents, and his head and hands hewn off and delivered to the authorities. But his failed rebellion, like those of other Scottish rebel leaders before and after, grew in majesty and romance after his death. Followers of his anti–English Presbyterianism referred to themselves as "Cameronians" and continued their war against English rule.

The English struck hard to wipe the rebels out. The Covenanters were concentrated in southeastern (lowland) Scotland. In 1665 the "Five Mile Act" banned Covenanter ministers from coming within five miles of their former churches. Outlawed ministers continued to hold their church services, called *conventicles,* in secret services conducted in mountain passes, highland ravines or remote caves. English authorities hunted down these illegal church services, hanged the men and drowned the women. In a famous speech in Parliament in April 1685, the English Lord Chancellor declared, "We have a new sect sprung up among us from the dunghill, the very dreggs of the people who kill by pretended inspiration ... whose idol is that accursed paper the Covenant."[3] The Solemn League and Covenant was publicly burned by the royal hangman. To publicly avow allegiance to the Solemn League and Covenant was High Treason.

During a period known in Scotland as the "Killing Time," followers of Cameron were hunted down like rabbits on the treeless Scottish moors. A contemporary described "bloody butchering, beheading, mangling, dismembering alive, quartering upon scaffolds, imprisoning, laying in irons, torturing by boots, thumbkinds, fire-matches, cutting pieces out of the ears of others, banishing and selling as slaves old and young men and women in great numbers ... forfeiting, robbing, spoiling, pillaging their goods, [and] casting them out of their habitations."[4] As a political force, the Covenanters were essentially extirpated.

Unwilling to submit or yield, the few remaining Covenanter leaders fled abroad, first to Ireland and then, during the mass Scots-Irish emigration from the 1740s to the 1760s, to America. Even in colonial America, which was a patchwork of outcast religions, the Covenanters were considered bizarre and extreme radicals, and as such were constantly spied upon or reported to the authorities. To be left in peace, many Covenanter leaders settled in the remote wilderness. In areas such as the Carolina backcountry they kept Cameron's flag flying and nursed their unrequited hatred of the English. One such Covenanter was an Irish minister named Alexander Craighead.

Craighead was born in March 1707 in Donegal, Ireland, the third son of a third-generation Presbyterian minister named Thomas Craighead. Thomas brought his family to America in October of 1715 when Alexander was seven years old. Thomas was a charismatic preacher whose "impassioned sermons" were so powerful that his audience was "melted to tears, and the emotions of his hearers became so intense that they were unwilling to disperse."[5] Thomas was also an angry and volatile man. One historian politely said he "had the unhappy gift of discord" and led "a somewhat stormy life," but the reality is that he was deeply troubled, just as his son would be.[6] Thomas' internal demons manifested themselves in strict and unforgiving religious views. In 1735, he barred his own wife from receiving communion due to her insufficient piety, an act that was so "excoriating and unconscionable," according to church records, "that we cannot forbear supposing that he is under some dreadful delusion of Satan, if not a delirium in his head."[7]

His son, Alexander Craighead, seems to have been cast from the same mold. The younger Craighead has been described as "colorful," "naturally ardent and impetuous," and "a stormy petrel."[8] But to most of his contemporaries he was simply angry, spiteful and even possibly insane (as many of his contemporaries believed).[9] "[S]ome may take liberty to say that I am very fickle," Craighead wrote of himself, "and want to promote divisions."[10] In modern terms, his behavior suggests Craighead might have been bipolar, or manic-depressive. He not only carried on his father's personality traits but also his narrow and hard-line

Presbyterianism. "True Presbyterians," Craighead explained, "have been frequently termed *Cameronians*" and "continued steadfast in the Faith."[11] These views would set Craighead on a life-long collision course with political and religious authorities of all kinds.

Craighead's ministering career began in Lancaster County, Pennsylvania. In 1735, he became minister at Middle Octorara Presbyterian Church. It was a period called the "Great Awakening" in the American colonies, a widespread and intense spiritual movement. Settlers traveled many miles to listen to itinerant pastors preaching salvation. Within the Presbyterian denomination, adherents to this modern, revivalist and more populist style were called "New Side" or "New Light" preachers. Their preaching style was described as "warm, vivid, energetic and direct," in contrast to the more formal, stylistic and cold sermons of the old guard.[12] New Light ministers rode through the woods singing gospel songs and preached two or three times a day, sometimes to gatherings of three, four or five thousand people at a time. The congregation would stand, shout and cry. Audience members were disturbed by "incidents of weeping, screaming, fainting" and other "bodily commotions like 'epileptic fits.'"[13]

New Light preachers were controversial, not only due to their evangelical style but also because their views were often associated with anti–English radicalism. "In the Southern colonies where the Episcopal Church was established and where Dissenters faced certain legal disabilities," writes one scholar, "the 'New Lights' who went into the back country first as itinerants and then as settled pastors, often roused sharp opposition from the authorities of church and state."[14] One disapproving minister wrote in 1749 that the New Lights had been "*foremost* in propagating the Principles of Sedition, and Disobedience to authority.... I make no Doubt but it had an unhappy influence upon the People, and encouraged many to despise Government, and to speak Evil of Dignities."[15]

Due to the unapologetic, often seditious character of their teachings, New Lights thrived in the frontier, where they could preach as they wished without fear of being arrested. The "greatest part" of the province of South Carolina had been overrun with "Irish Presbyterians from Belfast, or Pennsylvania," wrote one observer. Among these were a "Great Number of new Lights ... roving Teachers that stir up the Minds of the People against the Establish'd Church, and her Ministers."[16] "The Country is very much over spread with New Light Whitefield followers," complained one despairing Anglican in 1747, particularly "Covenanters who receive their Sacrament with a gun charg'd and drawn sword; & profess they'l fight for Christ against Civil Magistrates."[17]

To New Light preachers politics and religion were not different spheres to be kept separate, but a unified whole, opposite sides of the same coin. John Knox had asserted in his first confession of faith "the right and duty of the people to resist the tyranny of their rulers."[18] To Knox, Christ was sovereign over *all* men — kings included. The general assembly of the Church of Scotland had resolved in 1649 that "arbitrary government and unlimited power are the foundations of all the corruptions in Church and State" and "boundless and unlimited power is to be acknowledged in no king nor magistrate."[19] Both the king and his citizens were bound in a covenant of "mutual obligation" to one another: "As both of them are tied to God, so each of them is tied the one to the other for the performance of mutual and reciprocal duties."[20] As such, resistance to tyranny was obedience to God's will. If the unrighteous governed, the citizens had a duty to resist them — a duty commanded by God. In an era of absolute monarchy, this was a highly seditious view.

The ramifications of Knox's political views were fundamental to New Lights such as Craighead. The English kings, Craighead believed, were usurpers who had lost their legitimacy to rule as a result of their having abandoned true Protestantism in favor of satanic Anglicanism. In his sermons, Craighead denied King James I had "any legal Right to rule over this Realm, by Reason of his Popish Principles."[21] He described King George I as "an outlandish Lutheran" and King George II as a "sworn Prelaticks, the Head of Malignants, and Protectors of Sectarian Heretics." These radical views were not for everyone. But in Pennsylvania, Craighead found a community of Scots-Irish who were inclined to take their religion neat. "No preacher goes to those People (who are very numerous)," wrote one contemporary in Lancaster County, "but a mad fellow (one Craighead), a furious leveler who labors to confound their opinions both Religious & Civil."[22]

Craighead practiced as intensely as he preached. In November 1740, the Donegal Presbytery (which had jurisdiction over Craighead's parish) received a complaint that Craighead was "intruding [beyond] ye bounds of his [congregation] without any invitation."[23] In other words, he was meddling in the affairs of other parishes.[24] Other complaints followed. Several members of his own congregation complained of his aggressiveness, intolerance and "bad conduct." He was "imposing new terms of communion on his people at the baptism of their children,"[25] by requiring that they subscribe to the Solemn League and Covenant. He denied communion to those who disagreed with him and made "other confessions unbecoming his chamber."[26]

On December 9, 1740, Presbyterian Church elders traveled to remote Middle Octorara to investigate Craighead and the charges that had been made against him. Instead of explaining his actions to the church elders, Craighead attacked them. He circulated a paper accusing them of "whoredom, drunkenness, Swearing, Sabth breaking, lying &c."[27] While the Presbytery met in the church, Craighead incited the crowd outside with "circumlocutions and harangues."

"Mr. Craighead utterly and absolutely declined our authority," concluded the minutes of the Donegal Presbytery, with "notorious and disorderly conduct."[28] Through his "liti-

"**No War is proclaimed without a drawn Sword.**" Painting of Alexander Craighead preaching in the backcountry, by Will Puckett, 2012 (courtesy Will Puckett).

giously interrupting the [meeting] for a long time in their proceedings ... & conniving at ye peoples tumultuous behavior, whereby [were] we obliged to break up in an abrupt manner. In sum, we cannot but look on Mr. Craighead's whole conduct on ye above instances to be extremely irregular and disorderly, So that we have not known a parallel instance Since we have been capable to mark anything on the world."[29] Craighead was expelled from the synod. Undeterred, he formed a new and competing presbytery, one in accordance with his own principles. As a condition to belonging to his new synod, Craighead demanded that its members pledge allegiance to the Solemn League and Covenant. They refused. Craighead split *again*, this time withdrawing entirely from the Presbyterian Church, which he proceeded to attack in a series of lengthy articles and pamphlets.

One of his sermons — published anonymously during this period — came to the attention of the royal governor of Pennsylvania. On May 25, 1743, Thomas Cookson, an agent of the governor, brought the offending paper before the Philadelphia Synod and conveyed the authorities' displeasure with its contents. The synod, deferring all regular business, listened with growing astonishment as Cookson read the paper. "It was unanimously agreed," according to the meeting minutes:

> That it is full of treason, sedition, and distraction, and grievous perverting of the sacred oracles to the ruin of all societies and civil government ... we hereby unanimously, with the greatest sincerity, declare that we detest this paper, and with it all principles and practices that tend to destroy the civil and religious rights of mankind, or to foment or encourage sedition or dissatisfaction with the civil government that we are now under, or rebellion, treason, or any thing that is disloyal.[30]

Besieged on all sides by enemies, both spiritual and political, Craighead felt trapped. He searched his conscience for a solution. Where could he go to live a pure life, one undefiled by the material and corrupt world, away from Anglican priests and English lords? The answer was obvious — into the wild. In the desolate backcountry, he could live according to the word of God.

On November 11, 1743, Craighead gathered all the members of the Covenanter societies at Middle Octorara and announced his decision. He told them that he looked upon it as his "duty to separate ourselves from the corrupt Constitution of both Church and State, and not to touch, taste, or handle these Abominations, lest by partaking with them in their Sins, we be made Partakers with them in their Plagues." He could no longer tolerate "the apostate, perjured and blood-guilty Condition of Church and State." By abandoning civilization they could escape the "errors and Immoralities that abound in this corrupt and apostate Age." He asked those who were brave and devout enough to join him in his self-imposed exile. Then they drew swords in a symbolic renewal of the Solemn League and Covenant, to symbolize their commitment, just as Cameron and their other "spiritual forebears had done."[31]

"[O]ur renowned Ancestors were constrained to draw the Sword in the Defense of their own Lives," said Craighead. "Our drawing of the Sword is to testify to the World; that we are one in Judgment with them, and that we are to this Day willing to maintain the same defensive War in defending our Religion and ourselves against all Opposers thereof, although the Defense of these should cost us our Lives."[32] It was, as one writer put it, a "declaration of independence."[33] It was also a Declaration of War — a spiritual war, perhaps, but a war all the same, just as Craighead intended it to be. "[N]o War is proclaimed without a drawn Sword," he defiantly explained, "and there is no Reason that this should be singular in this particular."[34]

Craighead and his followers headed southwest into the Shenandoah Valley, perhaps using heavy horse-drawn wagons built in the village of Conestoga. Sometime around 1750 they settled just south of present-day Lexington, Virginia. The authorities regarded Craighead and his sectarian followers as dangerous radicals and their appearance in Virginia was not welcome. An executive council meeting in April 1747 denounced the "Itinerant Preachers lately crept into this Colony" and the propagation of their "Shocking Doctrines."[35] The council ordered a "Proclamation forthwith issue requiring all Magistrates and Officers to discourage and prohibit as far as legally they can all Itinerant Preachers whether New Light men Morravians or Methodists from Teaching Preaching or holding any Meeting in the Colony."[36]

Craighead's preaching soon came to the attention of royal officials. In June 1752, two justices of the peace complained to executive council that "the Revd Mr Alexander Creaghead has taught and maintained treasonable positions and preached and published pernicious doctrines."[37] At this point, Craighead's former colleagues in the Philadelphia Synod felt it necessary to distance themselves from him. Craighead and his followers, they pointed out to the authorities, had earlier been expelled "by Reason of their divisive, censorious and uncharitable Doctrine and practices."[38]

Craighead had worn out his welcome in Virginia. But it was at this time that "a call was presented to the Presbytery from Rocky-river N. Carolina, requesting that Mr. Craighead might take the pastoral care of them."[39] Rocky River, like Sugar Creek, was part of the frontier settlements in Mecklenburg nearly a month's ride south in the Carolina backcountry. This was his opportunity. There were no permanent ministers in the region. The area was being steadily populated with Scots-Irish: his people. Craighead could preach as he wanted, without fear of being spied on by Anglican traitors. He and his followers soon made haste for Carolina. At least four young men who would later become prominent Whig leaders in the area (Henry Downs, Zaccheus Wilson, Benjamin Patton and William Graham) are thought to have come with Craighead.

When Craighead arrived in Mecklenburg he found a scattering of Scots-Irish settlers living in log cabins. The first of these settlers had arrived only nine years before. It was virgin territory. "The church he was to preach was built of logs and stood on a rise, near some springs," records a history of Sugar Creek Presbyterian Church, one of at least two churches where Craighead preached.[40] When he was not preaching at Sugar Creek or Rocky River, Craighead saddled his quarter horse and rode along the narrow Indian paths to preach to far-flung settlers in the forest. When the weather was fine he would preach outside to groups of forty or fifty people. When it rained or snowed, dozens would crowd under boughs of oak trees for shelter to listen to him. Here he "found a people remote from the seat of authority ... [and] so united in their general principles of religion and church government, that he was the teacher of the whole population." Among the settlers Craighead "poured forth his principles of religious and civil government, undisturbed by the jealousy of the government, too distant to be aware of his doings, or too careless to be interested in the poor and distant emigrants on the Catawba."[41]

Craighead's influence on the frontiersmen was powerful, and others from miles around took notice. One Anglican observer voiced his alarm that Craighead and others "willingly put the Solemn League and Covenant now in force — Nay, their Teachers press it on them, and say that [it] is as binding ... as the Gospel it Self, for it is a Covenant enter'd into with God, from which they cannot recede."[42] Another Anglican missionary, writing in 1765, described the Mecklenburg settlers as "entire dissenters *of the most rigid kind*" and "in general greatly averse to the Church of England."[43] In fact, so hostile were they to the prevailing laws that made it illegal for anyone but Anglican missionaries to conduct marriages (known as the Marriage and Vestry Acts) that the Mecklenburg settlers regarded them "as oppressive as the Stamp Act and were determined to prevent its taking place there, by opposing the settlement of any Minister of the Church of England that might be sent amongst them."[44]

The Marriage and Vestry Acts were a source of constant outrage and anger to Craighead and his congregation. Because there were almost no Anglican ministers in the area (nor were they welcome), couples had to travel many miles to be legally wed. It also had the result that if a woman was pregnant, it might be many months before she could be married, resulting in her children being born out of wedlock. For these reasons the settlers were "highly injured and aggrieved by the marriage act" which "scandalizes the Presbyterian clergy ... obstructs the natural and inalienable right of marriage and tends to introduce immorality."[45]

To add insult to injury, the British levied taxes (10 shillings annually per "taxable soul") to support the construction of Anglican churches and hire priests. To the Presbyterians, this was not only a financial burden but also an issue of conscience. Their money was going to

Grave of the Rev. Alexander Craighead in Sugar Creek (old) burying ground. The small plot is in a rundown area of town, locked behind a chain-link fence and largely forgotten, as is Craighead himself (photograph by the author).

support and propagate not only a false but a hostile religion. They bitterly resented "the enforced payment of tithes to the Episcopal clergy to sustain a theocracy which Presbyterians believed to be contrary to the laws of God, and knew to be destructive of their own rights and liberties."[46]

A petition from the "inhabitants of Mecklenburg County, of the Presbyterian denomination" to Governor Tryon in 1769 complained that they were "highly aggrieved by the exorbitant power of the vestry, to tax us with the enormous sum of ten shillings each taxable; which is more than double the charge of Government." Why should Presbyterians pay to support Anglicans, they asked: "We think it as reasonable that those who hold to the Episcopal Church should pay their clergy without our assistance as that we, who hold to the church of Scotland should pay our clergy without their assistance."[47] It was a senseless policy, they believed, as "not one twentieth part of the inhabitants" were Anglican anyway. Even if there were "an Episcopal clergyman in this Parish, his labours would be useless."[48]

Their incessant complaints and quasi-treasonable political beliefs led many English to regard the Presbyterians as incorrigible rebels. "I fix all of the blame for these extraordinary proceedings on the Presbyterians," wrote one monarchist to King George III just prior to the outbreak of the Revolution. "The Presbyterians have been the chief and principle instruments in all of these flaming measures. They always do and ever will act against government from that restless and turbulent anti-monarchical spirit which has always distinguished them everywhere."[49] Similarly, a colleague of the Earl of Dartmouth wrote him in late 1776 that "Presbyterianism is really at the bottom of this whole conspiracy, has supplied it with Vigour, and will never rest, till something is decided on it."[50]

Craighead did not live to see the final, all-out battle between Presbyterian "vigour" and English authority. He died in March 1766 at the age of fifty-nine. His was the first marked grave in Mecklenburg County and was in the old cemetery at Sugar Creek, where his headstone stands to this day. Although he did not live to see rebellion in the Carolinas, Craighead is credited by many as having led the way through his revolutionary teachings. Not surprisingly, many of the most prominent Whig leaders in the region in 1775 were parishioners of Craighead's, including Abraham Alexander and the Reverend Hezekiah James Balch. "[T]he Sugar Creek Congregation loved Craighead," records a *History of the Sugaw Creek Presbyterian Church*.[51] So respected was Craighead, that in 1791 the settlers called his grandson, Samuel Craighead Caldwell, to serve as their minister. Caldwell served for 35 years. Craighead's great-grandson, John Madison McKnitt Caldwell, served as minister at Sugar Creek from 1837 until 1845.

According to historian Charles Hanna, Craighead "was the foremost American of his day in advocating those principles of civil liberty under a republican form of government, to confirm which the Revolutionary War was fought."[52] But "Craighead's principal legacy," in the words of historian Dan Morrill, "was to instill among the people of his congregations a fierce determination to resist the imposition of unwanted authority from outside the community, especially from the State Capital in New Bern or from London."[53] Craighead had taught them that resistance to tyranny was obedience to God; and that this radical view was supported by scripture. As McKnitt would later put it, using words that could have come from Craighead himself, "whatever was the Voice of the *People* was the voice of *God*." The echo of Craighead's teachings would reverberate throughout the Carolina backcountry as tensions rose between England and her colonies.

4

"Brutal Sons of Bitches"
Thomas Polk and
the Sugar Creek War

Shall not the war of Sugar Creek be handed down to posterity? ... [H]ad I been pres-
ent — I most assuredly & without any ceremony had been murdered.
—Letter from Henry Eustace McCulloh to
Edmund Fanning, May 9, 1765

To the "unwanted authorities" — that is, the English — watching from afar, the Carolina backcountry appeared to be swarming with radical sectarians. In particular, the Scots-Irish were spreading so far and so fast in the Carolinas that the Anglican Church could not keep up. And wherever they went, they spread a virulent strain of Republicanism. The entire province was in danger of becoming a second Scotland — or worse, a New Ulster. "Cousin America has eloped with a Presbyterian parson," the writer and member of Parliament Horace Walpole wrote to a friend in August 1775.[1] The British government was determined that "Cousin America" break off this inappropriate engagement. Religious dissenters in Carolina, be they Quakers, Baptists, Moravians or Presbyterians, were to be passively discouraged if not actively suppressed.

The result was a simmering, largely nonviolent civil war in the backcountry for the hearts and minds of the people fought between the Anglicans and the Presbyterians. The "perverse persecuting Spirit of the Presbyterians," wrote the Anglican clergyman Charles Woodmason, an itinerant minister in the Carolina piedmont in the mid–1760s, "displays it Self much more here than in Scotland. It is dang'rous to live among, or near any of them — for if they cannot cheat, rob, defraud or injure You in Your Goods — they will belye, defame, lessen, blacken, disparage the most valuable Person breathing, not of their Communion, in his Character, Good Name, or Reputation and Credit. They have almost worm'd out all the [Anglican] Church People — who cannot bear to live among such a Sett of Vile unaccountable Wretches."[2]

Woodmason was a cantankerous malcontent who clearly didn't like anyone. In addition, he spent considerable time justifying the utter failure of his missionary efforts in the back-country. With that said, his journal, kept between 1765 and 1768, is a fascinating and often hilarious account of the harassment, threats and badgering by the Presbyterians he so despised. "I had appointed a Congregation to meet me at the Head of Hanging Rock Creek — Where I arriv'd on Tuesday evening," Woodmason recorded in February 1766. There he "found the Houses filled with debauch'd licentious fellows and Scot Presbyterians who had hir'd these lawless Ruffians to insult me, which they did with Impunity — Telling me, they wanted no D[amne]d Black Gown Sons of Bitches among them — and threatening to lay me behind the Fire, which they assuredly would have done had not some travelers alighted very opportunely, and taken me under Protection — These Men sat up with, and guarded me all the Night — In the Morning the lawless Rabble moved off on seeing the [Anglican] Church People appear, of whom had a large Congregation. But the Service was greatly interrupted by a Gang of Presbyterians who kept hallooing and whooping [outside the] Door like Indians."[3]

The Presbyterians broke into Woodmason's home and stole his sermons, hid the keys to meeting houses where he intended to preach, gave him wrong directions to get him lost, refused to provide him shelter on his travels; and organized riots to disrupt his services. At a sermon just after Christmas, "they hir'd a Band of rude fellows to come to Service who brought with them 57 Dogs (for I counted them) which in Time of Service they set fighting, and I was obliged to Stop."[4] On another occasion, a "Licentious Gang of Presbyterians stopt the Governors Messenger — broke open my Packet to see the Contents and would have whipp'd the Man, if not prevented."[5]

He recounted another episode. "This Day we had another Specimen of the Envy Malice and Temper of the Presbyterians," he wrote in December 1767. "They gave away 2 Barrels of Whisky to the Populace to make drink, and for to disturb the Service.... The Company got drunk by 10 [o']Clock and we could hear them firing, hooping, and hallowing like Indians."[6] When it wasn't the Presbyterians, other "Sects" harassed him. One night, someone stole his ceremonial black gown and slipped into bed with a woman, "making her give out next day, that the Parson came to Bed to her." This, he believed, was a "scheme laid by the Baptists."[7]

There was nothing he could do to stop these assaults; the backcountry was "infested" with Presbyterians. "It is in vain to take up or commit these lawless Ruffians," he wrote, "for they have nothing, and the Charge of sending of them to Charlestown, would take me a Years Salary — We are without any Law, or Order — And as all the Magistrates are Presbyterians, I could not get a Warrant — If I got Warrants as the Constables are Presbyterians likewise, I could not get them serv'd — If serv'd, the Guard would let them escape."[8]

In addition to religious tension, another major cause of the periodic flare-ups in the backcountry, even of actual violence, was the issue of land — or more specifically the issue of who owned it. Land ownership in the Piedmont was confused, to say the least. "Land matters in North Carolina are ... in unbelievable confusion," Bishop Spangenburg wrote in his diary, "and I do not see how end-less lawsuits are to be avoided."[9] The boundary lines between North and South Carolina were not settled. Title might lie with the Royal Colony of South Carolina, the Royal Colony of North Carolina or Lord Granville; in many cases it was not clear. Because it was not clear who was the actual owner, settlers were reluctant to pay for a parcel in case they were wrong about who the actual owner was. Fraud was also common, with settlers being charged more than once by various "true owners." "We do not know what land is vacant, and can only take for granted the word of the surveyor who says that such and such a piece has already been claimed," wrote Spangenburg.[10] Many of the settlers might have been happy to pay for their land in order to confirm title, but the confused state of affairs made this difficult.

Vast tracts in the Carolina piedmont were owned by various absentee English landowners. But because the lands were so remote, definitive boundary lines had not been set out, so in many cases it was not exactly clear which settlers had a legal right to be there and who did not. And for that matter, some settlers had no right to be there at all. Legally speaking, they were simply trespassers. Usually, this confused state of affairs did not matter. The landlords were far away, and so daily life simply went on quietly in the backcountry without outside interference. From time to time, however, the landowners sent agents to set off correct boundaries and collect back rent from the settlers. This caused much agitation and stress amongst the settlers. The historian Marjoleine Kars described it:

> Such families had invested much labor clearing fields, building shelter and fences, and planting orchards. When they were pressed to buy their farms for inflated prices or else leave their improvements, they, like the Indians in the face of European encroachment, had limited choices, all of them difficult. They could move on, hoping to find free land elsewhere, meanwhile losing the investment of their labor and resources. They could, if they were able, pay the inflated purchase price. Or they could resist the speculator's claims, aiming to either lower the price or scare him off altogether.[11]

In 1765, the Scots-Irish settlers in Mecklenburg were confronted with exactly this dilemma when an English land agent arrived to set off boundaries and collect past dues owed. The result was a series of riots, assaults and beatings later somewhat grandly called the "Sugar Creek War." And although no one was actually killed in the "war," the skirmishes that occurred demonstrated the settlers' willingness to resist outside English authority, and their clannish mentality. It also marked the first major involvement of a local figure, a young, Scots-Irish settler named Thomas Polk.[12]

The origins of the Sugar Creek War went back to May 19, 1737, when the British Crown granted two London merchants, Murray Crymble and James Huey, warrants — meaning purchase options — for 1,200,000 acres of land in the North Carolina piedmont. The warrants were conditional upon their ability to lure 6,000 Protestants to settle there, each to make annual payments to the owners of four shillings per 100 acres. These payments, called "quit rents," were an annual tax in perpetuity owed by the landowners to the Crown. The quit rent had its roots in medieval duties; once paid it "quit" the owner from any further feudal military duty. By this period, however, it was in essence merely an annual tax on the land.[13]

Crymble and Huey were mere go-betweens, however; the real owners were Henry McCulloh and his business cronies. McCulloh was a wealthy London merchant and land speculator. Tract nos. 1 and 3 of McCulloh's grant (comprising much of the future Mecklenburg County) were assigned to one of McCulloh's associates, George Augustus Selwyn (for whom a road and school are now named in Charlotte). Selwyn's sprawling tracts encompassed the Scots-Irish settlements along a small, shallow and muddy creek called Sugar Creek. The landowners had received reports from time to time that Scots-Irish settlers were squatting on their land. But without an on-the-ground agent to enforce their property rights and to compel payment of the quit rents, there was nothing they could do about it. The owners had to come up with a plan to regain some semblance of control over the area and to collect payment from the settlers squatting illegally there. But how?

The Carolina tracts were unmapped, distant and difficult to reach. Few survey lines had been drawn in the backcountry, so it was unclear who owned which parcels or where the boundaries between them lay. For that matter, it was not even known where the boundary line between North and South Carolina lay and thus whose jurisdiction the various settlements fell under. Settlers would "hold to the South"—claiming they were in South Carolina—when North Carolina governmental agents arrived, and of course do the opposite when South Carolina officials came through. "South Carolina surveyors were in the territory locating grants issued by that Province, North Carolina surveyors were there locating lands under her grants, and McCulloh's surveyors were also there in his interest," notes the *Colonial History of North Carolina*.[14] Land agents, surveyors and government officials roamed the dirt paths in the area attempting to map and survey who owned what, but no one really knew. For their part, the settlers were anxious to obtain clear title ("in fee simple") to the land, but there was no legal mechanism to do so. Both the tenants on the land (whether there "legally" or not) and the owners were stuck due to the feudal nature of the property laws. The whole situation was a mess.

Even if the lands were properly surveyed and identified, forcing the settlers to pay quit rents was not going to be easy. It was also quite dangerous. The settlers were poor, viscerally anti–English, and potentially violent. The areas in which they lived were distant and lawless. Not surprisingly, when agents of the Crown arrived in the region from time to time, "disorders were frequent and violent collisions, in some of which lives were lost," according to the *Colonial History*.[15] In one incident in 1762, the sheriff of Anson County, acting "in the King's name" attempted to restore order, but the settlers "damned the King and his peace and beat and wounded several of those whom the Sheriff had called to his assistance." Warrants for arrest of the rioters were returned annotated "not executed" as a result of the "threats and frequent abuse committed upon the officers of justice and the protection they met with from the South Carolina government."[16] Even Governor Dobbs himself was "personally treated with the greatest indignity" when he visited the Sugar Creek settlers.[17] Collecting quit rent was not a job for the faint of heart. In danger or not, McCulloh and his business associates were not going to give up their property without a fight. McCulloh then retained Colonel Nathaniel Alexander of Mecklenburg County and John Frohock of Rowan County as commissioners to conduct a survey of who was living on their lands and to report back. To oversee their work, McCulloh sent his son, Henry Eustace McCulloh, to Carolina.

The younger McCulloh would describe himself at the time as "Young in Life, Knowledge, and Experience, and totally unacquainted with the real circumstances of his Fathers affairs" when he arrived in this "strange Country" in 1761.[18] This was an understatement. Then in his mid–twenties, McCulloh was arrogant, brash and lecherous, almost the very stereotype of the rapacious English snot-nosed aristocrat. His twin passions were money and women, and in his travels in Carolina, he saw an opportunity to indulge his appetite for both. Writing from eastern North Carolina to his friend Edmund Fanning in Hillsboro, he noted "[t]hough I lead here a life of absolute Ease and Freedom, I long after the Flesh and the Proc [i.e., money] of thy Western regions."[19] To another he wrote, "Of nights, I follow Good King David's Example. Solace myself in the flesh way." The backcountry would allow him an opportunity to sample women across the state while shaking down the settlers living in the Piedmont, many of whom had fled to America to escape English bloodsuckers like, well, Henry Eustace McCulloh.

McCulloh's task, as he saw it, was simple and fair. Many of the settlers had come to the region after being enticed by offers of 100 acres per £5 sterling. Upon arriving, no one had demanded payment, and consequently they had not paid. Now McCulloh was here to make them an offer they couldn't refuse: collection of quit rents past due in exchange for leniency. To begin, he needed to survey the land and run boundary lines demarking tracts. Then he could survey each claimed tract and sell the land to the occupant, giving him a clear title in exchange for the purchase money and annual quit rent.

Not surprisingly, he was not warmly welcomed on arriving in the Piedmont. Because boundary lines had never been run, marking off territory usually meant taking lands from one settler and assigning them to another. In Mecklenburg, McCulloh observed that "many of the Settlers upon Mr. Selwyns Lands ... oppose their running any Lines." He also began to receive anonymous warnings and "the greatest threats against his Life and Person." Undeterred, McCulloh contacted local citizens who, through bribery or coercion, would help him. Accompanied with armed guards McCulloh "proceeded to run the said Boundary Lines," which he did "unmolested." His next step was to make a formal offer to them of how much per acre the land would cost. As it would be "extremely burdensome to him to make his Terms known to every individual in the Tract," McCulloh "recommended it to the Settlers to have a meeting and to choose and Authorize 4 Persons to meet and treat with him on the Subject."

One of the four designated to negotiate with McCulloh was Thomas Polk. Although the two men were almost the same age, the contrast between McCulloh and Polk could not have been more striking. Unlike the wealthy English dandy, born into wealth and privilege, Polk was a self-made man. Where McCulloh was effete and whiny, Polk was charismatic and rugged — the personification of the colonial frontier leader.

There are only a few existing drawings of Thomas Polk, but whether they are accurate or not is unknown. In one, Polk is shown as clean-cut and with dark eyes, a high forehead, swept-back dark hair, long sideburns, and the chin of a boxer. He had the rough but affable demeanor of a Wild West politician, which in many ways is was what he was. Though self-taught, Polk was literate, as were most of the Presbyterian settlers; several thoughtful letters of his have survived. Polk was an instinctive leader, nor was he afraid to make enemies. "I was not a little obnoxious to a vast majority of the Province in which I lived," he later wrote.[20] Tough, aggressive and mean, Polk was also the de facto leader of the poor Scots-Irish settlers in the region. Or as McCulloh later put it, Polk was "the only Man who has any pretense to sense or weight among these deluded People."[21]

The essence of McCulloh's terms to Polk and the other were as follows: First, each settler would have a right of first refusal, whereby he could match any offer made by another settler for his land. In other words, he was going to open every man's property up to auction to the highest bidder. Second, the settlers would have a three-year right to unwind the transaction and receive back their payments — both principal and interest. This, he believed, would absolutely cease all the settler's objections. It was, after all, a 100 percent money back guarantee. Third, each plat would be sold at "fair market value" (as determined by McCul-

Opposite: Detail from Henry McCulloh's surveying book circa 1763. "Shall not the war of Sugar Creek be handed down to posterity?" he asked (courtesy Southern Historical Collection, Wilson Library, University of North Carolina at Chapel Hill).

General Plan of Surveys from No. 40 to No. 54, inclusive

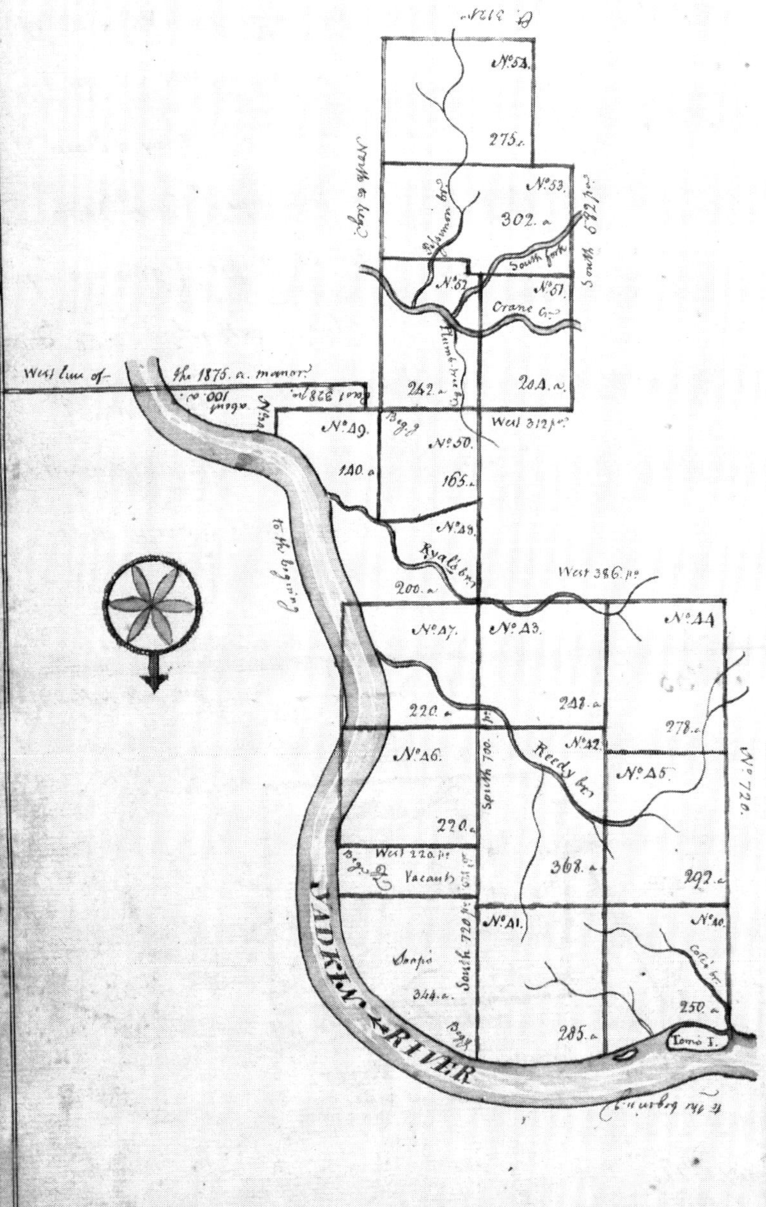

Plotted per Scale 200 po. to one Inch.

loh), between £8–£12 Sterling per hundred acres in 200 acre installments (although McCulloh was prepared to come down to "£5 and so in proportion according to Quality"). Moreover, "in the interests of fairness" McCulloh was further prepared to give a 30 percent discount to applicable buyers. Installment payments would also be permitted. Finally, back quit-rents from the time of settlement would be paid in full by the settlers. No further settlements on Selwyn's lands would be permitted until McCulloh had resolved these issues.

These were the "reasonable and equitable" terms McCulloh proposed. Then, mounting his horse, he announced that he would return in January to lay off the boundaries and settle all accounts. After he left, there was an uproar. Out of the blue, this arrogant young man had arrived demanding cash for the lands the settlers had tilled, improved and worked with their own hands. They had fled Ireland to escape grasping English landlords and now here they were again.

In late February 1765, McCulloh returned to Mecklenburg. Perhaps indulging in some wishful thinking McCulloh did not imagine he "should meet with the least opposition from the Settlers." The settlers had word he was coming, and, on March 4, "30 & 40 of the Settlers" had gathered, "with a design to oppose his coming upon the Tract." An angry crowd awaited his arrival. There were one hundred and fifty settlers "as near as he could judge." They were dressed in buckskin with bearskin hats. They carried knives and axes and a few had pistols. McCulloh sensed that the crowd bore him "ill return to his kind intentions." He had faced angry mobs before, but his heart must have raced as he rode slowly toward the sullen mob waiting for him at Alexander's farmhouse.

McCulloh did have one thing in his favor — the law. As a technical matter, he was in the right. These *were* Selwyn's lands and the settlers living there *were*, in point of fact, trespassing. Facing the hostile crowd, McCulloh held up copies of Selwyn's deeds and admonished the crowd of the "folly and consequences" of their failure to comply with his demands. The settlers were intimidated, but only for a moment. Polk and his henchmen "surrounded him." They had a counteroffer to propose, and it was also one that McCulloh couldn't refuse. With "the utmost insolence [and] manifest designs of terrifying him [and] contemptuous expressions of defiance," Polk offered him £10 per hundred acres.

By now McCulloh was surrounded, the crowd acting "more like Wolves than rational Beings." Shouting with anger, they pushed and jostled the young man, who was alone in a sea of hostile frontiersmen "continually gathering round him and talking to him in the most insulting manner." McCulloh maintained his composure, announcing his intention to begin surveying the next day. Some of the crowd "had the insolence to defy [him] in the most affecting manner, and others to tell him by way of friendly advice (as they insultingly pretended) not to try, for that if he did, the best usage he should expect to meet with, would be to be tied Neck and heels and be carried over the Yadkin, and that he might think himself happy if he got off so." The battle lines had been drawn.

The next morning, March 6, McCulloh rose from his bed to carry out his promise of beginning his surveys. The first thing he saw was "two of the Persons who had been there the day before sitting upon the Fence with Guns in their hands." A crowd began to gather. Polk was among them. In "taunting Language and insolent Behavior," Polk told McCulloh he "might depend upon it neither he nor the People would ever suffer any Sheriff or other Officer" to permit the land to be surveyed. McCulloh was "[a]mazed at such a Conduct from a person [he] little expected it from." He perceived "the greatest probability of their design to injure either his Life or Person." He called them "a parcel of Blockheads" and tried to walk away to begin his surveys.

Polk followed him, along with "100 more of his Gang many of whom were Armed with Guns." They surrounded the young man "in a most ignominious and taunting manner; and among other pieces of Insolence some of them asked [him] whether he had not great honor done him, and whether he thought he would have as many Men attend him to his Grave or not?" McCulloh, reckless or extremely brave, refused to be deterred. He proceeded to fix his compass onto his surveying staff and began to lay a chain down to walk out boundary lines. Polk's gang "gathered tumultuously round them, and notwithstanding [that McCulloh] made a solemn and a legal Proclamation in the Majesty's sacred Name to disperse the Riot," the crowd "paid no regard" and "contemptuously seized and broke the Surveying Chain in several pieces." Polk himself "with his own hands took the Compass off the Staff."

It was a pivotal moment, and could easily have ended with McCulloh's murder by an angry mob. "For many hours," McCulloh wrote, he was uncertain "whether that day was to have been the last of his Life or not." Perhaps realizing the gravity of the situation — and the consequences of treason and riot — the crowd went no further. McCulloh also got the message: "To persist would be to no other purpose than to incur the greatest risk of losing his Life." He fled Mecklenburg County immediately thereafter.

McCulloh had only been temporarily defeated, however. "Determined to revenge the settlers' challenge to his authority he lost no time in starting in Salisbury superior court further ejectment suits against some of the insurgents, in order, as he claimed to the governor and his fellow council members, to make 'Examples of some of the Ringleaders.'"[22] The settlers responded by writing to the governor and accusing McCulloh of simple extortion. In early April 1765 the lieutenant governor ordered the young Englishman to "desist from any Steps in Law to dispossess these People, 'till we meet at the General Assembly" to discuss such measures "as will tend to the quieting the Minds of the Inhabitants, and securing the Peace of His Majesty's Province."[23]

Perhaps emboldened by the support of the governor, the settlers escalated their resistance to McCulloh's work. The next month, in May 1765, McCulloh's surveyors, including John Frohock, Abraham Alexander and James Norris, were physically assaulted as they made plans to run boundary lines. The attackers, their faces blackened with tar and soot to avoid identification, "outrageously beat and abused" McCulloh's hired help.[24] Clearly, opposition to McCulloh had intensified. Instead of the threats and obstruction such as Polk had led, the settlers were now willing to engage in violence against the outsiders.

"More adventures yet," McCulloh wrote a friend shortly after the attack. "John Frohock says I can hardly form an Idea equal to the horror of their Behavior and Appearance." Frohock himself was beaten quite badly: "It made my heart quite full, when I first saw poor John," McCulloh wrote. "[H]e got one damnable swipe across the Nose and Mouth." "Abraham they say is striped from the nape of his neck to the Waistband of his Breeches, like a draft Board; poor Jimmy Alexander had very near had daylight let into his skull."[25] (In modern terms, Frohock had been hit in the face with some sort of blunt instrument, Abraham had been whipped from neck to waist so that his back looked like a checker board and Jimmy had been hit in the head with some instrument which broke his skull.) Fortunately for him, McCulloh had not been with his minions when they were attacked, because he would not have escaped with a simple beating. "Providentially detained by particular business

I was not there," he wrote, "had I been present — I most assuredly & without any ceremony had been murdered." The mob, he was told, had brought guns "for that particular purpose.— They declare solemnly — publicly, they will put me to Death."[26]

"Shall not the war of Sugar Creek be handed down to posterity?" McCulloh inquired rhetorically (and more than a bit melodramatically) of his friend Frohock. "Can the annals of the history of this Country, parallel this affair?"[27] His mission had ended in total failure. Now, overcome with self-pity and frustration, McCulloh was at a total loss as to what to do. "Is not my life in the greatest peril? — my friends cruelly abused for being so? — What am I to do?"[28]

The situation had the potential to get out of control, and so the governor was forced to become involved. On the one hand, the last thing he needed was a rogue agent stirring up a rebellion among the dissenters in the backcountry. This had the potential to burst into outright rebellion and violence, which he would then have to put down. On the other hand, assault and battery were unacceptable, and McCulloh and his family had powerful friends and allies in London. Although he was a pest, McCulloh did have the law on his side, and that could not simply be ignored.

On May 18, 1765, Lieutenant Governor Tryon announced, "[I]n the County of Mecklenburg several Rioters to the number of twelve or more, blacked and disguised and armed with Guns and Clubs to the Great Breach and Disturbance of His Majestys Peace and Government, did violently outrageously and riotously assault and beat John Frohock Esqr and others employed by the Honble Henry Eustace McCulloh in surveying and running out some surveys for persons settled in the Lands belonging to George Augustus Selwyn." The governor was keen for "the discovery of the said Rioters and that they be punished agreeable to Law."[29] If any rioters were to turn themselves and the others in, they would be exonerated.

No one came forward. McCulloh increased the pressure to defeat "King Polk." He asked Edmund Fanning to issue a writ of ejectment against him and to sue him for £1,000, a sum representing the lost rents during Polk's time on the land. "Have him [Polk] taken upon another for the mesne profits — £1,000 — don't fail." He also attempted to get Polk's commission as a magistrate revoked. "Damn thee, Tom Polk," McCulloh wrote, "if I don't conquer thee."[30]

In January 1766, a compromise was reached. Nearly half the settlers, including Polk, agreed to buy the land from McCulloh for £13 proclamation money per 100 acres. This was less than McCulloh had wanted, but more than the settlers' earlier counteroffer. The Sugar Creek War was over. But who had won?

In the short term, it could be argued that McCulloh was the victor. He had forced the issue and won a settlement from the Mecklenburg settlers. In the process, he seemed to have co-opted Polk, who later served as his land agent in Mecklenburg. But in the long run, things turned out quite different. "In the end," writes Kars, McCulloh was the "financial loser" of the Sugar Creek War. "The American Revolution completely undercut his business schemes and his lands were confiscated. While he eventual received £12,047 in compensation, he had lost many times that much. Clearly, in putting his hopes on the eventually victory of the king, McCulloh had bet on the wrong horse. He died in an asylum around 1810. The clear winners in the Sugar Creek War were the local power brokers who served as McCulloh's agents," such as Polk.[31]

The grave of Thomas Polk in uptown Charlotte. Polk was "the sole apparent Cause of the Opposition" McCulloh faced in the Sugar Creek War (photograph by the author).

The Sugar Creek War established Polk as the leading figure in the area. And while it appeared that he had been co-opted by McCulloh, perhaps the opposite was also true. Just a year later, on January 15, 1767, Polk, Frohock and Abraham Alexander, as "Trustees and Directors of the town of Charlotte" bought 360 acres from McCulloh's employer, George Augustus Selwyn, in exchange for "ninety pounds, proclamation money." The founding deed, a page and a half of tightly written cursive, signed by McCulloh as Selwyn's agent, defined the boundaries of the new town as "beginning at a White Oak about 150 yards from Thomas Polk's line."[32] A year later, the town of Charlotte was created. So while McCulloh got his money, Polk and the settlers gained a new town in bargain — and the center of town began in Polk's front yard.

Nor was there any doubt that Polk was responsible for the victory. Polk, McCulloh wrote, was the unquestioned "Leader and Spokesman of that unthinking Multitude" and "the sole apparent Cause of the Opposition" he had faced. In fact, McCulloh had been "creditably informed, that if [Polk] had not declared himself for them the second day," the backwoods peasants "would have submitted."[33]

In a report to the governor giving his side of the events on Sugar Creek in May 1765, McCulloh recommended that the authorities expel Polk from Mecklenburg, even from the province itself, lest he continue to cause trouble. This was his formal recommendation to the governor. In private, however, McCulloh's views were even blunter. Polk and his followers in Mecklenburg, McCulloh wrote, "may be damned for a pack of ungrateful brutal Sons of Bitches."[34]

PART II. HIGH TREASON (1775–1781)

5

"General frenzy"
Polk Summons a Meeting

Pursuant to the Order of Col. Tho. Polk to each Captain of Militia in his regiment of
Mecklenburg County, to elect nominate and appoint 2 persons of their militia company, clothed with ample powers to devise ways & means to extricate themselves and
ward off the dreadfull impending storm bursting on them by the British Nation.
— "Rough Notes" of John McKnitt Alexander, Date Unknown

The Mecklenburg County courthouse stood in the middle of the small village of Charlotte. As was customary in market towns of that era, it had been built in the intersection
of the two main streets. It was a rustic, one-room structure standing atop six red brick
pillars roughly ten feet tall. It had been built sometime prior to 1768 along the main north-
south Indian trading path near the home of Thomas Polk. The path — named "Tryon" in
honor of Royal Governor William Tryon — ran along a heavily wooded ridgeline towards
Salisbury, just over forty miles north of Charlotte. At Salisbury, the path merged with the
Great Wagon Road to Philadelphia.

Although Charlotte was located near the western edge of Mecklenburg County, the
courthouse was its political and commercial center. Distances to other towns, such as Salisbury or Camden, were measured from a marker placed beneath it. The town common
was the mustering point for the county militia. Official proclamations, announcements or
circulars were read from the courthouse steps. Legal notices, summons and writs (as well as
wolf pelts, for which a bounty was paid) were nailed to its doors.

Beneath the courthouse, a market was held, usually quarterly. Farmers, itinerant merchants
from the surrounding counties, and local Indians bought and sold a variety of goods and livestock there: firearms, liquor, corn, deerskins, beaver and bear pelts, as well as hogs, sheep,
cattle and horses (plus fresh shad when they were running in the Catawba River). The market
was raucous and smelly. At one point the community leaders undertook to "inclose the under
part of the Court house So as to keep out Suttlers [traders], Horses, Sheep, Hogs and other
things that may have any tendency to make it disagreeable as an exchange."[1] In the muddy
common nearby, idle or intoxicated townspeople engaged in the "frequent firing of Guns, Running Horse Races and playing at Long Bullets" (the latter a game in which a 28-ounce iron
ball roughly the size of a tennis ball was hurled down the road). These pastimes, noted the
authorities, had a "dangerous Tendency" towards personal injury and property damage.[2]

At first glance, the courthouse personified governance — and in particular British rule and British law. It was a symbol of civilization amidst a vast wilderness. But on closer examination, it had a deeper symbolism. The courthouse had been built with no outside assistance, evidencing the self-contained nature of life in the backcountry. Although the courthouse towered over the town common, the building itself was primitive, unpainted and hollow. A provincial court (specifically, the quarterly sessions of the "Inferior Court of Pleas") was held there on the third Tuesday in January, April, October and July of each year, but the officers who met there were all local citizens. Looking more closely, the courthouse did not embody British authority, but in many respects just the opposite. Local citizens had built the courthouse, and within it, they governed themselves.

The county was governed by "magistrates." It was essentially the executive, legislative and judicial bodies all rolled into one. Three magistrates — also known as "justices" or "JPs" — held court for a particular term. A few of these magistrates were lawyers but most were not. They simply brought their common sense and view of fairness to the issues they were faced with. Although they were appointed for life by the royal governor, it was at the request of the citizens of the county. While the franchise was limited to white, property-owning men, for the time and place Mecklenburg was magnificently democratic. Indeed, as historians Morison and Commanger wrote in *The Growth of the American Republic*, western North Carolina "was more democratic than any other section of the American colonies, excepting possibly Vermont."[3]

The magistrates wielded enormous power over the day-to-day life of their fellow citizens. "The powers, authorities and trusts belonging to [the magistrates] are many and important," reported Gordon in his 1767 report to Governor Tyron.[4] "They annually audit and pass the Sheriffs accounts of the public money" and were responsible for "building and repairing bridges, making and repairing high roads, repairing courthouses, jails and other public works." Their "jurisdiction is extensive and their proceedings summary in all questions which regard servants and slaves and touching their complaints of ill-usage," Gordon reported.[5]

The magistrates also regulated the taverns and inns along the public roads. In July 1778, they "[o]rdered that the Clerk immediately send notice to different parts of the County by publick advertisements therein that all person who keep tippling Houses or retail Liquors shall be prosecuted unless they apply at next Court and first obtain a License for that purpose."[6] Tariffs setting forth the regulated prices for food, drinks and lodging were required to be posted. In April 1775, Mecklenburg's magistrates fixed the cost of whisky and brandy at 5 shillings per gallon; West Indian rum 12 shillings per gallon; "good claret" and Madeira 6 shillings, 8 pence per bottle; and "strong beer imported" 2 shillings, 6 pence per bottle (while "strong beer of this Province" was only 6 pence).[7]

The magistrates validated and acknowledged deeds for real and personal property, maintained the public roads, oversaw and distributed the public treasury, appointed grand and petit juries for trials in the District Court in Salisbury, granted orders distributing properties for those who died intestate, and imposed and collected taxes.[8] Most important, the magistrates kept public order. Jurisdiction of the court in civil cases was limited to matters involving less than £20, while in criminal cases it could impose fines of £20 or less. While the court in Mecklenburg did not hear capital cases, according to Gordon, "they often inflict corporal punishment, such as pillory whipping and others that don't extend to life."[9] In short, all the mundane but essential functions of daily government were performed by local citizens of the county. The people on the frontier were not independent of British rule, but as a practical matter British governance was distant and remote. On a day-to-day basis, they governed themselves. In fact, the only thing that the frontiersmen usually *required* from the British authorities was permission — permission to charter a school, permission to build a mill, permission to perform a marriage ceremony. The government didn't do anything *for* them. Largely it only hindered them.

Obtaining permission from the regional authorities (for example, to charter a school or build a new courthouse) was slow and complicated. The assembly generally followed the recommendation of a county's delegates for local matters, but the governor's Council and the Governor himself had to agree and finally each bill had to be approved by the king. This could take several years. Mecklenburg's representatives introduced three bills (in November 1766, January 1768 and November 1768) before the town of Charlotte was finally sanctioned by the governor. Further slowing down the legislative process was the fact that any legislation passed in the North Carolina general assembly had then to be transmitted to the king via the Board of Trade and his Privy Council in London for final approval. (Perhaps not surprisingly then, the first two grievances made against the king in the Declaration of Independence were that the king "has refused his assent to laws the most wholesome and necessary for the public good" and had "forbidden his governors to pass laws of immediate & pressing importance, unless suspended in their operation till his assent should be obtained.")

As the colonies expanded, the authorities in London were unable to swiftly respond to the needs of the far-flung colonists. New courts could not be approved quickly enough to accommodate the new settlers. As a result, access to the courts was difficult and laws were unevenly applied. In July 1774 Governor Martin bemoaned "the discontent manifested and declared by a great part of the Inhabitants of this Country ... with regard to the Court-Laws."[10] Settlers sometimes took the law into their own hands, leading to anarchy and lawlessness in the backcountry. Increasing the settlers' frustration, not only did central government fail to perform its basic functions, such as administering justice in a timely . manner, but increasingly it also imposed new burdens and restrictions on them.

The most detested was taxation. Like owning a professional sports team in the modern world, being an absentee landlord of large tracts of wilderness in continental North America was the hobby of rich men — and like owning a sports franchise, it nearly always lost money. Financial issues had compelled the Lords Proprietors to sell their lands back to the king. Once the Province of North Carolina reverted to direct Crown rule, these net operating losses were absorbed by His Majesty's Exchequer.

In an attempt to break even, the Crown imposed usage, licensing, patent and other taxes and fees. The most famous was the Stamp Act of 1765. The Stamp Act was the first attempt by Parliament to impose direct taxes on intercolonial goods (meaning goods sold solely within the American colonies), as opposed to commerce between the colonies and Great Britain. The Stamp Act was badly received throughout the colonies. Demonstrations and sometimes riots occurred throughout North Carolina.

On November 16, 1766, in Wilmington a mob of over three hundred men, beating drums and carrying flags and torches, appeared at a local inn where Dr. William Houston, the newly appointed stamp collector, was staying. They convinced him to take a walk with them to the local courthouse where he was "invited" to resign his position. Given the size and temper of the crowd, this was probably not a difficult decision. Houston resigned on the spot, following which he was carried in an armchair back to his inn and toasted by his admirers with "the best Liquors to be had."[11] Similar demonstrations, and often more violent ones, occurred throughout the American colonies.

The Stamp Act was repealed, but a tax on tea was not, leading to additional riots and unrest. The tea tax of course was merely symbolic of the bigger principle. The real issue was whether Parliament had a constitutional right to tax goods and services in the American colonies despite the fact that no American citizens could vote for or send representatives to Parliament. Both sides dug in. Parliament was determined to defend its right to levy taxes in America while the Americans vehemently objected. *No taxation without representation* became the Americans' motto.

In addition to taxes imposed by Parliament, provincial officials imposed a bewildering and seemingly all-encompassing list of taxes, fees and fines. There was a "publick" or "provincial" head tax in each county to support public expenditures or other "pressing public needs." All of the legal officials except for the royal governor were supported entirely by transaction fees and none drew a salary. Thus there were a plethora of fees required to support them. There were fees for having the governor's secretary draw up certificates for probate of wills and for bills of sale. There were fees for letters of administration; fees for registers of shipping; fees for testimonials under the colony seal; and fees for civil commissions. There were fees to run a tavern (20 shillings); fees to "retail wine or spirituous liquors"; and fees to get married (also 20 shillings). There were even different registration fees, depending on whether the governor's large or small seal was required for a particular transaction. There was, it must have seemed, a fee or tax on everything.

In the payment of taxes, the local authorities required hard currency — gold or silver coin or specie — which was hard to come by, especially in the backcountry. In that area the economy was largely based on bartering goods and services (such as medical or legal assistance) for livestock or commodity goods. If a settler did not have enough hard money when the tax collector arrived the authorities might take his home or property and auction it off to pay his tax bill.[12] And given the broad authority granted to tax collectors — who were paid based upon what they were able to collect — corruption and abuse were rife. "As often as not," says *North Carolina: A History*, "friends of the sheriff ended up in possession of many desirable farms when owners could not pay taxes in silver."[13] As a result, tax collectors were routinely assaulted and even murdered in the course of their duties.

This combustible mixture of taxation, corruption and unhappiness exploded in what was called the Regulator Rebellion. The principal causes of the uprising were the terrible poverty and impossible living conditions of the rural population, combined with high taxes and corruption of local officials. As more and more settlers entered the central Piedmont, land became scarcer and more expensive. A series of droughts caused crops to fail year after year. Farmers had no products to sell. As their earnings plummeted, they became more and more indebted to landlords and speculators who offered to loan them money on easy credit but at exorbitant rates.

Despite the hard times, taxes continued to rise. Corrupt tax collectors and government officials seized farms and livestock on the spot when farmers were unable or unwilling to pay. Farms were confiscated and families ejected from their homes. The Piedmont became full of armed bands of destitute, angry, homeless men — men with nothing to lose, men with a grudge. The entire system seemed to be rigged in favor of the rich and powerful against the poor and oppressed. It was Ireland all over again. And just as in Ireland, things soon reached a tipping point. Mobs of farmers roamed the Carolina piedmont, terrorizing property owners, judges, tax collectors and sheriffs. In one county in central North Carolina it was estimated that of 8,000 male inhabitants, as many as 6,000 took up arms against the local government. It came to be known as the "Regulator" uprising because its leaders wanted to regulate their own affairs.

By the spring of 1767, it was unclear how far the unrest could spread and where it might end. Thus far, the backcountry settlers on the western frontier had stayed quiet. But Governor Tryon knew that the dissident Presbyterian Scots were no great fans of British rule; the Sugar Creek War had shown him that. Their loyalty was inherently unstable. If Governor Tryon was forced to call out the county militias to put down the Regulators by force, would they obey? If Mecklenburg and the frontier counties threw in with the Regulators, royal troops might have to be brought from England. In theory, the Province might even be lost.

Many in Mecklenburg (especially the poorer farmers) strongly sympathized with many of the Regulators' complaints. In fact, in May 1768 Governor Tryon received word that two Regulator sympathizers had been in Mecklenburg "spreading through the Inhabitants the Sedition that prevailed in the South part of Orange County."[14] However, most people in the area simply wanted to stay out of the whole mess. They had just gone through the Sugar Creek War and no doubt had little enthusiasm for another conflict. Mecklenburg had its own problems; why be drawn into the problems of others?

In addition, local leaders were put off by the Regulators' casual violence and anarchistic tendencies. The Regulators' targets for beatings and whippings were figures of authority and power in the province — wealthy landlords, lawyers and magistrates. In other words, people like Thomas Polk and John McKnitt Alexander. In addition, the bulk of the Regulator movement were Baptists or Quakers, who found little sympathy among the Presbyterians. "Though allegedly privately sympathetic to the plight of Piedmont farmers, they warned from the pulpit that any Presbyterians who joined the Regulation 'departed from the invariable Principals of their Profession.'" Some Presbyterian ministers privately assured Governor Tryon that they would act to "prevent the Infection spreading among the People of our charge, and among the whole Presbyterian Body in the Province as far as Our Influence will extend."[15]

But perhaps most important, many must have perceived that the Regulators had little chance of success. They were unorganized and undisciplined. While they might be able to ignite a rebellion against local officials, what real chance of success did they have against the full power of the British government? If the troubles in the Piedmont were a replay of Ireland, Polk knew how that story ended. All of them did. For these reasons, "[n]ot surprisingly, many prominent upwardly mobile Presbyterians actively supported the governor against the Regulators and found themselves handsomely rewarded."[16]

The backcountry settlers had no special love for Governor Tryon or his government. But he was the devil they knew. The Regulators, on the other hand, were men born of desperate circumstances, driven to rebellion by poverty and oppression. But in the end, their rebellion would be put down. If and when they lost, British retribution would be terrible.

All in all, the Regulators had little to offer the people of Mecklenburg. But Governor Tryon did. Tryon could offer them concessions from the British Crown, concessions which London would otherwise have no reason to give. Tryon could give them a small, but increased, measure of autonomy. He could allow them greater religious and political freedom. He could permit Presbyterian ministers to conduct marriages. It was certainly a better deal than anything the destitute peasant farmers could offer them.

So Tryon and the Mecklenburg settlers cut a deal. The backcountry militia would support the governor against the Regulators. In return, Tryon would repeal the Marriage and Vestry Acts. Second, Tryon would permit them to build a school in Charlotte — a Presbyterian school, so that the settlers did not have to send their children to New Jersey to be educated.

We don't know what was said or how a deal was struck, but we do know — because the subsequent facts show it — that a deal *was* struck. Tryon needed Polk and the backwoodsmen to hold the province. Polk needed Tryon to squeeze concessions out of London. It was a marriage of convenience, the English governor and the Scots-Irish frontiersmen, but politics makes strange bedfellows. Tryon's tactic was noticed at the time, with some Regulators complaining bitterly that "the Governor gives Commissions making one Col. Alexander, and another Captain Alexander, another Alexander Esq. Justice of the Peace, &c&c — And all this to take in a large body of Presbyterians."[17]

As Tryon had feared, in the spring of 1768 the Regulator rebellion spread and he was forced to call up the backcountry militia. In July 1768, Polk and the Mecklenburg militia joined a large detachment of militia (1,461 men in total, mainly from Rowan, Mecklenburg and Granville counties) and marched to Hillsboro. The Regulators had roughly 3,700 men in the area and were threatening to attack the courthouse. After two days, the Regulator army quietly disbanded and returned to their homes. The arrival in force of the militia quelled an outbreak of violence and sent a clear message that the frontiersmen could be counted on to support the governor if things escalated further.

The Mecklenburg militia had responded to the governor's request for assistance. Now it was Tryon's turn to keep up his end of the bargain. In return for Polk's support during the Hillsboro campaign, Tryon agreed to approve two laws as soon as the assembly passed them and to recommend them to the king for approval. The first would permit the chartering of a new college in Charlotte, the first of its kind in the South. The second would repeal the hated Marriage and Vestry Acts, which prohibited Presbyterian ministers from conducting marriages.

Polk was elected a representative from Mecklenburg County to the general assembly, and when the assembly next met, in December 1770, he moved a bill for the "founding, establishing, and endowing of Queen's College, in the Town of Charlotte in Mecklenburg County." The purpose of the new school was to impart a "competent knowledge of the Greek, Hebrew and Latin Languages to imbibe the principles of Science and virtue and to obtain under learned, pious and exemplary teachers ... a regular and finished education in order to qualify them for the service of their friends and Country." Funding for the college would be paid by a duty of six pence per gallon of rum "and other spirituous Liquors" brought into the county.[18]

Fourteen trustees of the new college were named, including Thomas Polk, John McKnitt Alexander and Waightstill Avery. The trustees were empowered to create and enforce such rules "as near as may be agreeable to the Laws & Customs of the Universities of Oxford

& Cambridge or those of the Colleges in America."[19] On January 15, 1771, the act establishing a new school in Charlotte was signed by Richard Caswell, speaker of the assembly, James Hassell, president of the Governor's Council, and, at the end of the session, Governor Tryon himself. A second act repealing the Marriage and Vestry Acts was also passed by the assembly and submitted to the governor for his approval. Both acts were now law. Mecklenburg was permitted to establish its own school. Presbyterian ministers were free to conduct marriages in the backcountry.

Or were they? Although the general assembly has passed the acts and the governor had signed them, they did not yet have the full power of law. Every act had to be sent to the Board of Trade in London for approval. The Board of Trade would then recommend to King George III whether he should give his royal approval or not. But until the king approved or disallowed the acts, they were only provisional. In most cases, approval by the Board of Trade was a formality, particularly if the act were championed by the governor. But nothing was certain. London was far away and divorced from the political realities on the ground in America. An act which seemed necessary and appropriate to the people in the colonies might be disallowed for reasons that seemed arbitrary to the colonists themselves. For example, a particular act might offend powerful political or commercial interests which could cause the board to recommend that it be disallowed. There was no telling for sure how the authorities in Whitehall and Westminster would react.

For these reasons, political sensitivity and tact were required, particularly regarding any act that affected the Anglican Church—as the act repealing the Marriage and Vestry Acts surely did. Education was also a sensitive matter. A new school in an area filled with dissenters might be used to indoctrinate children in radical views. The Crown was therefore reluctant to charter new schools, unless they were clearly aligned with British rule and the Anglican faith.

Recognizing these realities, Polk and his colleagues had proposed naming the new school "Queen's College" in honor of King George's wife. In addition, its charter specifically provided that "no person shall be admitted to be President of the said College but who is of the Established Church."[20] It was supposed that this would placate any fears in London that the new school would be a breeding ground for radical republicanism of the Craighead strain.

In a cover letter to the board dated March 12, 1771, enclosing the acts, Tryon made the case for their approval. Regarding Queen's College he wrote, "The necessity for such an institution in this country is obvious."[21] Although there were two schools in the province chartered by the king and permitted to grant degrees (one in Edenton and a second in New Bern) both were far away on the eastern coast, and neither was a Presbyterian institution. There was no comparable college in the backcountry. "[T]he Fellows, Trustees and Tutors I apprehend will be generally Presbyterians," Tryon wrote, "the college being promoted by a respectable settlement of that persuasion [Presbyterians] from which a considerable body marched to Hillsborough in September 1768 in support of government."[22] He reiterated that the president of the new school would be required by the charter to be an Anglican. And it was, after all, named *Queen's College.*

Tryon recognized that the act permitting Presbyterian ministers to conduct marriages was even trickier. This act stepped directly on the toes of the Anglican hierarchy. Tryon foresaw "great objections" from the Bishop of London and other Anglican power brokers.

Nonetheless, the demographic realities of the province made the act necessary as well, he argued. A review of the composition of the delegates of the general assembly, he wrote, "plainly evinced [that] the Presbyterians were the strongest party in the House." London might not like it, but revoking the Marriage and Vestry Acts was plainly in accordance with the wishes of the majority of the settlers. More important, Tryon wrote, they had earned it. "[T]he attachment the Presbyterians have shown to government," he argued, "merit the indulgence of this Act."[23] Tryon could not cause the Board of Trade (or the king of course) to approve either act. Whatever the king's pleasure, it was now out of the governor's hands. But he had lived up to his end of the bargain with Polk and the Mecklenburgers.

At the same time that Tryon was writing to London in support of Queen's College and the repeal of the hated anti–Presbyterian measures, the Regulator Rebellion was reaching a boiling point. By December 1770, entire counties were

Governor William Tryon. "[T]he attachment the Presbyterians have shown to government," Tryon wrote to King George III arguing for repeal of the Marriage and Vestry Acts, "merit the indulgence of this Act" (courtesy of the State Archives of North Carolina).

in open rebellion against the government. On January 19, 1771, four days after the general assembly gave the third reading to the act authorizing Queen's College, a council was held in the governor's palace at New Bern to discuss the unrest. Tryon was told that "people in the County of Orange who style themselves Regulators are still assembling themselves to the great terror and fear of the inhabitants."[24] Armed bands numbering in the thousands arrested local officials and attacked courthouses and the homes of judges and other prominent government officials. The province had the potential of disintegrating into total anarchy.

By March 1771 the uprising had spread to the very doorstep of Mecklenburg. A "most dangerous and lawless Insurrection" was brewing in nearby Salisbury, John Frohock wrote to Tryon on March 18, 1771.[25] A band of "four or five hundred" Regulators were "incamped in the Woods on this side of the [Y]Adkin River," north of the county. Frohock had heard that they had "formed a design to visit Salisbury Superior Court," possibly to burn it down or to capture the lawyers and judges there. "We went to them," Frohock reported, and "found some of them Armed and others unarmed [and] desired to know their Designs and what they wanted."

The Regulator leaders claimed that they had "no Intention to disturb the Court or to injure the Person or property of any one," Frohock wrote, "though there were several Threats and Menaces of whipping flung out by the lower Characters." Frohock believed that the silent majority of people in Mecklenburg and Rowan were tired of the roving bands and had grown "sick of Regulation and want peace upon any tolerable Terms," although, he wrote, a "Spirit of sedition" was being whipped up "with much industry among the lower class of Inhabitants here, who are loud in their clamors against the officers."

If the mob were to attack the Salisbury courthouse, however, the authorities were ready. Colonel Alexander and Captain Polk, Frohock reported, had "appeared from Mecklenburg with Seventy or Eighty men" to defend public order, "to whom the Thanks of this County are justly due."[26] Polk continued to live up to his end of the bargain he had made with Tryon.

Waightstill Avery was not so lucky. Avery was a well-educated lawyer and landowner, just the sort of person the Regulators hated. Around nine or ten in the morning on March 6, 1771, near the ferryman's house on the Yadkin, Avery saw "Thirty or Forty of those People who style themselves Regulators" and was seized and marched under guard to the Regulators' main camp.[27] While held prisoner, Avery overheard the Regulator leaders holding a council of war. They said many "opprobrious things against the Governor [and] the Judges of the Superior Court," he recalled, as well as "against the House of Assembly and other persons in Office."

Due to a Riot Act that the assembly had recently passed — an act directly aimed at giving Tryon the military authority to suppress the Regulator mobs — "the people are more enraged than ever." "If they had not made that Act we might have suffered some of them to live," Avery overheard someone say. "A Riotous Act! there never was any such Act in the laws of England or any other Country but France." Said others, "They'll bring the Inquisition next."

"Now we shall be forced to kill all the Clerks and lawyers," he also heard, "and we will kill them and I'll be damned if they are not put to death." "When news was brought that Captain Rutherford at the head of his Company was parading in the Streets of Salisbury," Avery recalled, the leaders of the gang demanded "very hard and strenuously that the whole Body of the Regulators then present should march into Salisbury with their Arms and fight them." "We can kill them," they said. "We will teach them to oppose us."[28] Despite the threats, Avery escaped the Regulator camp unharmed and the proposed attack on the Salisbury courthouse did not take place.

But two months later, in May 1771, the Regulators again gathered in force. This time they threatened to march on New Bern, seize the governor and burn the town. Responding to this provocation, Governor Tryon called out the militia, mustering just over a thousand men and marching to Hillsboro, where the Regulators were gathering. Polk and other local leaders in Rowan and Mecklenburg were urgently requested to gather men and weapons to meet the uprising. Time was short, however, and Tryon had already reached Hillsboro before Polk's militia set out from Salisbury. En route, the Mecklenburg militia met a large body of Regulators and halted. Tryon moved his forces south to assist them and intercepted the Regulators near Alamance Creek.

There, on May 16, 1771, the main body of Tryon's militia confronted a Regulator army of nearly 2,000. The governor demanded of them to "quietly lay down your arms," and "surrender up your leaders, to the laws of your country and rest on the leniency of the Government." They were given one hour to comply in order to prevent an effusion of blood and were reminded that they were "at this time in a state of rebellion against your King, your country, and your laws."[29]

"Fire and be damned!" the Regulators responded. Tryon obliged them. The superior military training, organization and equipment, including cannon, of Tryon's militia were too much for the unorganized farmers. Within just a few minutes, nine Regulators were killed and dozens, perhaps as many as a hundred or more, lay wounded and bleeding on the field. Tryon's losses are not known. What was clear, however, was that the rebellion had been smashed. A dozen of the Regulator leaders were captured and would shortly be put on trial for treason, with six being subsequently executed. The farmers were disarmed and forced to swear loyalty oaths to the king. The Regulator uprising was over.

In the spring of 1772, the Board of Trade began its review of the two acts Tryon had sent them on behalf of the people of Mecklenburg. When they had been passed and signed by Governor Tryon, more than a year earlier, Polk and others probably expected that the act authorizing Queen's College would be approved, while the act permitting Presbyterian ministers to perform marriage ceremonies would be disallowed. If both passed, all the better, but they no doubt considered this a long shot. What probably *no one* expected, however, was that London would reject *both* acts, which is exactly what happened.

"May it please your Majesty," began the board's report of February 26, 1772, "we have had under our consideration four Acts passed in your Majesty's Province of North Carolina."[30] One was the bill "establishing and endorsing of Queen's College in the Mecklenburg County." The second authorized "Presbyterian Ministers regularly called to any congregation within this Province to solemnize the Rites of Matrimony."[31]

In his cover letter to the Board of Trade, Governor Tryon had noted that "the necessity for such an institution" as Queen's College was "obvious" and reiterated that a "considerable Body" of Mecklenburg Presbyterians had supported the government during the Regulator uprising the year before. The Board of Trade, however, was unimpressed with Tryon's arguments. "From the Prevalency of the Presbyterian persuasion within the County of Mecklenburgh," it noted, "we may venture to conclude, that this College if allowed to be incorporated will, in effect operate as a Seminary for the education and Instruction of youth in the Principles of the Presbyterian Church."[32]

Permitting the Presbyterians to have such a school, they concluded, would only "add Incouragement to toleration [to] a sect of Dissenters from the Established Church who have already extended themselves over that Province in very considerable numbers."[33] This was intolerable. While the board was aware of His Majesty's "tolerating Spirit" and "disposed as we particularly are in the Case before us, to recommend to every reasonable Mark of favour and protection a Body of Subjects who by the Governor's Report have behaved with such loyalty and zeal during the late Troubles & disorders," nevertheless ... no. Or as the Board put it, "We do not hesitate humbly to recommend to your Majesty ... Royal disallowance of this Act."[34]

The second act whereby "Presbyterian Ministers [would be] allowed to celebrate the Rites of Marriage" was even worse. The board found the act "exceptionable," as it would permit a "tolerated Religion"—meaning Presbyterian—"to operate at the expense of the established"—meaning Anglican. This was a slam dunk "no." Absent exigent circumstances, the recommendations of the Board of Trade were adopted by the king as policy. In a letter from the Privy Council dated April 22, 1772, the will of the king was made known. "The

Queen's College, as imagined by artist Dan Nance. Established in 1771, the school's charter was revoked by King George III a year later to the anger of the local settlers. Today a plaque marks the spot in uptown Charlotte (courtesy Dan Nance).

said Acts," announced the Privy Council on behalf of the king "are hereby disallowed [and] declared void and of none effect."[35]

And that was that. There would be no college in Mecklenburg. The Marriage and Vestry Acts would remain the law of the land.

It would take some time for the news to reach Mecklenburg. The king's decision would have to be transmitted across the Atlantic to the governor in North Carolina. This could easily take four to five months. The governor then would issue a royal proclamation announcing the king's decision, which in turn would have to be carried by horse into the backcountry — another two to three months. In fact, it took over fourteen months before the governor announced the news to the citizens of Mecklenburg. In late June 1773 the governor issued the following Proclamation: "I do in pursuance of His Majesty's Royal Commands issue this Proclamation, hereby declaring the said Act[s] Disallowed, Void, and of none effect whereof all Persons are required to take notice and govern themselves accordingly."[36]

We don't know how long it took for the news to reach Mecklenburg, but it must have been that fall. At some point a messenger arrived with a copy of the royal proclamation, which was then read from the courthouse steps or nailed to the door of one of the local taverns. We don't have any record of Polk's reaction on receiving the news, but we can guess. He had been double-crossed.

As it happened, however, the signature at the bottom of the governor's proclamation of June 1773 was not that of William Tryon. After the Battle of Alamance, and while the two acts were pending in London, he finally obtained his long-sought appointment as royal governor of New York, a significant advancement in his career. His replacement was a man named Josiah Martin. Martin was in every respect the wrong man at the wrong time. Where Tryon had been pragmatic, decisive and strong, his replacement was whiny, weak and indecisive. In any event, Governor Martin's announcement lost him whatever friends he had along the western frontier; and given the events that were about to unfold, Martin was going to need all the friends he could get.

Protests against the tea tax continued to increase. In February 1775, Parliament declared the colony of Massachusetts Bay to be in a state of "actual Rebellion" and approved measures "to enforce the late acts of Parliament against America."[37] Parliament's threat to restore order in Boston by force unified the colonies in resistance to British rule. Five years had passed since the Boston Massacre and fourteen since the Boston Tea Party, but now the American colonies appeared ready to explode. "It is *no longer practical* to resist the Iron hand of oppression," read a circular letter sent to the Committees of Public Safety in South Carolina in April 1775.[38] "One general fact runs through all the colonies from Boston to Charlestown," read one report that same month, "which is that of resistance; the spirit of opposing the pretensions of the mother country is uniform through them all."[39] "[T]his arbitrary conduct on the other side of the Water," declared another Carolina paper, "has driven the people of this Capital and the neighboring Country TO DESPAIR of *a redress of American Grievances,* without an EFFUSION OF AMERICAN BLOOD."[40]

In Mecklenburg, they took up a voluntary subscription to send money and aid to Boston. Many agreed to contribute cattle. So passionate were the feelings of the people in the county, wrote McKnitt, that "had there then been a plan of government for their driving [oxen] to Boston, 100 would [have] been given in the county in one week."[41] Boston returned a note to the people of Mecklenburg thanking them for their goodwill. The colonies were ready to explode, and all it needed was a spark. "In the present state of general frenzy," Lord Dartmouth wrote to Governor Martin on May 3, 1775, "it is his Majesty's Pleasure that you do pursue every step" to calm the public. "I hope we may yet avoid the necessity of drawing the Sword," Dartmouth continued, "but it is prudent to provide as far as we are able against every possible mischief."[42]

It was amidst this dark and angry background that Polk sent a summons "to each Captain of Militia in his regiment of Mecklenburg County to elect nominate and appoint two persons" for a meeting to be held in the Mecklenburg County courthouse, on Friday, May 19, 1775.[43] The purpose of the meeting, McKnitt later wrote, was "to devise ways & means to extricate themselves and ward off the dreadfull impending storm bursting on them by the British Nation."[44] Almost exactly ten years earlier, in the spring of 1765, an arrogant, grasping Englishman named Henry McCulloh had arrived in Mecklenburg, threatening to take their lands, revoke their freedoms and hang those who dissented. Now it all seemed to be happening again, but on a larger scale.

6

"Fury and revenge"
May 19, 1775

After a short conference about their suffering brethren besieged and suffering every hardship in Boston and the American Blood running in Lexington &c the Electrical fire flew into every breast.
—"Rough Notes" of John McKnitt Alexander, Date Unknown

And thus it was that John McKnitt Alexander of northern Mecklenburg County found himself riding to Charlotte early on the morning of Friday, May 19, 1775, to attend the meeting scheduled for later that day. McKnitt was forty-two years old and, like many other frontier settlers, he presented a rugged appearance, the result of long days outside in the Carolina sun, plowing and planting, overseeing his slaves, mending fences around his property or riding for miles to attend to various commercial matters. These included surveying properties or buying various staples such as sugar, salt, cloth and needles in the surrounding counties.

He was a tall man, roughly six feet in height and, as remembered by his grandson, Dr. James Ramsey, "very symmetrical in his person." He "had a fine forehead and the most brilliant black eyes I have ever seen," Ramsey described him, and "was a man of great public spirit and enterprise," with "a vigorous intellect" and "self-reliant and energetic."[1] A neighbor of McKnitt described him as having a dark complexion, with a "good, intelligent face" and being "dignified, sensible and neat and tidy in dress."[2] According to Ramsey, "Everybody that knew us both always said I was his exact *facsimile* [in] stature, weight, complexion, temperament, intellect [and] tastes."[3] If it were true that McKnitt looked like Ramsey, McKnitt was lean and stern with the typical hard-drawn look of a frontier farmer. Tall, sinewy and weather-beaten, McKnitt was also acorn hard. Toughness was a family trait, and one the Alexanders took pride in. The family shared a Calvinist stoicism to suffering and an Irish resignation to loss.

McKnitt's toughness carried him well into his eighties, through a life that had as much turmoil and hardship as a Hollywood action movie. During his nearly nine decades of life, McKnitt worked in the unforgiving Piedmont summers; lived through the civil war that pitted neighbors against one another during the Revolution; twice survived the looting and pillaging of the region by British soldiers; endured the hardships that followed the War; watched as his life's work was lost in a house fire in April 1800; and then buried his wife, his friends and most of those of his generation, some of whom, such as Ephraim Brevard, died in his very house. His was a hard, uncompromising life, but McKnitt did not complain. By faith, upbringing and temperament, he took it.

We think of the earliest settlers in the Carolina backcountry as immigrants, and many of them were. But McKnitt was a third generation American whose only ties to the Old World were those of culture, language and historical memory. He was not an American — there was no such thing. If asked, he probably would have said he was a Scotsman, or a Carolinian, or even a Mecklenburger. At the time, the strongest affiliation he and most others had was to their town or region.

McKnitt was born on June 6, 1733, in Cecil County, in the northeastern corner of Maryland, at the head of Elk where the Elk River flows into the Chesapeake Bay near present-day Wilmington, Delaware. He was the youngest son of second generation Scots-Irish settlers. According to family tradition his grandfather, Joseph Alexander, had sailed from Ulster on the ship *Welcome*, anchoring in the Chesapeake on September 21, 1679.[4] His grandfather, Joseph Alexander, was

Photograph of John McKnitt Alexander's grandson, J.G.M. Ramsey. According to Ramsey, "everybody that knew us both always said I was his exact facsimile [in] stature, weight [and] complexion" (the Tennessee Historical Society).

forty years old when he arrived in the American colonies. He established a tannery on the bank of the Elk River in a settlement called "New Munster" and married Abigail McKnight (also spelled *McNite*, *McKnitt* or *McKnit*), whose maiden name appears in her descendants generation after generation.

Joseph Alexander died in 1730, at which point his New Munster property of 710 acres — patented with the record office as the "Joseph and James Settlement"–and his tanning business passed to his son James, McKnitt's father. James' first wife, Margaret — McKnitt's mother — died young, possibly in childbirth or from one of the illnesses which periodically swept through the frontier settlements claiming many lives, sometimes devastating (or eradicating) entire communities. James Alexander was a prominent citizen and community leader, a ruling Presbyterian elder at Christiana Church, a military officer (as coronet in the Cecil County Horse and Foot Militia), and a successful businessman and landowner. He acquired extensive real estate holdings around the Maryland tidewater. In 1721, he patented 170 acres, which he called "James Inheritance," and in 1724 forty-four acres, which he called "the Fortress." As more new settlers landed in Maryland and Delaware, property became scarcer and more expensive. James began to look elsewhere. Like many others, his eyes turned south.

Sometime around 1750 James Alexander traveled south into the gently rolling grasslands of the southern Piedmont. The area was almost entirely unsettled, as the royal governor, Gabriel Johnson, had just opened it for settlement in 1749. That year James laid claim to several acres of fertile, flat and densely wooded land along a small brook called Long Creek in Anson County, North Carolina (later part of Mecklenburg County). Four years later, in 1754, one of James' sons, John McKnitt Alexander, came from Maryland to take possession of his father's Long Creek tract. McKnitt was then twenty-one years old. Two of his brothers, Hezekiah and Ezekiel Alexander, four sisters (Jemima Sharp, Elizabeth Sample, Abigail Bradley and Margaret McCoy) and his brother's widow (Catherine Alexander), along with their families, followed McKnitt to the sparsely populated acres along Long Creek over the years that followed.

Establishing oneself in the backcountry meant starting from scratch, doing hard work clearing and planting the land and, to be a real success, pursuing a craft or trade. McKnitt had been apprenticed as a young man as a weaver and tailor, so when he arrived in the fledgling Mecklenburg settlement along Long Creek, he put these skills to good use, sewing and selling clothes for the newly arriving settlers. He made gowns, jackets, hats and handkerchiefs, and sold broadcloth, buttons, thimbles and knitting needles. In January 1767 he made a great-coat of mohair (hair from an Angora goat) with nine large buttons for Andrew Bowman. In this trade he used bolting cloth, a sturdy silk used for embroidery; corduroy, for waistcoats and breeches; fine woven linen, or cambric, for shirts, nightgowns and aprons; felt, cotton, linen and wool for hats, mittens, bed furnishings, window curtains and gowns; fine woolen broadcloth for suits and jackets; and buckskin (that is, deer skin), for breeches.

McKnitt became an all-around businessman, engaging in a variety of trades to make ends meet. He became a surveyor. Surveying was a lucrative profession, as virtually all of the surrounding area remained unmapped and unclaimed. Carrying a staff, compass and measuring chain, along with his crew of chain and axe men, McKnitt traveled widely throughout the region, marking out boundary lines for the registering or transferring of property. Through his contacts and travels, McKnitt acquired access to other goods, such as whiskey, rum, oats, sugar, allspice and beef, commodities which he sold to his neighbors. As one example, on May 13, 1765, he sold Daniel Alexander one hat, nine cups, a dozen buttons, one quart of whiskey, five pounds of tobacco and one strainer.

He brewed peach brandy and whiskey in a still at the base of the hill. In November 1769 he charged Joseph Sample £5, 15 shillings, 9 pence — a premium — for "good old Whiskey." (One quart of four-year-old peach brandy ran 2 shillings, 6 pence.) In January 1778 he charged David Maffoot 4 shillings for "one day hunting for liquor and bringing it from Major Davidson's" nearby home at Rural Hill. In 1769 he charged a customer £1, 12 shillings for "use of a cart, still vessels etc. etc. for making 32 gallons of very strong peach brandy."

In September 1762, McKnitt married Jean Bain, or Bean. Her father was a weaver from Chester County, Pennsylvania, near Cecil County, Maryland (where McKnitt was raised), and like the Alexanders, Bain owned land in Mecklenburg. We do not know whether McKnitt and Jean met in Maryland before coming to Mecklenburg, but we do know that they had a successful marriage and that she bore him three daughters (Margaret, Jean Bain and Abigail Bain) and two sons, William and Joseph.

Over the years McKnitt continued to acquire land around Long Creek. On April 23, 1765, he bought 509 acres from Lord Augustus Selwyn, an absentee English speculator who originally owned much of Mecklenburg County, and another 300 acres on McIntyre's Creek. In October 1768, he acquired 640 acres on the Broad River, in present-day Cleveland County, west of Charlotte. By 1775, he was one of the largest landowners in the region.

McKnitt built a log plantation home for his growing family. Various outbuildings, such as a smokehouse, stables, a corn crib, still, barns, slave quarters, chicken coops, hog pens, and, later, separate homes for his grown-up children were added over the years. Although it was a wooden frontier home, simple and plain in appearance, it was handsome and well-appointed for its time and place — a testament to McKnitt's commercial success. In his hall stood a cherry Queen Ann style parlor table and nearby a tall, hand-crafted clock made by William Gillespie of New London, Pennsylvania, a clockmaker whose products were expensive and prized. With a moondial face of brass, perfectly balanced hour, minute and second hands and filigreed spandrels in each corner, the Gillespie clock was an indication of McKnitt's prosperity and taste for quality and workmanship.

The Alexander home was a beehive of commercial and political activity. Sprawling over several thousand acres, it was visited by the great and the good, who came to seek counsel from McKnitt, enjoy his homemade brandy, and discuss commercial opportunities or the events of the day. So large and well known became the Alexander family's holdings that "Alexandriana" appeared on maps of the region in the early nineteenth century. Even as late as 1846, when the fourth edition of Yount and Mitchell's *Grand Map of the American Republic* was published, it appeared as a stand-alone place name, alongside such incorporated cities as Salisbury, Concord and Charlotte.

McKnitt was self-educated, which was common, and well read (both in scripture and politics). "His manner of speaking was calm and deliberate," recalled his grandson, "but exceedingly earnest and emphatic."[5] He had a respectable library for the area, including contemporary works by the English jurist Blackstone and likely a thick collection of sermons by the Rev. William Fenner, printed in 1656 in Giltspur Street, London. He was "exceedingly fond of books" and "read early and late with intense avidity," so much so that he lost his eyesight prior to his death.[6] On the inside of each of his books, in the top right corner, McKnitt clearly and gracefully signed his name in his customary fashion, underlining it with a clear line, broken in the middle like a lightning-bolt: *JMkAlexander.* Through his successful business affairs, civic involvement and political offices, McKnitt "became a man of substantial influence," in the words of one modern writer.[7] Colonel John H. Wheeler, a nineteenth-century historian of North Carolina, described McKnitt as "enterprising, shrewd and honorable."[8]

McKnitt was regularly elected or appointed to positions of prominence in the community, including delegate to the Provincial Congress at Halifax (August 1775); captain of the Mecklenburg County militia (September 1776 and April 1777); Mecklenburg's first county senator (1777); justice of the peace (1778); register of deeds (1792–1808); treasurer of the North Carolina Presbyterian Synod (1793); clerk and master of court (1782–1792); and trustee for the county (1808). Perhaps the most fitting description is one given by a biographer of his grandson, Dr. Ramsey, but which could equally apply to McKnitt himself: "He was a fit

John McKnitt Alexander's plantation, Alexandriana, is today a small park just north of Charlotte. Nothing remains of the original homes (photograph by the author).

representative of a Southern tradition, running back through Thomas Jefferson even to William Byrd the first, of cultured gentlemen who read the classics in their own libraries, took an active part in politics, contributed to the intellectual advancement of their communities, and stood in the forefront of movements for civic improvement."[9]

As more Scots-Irish Presbyterian families poured into Mecklenburg County, one of their first orders of business was establishing Presbyterian meeting houses (they could not be called *churches* as that term could be used only for establishments of the Anglican faith). In that part of the county, at first, the settlers held services under the spreading boughs of a large oak at the home of a neighbor of McKnitt's, a tanner named Richard Barry. As their numbers grew and a proper and more formal church was required, McKnitt donated several acres, where the settlers built a log church, formally dedicating it around 1765. Children threw stones in a sandy creek nearby or lifted small rocks to search for white crayfish beneath, while churchgoers watered their horses or washed their feet before daily services. It was named Hopewell, possibly after a church McKnitt had attended in Maryland as a boy.

McKnitt drew out a proposed interior seating arrangement for Hopewell by hand, methodically laying out the pews (twenty-four in all, sixteen facing forward, two rows of eight facing sideways, each 11 feet four inches long) and pricing the wood necessary for their construction. He served as a church elder at Hopewell until his death on July 10, 1817, and was buried in the quiet cemetery in front of the church, beside his wife, Jean Bean.[10]

On the morning of May 19, 1775, perhaps the most important event of McKnitt's life was at hand. As the mid–morning sun continued to ascend to its zenith, two dozen other militia officers were also riding along narrow forest paths to attend the meeting Col. Polk had called for that day in Charlotte. They were of varying social ranks and professions: blacksmiths, ministers, lawyers and farmers. They were also of varying nationalities. Although many, like McKnitt, were second or third generation colonial Americans, others were recent immigrants from Britain, such as Matthew McClure (Irish), John Queary (Scottish) and David Reese (Welsh). All were property-owning white men, and almost all were Scots-Irish (one notable exception being John Phifer, a Swiss Lutheran and a leading citizen of the county).

All were militiamen and a few were experienced military officers. They were frontiersmen, serious men, and men of accomplishment. One was an ordained Presbyterian minister. One was a doctor, and three were Crown lawyers. Four had previously served as elected delegates to the Provincial General Assembly. And almost to a man, they were devout Presbyterians, many of them of the militant Craighead viewpoint. Three of them were graduates of Nassau Hall, a small Presbyterian log cabin college in New Jersey originally established to train ministers. (It was later renamed the College of New Jersey, and thereafter Princeton University.) One Nassau graduate was a young attorney named Waightstill Avery. In addition to a quick wit he had a sharp tongue, so sharp, indeed, he was once challenged to a duel by another member of the Mecklenburg bar whom he had insulted. On the morning of the duel, tempers having cooled, both lawyers elected to fire over one another's heads — a common practice at the time. This spared the life of either North Carolina's first attorney general — Avery himself — or of his opponent, a young and hotheaded attorney from south of town named Andrew Jackson, later America's seventh president.

A Nassau Hall classmate of Avery's with the delightful Old Testament name of Hezekiah James Balch was also en route to Charlotte that morning. Rev. Balch was then thirty years old, and like Avery he was an excellent writer and speaker and regarded as a Whig. Balch had been one of the founders of the Cliosophic Society at Nassau Hall, a literary and debating club that exists to this day. In 1767 the Presbytery of Donegal in Pennsylvania licensed him to preach the gospel and two years later he was called to two congregations — Rocky River and Poplar Tent — where he acted as the successor to Rev. Craighead, his spiritual mentor.

The third Nassau Hall graduate represented that day was Ephraim Brevard, who had just turned thirty and was a doctor and teacher. His peers considered him brilliant, and a good writer, possibly the best in those parts. Brevard had lost an eye in his youth, by one account while playing in the woods. Despite this infirmity he had attended a Virginia preparatory school (later known as Hampden-Sydney) before attending Nassau Hall two years after Avery and Balch.

It was not a coincidence that three of the local Whig leaders were graduates of Nassau Hall. Originally founded by a Presbyterian minister, the school was named after William of Orange and of the house of Nassau, the Dutch monarch who, with his wife, Mary, had overthrown the Catholic James II in the Glorious Revolution of 1688 to become rulers of England. Nassau Hall was a hotbed of radical Presbyterianism. The trustees and tutors were largely New Light Presbyterians, the same evangelical sect to which Alexander Craighead had at one point belonged (before he split with them to found his own even more radical group). The political climate at the school was Calvinist and republican, teaching the rights of man, the consent of the governed, and the limited power of monarchs. In 1768, the year

Brevard graduated from Nassau Hall, its president was a well-known Scottish minister named John Witherspoon. A passionate orator, writer and theologian (he wrote three books on theology), Witherspoon was a leading American radical of the Presbyterian school. In July 1776, he would become the only ordained clergyman to sign the Declaration of Independence.

A second lawyer attending the meeting was William Kennon, a fortyish lawyer from Salisbury. Kennon was a well-known Whig and had been a vocal critic of the Stamp Act. On August 8, 1774, Kennon had been appointed a deputy of the Rowan Committee of Safety "to meet such Deputies as shall be appointed by the other Counties and Corporations within this Colony" in leading protests against the tea tax imposed by Parliament. The committee had adopted and published a number of anti–British resolutions over the years, many written by Kennon himself. In one resolution, they resolved that it was the "[d]uty and Interest of all the American Colonies, firmly to unite in an indissoluble Union and Association to oppose by every Just and proper means the Infringement of their common Rights and Privileges."[11]

As it happened, five of those riding to Charlotte for the meeting were relatives of McKnitt, including his cousin Abraham and his brother Hezekiah. As evidenced by their sheer numbers, the Alexanders were the most populous and influential family in the region. In many respects, Mecklenburg County was almost a private Alexander fiefdom. Alexanders were everywhere. Abraham Alexander was one of three "trustees and directors" named in Selwyn's original deed to the City of Charlotte. In 1771, four Alexanders (Abraham, Hezekiah, McKnitt and Joseph) were among fourteen citizens named trustees charged with "founding establishing and endowing Queen's College in Charlotte Town."[12]

When the general assembly passed "an Act for establishing the Court House in the Town of Charlotte, in Mecklenburg County" in 1774, an Alexander (Isaac) was named trustee. The bench for the Inferior Court of Pleas and Quarter Session for October 1774 listed two Alexanders (Hezekiah and Abraham) among the three judges; two other Alexanders (James and Chas) were seated on the Grand Jury. Alexanders served as magistrates, militia captains, "venirimen" (grand jurymen) for the district court in Salisbury, bondsmen, surveyors and assessors, and witnesses and securities for deeds. In a trial in Mecklenburg on July 14, 1779, four of the ten judges were Alexanders. Four other Alexanders were among the tax collectors appointed in October 1777. In the first U.S. census, taken in 1790, one district (Number 4, comprising the Sugar Creek Church District, which included the town of Charlotte) listed fifteen Alexanders as heads of families (of 95 total, or approximately 15 percent). Not surprisingly when the first history of Mecklenburg County was published in 1902, it was an Alexander (John Brevard) who wrote it.[13]

By late morning on Friday, May 19, the delegates had tethered their horses near the log courthouse in the Charlotte town common. To enter the courthouse, they climbed one of two simple exterior wooden staircases that faced each other on either side of an inverted "V." At the top of the staircase was a small standing platform. From there, looking away from the courthouse, they could look north, up the Salisbury road, or east, down a descending ridge that fell towards the slow-moving, brown Sugar Creek a mile away. No original record of who entered the courthouse that day and took part in the meeting that followed survives, but later accounts give between twenty-six and thirty-two attendees. Of those, the names of the leaders are generally consistent in all of the accounts: Polk, McKnitt, Brevard and Balch.[14] Nine of those who attended (or one-third of the total delegates) were Presbyterian elders, such as Abraham Alexander and David Reese.[15]

Other delegates included Henry Downs, a surveyor and tax assessor; McKnitt's neighbor Richard Barry; John Foard, a Scotsman; Neill Morrison, whose son, William, would later fight at the battle of Camden; John Phifer, whose family had been leaders of the Swiss Lutheran community along Buffalo Creek; and Zaccheus Wilson, who was later selected as a delegate of Mecklenburg to the State Constitutional Convention in Halifax in April 1776. Of some who were reported to have attended, such as Charles Alexander, Richard Harris, and Benjamin Patton, almost nothing is known.

It is not known for sure whether John Davidson, a neighbor of McKnitt's, attended, although he stated that he did (and at least one witness concurred). Another witness claimed that William Davidson, Samuel Martin, Ezekiel Polk (Thomas Polk's brother), William Wilson and Duncan Ochiltree attended, but no other accounts corroborate this.[16] (The confusion results from the fact that the list of delegates was assembled many years after the fact.) Perhaps Davidson, Martin and the others were simply in town as part of the large crowds that had gathered; perhaps they attended later meetings; perhaps the witnesses just got it wrong. Whatever the truth, most accounts give a total of twenty-six delegates in attendance on May 19 (and most accounts exclude the five — William Davidson, Samuel Martin, Ezekiel Polk, William Wilson and Duncan Ochiltree — noted above). The true list of those in attendance, and what exactly they discussed and resolved, will simply never be known.

Whoever attended, the delegates knew they had been summoned to discuss grave and dangerous issues — specifically, the threat of civil war that was looming, as neighbors were forced to choose between the patriots in Boston and the king in London. The agenda for the meeting, however, was quickly overtaken by events. Shortly after the meeting began, a horseman arrived in the town common bearing shocking news. One month to the day earlier — on April 19, 1775 — British troops had fired upon colonial militia at Concord and Lexington, Massachusetts. Open warfare between the British and the American colonists had begun. The time to choose sides, and to take action, was upon them all.

7

"There was not a dissenting voice"
The Mecklenburg Declaration Is Made

We (the County) by a solemn and awfull vote, Dissolved (abjured) our allegiance to
King George and the British Nation.
—"Rough Notes" of John McKnitt Alexander, Date Unknown

News traveled by the speed of horse from Boston. Express riders — so-called not because
of their speed but because they rode for the express purpose of delivery of news — rode in
every direction throughout the colonies, bringing news of Lexington. "To all Friends of
American Liberty," began one message from the Committee of Safety of Watertown, Massachusetts, dated April 19, "this morning before break of day a Brigade consisting of about
one thousand or twelve hundred men landed at Phipp's farm at Cambridge, and marched
to Lexington, where they found a Company of our Colony Militia in arms upon whom
they fired without any provocation and killed six men and wounded four others.... I have
spoken with several who have seen the dead and wounded."[1]

From town to town the rider carried the news of Lexington. At each stop, the recipients
would attest a "true copy" had been received — confirmation that the rider had discharged
his errand. By May 2, 1775, the news had arrived in Williamsburg, Virginia, with instructions to "forward the papers to the Southward." On May 4, the news was received in Edenton, North Carolina, two days later in Bath, and two days after that at the coast, in
Wilmington. The urgency of the message was evident:

Wilmington, May 8th 1775, 4 O'clock Afternoon.— Dear Sir: I take the liberty to forward by
express the enclosed papers which were received at 3 o'clock this afternoon.... For God's sake send
the man on without the least delay and write to Mr. Marion to forward it by night and day.[2]

From Wilmington, North Carolina, it went to Charleston, with the following instructions:

I take the liberty to forward by express the enclosed Papers which I just received from Wilmington and I must entreat you to forward them to your community at Georgetown to be conveyed
to Charlestown from yours with all speed. Enclosed is the Newspaper giving an account of the
beginning of the battle and a letter of what happened after. Pray don't neglect a moment in for-
warding.[3]

When the news of Lexington reached Charleston, South Carolina, it electrified the city. A
newspaper in Charleston reported:

[O]n the part of the Americans about thirty were killed, and three or four taken prisoners, not a single wounded man being found alive, the troops having, with a barbarity disgraceful to the character of British soldiers, killed all the wounded Americans: That at Lexington they burned four dwellings and two out houses; an aged man, whom they found sick in his bed, was run through with a bayonet, and two aged and infirm persons where shot in another house.[4]

Apparently, as is the usual case, the story had grown as it progressed farther from the battle site. In late June the *South Carolina and American General Gazette*, reported: "The cause of America is now become so serious that every American considers it as a struggle from which they shall obtain a release by an ample redress of their grievances, or a redress by the sword. The only alternative which every American thinks of is Liberty or Death."[5] In South Carolina, the Provincial Congress named Thursday, July 27 "a Day of FASTING and PRAYER; to humble ourselves before Almighty God, and implore his Favour to this oppressed Country, and Success upon all Endeavours for the Security of the Liberties of the American Colonies."[6]

Well before the news of Lexington was received, committees of correspondence or intelligence had already been established throughout the colonies to communicate information of political developments. On April 26, 1775, the general committee of Charleston appointed seven men — one of whom was Charles Pinckney, later a signer of the National Declaration of Independence — to constitute a committee of intelligence, whose purpose was "to correspond with, and communicate to, the Inhabitants of the interior and back Parts of this Colony, every kind of necessary Information." It was of the "highest importance," the Committee concluded, "that the committees in the interior parts of the Colony, and that, through them, the People at large, should from time to time, be informed of all such affairs and transactions as have any relation to the American Cause."[7]

On June 3, 1775, the Provincial Congress of South Carolina unanimously adopted the following resolution:

The actual Commencement of Hostilities against this Continent, by the British Troops, in the bloody Scene on the 19th of April last, near Boston; the Increase of arbitrary Impositions from a wicked and despotick Ministry, and the Dread of instigated Insurrections in the Colonies, were Cause sufficient to drive an oppressed People to the Use of Arms; We therefore, the Subscribers, Inhabitants of South-Carolina, holding ourselves bound by that most sacred of all Obligations; the Duty of good Citizens towards an injured Country; and thoroughly convinced, that, under our present distressed Circumstances, we shall be justified before God and Man, in resisting Force by Force.[8]

The Committee pledged its resolve to "go forth, and be ready to Sacrifice our Lives and Fortunes to secure [the] Freedom and Safety" of the American colonies.[9] During the night of April 21, the Charleston armory and magazine was opened by patriotic citizens, the committee reported favorably, "and a considerable quantity of arms and ammunition were taken, without doubt, for the ends for which they were originally procured — THE PUBLIC SAFETY."[10]

The Board of Trade and other British politicians and officials in London, relying on loyalists in America, had expected that the use of force in Lexington would cow the colonists into submission. The opposite proved to be the case. "The account of the Skirmish or Engagement between the King's Troops and the Provincials of Massachusetts near Lexington on the 19th of last month," dryly wrote William Bull, the lieutenant governor of South Carolina, to the Earl of Dartmouth in a letter dated May 15, 1775, "seems to produce effects here very different from intimidation."[11]

Meanwhile, express riders were carrying the news into the interior backcountry by many paths, including the Great Philadelphia Wagon Road. On May 17, 1775, in the Moravian settlement at Salem, North Carolina (today Winston-Salem), Brother Richter, returning from Philadelphia, brought with him a packet of letters, papers and church periodicals. The letters were dated April 25 and May 1, and "among other things mentioned the unpleasant fact that about April 19 there had been a skirmish near Boston between the royal troops and the Provincial Militia."[12] Salem was less than three days' ride from Charlotte.

In Charlotte the representatives convened on May 19 in the county courthouse, unaware of the news of the battle of Lexington but concerned that events in the colonies were headed in a bad direction. Community meetings of this type had occurred regularly throughout 1774 and 1775, as various communities attempted to reach a consensus on how to respond to events. Various resolutions denouncing British acts in Boston and declaring sympathy for the cause of American liberty commonly circulated among various towns. "During the Winter and Spring preceding [May 19, 1775], several popular meetings of the people were held in Charlotte; two of which I attended," one witness later recalled. "Papers were read, grievances stated, and public measures discussed. As printing was not then common in the South, the papers were mostly manuscript."[13]

The meeting on May 19 was larger than usual, however. One witness recalled that "a much larger number of citizens attended in Charlotte than at any former meeting — perhaps half the men in the county."[14] The delegates crowded the stairwells leading to the primitive unpainted room inside. "There was some difficulty in choosing the commissioners. To have chosen all thought to be worthy would have rendered the meeting too numerous," another recalled.[15] Sometime that day, an express rider arrived at the courthouse, which stood square in the center of the road and was thronged with a crowd of thirty or so people. His appearance and the reading aloud of the circular was electric. No original minutes of the meeting still exist. There is no account of what was said or by whom. The written records that do remain are ambiguous. Not that there is a total lack of direct evidence, about the meeting in Charlotte. Many years later, eyewitnesses who were in Charlotte that day, either as direct participants or as bystanders, gave their sworn accounts. Because no primary written records from the meeting exist, all that we have to go on nearly two hundred and fifty years later as to what happened in Charlotte on May 19–20, 1775, are the firsthand accounts of these key witnesses.

The first such witness was Joseph Graham, who in 1775 was a student at Queen's College. "I was then a lad about half grown," he recalled of that day, and "was present on that occasion [as] a looker on." "On the 20th of May, 1775," Graham continued, "[t]he news of the Battle of Lexington, the 19th of April preceding, had arrived. There appeared among the people much excitement."[16]

Another witness, named Humphrey Hunter, a highly respected historian, remembered, "I was 20 years and 14 days of age, a very deeply interested spectator" on that "memorable day." Hunter remembered that on May 19 "a far larger number than two out of each [militia] company were present" when the express rider arrived with the news of Lexington.[17] Hunter was born in Ireland and later emigrated to the American colonies. During the Revolution, he fought at the battle of Camden, where he was taken prisoner, while the American commander, General Horatio Gates, fled without pausing, all the way to Hillsboro, following the battle. Hunter became a Presbyterian minister and historian, writing a history of Revolutionary events in the southern colonies, including a vivid and often quoted account of the death of Baron de Kalb at the Battle of Camden.

According to both Graham and Hunter's accounts, arrival of news of the Battle of Lexington threw the meeting in Charlotte into chaos and confusion. Graham recalled that there was "much animated discussion."[18] As McKnitt put it, "We *smelt* and *felt the Blood* & carnage of Lexington, which raised all the passions into *fury* and *revenge*."[19] In order to "preserve order" in the courthouse it was necessary to appoint a chairman of the meeting. According to Graham and almost all other witnesses, Abraham Alexander was given this role.

At fifty-eight years of age, Abraham Alexander was the elder statesman of Mecklenburg and the logical choice. He was well known to his fellow citizens and had served often as a magistrate in that very courthouse. He helped found Sugar Creek Presbyterian Church and had been a close friend of Alexander Craighead. Alexander and Thomas Polk had served as delegates from Mecklenburg County to the Colonial Assembly in New Bern, from 1769 to 1771 under Governor Tryon. The two of them had worked closely on all of the major issues that had touched Mecklenburg in the last dozen years, including the Tryon Committee to recommend land dispositions following the Sugar Creek War and the founding of Queen's College. It would have been difficult, if not impossible, to have selected two men more in favor of separating from the British than Thomas Polk and Abraham Alexander.

With the elder Alexander in charge, someone was then selected to keep the minutes. By most accounts, including his own, this role was given to John McKnitt Alexander. (Some later recalled that Ephraim Brevard was secretary; at least one other recalled that both served in the role.) Tradition would take hold that McKnitt was the secretary of the convention, and the fact that he kept notes of the meeting and took possession of the original minutes seems to confirm this.

"The Chair being occupied, and the Clerks seated, the House was called to order and proceeded to business."[20] According to Graham, "After reading a number of papers as usual, and much animated discussion, the question was taken, and they resolved to declare themselves independent. One among other reasons offered, that the King or Ministry had, by proclamation or some edict, declared the Colonies out of the protection of the British Crown; they ought, therefore, to declare themselves out of his protection, and resolve on independence."[21]

According to Hunter's account, there was "a full, a free, and dispassionate discussion obtained on the various subjects for which the delegation had been convened."[22] McKnitt described the delegates as having a "free discussion in order to give relief to suffering America and protect our just & natural right[s]."[23]

A special committee was set up to draft the actual resolutions voted on by the delegates. The committee comprised the two Nassau Hall classmates, the Rev. Hezekiah Balch and the doctor Ephraim Brevard, as well as the Whig lawyer from Salisbury, William Kennon. The three recused themselves a block south of the courthouse in — irony of ironies — the wooden building that had housed Queen's College before the King rescinded its charter. Hunter recalled the following:

> Those resolves [in favor of independence] having been concurred in, bye-laws and regulations for the government of a standing Committee of Public Safety were enacted and acknowledged. Then a select committee was appointed, to report on the ensuing day a full and definite statement of grievances, together with a more correct and formal draft of the Declaration of Inde-

pendence. The proceedings having been thus arranged and somewhat in readiness for promulgation, the Delegation then adjourned until to-morrow [Saturday, May 20], at 12 o'clock.[24]

While the three-member drafting committee retired to Queen's College the delegates in the courthouse continued to deliberate. Graham gives the only detailed account of the actual deliberations that occurred that day. Because it is so vivid, it is worth quoting in full:

> [A] sub-committee, consisting of Doctor Ephraim Brevard, a Mr. Kennon, an attorney, and a third person, whom I do not recollect [likely Rev. Balch], were appointed to draft their Declaration. They retired from the court house for some time; but the committee continued in session in it.
>
> One circumstance occurred I distinctly remember: A member of the committee, who had said but little before, addressed the Chairman as follows: "If you resolve on independence, how shall we all be absolved from the obligations of the oath we took to be true to King George the 3d about four years ago, after the Regulation battle, when we were sworn whole militia companies together. I should be glad to know how gentlemen can clear their consciences after taking that oath." This speech produced confusion. The Chairman could scarcely preserve order, so many wished to reply.
>
> There appeared great indignation and contempt at the speech of the member. Some said it was nonsense; others that allegiance and protection were reciprocal; when protection was withdrawn, allegiance ceased; that the oath was only binding while the King protected us in the enjoyment of our rights and liberties as they existed at the time it was taken; which he had not done, but now declared us out of his protection; therefore was not binding. Any man who would interpret it otherwise, was a fool. By way of illustration, (pointing to a green tree near the court house,) stated, if he was sworn to do any thing as long as the leaves continued on that tree, it was so long biding; but when the leaves fell, he was discharged from its obligation. This was said to be certainly applicable in the present case. Out of respect for a worthy citizen, long since deceased, and his respectable connexions, I forbear to mention names; for, though he was a friend to the cause, a suspicion rested on him in the public mind for some time after.
>
> The sub-committee appointed to draft the resolutions returned, and Doctor Ephraim Brevard read their report.[25]

Graham and Hunter left the most detailed accounts of the events of that day, but not the only ones. "I was present in Charlotte on the 19th and 20th days of May, 1775," wrote Isaac Alexander on October 8, 1830, "when a regular deputation from all the Captains' companies of militia in the county of Mecklenburg ... met to consult and take measures for the peace and tranquility of the citizens of said county, and who appointed Abraham Alexander their Chairman, and Doctor Ephraim Brevard Secretary; who, after due consultation, declared themselves absolved from their allegiance to the King of Great Britain, and drew up a Declaration of their Independence, which was unanimously adopted."[26]

Another individual, Major John Davidson, testified that he was a delegate and recalled, "When the members met, and were perfectly organized for business, a motion was made to declare ourselves independent of the Crown of Great Britain, which was carried by a large majority."[27] According to other eyewitnesses, "the Delegates continued in session until in the night of that day [May 19]" and "on the 20th they again met, with a committee, under the direction of the Delegates, [which] had formed several resolves, which were read, and which went to declare themselves, and the people of Mecklenburg county, Free and Independent of the King and Parliament of Great Britain."[28]

What resolves did Brevard read to the delegates? We will never know for sure because the original papers are lost. But according to many witnesses, and some fragmentary papers found later among McKnitt's possession, Brevard read five resolutions to the delegates, the substance of which was as follows:

- First, that "whosoever directly or indirectly abetted, or in any way, form or manner, countenanced the unchartered and dangerous invasion of our rights, as claimed by Great Britain, is an enemy to this country — to America — and to the inherent and inalienable rights of man." The first resolution was a general statement of intent — you were either with the Whigs in Mecklenburg, or you were against them.
- Second, "we the citizens of Mecklenburg county, do hereby dissolve the political bands which have connected us to the Mother Country, and hereby absolve ourselves from all allegiance to the British Crown, and abjure all political connection, contract, or association, with that nation, who have wantonly trampled on our rights and liberties — and inhumanly shed the innocent blood of American patriots at Lexington."
- Having dissolved all ties to Great Britain, the militia leaders resolved "we do hereby declare ourselves a free and independent people" and "are, and of right ought to be, a sovereign and self-governing Association, under the control of no power other than that of our God and the General Government of the Congress." As devout Presbyterians, God came first, but right after was the Second Continental Congress, which was meeting in Philadelphia. To these ends, as well as "the maintenance of which independence, we solemnly pledge to each other, our mutual co-operation, our lives, our fortunes, and our most sacred honor."
- The fourth resolution declared, "as we now acknowledge the existence and control of no law or legal officer, civil or military, within this country, we do hereby ordain and adopt, as a rule of life, all, each and every of our former laws." By former laws, they meant the common laws and charter granted to them by the Lords Proprietors, laws that existed before the Crown took over governance of the Colony. The chief promise of the charter was religious independence, which the Presbyterians of Mecklenburg had always zealously protected. Finally, they noted, "the Crown of Great Britain never can be considered as holding rights, privileges, immunities, or "authority there" over them any longer.[29]

Of the four resolutions, three had announced in different ways the dissolution, voiding and cessation of British rule in Mecklenburg County. They were now "free and independent," and technically without laws or administration for public order. For that reason, the fifth and final resolution of the Mecklenburg Declaration put in place a provisional government for the County — specifically, self-governance by each one of them, acting as independent magistrates:

It is also further decreed, that all, each and every military officer in this county, is hereby reinstated to his former command and authority, he acting comformably to these regulations. And that every member present of this delegation shall henceforth be a civil officer, viz. a Justice of the Peace, in the character of a "Committee-man," to issue process, hear and determine all matters of controversy. [The mission of the Committee was] to preserve peace, and union, and harmony in said county; and to use every exertion to spread the love of country and fire of freedom throughout America, until a more general and organized government be established in this province.

In other words, British rule was abolished; and until the Congress stepped in and established a new government in North Carolina, the people of Mecklenburg County would govern themselves. To that end, a "selection from the members present shall constitute a Committee of public safety" for Mecklenburg County. These five resolutions would come to be known as the Mecklenburg Declaration of Independence.

Despite the fact that many of them had sat up all night in the courthouse, the delegates were "neither sleepy, hungry, nor fatigued."[30] McKnitt put it in more vivid terms: "[A]fter a short conference about their suffering brethren besieged and suffering every hardship in Boston and the American Blood running in Lexington," he wrote, "the *Electrical fire* flew into every breast," and "by a *solemn* and *awfull* vote, [we] Dissolved (abjured) our allegiance to King George and the British Nation."[31]

Hunter said, "The resolves, bye-laws and regulations were read by John M'Knitt Alexander. It was then announced from the Chair, are you all agreed? There was not a dissenting voice."[32] Others attested: "[The] Declaration was signed by every member of the Delegation, under the shouts and huzzas of a very large assembly of the people of the county, who had come to know the issue of the meeting."[33] The declaration was "publicly declared," recalled Samuel Wilson. "This was done before a large collection of people, who highly approved of it. I was then and there present, and heard it read from the Court House door."[34] Graham recorded the following:

It was unanimously adopted, and shortly after it was moved and seconded to have [the] proclamation made and the people collected, that the proceedings be read at the court house door, in order that all might hear them. It was done, and they were received with enthusiasm. It was

Dan Nance's painting of Colonel Thomas Polk reading the Mecklenburg Declaration from the courthouse steps at noon on May 20, 1775. The declaration was "received with every demonstration of joy by the inhabitants," according to James Jack (courtesy Dan Nance).

then proposed by some one aloud to give three cheers and throw up their hats. It was immediately adopted, and the hats thrown. Several of them lit on the court house roof. The owners had some difficulty to reclaim them. The foregoing is all from personal knowledge.[35]

"[T]he whole proceedings were read distinctly and audibly, at the Court-House door, by Col. Thomas Polk, to a large, respectable and approving assemblage of citizens, who were present, and gave sanction to the business of the day," as Hunter told the story.[36] "When the resolutions were finally agreed on," recalled a tavern owner named James Jack, "they were publicly proclaimed from the court-house door in the town of Charlotte, and received with every demonstration of joy by the inhabitants."[37]

It was noon on May 20, 1775. Mecklenburg County had declared itself "free and independent" of the rule of Great Britain. If the witnesses' stories were accurate, it was the first declaration of independence in the American colonies. Whether it *was* true, however, would in time become the subject of a ferocious debate.

8

"A rash act"
Treason and Second Thoughts

TREASON ... a betraying, treachery, or breach of faith ... when disloyalty so rears its crest, as to attack even majesty itself, it is called by way of eminent distinction high treason.

—Blackstone's *Commentaries on the Laws of England*, 1765

Among McKnitt's very few original surviving possessions is a copy of *Commentaries on the Laws of England* by Sir William Blackstone. Blackstone's *Commentaries* (known to generations of law students simply as *Blackstone's*) was originally published between 1765 and 1769 and today is considered the leading and definitive work on the development of English common law. This edition of *Blackstone's* was printed in England, shipped to America, and arrived in Charleston and Philadelphia in March 1772, where it sold for two dollars. Twenty-eight years later McKnitt gave it to his son, for in the top right corner of the first page of McKnitt's copy, in his crisp, flowing handwriting is written: "Joseph Alexander his book by the division I made on March 25, 1800 — J McKnitt Alexander."

McKnitt would no doubt have been familiar with Book IV of *Blackstone's*, which dealt with "public wrongs," meaning criminal acts, as well as crimes against the government, crimes such as treason. "[E]very public offence is also a private wrong," stated Blackstone, "and somewhat more; it affects the individual, and it likewise affects the community. Thus treason in imagining the king's death involves in it conspiracy against an individual, which is also a civil injury; but, as this species of treason in its consequences principally tends to the dissolution of government, and the destruction thereby of the order and peace of society, this denominates it a crime of the highest magnitude."[1]

A crime of the highest magnitude. In other words, High Treason. This concept in English jurisprudence dated back to the Treason Act of 1351, a law decreed by King Edward III but one that remains in force in the United Kingdom today (albeit in amended form). The law of High Treason as it existed in 1775 provided as follows: "[I]f a Man do levy War against our Lord the King in his Realm, or be adherent to the King's Enemies in his Realm, giving to them Aid and Comfort in the Realm, or elsewhere, and thereof be proveably attainted of open Deed by People of their Condition ... it ought to be judged Treason which extends to our Lord the King, and his Royal Majesty."[2]

Levying war against the king could take many forms. As Blackstone explained, "This may be done by taking arms, not only to dethrone the king, but under pretence to reform religion, or the laws, or to remove evil counselors, or other grievances whether real or pretended."[3] The motives for "levying war" against the Crown were irrelevant, Blackstone explained. "For the law does not, neither can it, permit any private man, or set of men, to interfere forcibly in matters of such high importance."[4] Nothing could justify resistance "for private or particular grievances."[5]

High Treason was the worst crime that could be committed and punishment for it was swift and merciless. If there were favorable extenuating circumstances, the convicted would be simply hanged. If not, an excruciating and agonizing death awaited — a death worthy of a traitor, which by law included disembowelment and dismemberment while the criminal was still alive. High Treason was more than an abstract judicial concept to McKnitt and his fellow citizens in North Carolina. They had seen the concept applied firsthand just four years earlier when the Regulators had been crushed at the Battle of Alamance and the Regulator leaders, including Benjamin Merrill, were sentenced to death.

In the case of Merrill the presiding judge at his trial had given his sentence according to the customary formula: "I must now close my afflicting Duty, by pronouncing upon you the awful Sentence of the Law which is, that you Benjamin Merrill, be carried to the Place from whence you came, that you be drawn from thence to the Place of Execution, where you are to be hanged by the Neck; that you be cut down while yet alive, that your Bowels be taken out and burnt before your Face, that your Head be cut off, your Body divided into Four Quarters."[6]

Now, four years nearly to the day following the Battle of Alamance, the Mecklenburg leaders were in Merrill's position. They had committed High Treason. If caught they would suffer Merrill's fate. This must have haunted them as they contemplated what to do next. For the ringleaders — Polk, McKnitt and Brevard — it was too late to turn back. They immediately took steps to consolidate their power and root out any loyalists among them. The fifth resolution of the Mecklenburg Declaration had decreed that a Committee of Public Safety was to be established "until a more general & organized government be established in this province." Each delegate was appointed a member of the Committee of Public Safety — or a "Select-Man" or "Committee-Man" — with the power to arrest traitors.

A "Special Court of Enquiry" — as McKnitt described it, "a civil court, founded on military process" — was established to enforce obedience to the new order.[7] Traitors or suspicious persons were to be arrested on orders of the safety committee and turned over to the state authorities. In essence, the county was put under martial law. As several participants described it, the committee of safety was "clothed with civil and military power, and under their authority several disaffected persons in Rowan, and Tryon (now Lincoln county,) were sent for, examined, and conveyed (after it was satisfactory proven they were inimical [loyalists]) to Camden, in South Carolina, for safe-keeping."[8] Another witness, a young militia private named John Simeson, later recalled that, "I myself heard a dispute take place on the bench, and an acting magistrate was actually taken and sent to prison by an order of the Chairman."[9]

"[B]efore this judicature all suspicious persons were made to appear," McKnitt wrote, "formally tried and banished ... or continued under guard." The power and jurisdiction of the special court "was as unlimited as Toryism — and its Decrees as final as the confidence and patriotism of the County."[10] Citizens were forced to carry with them a written attestation of their loyalty to the patriot cause. One such certificate dated November 28, 1775, signed by Abraham Alexander as chairman of the Committee of Public Safety, reads: "These may certify to all whom they may concern, that the bearer hereof, William Henderson, is allowed here to be a true friend to liberty."[11]

Word quickly spread of the coup d'etat in Mecklenburg. In June 1775, the Moravian pastor Johann Michael Graff wrote to his superiors in Germany:

[A]round us the unrest constantly increases.

In Mecklenburg County, where they have unseated all Magistrates and put Select Men in their places, they are threatening to force people, and us in particular, to sign a Declaration stating whether we hold with the King or with Boston, but we think that for the present these are only threats. If a higher authority should ask for such a Declaration of us, we think we will follow the form of the Declaration made by the Congress in Philadelphia concerning King George III, but say nothing whatever about the points at issue, which we do not understand. If a tax is laid on the people and we are expected to share in it, it will probably be better to bear what cannot be changed, than to refuse and so come into a much worse position. Such a course brought us fairly well through the recent Regulator confusion.[12]

The same month, two lawyers named John Ross Dunn and Benjamin Booth from neighboring Rowan County were seized, tried and deported on order of the committee of safety. The basis for Dunn's arrest was laid earlier that year. By his own account, he had been minding his own business when "a Certain William Temple Coles" approached him. Coles read out loud "Resolves or Protests, entered into by the people of New York and declaring their disapprobation to the Measures then Carrying on by the people at Boston & in opposition to the British Acts of Parliament, Touching the Tea act and other Acts." They were pro–British resolutions.[13] Coles approved of these "Very Much, and then said he thought it was Very Necessary and becoming the people of our Province" to make similar resolves. Coles asked Booth if he would draw up "something of that nature" on behalf of the loyalists of Rowan County. Booth agreed to do so. Later, Coles produced "a paper Containing a Declaration of Allegiance, fidelity and obedience to his Majesty and Submission to the British Acts of Parliament in General similar to that published at New York."

"Shortly afterwards," Dunn recalled, "being at Mecklenburg Court I had learned that Mr [Waightstill] Avery had by some means procured a copy" of these pro–British resolves. "I was also told that Mr Avery had Read it to the whole Presbyterian Congregation at their Meeting at Mecklenburg." Dunn liked to drink and, like lawyers of every age, he liked to talk. It was a bad combination. At Hatfield's Tavern in Salisbury one evening Dunn began "arguing warmly in favor of Ministerial measures" against America. According to a witness, Dunn argued "the Americans ... had no right to prescribe to the Prince and Parliament!" At times Dunn's comments were so incautious that "nothing but drunkenness could excuse him." As perhaps the last straw, local Whigs observed with suspicion that Dunn had a stray dog he named Tory.[14]

The Mecklenburg militia leaders took action to have both Booth and Dunn arrested. Dunn testified that toward the end of July 1775, he was "just recovering out of a fit of Sickness and at my own house in Salisbury ... [when] a number of Armed persons Entered ... [and] Seized upon my person."[15] He was taken away under guard. A few minutes later he "saw Mr. Booth Conducted in the same manner to the Same house." where they were held long into the night under the watchful eye of several armed Whig militiamen. "Shortly

The arrest of the loyalists Booth and Dunn in June 1775 as depicted by Will Puckett. Dunn's dog named Tory is in the foreground (courtesy Will Puckett).

afterwards William Kennon, Attorney at Law and Adlai Osbourn entered the room." Some sympathetic Salisbury merchants asked "for what reason, or by what authority, or by whose order" the two men had been taken into custody. Kennon answered, "It was at the desire of some Gentlemen from the Southward ... in Order to Examine us with regard to our Political Sentiments, with regard to the American Cause of liberty."

Later that night, nearly "thirty or forty Armed men from Mecklenburg and Tryon Counties" arrived to escort the two men to Charlotte. About two in the morning, they were "escorted by this Guard to Mecklenburg Court house where we Arrived in the evening of the next day." There they were tried, convicted and sentenced by the court of enquiry. The next day, Dunn recalled, an "armed force of about Sixty horsemen were Ordered to Convey me to Camden [South Carolina]." From Camden they were then deported to Charleston and detained for over a year — as Dunn put it, "in Direct Violation of those Rights and Privileges which Americans contend with Great Britain for at this Time."[16]

The arrest and expulsion of Booth and Dunn no doubt sent a message to other loyalists in the region about what awaited them. It also showed the power and reach of the Mecklenburg Committee of Public Safety. McKnitt later argued that although these measures were admittedly "arbitrary" they were necessary in "the cause of peace." Others were not so sure. The summary arrest and deportation of two citizens without public trial might have made some wonder if the committee of safety had gone too far. Most of the people wanted a quiet life. They saw trouble coming and wished for it to pass as quickly and painlessly as possible. They saw Polk and his cohorts as troublemakers and rabble-rousers, and feared that no good would come from the actions they had taken. "The timid, the Friends of the established Government, & the moderate, as they were called at that Period composed the bulk of the Inhabitants," Polk wrote in a letter to George Washington of June 26, 1778, "and by them was my forward zeal universally condemned."[17]

"There existed at that time at least three classes of Whigs, and three of Tories," recalled one observer. "The first class of Whigs were those who determined to fight it out to the last, let the consequence be what it might; the second class were those who would fight a little when the wind was favorable, but so soon as it shifted to an unfavorable point would draw back and give up all for lost; the third class were those who were favorable to the cause, provided it prospered and they could enjoy the benefit but would not risk one hair of their heads to attain it."[18] And then there were those who disagreed that the county should be "free and independent" in the first place. That same summer, Royal Governor Martin reported that he had received "a Messenger from a considerable Body of Germans, settled in the County of Mecklenburg, who brought me a loyal declaration against the Very extraordinary and traitorous resolves of the Committee of that County."[19]

It must have troubled even some of the most ardent Whigs that an unelected convention had taken such an unprecedented course of action. John Simeson recalled that he "heard Col. Polk have two warm disputes with two men of the county, who said the measures were rash and unnecessary."[20] A handful of the most extreme, anti–British leaders of the county had renounced their allegiance to the mother country in violation of oaths they had taken as militia officers and officers of the court and taken all power into their own hands. Nor was this necessarily a democratic act. Although the delegates had debated and voted on this act among themselves, it was not clear by what authority the delegates had any right to do so. Nor was there any subsequent vote by the people of the county to ratify or approve what they had done. To many, this was a divisive and dangerous course of action, one that many of their fellow citizens no doubt strongly disagreed with or at least considered provocative or unwise. After all, as Dunn pointed out, wasn't it arbitrary and tyrannical power that the Mecklenburgers were rebelling against?

As the initial passions of "fury and revenge" cooled, even the most staunch Whigs must have privately had second thoughts. McKnitt's handwritten notes give a clue to the cooling ardor among the delegates as they thought about what to do next. One fragment, torn in key places, implies that a second meeting was held in late May to attempt to rally the fainthearted. The fragmentary passage reads:

... allowing the 19th May to be a *rash Act* ...
... effects in binding all the middle & west ...
... firm Whigs — no Torys but ...
... not fully represented in the first....[21]

Not fully represented in the first.... First what? The missing word seems to be *meeting*. If so, McKnitt seems to be saying that a second meeting took place, in which "no Torys" were permitted to attend but other prominent Whigs who had not been "fully represented in the first" meeting on May 20 were present.[22]

A second clue regarding the state of mind is a letter from the committee of safety for neighboring Rowan County to the committee of safety in Mecklenburg written sometime in June 1775. The committee in Rowan noted "the alarming state of American freedom" drove them to desire greater communication "that the greater unity may be in supporting the common cause." They inquired about Mecklenburg's intentions and requested "an account of your proceedings, promising you a like Return."[23] The letter from Rowan concluded with a call to common prayer, and in particular a cryptic plea:

> We beseech you likewise that with us you would lift your Hearts in undissembled prayers to the Disposer of all Events, that He would by his providence interpose *against the Counsels of designing Men* [emphasis added], that we may have our Constitution as contained in the Magna Charta, the charter of the forest, the Habeas Corpus Act and the charter we brought over with us handed down unsullied to posterity, and that under God the present House of Hanover in legal succession may be the Defender of it.[24]

The Rowan letter is not a call to insurrection, but the opposite — a plea to the committee in Mecklenburg to calm things down. Reading between the lines, it would seem that the "designing Men" they are warning of — a common code phrase for the King's ministers — were, in this case, not the advisors to King George, but rather Polk, McKnitt and the other leaders of Mecklenburg. That this interpretation might be correct is indicated by an address from the same committee of safety to the Rowan County militia that same month. It began by reiterating that the people of Rowan remained "his Majesty's Loyal subjects" and that "his Majesty George the third is lawful and rightful King of Great Britain and the Dominions thereunto belonging."[25] The mood in the region, at least in nearby Rowan County, seemed to be cooling.

Rash and unnecessary. These words must have been on many lips as the hot summer of 1775 settled over the Piedmont. The delegates meeting on May 19 had not been given authority to declare independence when Polk summoned the meeting; indeed the very idea would have been unimaginable at the time. The news from Lexington had changed all that. With emotions running high and nervous energy in the air, the delegates had embarked upon the most radical act that could be contemplated. They had committed High Treason, and by inference the entire county had as well. By their actions every man who participated in the convention had exposed his life, his property and his family — and by extension the lives, property and families of his fellow citizens — to the gravest of dangers. Just four years earlier Merrill and his followers had been hanged for rebellion against the Crown. Why would their fate be any different?

Not only were their actions "rash" in the sense they were taken in haste and in high emotion, but they were also rash in their consequences. After all, if British rule were "voided" in Mecklenburg, who was in charge? The resolutions had provided that the committee of safety was to govern until the Congress established a new government in the province. But when would that be? And what were they to do until then? The people of Mecklenburg were in uncharted waters.

Normally, the next highest democratic institution would have been the North Carolina General Assembly. However, in the summer of 1775 it was not in session. Governor Martin had dissolved its last meeting after only four days and had given no indication of calling it again. Consequently it was not clear who was in charge of the province, if anyone. With the general assembly not in session, the only government to look to was the Second Continental Congress, which had been meeting in Philadelphia since May 10. North Carolina had sent three representatives to the Congress: Richard Caswell, William Hooper and Joseph Hughes. In the absence of a general assembly, these three men were the only elected officials representing North Carolina.

Legally and logically, Mecklenburg County could not take any step towards self-government without discussing it with these delegates. After all, if the county declared independence from British rule but North Carolina's own delegates did not approve, what was the point? At some point, someone in Mecklenburg suggested that the proper course, the safe course, the democratic course, was for the committee of safety to deliver the resolutions to its elected representatives to "get Congress to sanction or approve them."[26] This would give the committee of safety a correct and legal basis for its action. It would silence any doubters. It might also move Congress to take similar steps. This was easier said than done, however. Someone had to be willing to carry these instruments of treason over 550 miles, alone and in secret, to Philadelphia.

9

"I set out the following month, say June"
The Ride of Captain James Jack

A copy of these Resolves I am informed were sent off by express to the Congress at
Philadelphia as soon as they were passed in the Committee.
—Letter from Governor Martin to William Legge,
the Earl of Dartmouth, June 30, 1775

A few days following the meeting of May 19, wrote McKnitt, "a considerable part of [the] Committee Men convened" to decide what to do next.[1] Given their "rash" decisions on May 20 and the wavering views of some of the citizens, the committeemen concluded that the prudent course of action was to consult with their elected delegates in the Continental Congress. These three delegates were at the time the highest elected officials in the province and the only ones vested with democratic legitimacy to speak for the populace. But getting their guidance was not going to be easy. Philadelphia was over 550 miles away, and time was of the essence. After discussing what to do, the committeemen decided to designate a courier "to go express to Congress (then in Philadelphia) with a copy of all S^d. resolutions and laws &c and a letter to our 3 members there, Rich^d. Caswell, W^m. Hooper & Joseph Hughes, in order to get Congress to sanction or *approve* them."[2]

To do that, they needed a messenger, someone who was discrete, tenacious and, above all, dedicated to the patriot cause. In volunteering to carry the resolutions of the Mecklenburg convention, he would be carrying his own death warrant if he were to be caught by the British authorities—and not only his own death warrant, but a death warrant for all of those other men whose names were listed on the resolutions. Their lives would be in his hands.

The committee selected a forty-five-year-old tavern owner named James Jack. Jack— later and popularly known as "Captain Jack" due to his rank in the county militia—was the eldest son and one of nine children of Irish immigrants who came to America around 1730. His father, Patrick Jack, was born in Ballykelly, County Derby, Ireland, on September 19, 1700. His mother, Lillis (or Lillie) McAdoo, was said by those who knew her to be "one of the best of women," amiable, charitable and pious.[3]

Patrick and Lillie settled at first in Lancaster County, Pennsylvania, where Alexander

Craighead, John McKnitt Alexander and many other Mecklenburg settlers lived at the time. The Jack family moved to the Piedmont to escape the bloodshed and danger of Indian attacks during the French and Indian War, as did Craighead and many others. By 1760 the Jacks were living in a Presbyterian community west of Salisbury called Thyatira, a biblical name and the name of a church in Lancaster County, Pennsylvania.

In August 1772, the Jack family moved to Charlotte and set up shop near the town common. There they owned and managed a tavern known as Pat Jack's, a few hundred yards west of the courthouse. According to one historian, Pat Jack was said to "*crack* many an Irish joke, to the infinite delight of his numerous visitors."[4] No doubt the Jack tavern was the scene of much drinking and carrying-on.

James Jack had not been a delegate at the meeting on May 19 and the exact reason for his selection as a messenger to Philadelphia is not known. By his own account, he was "solicited to be the bearer of the proceedings to Congress,"[5] or recruited by the committee of public safety. As a tavern owner (and perhaps a merchant), Jack was probably familiar with the road to Philadelphia and had traveled it often enough that his presence would not arouse suspicions either on the road or in Philadelphia. Or Jack may have been solicited precisely because he was not a member of the convention of delegates. Many of the other

Painting of Captain Jack riding north to Philadelphia to deliver the Mecklenburg Declaration of Independence, by artist Chas Fagan. The courthouse can be seen behind Jack in the distance (courtesy Chas Fagan).

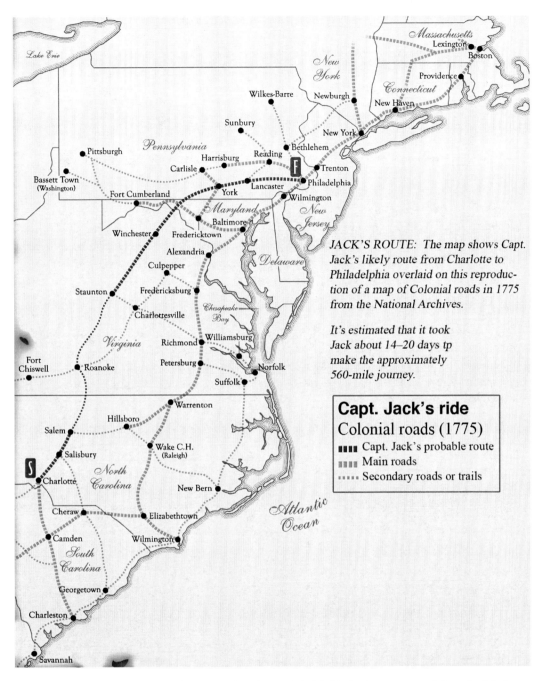

JACK'S ROUTE: The map shows Capt. Jack's likely route from Charlotte to Philadelphia overlaid on this reproduction of a map of Colonial roads in 1775 from the National Archives.

It's estimated that it took Jack about 14–20 days tp make the approximately 560-mile journey.

Capt. Jack's ride
Colonial roads (1775)
▮▮▮▮ Capt. Jack's probable route
▮▮▮▮ Main roads
•••••• Secondary roads or trails

The likely route of Captain Jack's 560-mile ride to Philadelphia in June 1775 to deliver the Mecklenburg Declaration of Independence (courtesy *Charlotte Observer*).

delegates, such as Hezekiah Alexander, Polk or Avery, were well known and would have been recognized if they ran into loyalists. Jack was less well known and would have more easily passed unnoticed.

Whatever the exact reason Jack was selected for the task, he accepted it. "[A] few days after the Delegates adjourned, Captain James Jack, of the town of Charlotte, was engaged to carry the resolves to the President of Congress, and to our Representatives—

one copy for each," witnesses later recalled.[6] According to Jack, "I set out the following month, say June."[7] Food, water and (where possible) lodging had to be found along the way. To pay for his trip, a voluntary subscription was established among the people of the county.

In good weather, and with a good horse, Jack would have been able to cover as much as fifty miles a day. However, in early June 1775 the weather in the Piedmont was violent and wet, which made the rough wagon road on which he was traveling difficult and nasty. "There has recently been much rain," recorded the Moravian journals for June 7, 1775. "Last night there was a very hard rain; about noon today the sun came out and it was oppressively hot, but about sunset there were more storms, and it rained heavily for three hours."[8] Travel was slow and generally miserable. When the storms broke, it became oppressively hot and humid. In the words of the later historian Hunter, Jack's ride was "long, lonesome and perilous."[9] In addition to the stormy weather there lay the threat of loyalists, who watched the roads and searched passing strangers.

James Collins was a teenager living on his family farm in York, South Carolina. "[T]imes began to be troublesome," Collins recalled, "and people began to divide into parties. Those that had been good friends in times past, became enemies; they began to watch each other with jealous eyes, and were designated by the names of Whig and Tory."[10] Collins volunteered to be a spy for the Whigs. It was a dangerous role. In his memoirs, Collins gives a good account of the methods of espionage at the time, possibly similar to those Jack employed:

> I had often been sent on business, by my father, in various directions through the country, and was frequently employed by others to hunt stray horses, etc., consequently I became acquainted with all the by-paths for 20 or 30 miles around ... [and] it was agreed that I should be made use of [by the Whigs] merely as a collector of news. In order to prepare me for business, I had to receive several lectures. I was furnished with documents — sometimes a list of several stray horses with marks and brands, sometimes with papers and other business. I was to attend all public places, make ... inquiry only about the business I was sent on, and pay strict attention to all that was passing in conversation and otherwise. I succeeded for some time without incurring the least suspicion.[11]

Friends and neighbors, even family members, ceased speaking with one another, and everywhere citizens gathered arms and stored gunpowder. Governor Martin complained that "spies and emissaries" of the patriots "keep the most strict and Vigilant watch upon every road and communication which leads towards me, that I have found myself defeated in almost every attempt I have made to correspond with the well affected people in the upper Country."[12] Loyalist delegates sent to meet the Governor that summer "to consult me about their safety, have been intercepted coming or going, and searched, detained, abused, and stript of any Papers they have had about them."[13] At every step along his ride to Philadelphia, Jack's odds of detection increased and his peril grew. Had he been caught in possession of the Mecklenburg papers, he would undoubtedly have been hanged for treason, possibly on the spot.

Senior British authorities, including the governor and the secretary of state for the colonies, were aware of Jack's mission, although they did not know his identity. In August 1775, Governor Martin wrote to the Earl of Dartmouth in London that he had been "informed" that "treasonable resolves" had been "sent off by express to the Congress at

Philadelphia as soon as they were passed in the Committee."[14] He might have learned this from informants in Mecklenburg, Salisbury or other stops along the way.

Jack's first stop was Salisbury, forty-odd miles, or roughly a day's ride, north of Mecklenburg. "In passing through Salisbury, the General Court was sitting," Jack recalled. "At the request of the court I handed a copy of the resolutions to Col. Kennon, an Attorney, and they were read aloud in open court." The following evening, as Jack remembered it, Major William Davidson and Waightstill Avery called on him at his lodgings, "and observed, they had heard of but one person, (a Mr. Beard) but approved of them."[15]

After Salisbury, the trading path crossed the Yadkin at Trading Ford. Often there were two or three paths at such river crossings, one for wagons, one for horses and cattle and the original Indian ford still used by those traveling on foot. After crossing this ford (the first of dozens) the next settlements were the well-laid-out and orderly Moravian towns in central Carolina. Leaving behind these settlements of neat fields and small, wooden cabins in the German style, the path (really a series of interconnected trails and side trails linked together like a spiderweb) crossed the shallow and rocky Dan River into Virginia.

In Virginia the trail ran generally north and then west, passing through a gap in the Blue Ridge Mountains at the Staunton River to the village of Staunton, a small outpost of a few scattered homes in an area then called the "Irish Tract." The path then took him northeast up the Shenandoah Valley (following what is today Interstate Highway 81). Here Jack passed scattered Quaker farms and Irish mud and daub houses and crossed the Fluvanna River at Looney's Ferry.

After Staunton, the next town of any size was Winchester, set amidst a rolling farm country of shattered granite rocks and low balds that resembled the treeless moors of Scotland. In Pennsylvania, the Wagon Road swung east through York and then Lancaster County. As he approached Philadelphia, farmhouses, taverns and villages became more common. So did the number of lumbering wagons headed south, behind which trailed horse and oxen. Compared to the frontier roads of the Piedmont, the Wagon Road in northern Virginia and southern Pennsylvania was a veritable interstate. Ahead lay Philadelphia. All in all, Jack rode 550-plus miles on his journey north.

An express rider, swapping horses every four or five days, would have been able to complete the journey in ten to twelve days. Stopping to rest his horse now and then, it probably took Jack just over two weeks. In any event, he is recorded to have reached the Moravian townships in central North Carolina by the first week of July on his return trip, so we know that the journey could not have taken much more than three weeks on the trip north, and probably about fifteen to twenty days.

We do not have any original evidence documenting what day Jack arrived in Philadelphia, how long he stayed, or what exactly he did there. We do know, however, that he got there. In 1830 several witnesses recalled that they had "frequently" heard William Alexander, deceased by that time, say that he was in Philadelphia "on mercantile business, in the early part of the summer of 1775, say in June," and that on the same day that "Gen. Washington left Philadelphia to take command of the Northern army" (June 23) he "met with Capt. James Jack, who informed him" that he had been sent on behalf of the committee of safety in Mecklenburg "as the agent or bearer of the Declaration of Independence made in Charlotte, on the twentieth of May [1775] by the citizens of Mecklenburg." Alexander said that

Jack had told him he had been given "instructions to present the same to the Delegates from North Carolina."[16]

The Alexander story quoted above was written many years later, when Alexander himself was dead and is based on what Alexander had said, as quoted by his sons. Legally this is known as hearsay evidence although even hearsay is admissible as evidence in certain situations. What is *not* hearsay, however, is the direct testimony of a witness — in this case, Jack himself. In a brief account in 1819, Jack wrote: "I then proceeded on to Philadelphia, and delivered the Mecklenburg Declaration of Independence of May, 1775, to Richard Caswell and William Hooper, the Delegates to Congress from the State of North Carolina."[17]

I delivered the Mecklenburg Declaration of Independence ... to Richard Caswell and William Hooper. Jack did *not* say that he also met with Joseph Hughes, North Carolina's third delegate — only with Caswell and Hooper. Also, Jack does not say he had an audience with the two men, only that he "delivered" the papers. Read literally, this might mean Jack simply dropped them off without further comment, in which case he was little more than a courier. Jack's brief testimony is all he is known to have ever written about his famous ride. His entire narrative is less than one page and omits a great deal. For example, it does not describe if he had a conversation with the delegates, or what was said.

Exactly what papers did he deliver? McKnitt wrote that Jack was tasked to carry with him "a copy of all S[ai]ᵈ resolutions and laws &c" as well as a "a letter to our 3 members there [in Philadelphia]."[18] McKnitt believed that "all S[ai]ᵈ resolutions and laws" included the Mecklenburg Declaration but exactly what the "laws &c" meant is not known. According to some contemporaries, Jack carried with him three copies of the Mecklenburg Declaration — one for each delegate — and perhaps a fourth for the Speaker of the House. The mystery of what Jack carried to Philadelphia, and what he told the delegates (if anything), has never been resolved and probably never will be.

Other than Jack's account and some second-hand ones, there is no written evidence of Jack in Philadelphia at all. The records of the Second Continental Congress do not mention Jack nor any messenger from Mecklenburg. The diaries, letters and papers of Caswell and Hooper (and Hughes for that matter) do not mention either any meeting with Jack or the Mecklenburg Declaration of Independence. The historical record is entirely silent. All we have is the testimony of Jack and a few of his contemporaries as witnesses.

The fullest historical account of the Jack story was written by Cyrus Hunter in *Sketches of Western North Carolina* in 1877, just after the centenary of the Mecklenburg Declaration of Independence:

Upon his arrival [Captain Jack] immediately obtained an interview with the North Carolina delegates (Caswell, Hooper and Hewes [*sic*]), and, after a little conversation on the state of the country, then agitating all minds, Captain Jack drew from his pocket the Mecklenburg resolutions of the 20th of May, 1775, with the remark: "Here, gentlemen, is a paper that I have been instructed to deliver to you, with the request that you should lay the same before Congress."

After the North Carolina delegates had carefully read the Mecklenburg resolutions, and approved of their patriotic sentiments so forcibly expressed, they informed Captain Jack they would keep the paper, and show it to several of their friends, remarking, at the same time, they did not think Congress was then prepared to act upon so important a measure as *absolute independence*.

On the next day, Captain Jack had another interview with the North Carolina delegates.

They informed him that they had consulted with several members of Congress (including Hancock, Jay and Jefferson), and that all agreed, while they approved of the patriotic spirit of the Mecklenburg resolutions, it would be premature to lay them officially before the House, as they still entertained some hopes of reconciliation with England.

It was clearly perceived by the North Carolina delegates and other members whom they consulted, that the citizens of Mecklenburg county were *in advance* of the general sentiment of Congress on the subject of independence; the phantasy of "reconciliation" still held forth its seductive allurements in 1775, and even during a portion of 1776; and hence, no record was made, or vote taken on the patriotic resolutions of Mecklenburg, and they became concealed from view in the blaze of the National Declaration bursting forth on the 4th of July, 1776, which only re-echoed and reaffirmed the truth and potency of sentiments proclaimed in Charlotte on the 20th of May, 1775.

Captain Jack finding the darling object of his long and toilsome journey could not be then accomplished, and that Congress was not prepared to vote on so bold a measure as *absolute independence*, just before leaving Philadelphia for home, somewhat excited, addressed the North Carolina delegates, and several other members of Congress, in the following patriotic words:

"*Gentlemen, you may debate here about 'reconciliations' and memorialize your king, but, bear it in mind, Mecklenburg owes no allegiance to, and is separated from the crown of Great Britain forever.*"[19]

This story became the locally accepted version of Captain Jack's ride for a century afterwards. It captures the spirit and daring of "Charlotte's Paul Revere" and the bold defiance of British rule by his fellow citizens in Mecklenburg.

But is it true? Hunter himself referred to these stories not as a history but as "Sketches." And he contradicts Jack's own, and much earlier, version (Hunter says he met with *all three* North Carolina delegates; Jack says he only met with two), which is not a great testimony to its accuracy. In addition, Jack's speech to the delegate appears in Hunter's version for the first time, nearly a century after the event, when Jack was long dead. While Hunter's version was loosely based on the known facts of Jack's ride, it seems clear that he embellished the story in a number of respects.

For that matter, is *any* of the Jack story true? Did he ride to Philadelphia at all? Some people later questioned the entire tale and suggested it was all a myth. However, based on his own testimony and that of various others, the evidence is convincing that Jack did ride to Philadelphia. The only question is what he was carrying in his saddlebags. Evidence of this ride includes a letter Royal Governor Martin wrote to London saying he had been "informed" that an express rider bearing certain "resolves" was sent from Mecklenburg to Philadelphia "as soon as they were passed in the committee." In addition, a dozen other witnesses corroborate Jack's ride.

Still, by the time the ride of Captain Jack became the subject of widespread public discussion in the mid–1800s most of the other firsthand participants — Caswell, Hooper and Hughes the most important — were dead. To skeptics who argued that the story was a myth, the evidence of the ride of Captain Jack was ignored or denied. That's where it was left for many years — a fascinating, if arguably dubious local legend, like George Washington cutting down the cherry tree. Without powerful conclusive evidence putting Jack in a certain place in the summer of 1775, that's where the story would have remained — a local fairy tale. That conclusive evidence would not be found for another hundred years.

Riding to Philadelphia and returning home, Jack passed through the Moravian settlements in the Wachovia tract near present Winston-Salem, North Carolina. The Moravians were quiet, extremely devout and determinedly nonpartisan. Although the colonies were in a state of growing unrest and incipient rebellion, the Moravians attempted to maintain an air of strict neutrality and principled calm. Moravian pastor Johann Michael Graff kept in regular communication with his superiors in Europe and sent them updates on the political situation in the colonies.[20] In late May 1775, Graff reported: "The critical condition of the English Colonies becomes constantly worse, though we personally have no reason to complain. It looks as though many persons would remain loyal to the Government, and from a number of settlements addresses have been sent to the Government, but we intend for the present to remain quiet."[21]

Graff and other Moravian elders also kept a meticulous and detailed diary of events, recording things such as strangers passing through, the weather, what was being planted and other news and gossip. In mid–June the Moravian diary notes, "Col. Armstrong came from Cross Creek [modern Fayetteville, North Carolina], and told us all sorts of things about the present unrest in the Colonies, the *confusion* constantly increases."[22] Three weeks later, on July 7, 1775, the diary records: "This afternoon a man from Mecklenburg, who had been sent from there *Express* to the Congress in Philadelphia, and was now returning, brought a circular, addressed to *Mr. Traugott Bagge.*"[23] The name of the rider is not given, but the timing and the circumstances of his journey ("sent there express to the Congress in Philadelphia") are unmistakable. The rider is James Jack. Indeed, a footnote in the *Records of the Moravians* states, "Undoubtedly Captain Jack."[24]

The Moravian diary corroborated the basic facts: he came from Mecklenburg; the purpose of his trip ("sent express to Philadelphia"), and the return date (July 7). This proved beyond peradventure that Jack had arrived in Philadelphia, completed his errand and was returning home. "Capt.ⁿ Jack returned to Charlotte in July, recalled McKnitt, bearing with him a "long, full, complanest letter from [the] 3 members"—Caswell, Hooper and Hughes—"recommending our *zeal, perseverance, order & forbearance.*"[25] "Congress never had our S[ai]ᵈ. laws on their table for discussion, though [a] copy was left with them by Captⁿ. Jack."[26] The committee of safety had sent Jack to Congress seeking its sanction or approval, but in the end they received neither. Jack did bring a message from Congress, however: Mecklenburg had been "premature." Independence would have to wait.

10

The Empire Strikes Back
"A most treasonable publication ... in Mecklenburg"

The Resolves of the Committee of Mecklenburgh, which your Lordship will find in the enclosed Newspaper, surpass all the horrid and treasonable publications that the inflammatory spirits of this Continent have yet produced.
    —Letter from Governor Martin to William Legge,
      the Earl of Dartmouth, June 30, 1775

The actions of Mecklenburg may have been "premature" but they had not gone unnoticed. In mid–June, Richard Cogdell, chairman of the Committee of Safety of New Bern, forwarded a newspaper to North Carolina Representative Richard Caswell at the Continental Congress in Philadelphia, noting, "You will observe the Mecklenburg Resolves exceed all other committees or the Congress itself." About a week later, on June 27, Sam Johnston wrote to Joseph Hughes, another N.C. delegate, "Tom Polk, too, is raising a very pretty spirit in the back country (see the newspapers). He has gone a little farther than I would choose to have gone, but perhaps no farther than is necessary."[1]

British authorities in North Carolina were also aware of the "spirit" in the backcountry, but that summer it was just one of the pressing matters they had to deal with: treason and rebellion were breaking out across the Carolinas. Following the news of the battle of Lexington in May, committees of safety from all parts of North Carolina held meetings in which they passed resolutions denouncing the British Crown. In reply, on June 16, Royal Governor Josiah Martin issued a proclamation in which he denied that Parliament intended to enslave the colonies, and he threatened retribution to traitors. It was not well received. Within the week, committees of safety representing five counties in the southeastern low country (New Hanover, Brunswick, Bladen, Duplin and Onslow) met in Wilmington to draft a response to the governor's proclamation. They prepared a counter-proclamation, which the delegates ordered to be printed in the public papers and in handbills.[2] "In our opinion," read the resolves, "his Excellency Josiah Martin, Esq., hath by the said Proclamation, and by the whole tenor of his conduct, since the unhappy disputes between Great Britain and the colonies, discovered himself to be an enemy to the happiness of this colony in particular, and to the freedom, rights and privileges of America in general."[3]

The stakes had been raised. As the Wilmington Resolves made clear, the success or failure of British rule in North Carolina that summer lay in the hands of His Excellency Josiah Martin. At first glance, that appeared positive for Great Britain. The governor was well connected: his father owned an estate in Antigua producing sugar, molasses and rum, and his brother Samuel was a barrister and member of the British House of Commons.[4] The Martin family had a long history of facing colonial uprisings. The family motto was *pro patria* ("for country"). An ancestor of the governor, Martin of Tours, had fought at the Battle of Hastings, while another relative had suppressed rebellions in Ireland during the reign of Elizabeth I. Other Martins had been less fortunate. His grandfather, a wealthy plantation owner on the Caribbean island of Antigua, was murdered in his bed on Christmas morning 1701 by his slaves.[5]

But a closer examination of Martin and his background spelled trouble for the future of British authority in North Carolina. In a contemporary portrait he has a long nose, dull eyes and a pudgy pink face seeming to embody the British aristocracy of the period — weak in mind and body. He looks arrogant and out of his depth, more like a man who would lose an Empire than a man who would create one. His behavior and career indicates this image was correct. As a student his father accused him of being "mulish in his tendencies, and tending much to ye vanity of dress and extravagance."[6] He was lazy and filled with self-pity. In February 1754, in what his biographer calls a "display of juvenile theatrics," the future governor complained of his "miserable & loathsome life" on the family estate in the Caribbean. "[U]nder my present circumstances," he wrote, "Death is preferable."[7]

By British law at that time, the eldest son inherited all estates, titles and incomes. The younger sons could go into law, the clergy or the military. Going into "trade" was out of the question as being totally unsuitable for the son of an aristocrat. Sons who failed at all of these were sometimes sent abroad as a "remittance-man," to receive an annual remittance so long as they did not return home and embarrass the family. With few options, Martin, like many a wastrel son of a wealthy family, opted for a career in the military (specifically the Fourth Foot Regiment of the Antiguan militia). His father hoped the service would give him "a better sphere of action" and cure him of his "two vices, that of women, and extravagance."[8] But by 1765 Martin's military career stalled and his future, in the words of his biographer, "looked bleak."[9]

"Poor Joe is much down in spirits by the fatigues in his Regiment," his father wrote privately to Samuel, "having no hopes of farther advancement in his profession." Josiah Martin resolved to "retreat to N. America" with a "deliberate view" to secure a post in colonial administration through the help of his brother Samuel's powerful political connections. His brother came through for him. In 1767 Martin was awarded a minor position as deputy quartermaster general for New York.[10] When Henry Moore, the royal governor of New York, died in the spring of 1770, Governor William Tryon of North Carolina was sent to replace him. This was a promotion that Tryon had been maneuvering for throughout his entire time in North Carolina. Through Samuel's lobbying, Josiah Martin was given the job of replacing Tryon as governor of North Carolina. Josiah wrote Samuel that he regarded the appointment as a "miracle."[11]

It was a hot, humid late summer day when Martin and his family arrived in New Bern, North Carolina, on Sunday, August 11, 1771. The new governor "admired the wild beauty of the land as it met the water," according to his biography. As the ship "approached the dock, Martin stood at the bow shading his eyes from the sunlight shimmering on the water and the trim white houses of New Bern. Through the humid heat he saw to his left the governor's residence, Tryon's Palace, rising above the humbler buildings. He surveyed his promised land and despite the discomfort of the heat and perspiration, he was pleased." Martin was thirty-four years old.[12]

That feeling would quickly pass. The Battle of Alamance was only three months in the past. The province simmered in a state of sullen anger. His new administration was starting out over £80,000 in debt, in part due to the building of the new "Governor's Palace," but largely due to the expense of fighting the Regulator Rebellion over the last several years. Martin proposed continuing a tax on rum, wine and other liquors that was set to expire at the end of 1771. The general assembly refused to extend the tax, but Martin instructed the local sheriffs to collect it anyway. It was, Martin reported to London, "a monstrous usurpation of authority that I think proves irrefragably the propensity of this people to democracy."[13] That was not a compliment. Relations between the new governor and the Whigs who comprised much of the general assembly began coldly and never thawed.

By the spring of 1775 it was an open secret that bloodshed would soon break out between the colony militia and British troops. As one committee in South Carolina put it, "There is but little probability of deciding the present unhappy public disputes, by the pacific measures we have hitherto pursued."[14] Governor Martin held conservative, unimaginative and unsympathetic views towards the colonist's demands for greater freedom. During the Stamp Act protests in 1765 while he was still living in Antigua, he had sneered at the "weak, timid, licentious mob[s]." Later he warned that repeal of the Stamp Act "so inspired this people with ideas of their power and authority" that the Americans would "dispute the Authority of Britain in every case." He believed that more coercive measures to demonstrate the "spirit of Govt" were necessary.[15] As the situation deteriorated in the colonies, Martin predicted he might soon need a restoration of his military rank, "when Civil Government should no longer be tenable," a situation which "the late frantic proceedings of the Northern Colonists, have at times, brought me to think possible."[16]

His relationship with the Whigs in the general assembly had broken down completely, leading Martin to first prorogue and then dismiss them. Whig leaders decided to call a meeting themselves. Newspapers and handbills were widely circulated requesting that the towns and counties elect delegates to a convention on April 3, 1775. Martin, aloof and alone, panicked. He denounced these "Unlawful Proceedings" and asked the people to "renounce, disclaim and discourage all such meetings cabals and illegal proceedings which artful and designing men shall attempt to engage them in, and which can only tend to introduce disorder and anarchy ... and to involve this province in confusion, disgrace and ruin."[17] No one listened to him and they proceeded with their meeting. The same month, Martin sent his family to safety in New York and took refuge in Fort Johnson at the mouth of the Cape Fear River. If the fort were attacked, he could escape by boarding the nearby British sloop of war *Cruizer*. Then the news of the battles of Lexington and Concord swept through the colonies, sending the situation into a "general frenzy."

On June 25, 1775, Martin called an urgent meeting of his Honorable Council to evaluate the alarming and deteriorating situation. Committees of safety and resolutions of rebellion were appearing all over the province like brushfires, not only in Mecklenburg but also in the coastal counties near Wilmington. The empire was determined to strike back, but where? Mecklenburg was a problem, but it was isolated on the frontier. With a loosely scattered population, no printing press, and little wealth, Mecklenburg had practically no influence over the province as a whole. Wilmington, however, was a different matter. It was a wealthy and populated port town and a center of commerce. Wilmington also had a printing press with which it could influence the rest of the province. Rebellion in Wilmington was a more urgent matter than what was happening on the frontier. And Wilmington, being a port city, was subject to the reach of British arms, specifically, the Royal Navy. If force was required, Wilmington lay in striking distance.

When the right honorable gentlemen had been greeted and seated, Martin "addressed the Council in the following Terms."[18] "[S]editious combinations" had been formed "and are still forming in several parts of this Colony," he began.[19] The "usurped Authority of Committees" in Wilmington and Mecklenburg called for action. In the backcountry, said Martin, there had been of late a "most treasonable publication of a Committee in the County of Mecklenburg, explicitly renouncing obedience to His Majesty's Government and all lawful authority whatsoever." These were "audacious and dangerous proceedings" which were "directly tending to the dissolution of the Constitution of this Province." His Majesty's Government, indeed the constitution of Great Britain itself, Martin concluded, had been "flagrantly insulted and violated" by a handful of rabble. They had, in short, committed High Treason.

The proceedings in Mecklenburg would not be tolerated. Order would be restored. But how? There was no money, no ammunition, no Regular British Soldiers. Outside the walls of Fort Johnson the population grew daily more sullen and, as Mecklenburg demonstrated, overtly hostile to the English gentlemen sheltering inside. Indeed, the very fort in which they were meeting, according to its own commander, "was in no state of defense." Originally defended by twenty-five men, it was now "reduced by desertion to less than half that number," and was "destitute of powder, & in no condition to afford a sure protection … in case of an attempt upon it." There was no ammunition for the guns, no replacements, not even any "funds allotted in this Country for such exigencies."

It surely was, Martin concluded, "an alarming conjuncture." He nevertheless expected his advisors "from your Duty to His Majesty and zeal for his service, and the good of your Country, not only your best advice, but your utmost influence in this to carry into execution most effectually the measures you may advise, for the support of the Rights of His Majesty's Crown, for the security and welfare of the People, and for the maintenance of the Laws and Constitution of this Province." Silence fell around the table. Someone coughed and chairs squeaked loudly, as each of his five advisors waited for someone else to speak first. Eventually, one of them broke the awkward silence. It was, he said, an "unhappy situation." Another noted pointlessly that it was a "time of commotion." But no one had any answers. They shrugged, and noted that Martin should do whatever he thought best. Another prolonged silence ensued in the meeting room.

Perhaps, proposed Martin, they could ask General Gage for funds to repair the fort and provide a garrison? It was unanimously agreed. The "most treasonable" citizens of Mecklenburg would be dealt with, Martin decided, once general order had been restored. Five days later, on June 30, 1775, Martin wrote a lengthy, detailed and obsequious report of events in North Carolina to his direct superior, the Earl of Dartmouth, British secretary of state for the American Department.[20]

The situation in New Bern, Martin wrote, had disintegrated following receipt of word of the battle at Lexington in Massachusetts Bay Colony. The "Account of the Affair of the 20th of April between a Detachment of the King's Troops and the People of the neighborhood of Boston ... reached me in little less time than two months after the event, and too late to operate against the infamous and false reports of that transaction which were circulated to this Distance from Boston in the space of 12 or 13 days." The "gross and abominable forgeries of the New England People, had taken deep root in the minds of the vulgar here universally and wrought a great change in the face of things, confirming the seditious in their evil purposes, and bringing over vast numbers of the fickle, wavering and unsteady multitude to their party."

So inflamed had the situation become, Martin wrote, that he was forced to leave the Royal Palace at New Bern and retire into Fort Johnson when he received word that a mob had gathered "stimulated by some of the Leaders in sedition" and "inflamed with liquour." They attempted "to seize and carry off the cannon behind my house, which they likewise made some slight attempt to break into." After "repeatedly demanding the Keys of it in vain of my servants, who in consequence of my orders (having notice of the intention of the rabble) had spiked the guns, to the great disappointment and discomfiture of the Assailants." On top of all this presumptuousness, wrote Martin, the "most unprovoked & unnatural Rebellion that has even been known" had broken out in Wilmington. He enclosed a newspaper to Dartmouth, describing the Wilmington resolves of June 21. "The Newspaper enclosed," the governor wrote, "your Lordship will find this Publication prescribes me as an Enemy to this Province in particular, and to America in General."

If the Wilmington resolutions were "impudent," the resolutions passed by Mecklenburg were worse. Again enclosing a newspaper with his letter to Dartmouth, Martin wrote:

> The Resolves of the Committee of Mecklenburgh, which your Lordship will find in the enclosed Newspaper, surpass all the horrid and treasonable publications that the inflammatory spirits of this Continent have yet produced, and your Lordship may depend its Authors and Abettors will not escape my due notice, whenever my hands are sufficiently strengthened to attempt the recovery of the lost authority of Government. A copy of these Resolves I am informed were sent off by express to the Congress at Philadelphia as soon as they were passed in the Committee.[21]

Sadly, concluded the forlorn governor, "it is to me at this time evident, and out of all doubt, that reason and argument can never restore the just power and authority of Government in America[:]

> The People now freely talk of Hostility toward Britain in the language of Aliens and avowed Enemies and I fear the means that British spirit at last resorts to for the chastisement of her more natural foes can only now reclaim her most unnatural children in these Colonies to a proper sense of their duty; and I must add too, my Lord, that in charity to them and in duty to my King and country I think myself bound to give it as my sincere opinion that the rod of correction cannot consistently with the good and interest of either be longer spared.[22]

Martin was surely right about one thing: British rule was not going to be restored to the province of North Carolina by "reason and argument" alone. In fact Martin could not even restore himself to the Governor's Palace in New Bern. Soon it was not even safe for him to set foot on North Carolina soil. Martin and his advisors were forced to flee from Fort Johnson to a British sloop in the Cape Fear River on July 14. Angered colonists demolished Fort Johnson. Four days later, on Tuesday, July 18, 1775, Martin and his council had a second war conference on board the *Cruizer*.[23]

Many topics were on that day's agenda. Rebellion had broken out across the entire royal province. But one of the most important questions for discussion was what to do about Mecklenburg. Although it was a remote and sparsely settled region, it was setting a bad precedent and could only encourage other malcontents. Although out-and-out rebellion in the faraway backcountry could have little immediate impact on British rule, Mecklenburg still had to be dealt with, and for this reason it was at the forefront of that day's conference.

Governor Martin began by noting that he had "received advices" that the citizens of Bladen County "were pursuing the Example of the People of Mecklenburg whose treasonable proceedings he had communicated to the Council at the last meeting." If Mecklenburg's example remained unchecked, Martin feared, the rot would spread. The authorities had "to check and prevent the growth of that spirit of disorder which at this time unhappily prevails in great part of the Province and especially in the County of Mecklenburg." Martin "desired the advice of Council on the measures expedient to be taken to counteract such unwarrantable and dangerous extravagancies."

The council was split. A few believed that "the deluded People of this Province (who have followed the Example of the neighboring Colonies) will see their error and return to their allegiance" to Great Britain. They counseled that a policy of moderation be adopted, "whereas every violent measure must increase the disturbances and be attended with the most fatal consequences." But not everyone agreed. According to the official minutes of the meeting, "James Hasell is of opinion that His Excellency should take every lawful measure in his power to suppress the unnatural Rebellion now fomenting in Mecklenburg and other parts of the Province in order to overturn the Constitution and His just prerogative." Governor Martin agreed with Hasell. Mecklenburg could not be ignored. It was setting an example of treason and defiance that was could be contagious.

Martin would develop this theme further in a lengthy diatribe he issued on August 15, 1775. Due to its defiant tone and its threats of retribution it became known as the "Fiery Proclamation."[24] The first sentence set the theme: "I have seen a publication in the *Cape Fear Mercury* which appears to be proceedings of a General Meeting of People stiling themselves Committees of the District of Wilmington," he began. He denounced the Wilmington Committee as "evil, pernicious and traitorous." Continuing the theme, Martin wrote: "I have also seen a most infamous publication in the *Cape Fear Mercury* importing to be resolves of a set of people stiling themselves a Committee for the County of Mecklenburg most traitorously declaring the entire dissolution of the Laws Government and Constitution of this country and setting up a system of rule and regulation repugnant to the Laws and subversive of His Majesty's Government."

The governor had also seen the circular letter from Caswell, Hooper and Hughes (the same letter that Captain Jack had brought with him back to Charlotte). "This publication begins with a recital of the most unparalled falsehoods that ever disgraced a sheet of paper," Martin wrote. Their letter was "a shallow concealment of horrid treason that I have no doubt every honest man will explode and treat with its merited contempt and abhorrence." He called for the loyal subjects to be on the lookout for "seditious Treasons and Traiterous Conspiracies" and to bring to justice "principals and accomplices therein."

Martin's proclamation was distributed throughout the province, read in taverns and churches, nailed to the doors of churches and courthouses and posted at public gathering places such as gristmills and ferries. The citizens were clearly not intimidated by Martin's proclamation, no matter how fiery. In August 1775 the province sent delegates to Hillsboro for a convention despite the threats of the governor. In their formal response to the Fiery Proclamation the delegates unanimously resolved: "That the said Paper is a false Scandalous, Scurrilous, malicious, and seditious Libel, tending to disunite the good people of this province, and to stir up Tumults and Insurrections, dangerous to the peace of His Majesty's Government, and the safety of the Inhabitants, and highly injurious to the Characters of several Gentlemen of acknowledged Virtue and Loyalty."[25] Any copies, they announced, were to be "burnt by the common Hangman."

For all Martin's strong words, however, privately he knew the game was up. There was no restoring order in the backcountry now, possibly not ever. In a letter to Lord Dartmouth in August 1775, just after he issued the Fiery Proclamation, Martin wrote as follows:

> My Lord I am reduced to the deplorable and disgraceful state of being a tame Spectator of Rebellion spreading over this Country.... Every device My Lord has been practiced by the seditious Committees to inflame the minds of the Inhabitants of this Country.... [T]he influence of Committees, My Lord, hath been so extended over the Inhabitants of the Lower part of this Country ... and they are at this day ... so generally possessed with the spirit of revolt that I consider it no longer possible to avail myself of the power of the friends of Government in the interior parts of it without the aid of two Battalions to force a communication with them.[26]

"In short," he concluded, "everything now convinces me that the time for restoring Lawful Government in this Province, by its own internal strength, is past and gone."

Governor Martin's involvement in the Mecklenburg saga is interesting, but what exactly it proves is not clear. Although he mentions "treasonable resolves," it is not known exactly what resolves he saw. On the other hand, his passionate denunciation of the "most treasonable" committee in Mecklenburg dispels one later myth: namely that it was impossible to believe that anyone in the colonies as early as the summer of 1775 was really considering American independence. Put another way, the false theory is that few colonists in 1775 really hated the British that much.

The entire history of the collapse of Governor's Martin's administration in the summer of 1775 shows that this supposition is incorrect. In fact, so strong was anti–British sentiment in the Carolinas that within a matter of weeks of receipt of the news of Lexington, the governor was forced to flee his mansion for the safety of a British ship. It was not safe for him to set foot on American soil even in the most loyal areas along the coast. And in the Presbyterian interior, the anti–British sentiment was even more vehement. Martin himself attributed much of the mischief in the colonies to the Presbyterians, who he wrote, "have ever been unfriendly to Monarchical Government."[27]

Other British figures who served in the Carolinas corroborate this view. Following the Revolution, British cavalry officer Lt. Col. Banastre Tarleton wrote his memoirs, *A History of the Campaigns of 1780 and 1781 in the Southern Provinces of North America*. Tarleton was perhaps the most hated British officer of the entire Revolutionary War, so much so that the phrase "Tarleton's Quarter" was commonly used to mean "no mercy." Tarleton's recollections of his brief period in the Mecklenburg backcountry vividly illustrate the feelings of the Scots-Irish settlers there.

In the autumn of 1780, Tarleton was encamped in Charlotte with Cornwallis' main body of troops, where they were harassed by snipers and irregular fighters. Assessing Lord Cornwallis' strategy to move through Charlotte, Tarleton wrote, "The route by Charlotte town, *through the most hostile quarter of the province* [emphasis added], on many accounts, was not advisable."[28]

"The town and environs abounded with inveterate enemies; the plantations in the neighborhood were small and uncultivated; the roads narrow, and crossed in every direction; and the whole face of the country covered with close and thick woods."[29] In short, the topography was perfect for guerilla fighters waging war against traditional troops. Worse, wrote Tarleton:

> [N]o estimation could be made of the sentiments of half the inhabitants of North Carolina, whilst the Royal army remained at Charlotte town.... The vigilance and animosity of these surrounding districts checked the exertions of the well affected, and totally destroyed all communication between the King's troops and the loyalists in the other parts of the province.
>
> No British commander could obtain any information, in that position, which would facilitate his designs, or guide his future conduct. Every report concerning the measures of the governor and assembly would undoubtedly be ambiguous; accounts of the preparations of the militia could only be vague and uncertain; and all intelligence of the real force and movements of the continentals must be totally unattainable.[30]

After spending only two weeks in Mecklenburg, Cornwallis, according to local legend, called Mecklenburg County a "damned hornets' nest."

"It was evident," concluded Tarleton, "and it had been frequently mentioned to the King's officers, that the counties of Mecklenburg and Rohan were more hostile to England than any others in America."[31] In discussing the veracity of the Mecklenburg Declaration of Independence, the motives and mindset of the inhabitants cannot be entirely dismissed.

Part III. Opening Arguments (1817–1829)

11

From Beyond the Grave
The "copy in an unknown hand"

The foregoing is a true copy of the papers on the above subject, left in my hands by
John M'Knitt Alexander, dec[ease]d.... [T]he original book was burned April, 1800.
— Dr. Joseph McKnitt Alexander, *Raleigh Register*, April 30, 1819

On Tuesday, May 20, 1817, it had been 35 years, seven months and one day since Major
General Lord Cornwallis surrendered to a combined Franco-American army at Yorktown,
Virginia, effectively ending major military operations in North America and the American
Revolution. By then nearly all of the men who had attended the convention in Charlotte
42 years earlier on May 20, 1775, were dead.

Lt. Col. Phifer died in 1778, not long after the war began.[1] Abraham Alexander, the
chairman of the convention, died in April 1786 at the age of seventy and was buried at
Sugar Creek Presbyterian Cemetery, not far from the graves of the Reverend Alexander
Craighead (in the old cemetery #1) and his relative Hezekiah Alexander (cemetery #2).
Adam Alexander, an original minuteman, was buried at a place called Rocky Springs east
of town, as were two other delegates, John Queary and John Foard.[2]

Thomas Polk passed away in 1794 and was buried beside his wife, Susanna, only a few
hundred yards from where his white clapboard home, a vaguely Tudor-looking cottage with
dormered garret windows and irregular chimneys, still stood.[3] General Robert Irwin died
two days before Christmas 1800 and was buried at Steele Creek Presbyterian cemetery. Irwin
had been instrumental as a leader of the Committee of Public Safety and as Mecklenburg's
delegate to the Provincial Congress at Halifax in April 1776, which had then declared independence on behalf of the state. Richard Barry, the tanner and neighbor of McKnitt, died
in August 1801, aged seventy-five, and lay buried at Hopewell cemetery.

By 1817 the three members of the drafting committee credited with having written the
Mecklenburg Declaration were dead or had left the area for parts unknown. Reverend
Hezekiah Balch, the Presbyterian minister, died in April 1776, aged just thirty, and was
buried north of Charlotte on a sloping hillside graveyard behind Poplar Tent Church.
William Kennon, the Salisbury lawyer and leader of the Rowan Committee of Public Safety,
moved to Georgia following the war, and there is no clue as to his whereabouts thereafter.
The death of Dr. Ephraim Brevard, the third member of the drafting committee, was

perhaps the most tragic of the main characters. Brevard was born in Maryland and moved to North Carolina at the age of four. He was raised in Rowan County, today Iredell County, near Mount Mourne and Centre Church. Blinded in one eye as a child, he later attended Nassau Hall. After he settled in Charlotte, Brevard married a daughter of Thomas Polk. They had one child named Martha. Shortly after Martha's birth, Brevard's wife died. Her death left Brevard devastated.

In addition to acting as a physician, Brevard taught at Queen's College in Charlotte. When hostilities with the British began in 1775, Brevard and two dozen of his students joined the county militia to take part in the attack upon a band of loyalists, mostly Highland Scots, gathering along the Cape Fear River. The loyalists were routed at Moore's Creek Bridge on February 27, 1776, before Brevard and the militia could play an active role. Four years later he volunteered to serve as a surgeon's mate (or assistant surgeon) under General Benjamin Lincoln, who commanded the patriot forces in Charleston.

Lincoln's army was surrounded and besieged, and Brevard was captured along with the entirety of Lincoln's army in May 1780. According to some accounts, Brevard was held prisoner on a British warship, where he became quite ill. For whatever reason, he was paroled by the British sometime in the spring of 1781. He was without money or means of transportation and began to walk home. There was no public transportation and practically no roads. He was walking through enemy territory which had been stripped bare by the advancing and retreating armies. It was over 175 miles from Charleston to his mother's home in Iredell County. As one later chronicler related the tale, "[D]uring his confinement in Charleston, as a prisoner of war, he suffered so much from impure air and unwholesome diet that his health gave way, and he returned home only to die."[4] He made it as far as McKnitt's home, sometime in the summer of 1781.[5]

He did not have long to live. In his final will, made on July 20, 1781, Brevard stated that he was "reduced to a dangerous degree of bodily weakness by disease & infirmity" and was "apprehensive that it may be the pleasure of the Divine being to call me from this world by means of my present illness."[6] Polk, McKnitt and others were with Brevard when he died, aged only 37. In his will, Brevard, the teacher, worried about Martha's education and requested that his executors "take all prudent care" to have Martha "decently, usefully and frugally educated, either with the family where she now lives or such other family as they shall think most for the advantage of the child's education." Upon his death, his clothes (breeches, spurs, a great-coat, a hat, gloves, stockings and some buttons) as well as his other meager possessions (a razor, an ink pot, a Bible, saddlebag and a book on French grammar) were sold off for the support of "my beloved daughter." To Polk, Brevard left his boots, underdrawers and jacket, as well as guardianship over his "orphan daughter."[7]

Brevard died at the height of the Revolutionary War in the South; it was a chaotic time, and death was common. To this day it is not known for certain where Dr. Ephraim Brevard — widely held by his contemporaries to be the principal author of the Mecklenburg Declaration of Independence — is buried. Some historians claim Brevard was buried at Hopewell, near Alexandriana. According to a long-standing local tradition, Brevard was buried in the public cemetery near the Charlotte town common (Settlers' Cemetery), where Polk and many of his family were buried. A third theory is that he was buried on the grounds of Queen's College. No one knows. Brevard's final resting place, like much of the history he represented, would be forgotten.[8]

Only a handful of the principal Mecklenburg patriot leaders remained alive by the spring of 1817. One was Waightstill Avery, the attorney and former dueling opponent of Andrew Jackson. In 1817 Avery was seventy-four and in poor health, living at his home, called Swan Pond, in Morganton in the foothills of the Blue Ridge Mountains. In September 1780, while occupying Charlotte, Lord Cornwallis ordered Avery's home burned down. According to the *Biographical History of North Carolina from Colonial Times to the Present*, by Samuel Ashe (1905), "[T]his evidence of displeasure was visited upon only a few of those whom Cornwallis considered leading offenders."[9] Following the Revolution, Avery served as the North Carolina's first attorney general. In addition to Avery, Zaccheus Wilson and William Graham remained alive.

Finally, there was John McKnitt Alexander. By this time he was eighty-four years old, gray-haired, infirm and blind. Old and blind he may have been, but that did not stop McKnitt from taking an active part in community affairs. Even as an old man he was called to testify in land disputes, due to his lifelong expertise as a surveyor. In this capacity, he came to know a lawyer in Salisbury named Cameron. The historian Foote would record the last recollections and impressions we have of McKnitt:

> Nearly blind with age and infirm, he was brought down to the court as an [*sic*] evidence in a land case.' The venerable old man sat in the bar-room, listening to the voices of the company, as they came in. "Is that you, Cameron?" said he, as the sound of his voice fell upon his ear. "I know that voice, though I cannot well see the man." Infirm, he was dignified: with white hair and almost sightless eyes, his mental powers remained. The past and the future were to him more than the present; in the one he had acted his part well, in the other he had hope; but the present had lost its beauty. He recounted, in the course of the interviews he had with the Judge, during the intervals of court, the events of the Revolution, particularly those in which Mecklenburg took the lead.[10]

McKnitt had maintained custody of all the original papers in his role as secretary of the convention. From time to time he wrote out copies by request and sent them to a few friends and historians to preserve for posterity. But by now almost all of the original records were gone, for on April 6, 1800, a fire destroyed McKnitt's house at Alexandriana and the original records from the convention. By this time McKnitt had given the house to his son Joseph and it is not known whether McKnitt was still living in the house at the time of the fire. Since some of his personal papers escaped the fire, it seems likely that he was living elsewhere.

It cannot be known exactly which papers were burned in the fire, but presumably they included the list of delegates who attended the meetings, the minutes from the meetings, and of greatest importance, the original text of the Mecklenburg Declaration of Independence. Following the fire, McKnitt acted to salvage whatever he could of the records that had survived.[11] Five months following the fire, in September 1800, McKnitt copied out the existing records and sent them to General William R. Davie. Davie and McKnitt had served together during the Revolution and were still close friends.

In 1800, when McKnitt copied out the records, Davie was perhaps the best-known man in North Carolina. Raised as an orphan in the Waxhaws, Davie had practiced law in Salisbury. When the Revolution began, he served as a cavalry officer. Davie fought the advancing dragoons during the Battle of Charlotte in September 1780 and led a series of delaying actions as the patriots retreated north along Tryon Street. He later attended the

Constitutional Convention of 1787 (leaving before the document was signed) and, in 1798 and 1799 served as North Carolina governor. He is also considered the founder of the University of North Carolina at Chapel Hill.

The copy of the Mecklenburg Declaration that McKnitt sent Davie came to be called the "Davie Copy," though whether it was copied from an existing record or written from McKnitt's memory later became the subject of a ferocious debate. As McKnitt himself wrote in the penultimate paragraph of the Davie Copy, "the original records of the transactions" no longer existed: "[A]ll those records and papers were burnt (with the house) on April 6, 1800."[12] Nevertheless, according to Cameron, McKnitt often remarked that "the copy of the [Mecklenburg] Declaration he had given to Davie [was] certainly correct."[13]

Despite the fact that the original papers had been destroyed, McKnitt was not worried that future historians would forget or disbelieve the story of the Mecklenburg Declaration of Independence. After all, it was common knowledge to the citizens living in the area. It was part of their collective memory. While participants still lived, no one considered it necessary to prove conclusively the existence of such documents. And the historiography was not as interested in the absolute, proven, truth as subsequent generations have been. How could something so widely remembered, so important, so dramatic, be forgotten? It wasn't possible. While McKnitt was said to lament "the loss of the original copy" of the Mecklenburg Declaration of Independence," he nonetheless "consoled himself by saying, that he had himself given a copy to General Davie some time before, which he knew to be correct."[14] McKnitt was confident that the historical record had been preserved. "*[T]he document is safe,*" he told his friends.[15]

McKnitt died on July 17, 1817, and was buried at Hopewell Cemetery, beside his wife. General William Lee Davidson, killed by a Tory bullet at the battle of Cowan's Ford in February 1781, lay nearby. So did three other delegates to the May convention: Richard Barry, Matthew McClure and William Graham.

McKnitt's death severed one of the last surviving links between the story of the Mecklenburg Declaration and the people who participated in it. By the time he died the major papers of the event were lost, and the principal eyewitnesses were dead. The entire episode seemed doomed to be swallowed up in the slow-moving but inexorable tide of time.

Not that history was entirely silent. In fact, a narrative of the American Revolution was already taking shape, but it was one that did not include the names of Thomas Polk or John McKnitt Alexander. Beyond the borders of Mecklenburg County, the events that occurred there in the spring of 1775 were entirely unknown. Certain events — such as the Battle of Lexington, Bunker Hill, Valley Forge, and Washington's night crossing of the Delaware — began to morph into legend. Not coincidentally, perhaps, these were events that occurred in the more populated northeast of America. Other events, particularly ones that occurred in the remote backcountry of the Carolinas, began to fade from common knowledge.

As the decades rolled by, the story of the American Revolution developed into a widely held if historically suspect narrative in which events and battles in New England and the middle colonies dominated. In the developing consensus view, the war in the rural South — the two battles at Savannah, the siege and fall of Charleston, Buford's massacre in the Waxhaws, and the battles of Camden, Kings Mountain, Cowpens, Cowan's Ford, Guilford Courthouse and Eutaw Springs — were glossed over as minor and confusing incidents in the overall story. In this version, the American Revolution began at the battle of Lexington; major battles were then fought in Boston, New York and Philadelphia; the winter at Valley Forge; and then ... Cornwallis surrendered at Yorktown. Various other incidents might have occurred, and, oh yes, there was the Battle at Saratoga, but they weren't worthy of particular attention. In short, if General Washington wasn't there, it just didn't matter.

To some degree, this was a result of regional prejudice. To the world outside the farms and mills of the rural Piedmont, the area was of no historical interest or importance. It was largely poor, undeveloped farmland in the backwards antebellum South. Frankly, if nothing had happened to trigger interest in or discussion of the Mecklenburg Declaration of Independence the entire story would have become a curiosity or a footnote in local history at best. More likely, all of it would have been entirely forgotten. With McKnitt's death in 1817, it was a story whose time seemed to have passed. What no one would have guessed was that the story of the Mecklenburg Declaration of Independence was about to explode into one of the most contentious historical controversies of the nineteenth century.

Events were set in motion in 1817 by William Wirt, a Virginia lawyer. Wirt was well educated, well read, and ambitious. He was admitted to the bar in 1792 and excelled as a lawyer. Over a long and illustrious career Wirt held a variety of distinguished legal posts, including clerk of the Virginia House of Delegates and chancellor of the Eastern District of Virginia. He became nationally known as one of three government prosecutors in Aaron Burr's trial for treason before the Supreme Court in 1807. In 1817 — the year McKnitt died — Wirt was appointed U.S. attorney general by President James Monroe, an office he held until 1829, the longest tenure of any AG to this day. In 1832, he ran for president on the Anti-Masonic Party ticket.

In addition to being a lawyer, Wirt was also a writer and amateur historian, and it was in this capacity that he inadvertently set events in motion to put Mecklenburg County at the center of a national historical controversy. In 1817 Wirt published *Sketches of the Life and Character of Patrick Henry*. This was the first work to contain many of Patrick Henry's most famous speeches, including "Give Me Liberty or Give Me Death."

Ironically, given the book's importance in the Mecklenburg Controversy, Wirt's book would *itself* become controversial, given that its subject — Patrick Henry — had died eighteen years before it was published. Wirt "first conceived" of writing Henry's biography in 1805, he claimed, six years after Henry had died. Wirt "knew nothing of Mr. Henry, personally," he conceded. He "had never seen him; and was of course, compelled to rely wholly on the information of others."[16] Many of Henry's speeches had never been published or even written down at that time; and, other than some newspapers articles and public records, the source of Wirt's information was primarily anecdotes or other testimony given to him by Henry's surviving friends. All of this would lead some to speculate as to whether Wirt was, at least to some degree, responsible for the substance of some of Henry's speeches.

Another major character in the Mecklenburg Declaration controversy, Thomas Jefferson, also had a major role in shaping Wirt's work. Jefferson "subsequently and repeatedly" assisted Wirt in writing the book, Wirt bragged.[17] In fact, Wirt attributed a large measure of his success in completing the book to Jefferson's "able counsel, in reconciling apparent contradictions and clearing away difficulties of fact."[18] Wirt's *Sketches* was a tremendous best seller, running into its third edition by 1818. As a native Virginian and aristocrat, Wirt had a specific and partisan slant on the Revolutionary period. First, he concluded, "The

American revolution is universally admitted to have begun in the upper circles of society. It turned on principles too remote and abstruse for vulgar apprehension or consideration."[19] In fact, had it been left to the "unenlightened mass," Wirt believed, there was "no doubt" that the Stamp Act "would have been paid without a question."[20] This was a pretty snobbish view of history and one that did not give any credit to the common man, much less the rural frontier folk of the Carolinas such as Polk and McKnitt.

And who gave the revolutionary impulse to the "upper circles" of society, Wirt asked? His answer was "unquestionably Patrick Henry."[21] Henry, Wirt asserted, was the spark that ignited the American Revolution. Consequently, as Henry was a Virginian, the State of Virginia deserved the majority of the credit in leading the American Revolution. "There was no colony which resisted, with more firmness and constancy, the pretensions of the British parliament than that of Virginia," he wrote.[22] Having led the way in resisting the Stamp Act, "[t]he impulse thus given by Virginia, was caught by the other colonies."[23] In Wirt's view, the American Revolution was a Virginian affair, led by Henry, a Virginian, and abetted by Jefferson, a Virginian (and his tacit coauthor). "The only state that has pretended to dispute the palm with Virginia," he wrote, was Massachusetts, although in Wirt's view their case was pretty weak.[24]

Virginia bias in Wirt's book was bound to irritate anyone who was not from Virginia and even many who were. Predictably, *Sketches* provoked a series of responses and an ongoing debate as to who should get the most credit for the American Revolution. The debate spread to Congress, where it received the attention of William Davidson, the congressman from Mecklenburg, who was appalled at the way Virginia politicians — goaded on by Wirt — were seizing a disproportionate amount of the credit for the American Revolution in the first quarter of the nineteenth century.

Davidson knew who deserved credit for the American Revolution: his constituents in the Great State of Mecklenburg. To this end he and North Carolina senator Nathaniel Macon began reaching out to the leading figures in Mecklenburg asking them to send information or documents in their possession regarding the Mecklenburg Declaration of Independence. Davidson and Macon intended to set the record straight.

Among those they approached was Dr. Joseph Alexander, the son of John McKnitt Alexander. In reply, Dr. Alexander sent Davidson a written summary of the events of May 20, 1775, which he had copied from some of his father's surviving papers. The document was a bombshell. Davidson shared the paper with Macon, who agreed that it was extraordinary. Macon sent it to the largest newspaper in the state, the *Raleigh Register and North Carolina Gazette*, for publication.

And thus it was that on April 30, 1819, the *Raleigh Register* published Dr. Alexander's account of the events of May 20, 1775. The editorial preface to Dr. Alexander's paper began with considerable understatement: "It is not probably known to many of our readers, that the citizens of Mecklenburg County, in this State, made a Declaration of Independence more than a year before Congress made theirs."[25]

Indeed this was not known. In fact, many of the readers may not have even heard of the name of the county itself, which is why the editors felt compelled to point out that it was in their own state. It continued: "[T]he following Document on the subject has lately come to the hands of the Editor from unquestionable authority, and is published that it may go down to posterity." The document read as follows[26]:

North Carolina, Mecklenburg County,
May 20, 1775.

In the spring of 1775, the leading characters of Mecklenburg county, stimulated by that enthusiastic patriotism which elevates the mind above considerations of individual aggrandizement, and scorning to shelter themselves from the impending storm by submission to lawless power, &c. &c. held several detached meetings, in each of which the individual sentiments were, "that the cause of Boston was the cause of all; that their destinies were indissolubly connected with those of their Eastern fellow-citizens — and that they must either submit to all the impositions which an unprincipled, and to them an unrepresented, Parliament might impose — or support their brethren who were doomed to sustain the first shock of that power, which, if successful there, would ultimately overwhelm all in the common calamity." Conformably to these principles, Colonel T. Polk, through solicitation, issued an order to each Captain's company in the county of Mecklenburg, (then comprising the present county of Cabarrus,) directing each militia company to elect two persons, and delegate to them ample power to devise ways and means to aid and assist their suffering brethren in Boston, and also generally to adopt measures to extricate themselves from the impending storm, and to secure unimpaired their inalienable rights, privileges and liberties, from the dominant grasp of British imposition and tyranny.

In conformity to said order, on the 19th of May, 1775, the said delegation met in Charlotte, vested with unlimited powers; at which time official news, by express, arrived of the battle of Lexington on that day of the preceding month. Every delegate felt the value and importance of the prize, and the awful and solemn crisis which had arrived — every bosom swelled with indignation at the malice, inveteracy, and insatiable revenge, developed in the late attack at Lexington. The universal sentiment was: let us not flatter ourselves that popular harangues, or resolves; that popular vapour will avert the storm, or vanquish our common enemy — let us deliberate — let us calculate the issue — the probable result; and then let us act with energy, as brethren leagued to preserve our property — our lives — and what is still more endearing, the liberties of America. *Abraham Alexander* was then elected Chairman, and *John M'Knitt Alexander*, Clerk. After a free and full discussion of the various objects for which the delegation had been convened, it was unanimously ordained–

1. *Resolved*, That whoever directly or indirectly abetted, or in any way, form or manner, countenanced the unchartered and dangerous invasion of our rights, as claimed by Great Britain, is an enemy to this country — to America — and to the inherent and inalienable rights of man.

2. *Resolved*, That we the citizens of Mecklenburg county, do hereby dissolve the political bands which have connected us to the Mother Country, and hereby absolve ourselves from all allegiance to the British Crown, and abjure all political connection, contract, or association, with that nation, who have wantonly trampled on our rights and liberties — and inhumanly shed the innocent blood of American patriots at Lexington.

3. *Resolved*, That we do hereby declare ourselves a free and independent people, are, and of right ought to be, a sovereign and self-governing Association, under the control of no power other than that of our God and the General Government of the Congress; to the maintenance of which independence, we solemnly pledge to each other, our mutual co-operation, our lives, our fortunes, and our most sacred honor.

4. *Resolved*, That as we now acknowledge the existence and control of no law or legal officer, civil or military, within this country, we do hereby ordain and adopt, as a rule of life, all, each and every of our former laws, wherein, nevertheless, the Crown of Great Britain never can be considered as holding rights, privileges, immunities, or authority therein.

5. *Resolved*, That it is also further decreed, that all, each and every military officer in this county, is hereby reinstated to his former command and authority, he acting conformably to these regulations. And that every member present of this delegation shall henceforth be a civil officer, viz. a Justice of the Peace, in the character of a "*Committee-man*," to issue process, hear and determine all matters of controversy, according to said adopted laws,

and to preserve peace, and union, and harmony, in said county,—and to use every exertion to spread the love of country and fire of freedom throughout America, until a more general and organized government be established in this province.

A number of bye laws were also added, merely to protect the association from confusion, and to regulate their general conduct as citizens. After sitting in the Court House all night, neither sleepy, hungry, nor fatigued, and after discussing every paragraph, they were all passed, sanctioned, and decreed, *unanimously*, about 2 o'clock, A.M. May 20. In a few days, a deputation of said delegation convened, when Capt. *James Jack*, of Charlotte, was deputed as express to the Congress at Philadelphia, with a copy of said Resolves and Proceedings, together with a letter addressed to our three representatives there, viz. *Richard Caswell, William Hooper and Joseph Hughes*—under express injunction, personally, and through the State representation, to use all possible means to have said proceedings sanctioned and approved by the General Congress. On the return of Captain Jack, the delegation learned that their proceedings were individually approved by the Members of Congress, but that it was deemed premature to lay them before the House. A joint letter from said three members of Congress was also received, complimentary of the zeal in the common cause, and recommending perseverance, order and energy.

The subsequent harmony, unanimity, and exertion in the cause of liberty and independence, evidently resulting from these regulations, and the continued exertion of said delegation, apparently tranquilised this section of the State, and met with the concurrence and high approbation of the Council of Safety, who held their sessions at Newbern and Wilmington, alternately, and who conformed the nomination and acts of the delegation in their official capacity.

From this delegation originated the Court of Enquiry of this county, who constituted and held their first session in Charlotte—they then held their meetings regularly at Charlotte, at Col. James Harris's, and at Col. Phifer's, alternately, one week at each place. It was a Civil Court founded on military process. Before this Judicature, all suspicious persons were made to appear, who were formally tried and banished, or continued under guard. Its jurisdiction was as unlimited as toryism, and its decrees as final as the confidence and patriotism of the county. Several were arrested and brought before them from Lincoln, Rowan and the adjacent counties.

After the narrative ended, Dr. Alexander added the following attestation: "The foregoing is a true copy of the papers on the above subject, left in my hands by John M'Knitt Alexander, dec'd. I find it mentioned on file that the original book was burned April, 1800. That a copy of the proceedings was sent to Hugh Williamson, in New York, then writing a History of North Carolina, and that a copy was sent to Gen. W.R. Davie." He signed his name as "J. M'Knitt," omitting the name Alexander as was his usual custom.

With minor and essentially immaterial iterations, the above narrative would serve as the definitive account for all future debate about the authenticity of the Mecklenburg Declaration. It is the Rosetta Stone of the whole story. All the key elements of the story are there: Thomas Polk summons two officers of each militia company for a meeting on May 19 in the courthouse in Charlotte; news of the massacre at Lexington arrives; Abraham Alexander is named chairman and his cousin, John McKnitt Alexander, clerk; five resolutions are unanimously adopted by the convention; the substance of them is that Mecklenburg County is declared "free and independent" of Great Britain; Captain James Jack is dispatched to carry the declaration to the three North Carolina delegates to the Second Continental Congress then meeting in Philadelphia; a series of bylaws are also drafted to govern the community; Captain Jack returns, with a message that the Congress has deemed their declaration premature; finally, a council of enquiry holds trial over local citizens believed loyal to England; two Tory lawyers, Booth and Dunn, are tried and sentenced to exile in South Carolina. These are the key elements, the critical facts, the recurring themes, that appear

The "copy in an unknown hand," anonymous and undated. "It matters not who may have thus copied the original record," wrote Dr. Joseph Alexander, "the entire sheet is most probably a copy taken long since from the original for some person ... and never sent on" (courtesy Southern Historical Collection, Wilson Library, University of North Carolina at Chapel Hill).

in each version of the story, facts and themes that would be debated, point by point, over the next hundred years.

But where did Dr. Alexander's account come from? The narrative and text was a "true copy," he claimed, but a "true copy" of what? It was not clear. Dr. Alexander noted that the "original book" was destroyed in the fire at Alexandriana nineteen years earlier. So it was clear that what he had provided was not a copy of the original. But what was it a copy of? And how had it survived the fire? Although the last paragraph of the article was a bit cryptic, Dr. Alexander noted that he had several "papers on the above subject," which had been "left in my hands by John M'Knitt Alexander."

Dr. Alexander did not explain this very well, but at the time he sent the account to Davidson, he had in fact *two* papers in his possession, both of which had survived the fire and exist to this day. (A third paper, called the "Davie Copy," would be found a few years later.) The first paper in Dr. Alexander's possession was a torn series of handwritten notes by his father, later called the "rough notes." The second was a "full sheet," as Dr. Alexander put it, well-preserved, legible and succinct. It was unsigned and undated. Dr. Alexander copied this second paper verbatim and sent it to William Davidson, who gave it to Macon, who then gave it to the *Raleigh Register*, in which it was published, almost word for word.[27] Where did this second paper come from? Who had written it, when and for what purpose? No one knew. Dr. Alexander noted that it was in an "unknown handwrite," and for that reason the paper to this day is known as the "copy in an unknown hand."[28] It was a voice from beyond the grave, but whose voice was it?

It was demonstrably *not* written by John McKnitt Alexander, nor in all probability by his son Dr. Joseph Alexander. Their handwriting is too different. Another possible author was William Polk. William was the only other individual known to have made copies of the original papers for other people. In 1960 the writer V.V. McNitt attempted to identify the author; despite thorough analysis, there were "inconclusive results."[29] (He tentatively concluded that William Polk may have been the author, although this seems extremely unlikely as *Polk himself* had corrected the record in at least one place when the paper was at one point in his possession.[30] And if Polk were the author, surely Dr. Alexander would have recognized his handwriting and identified him?) It is also impossible to know when the paper was written. In the first paragraph there is a parenthetical reference to "the present county of Cabarrus." Cabarrus County was formed in 1792, so it must have been written sometime after that. But in addition to being unsigned, the paper was undated.

Dr. Alexander had found these miscellaneous papers in his father's home bound up with a roll of Revolutionary War era pamphlets, which perhaps gave a clue to its age. As he put it, "the roll of pamphlets with which these two papers were found," he wrote (meaning the "copy in an unknown hand" and the "rough notes"), "were amongst his old surveying and other old papers [not found] until after his death." The roll of pamphlets in which they were found, he speculated, "may have been unrolled since 1788."[31]

To this day, the author, date and purpose of the "copy in an unknown hand" remains a mystery. Is it an authentic copy of the original minutes, taken before they were destroyed in the fire? Or was it written after the fact, perhaps made from whole cloth, perhaps even entirely invented? Is it an authentic record or the beginning of an elaborate hoax? These were the questions that would soon dominate the discussion. Whatever its provenance, Dr.

Alexander's transcription of the "copy in an unknown hand" burst like a Carolina thunderstorm upon an unsuspecting world.

The *Raleigh Register* story containing the Mecklenburg Declaration was in due course picked up by other papers, as was the common practice in those days. One of these, the *Essex Register* of Salem, Massachusetts, found its way into the hands of former president John Adams. The Mecklenburg Controversy was about to begin.

12

"He has copied the spirit, the sense, and the expressions of it Verbatim"
John Adams Accuses Thomas Jefferson of Plagiarism

> I was struck with so much astonishment on reading this document, that I could not help inclosing it immediately to Mr. Jefferson, who must have seen it, in the time of it.
>
> — Letter from John Adams to William Bentley, July 15, 1819

In the late spring of 1819, John Adams, second president of the American Republic, was living in semiretirement at his farm, which he called Peacefield, near Quincy, Massachusetts. He was eighty-three years old. One of Adams' principal interests at this time, late into his exceptional life, was an ongoing literary exchange with a former friend, later a bitter adversary, the third president of the United States, Thomas Jefferson.

The fact that the two former statesmen were in communication at all was remarkable, for prior to January 1812 they had not spoken in over a decade. Once friends, their relationship had been smashed entirely by political rivalry, conflicting philosophies, and diametrically opposed temperaments. They were polar opposites in every way: appearance, manner, views and background. Jefferson was an aloof aristocrat, a Southern slaveholder, a populist, and an idealistic revolutionary. Adams was practical, conservative and effusive, a Northerner, and a political realist. Jefferson was tall and lanky, with a head of red hair; Adams was stout and bald. Jefferson was quiet and shunned controversy; he said he "abhorred dispute." In fact, when he was serving in the Continental Congress he rarely spoke, and when he did his voice was so quiet as to be almost inaudible. "[D]uring the whole time I sat with him in Congress," wrote Adams, "I never heard him utter three sentences together."[1] Adams, by contrast, was loud, exuberant and impetuous; he had a violent temper and could be moody, overbearing and brash.

Then there were their political views. Jefferson was a populist. He believed in the popular will and the sovereign rights of the people. His greatest fear was a return to monarchism. Adams, especially after seeing the bloody riots of the French Revolution of 1789 up close, was not as starry-eyed as Jefferson about the inherent goodness of mankind. Adams feared anarchy, mob rule, and chaos. "You are afraid of the one, I, the few," Adams wrote Jefferson, following the signing of the U.S. Constitution. "You are apprehensive of monarchy; I, of aristocracy."[2] To Adams and the Federalists, Jefferson was a rabble-rouser, a demagogue, and an atheist. To Jefferson and the Democrats, Adams was a closet monarchist, a warmonger, unstable, perhaps mentally deranged.

Earlier in their careers they had been friends. Jefferson had corresponded with Adams' wife, Abigail, and was close to both of them. They shared news of personal successes and tragedies over many years together. Their diametrically opposed political philosophies were to spill over into enmity and outright confrontation when they served as cabinet ministers under President Washington, and thereafter fought each other to succeed him as president. Adams served as vice president; Jefferson as secretary of state. Serving together, under high pressure and in close quarters, their differing personalities and views repelled one another, like the north and south poles of a magnet. Something had to give, and ultimately Jefferson resigned as secretary of state on December 31, 1793. Of Jefferson's leaving, Adams wrote, "His want of candor, his obstinate prejudices of both aversion and attachment, his real partiality in spite of all his pretensions, his low notions about many things, have so utterly reconciled me to [his resignation] ... that I will not weep."[3]

On January 6, following Jefferson's departure, Adams noted, "good riddance of bad ware."[4] Upon Washington's departure in 1796 after two terms in office, Vice President Adams defeated secretary of state Jefferson to become the nation's second president. Four years later, following a bitter, partisan election, Jefferson defeated his former friend 73 electoral votes to 65. It was a bitter personal and political defeat for Adams: a defeat at the hands of a man he once loved as a brother, and whom Adams felt had betrayed him. Angry and depressed, Adams refused to attend Jefferson's inauguration in 1800. It was a wound that would never truly heal.

Adams wrote bitterly in forced retirement that Jefferson was a hypocrite, a fraud, and a "shadow man."[5] Although he had "always proffered great friendship," Jefferson had schemed and connived against him.[6] Revealing his innermost feelings, Adams had earlier accused Jefferson of supporting "almost every villain he could find who had been an enemy to me."[7] Now, in his private rage, compounded by his sense of failure, Adams cursed his rival and denounced his administration. Jefferson had "a total Incapacity for Government or War," he wrote, and was a failure both as governor and as president. Jefferson's presidency had left the new republic "infinitely worse than he found it," wrote Adams, "and that from his own ignorance or error."[8]

To others, he even disavowed any past friendship with Jefferson whatsoever. "You are much mistaken," he wrote to William Cunningham in 1804, "when you say that no man living has so much knowledge of Mr. Jefferson's transactions as myself." They were never friends, nor even close. "I know but little concerning him," Adams dismissively concluded.[9] But Adams' anger was that of a spurned friend. In every relationship there is the lover and the beloved; Adams was the former. He needed Jefferson's attention and respect; he craved his approval. In 1811, when a friend volunteered to broker reconciliation between them, Adams leapt at the opportunity. "I always loved Jefferson," he said, "and still love him."[10] Jefferson was more circumspect in his response. He observed that he "always knew [Adams] to be an honest man, often a great one, but sometimes incorrect and precipitate in his judgments."[11] Jefferson had often defended Adams' character, he wrote to Benjamin Rush, "but with the single exception as to his political opinions."[12] Thus pacified by mutual friends, despite their long-standing enmity, Adams reached out to Jefferson in a letter dated January 1, 1812, perhaps written as an old man's New Year's resolution. "You and I ought not to die," Adams wrote to Jefferson 18 months later, "before we have explained ourselves to each other."[13]

And so began a rare and exceptional exchange of letters between the two old men, the founders of the country—158 letters in total, of which 109 were written by Adams. The Jefferson-Adams letters were to become an American classic, indeed a milestone of Western literature. "They wrote of old friends and their own friendship," writes historian David McCullough in his magisterial work *John Adams*, "of great causes past, common memories, books, politics, education, philosophy, religion, the French, the British, the French Revolution, American Indians, the American navy, their families, their health, slavery — eventually — and their considered views on life, society, and always, repeatedly, the American Revolution."[14]

Adams, the lover in this complicated relationship, wrote the overwhelming majority of the letters — often several in a row — and set the intellectual agenda, sending Jefferson clippings that interested him; thoughts on political events, or his observations on history and art. Jefferson, the beloved, was cooler in his replies. While polite, many of his letters are condescending or stilted. Some seem written almost out of obligation. Nevertheless the lines of communication between them were open. And so it was, that Adams, in secluded retirement on his farm in Massachusetts, reading his local newspaper, the *Essex Register*, saw an article copied from the North Carolina newspaper *Raleigh Register* containing the account of the Mecklenburg Declaration of Independence. For a variety of reasons, and with mixed motivations, he forwarded it to Jefferson at his farm in Monticello.

"May I inclose you one of the greatest curiosities and one of the deepest mysteries that ever occurred to me?" Adams wrote Jefferson on June 22, 1819. "It is in the *Essex Register* of June 5, 1819. It is entitled the *Raleigh Register* [Mecklenburg] Declaration of Independence."[15] The Mecklenburg Declaration astonished Adams. "How is it possible that this paper should have been concealed from me to this day?" he asked rhetorically.

> Had it been communicated to me in the time of it, I know, if you do not know, that it would have been printed in every Whig newspaper upon this continent. You know, that if I had possessed it, I would have made the hall of Congress echo and reecho with it fifteen months before your Declaration of Independence. What a poor, ignorant, malicious, short-sighted, crapulous mass is Tom Paine's "Common Sense," in comparison with this paper! Had I known it, I would have commented upon it, from the day you entered Congress till the fourth of July, 1776. The genuine sense of America at that moment was never expressed so well before, nor since. Richard Caswell, William Hooper, and Joseph Hewes [*sic*], the then representatives of North Carolina in Congress, you knew as well as I, and you know that the unanimity of the States finally depended on the vote of Joseph Hewes, and was finally determined by him. And yet history is to ascribe the American Revolution to Thomas Paine! *Sat verbum sapienti!* [a word to the wise].[16]

The letter was characteristically Adams: breathless, overwrought and utterly oblivious of its audience. It also betrayed what modern psychologists might call a marked passive-aggressiveness towards Jefferson with veiled insinuations that Jefferson could not, and did not, miss. First was the insinuation that the Mecklenburg Declaration had been hidden from Adams and others — or, as he put it, "concealed" — perhaps by Jefferson or his allies. It was, Adams wrote, one of "the greatest curiosities" and "deepest mysteries" he had ever come across. The unspoken question hung in the air: had Jefferson hidden the Mecklenburg Declaration from him? Adams carried this theme farther, contrasting his own ignorance of the Mecklenburg Declaration's existence with the (perhaps) willful ignorance of Jefferson: "*Had it been communicated to me* in the time of it, *I know, if you do not know*, that it would have been printed in every Whig newspaper upon this continent. *You know*, that *if I had possessed it*, I would have made the hall of Congress echo and reecho with it fifteen months before *your* Declaration of Independence.... *Had I known it, I would have commented upon it, from the day you entered Congress* till the fourth of July, 1776." It's a strange passage. Adams uses the expression *had I known* (or similar expressions) four times in total — four times in six sentences. He also uses the expression *you know* (or similar expressions about Jefferson) *three times*. Why?

As his later, private writings on the subject make crystal clear, Adams' use of the phrases *had I known* and *you know* were not accidental. Adams believed Jefferson *did know* of the Mecklenburg Declaration and had hidden it from Adams and the world. Adams also suggested that Jefferson's concealment of the Mecklenburg Declaration had been responsible for delaying a national movement towards independence.

In fact Adams wasn't suggesting it, Adams was saying it: *Had I known it, I would have commented upon it, from the day you entered Congress till the fourth of July, 1776.* Read this carefully: Adams says he would have pushed the cause of the Mecklenburg Declaration, not from the moment Adams had *learned* of it, not from the moment *Adams* entered Congress, but from the moment *Jefferson* entered Congress until July 4 — the day that the national declaration was issued: the day of Jefferson's great triumph. The subtext was unmistakable: *You knew about this, and suppressed it. If you had not kept the Mecklenburg Declaration secret, I would have used it to lead a movement toward independence, not you. I would now have the credit for American independence, not you. And now I have found you out.*

The joy and enthusiasm that bubbles from Adams' letter has nothing to do with the Mecklenburg Declaration itself and everything to do with the fact that he believed that he had caught Jefferson in a cover-up. Adams always knew Jefferson was a phony — and now he had the proof. This "aha!" moment comes through in the next sentence in his letter: "*The genuine sense of America at that moment was never expressed so well before, nor since.*" In other words, the Mecklenburg Declaration contains the best, most succinct text of American independence, *not* the Declaration of July 4.

In this brief letter of only 229 words, Adams twice mentions the fact that the Mecklenburg Declaration predates Jefferson's Declaration of Independence and also manages two gratuitous insults of Jefferson's friend and ally, Thomas Paine, disparaging *Common Sense* ("poor, ignorant, malicious, short-sighted, crapulous mass") and mocking its historical importance in the Revolutionary movement ("and yet history is to ascribe the American Revolution to Thomas Paine!") The most generous reading of Adams' letter to Jefferson of June 22 is that Adams was excited and wrote rashly and without considering his words. In this interpretation, Adams believed that he had unearthed a historical mystery and thought Jefferson would be equally excited. He was, at a minimum, impolitic in his approach and failed to anticipate that Jefferson might interpret this as a political attack or as the disparagement of his life's work.

A less generous reading of the letter is that this was Adams' "gotcha" moment and his moment of revenge. He had caught Jefferson at last. It would have been impossible for

Adams, whatever he thought of Jefferson's qualities and accomplishments, not to harbor some sliver of animosity and resentment, not to feel some mischievous delight in seeing Jefferson squirm. After all, Jefferson had defeated Adams for president, had ended his political career, and had seized historical immortality in "writing" the Declaration of Independence. In politics, Jefferson had won and Adams had lost. Adams may have been a great statesman, writer and political thinker, but he was also human. For him not to enjoy what he must have felt was a moment of vindication and karmic revenge would have been impossible.

We also know from Adams' other letters at this time that this less generous interpretation of his letter of June 22 is the correct one. Adams believed he now had the proof that his long-time adversary was a fraud, for not only did Adams believe Jefferson had "concealed" the Mecklenburg Declaration from him — and from the world, for that matter — but Adams even believed that Jefferson had plagiarized from the Mecklenburg Declaration in drafting the July 4 declaration.

"He has copied the spirit, the sense, and the expressions of it verbatim." John Adams' incendiary accusation against Jefferson started the Mecklenburg Controversy. This 1826 portrait of Adams was made only a few years after the Mecklenburg Controversy began (Smithsonian American Art Museum, Adams-Clement Collection, gift of Mary Louisa Adams Clement in memory of her mother, Louisa Catherine Adams Clement).

Adams believed that he had discovered the first, original Declaration of Independence, written by a group of frontier farmers in remote Mecklenburg County, North Carolina, which Jefferson had stolen and passed off as his own work. If it were true, it was the intellectual crime of the century.

The source of Jefferson' supposed "brilliance" had been exposed. He had plagiarized the Mecklenburg Declaration of Independence. And Adams had caught him. *I know, if you do not know....* Did Adams really believe Jefferson had plagiarized from the Mecklenburg Declaration? Yes. Without question he did, for he told this to several friends. Without waiting for Jefferson to respond to his letter of June 22, Adams wrote to Reverend William Bentley of Salem, Massachusetts, three weeks later, on July 15.

Again, Adams' tone was breathless, almost manic. Adams clearly believed he was onto something, like a hero in a murder mystery who has seen the murderer fleeing the scene of the crime. In this private letter, Adams is more direct than in his oblique letter to Jefferson. "A few weeks ago I received an *Essex Register*, containing resolutions of independence by a county in North Carolina, fifteen months before the resolution of independence in Congress," he began. "I was struck with so much astonishment on reading this document, that I could not help inclosing it immediately to Mr. Jefferson, who *must have seen it, in the time of it, for he has copied the spirit, the sense, and the expressions of it* verbatim, *into his Declaration of the 4th of July, 1776* [emphasis added]."[17]

Adams was explicit: Jefferson must have seen it "in the time of it," meaning when it was written. What is more, Jefferson had copied, meaning stolen, its *"spirit, the sense, and the expressions of it* verbatim." Note Adams did not write *The similarities between the two documents are striking* nor *Jefferson might have seen this because it looks so similar to the National Declaration* nor *Wow, these look similar — could it be possible Jefferson copied this?* Read again what Adams wrote: *He* has *copied the spirit, the sense, and the expressions of it verbatim.* Not "might have copied" nor "could have copied" nor "possibly copied," but *"has* copied." Adams had no doubts. Jefferson had ripped off the Mecklenburg Declaration. If Adams believed this — and there is no doubt that he did, at least when he wrote to the Reverend Bentley — it could only lead to one conclusion.

Adams had concluded that at some point Jefferson had received a copy of the Mecklenburg Declaration. Possibly he saw it in a newspaper at the time or perhaps someone delivered a copy to him. He may have been shown it by the North Carolina delegation. However he received it, Jefferson had not spoken of it, and he had not raised it in Congress. Perhaps, Adams surmised, he had hushed it up. Either way, the story of the Mecklenburg Declaration had been buried. Furthermore, if Jefferson had not suppressed the declaration, some other national leader — possibly Adams himself? — would have taken on the cause of the people in Mecklenburg and moved for outright American independence in the summer of 1775.

Looked at another way, Jefferson, the great Democrat, the great leader of the people, had suppressed an authentic, genuine movement for national independence — the "genuine sense of America, at that time," as Adams put it. If this were true, far from leading the independence movement, Jefferson had tried to suppress it, even to smother it in its cradle. Only when events moved beyond his ability to control them, over a year later, did Jefferson embrace the cause. And when he did, he took the words and expressions of the Mecklenburg Declaration and lifted them — "verbatim," as Adams put it — and claimed them for his own. Jefferson, in short, was a fraud.

Adams poured out his developing conspiracy theory in his letter of July 15 to Bentley. "Had I seen that declaration at the time of it, it should have been printed in every Whig newspaper on this continent," he wrote. "Its total concealment from me is a mystery, which can be unriddled only by the timidity of the delegates in Congress from North Carolina, by the influence of Quakers and proprietary gentlemen in Pennsylvania, the remaining art and power of Toryism throughout the continent at that time. That [Mecklenburg] declaration would have had more effect than Tom Paine's *Common Sense,* which appeared so long after it."[18]

Adams believed he was on to something, and he wanted to spread the word. He implored Bentley, "I pray you to intercede with the printers to transmit me half a dozen copies of that Register, which contains it, and I will immediately transmit the money for them, whatever they may cost."[19] Adams realized that if the Mecklenburg Declaration could be shown to be real, not only would this cast Jefferson's work into shadow, but it would also correct the historical record (and avenge an old wrong) on his other old enemy, Thomas Paine. The Mecklenburg Declaration, concluded Adams, "must be more universally made known to the present and future generation."[20]

Plagiarism was an explosive, even if unsubstantiated, charge, especially so when made by one former president against another. Furthermore, Adams expected that his correspondence would be made public at some point in the future (he was speaking to the ages), further underscoring Adams' belief that he was correct about Jefferson.

What made Adams so sure? He did not spell out line by line the specific reasons for his firm conviction that the national Declaration of Independence was modeled on the Mecklenburg Declaration, but a review of the overall literary structure, as well as certain key phrases, reveals extraordinary — even spooky — similarities.

First, unlike many other pre–1776 resolutions or resolves published by various political bodies, the Mecklenburg Declaration was succinct, compact, and to the point. There were five resolutions, all of which (other than the fifth and concluding phrase) were only one sentence in length. Unlike the national declaration, which set forth a laundry list of grievances against British authority, the Mecklenburg Declaration summed up in one sentence the rationale for American independence. Simply, the British had engaged in an "unchartered and dangerous invasion of our rights." It was a model of classical, elegant and compact literary structure. Second, like the national declaration, the tone of the Mecklenburg Declaration was martial and sharp ("inherent and inalienable rights of man"), and the verbs were direct and active ("do hereby dissolve," "abjure," "declare"). Finally, there was the language itself.

Three passages in particular would have struck Adams as imitative of the national declaration. Here they are compared side by side:

Mecklenburg Declaration	**July 4 Declaration**
That whosoever directly or indirectly abetted, or in any way, form or manner, countenanced the unchartered and dangerous invasion of our rights, as claimed by Great Britain, is an enemy to this country, to America, and to *the inherent and inalienable rights of man.* [First Resolve]	We hold these truths to be self-evident, that all men are created equal, that they are endowed by their Creator with *certain unalienable Rights, that* among these are Life, Liberty and the pursuit of Happiness.
do hereby *dissolve* the political bands which have connected us to the mother country, and hereby *absolve* ourselves from all allegiance to the British Crown. [Second Resolve]	they are *absolved* from all allegiance to the British Crown, and that all political connection between them and the State of Great Britain, is and ought to be totally *dissolved.*
do hereby declare ourselves a *free and independent* people; *are, and of right ought to be,* a sovereign and self-governing Association. [Third Resolve]	That these united Colonies *are, and of Right ought to be Free and Independent* States.
we solemnly pledge to each other our mutual cooperation, *our lives, our fortunes, and our most sacred honor.* [Third Resolve]	And for the support of this Declaration, with a firm reliance on the protection of Divine Providence, we mutually pledge to each other *our Lives, our Fortunes, and our sacred Honor.*

It was, to quote Jefferson, self-evident. Jefferson had plagiarized from this hitherto unknown document. Adams had no doubts. "Either these resolutions are a plagiarism from Mr. Jefferson's Declaration of Independence, or Mr. Jefferson's Declaration of Independence is a plagiarism from those resolutions," he wrote to Bentley in a second letter on August 21.[21]

Adams would later back away (slightly) from these initial incendiary accusations. But it was too late. He had framed the argument for all time. Adams' accusations and insinuations against Jefferson would cast all future discussion of the Mecklenburg Declaration in an incendiary, even conspiratorial, context. The Mecklenburg Declaration could not be discussed without responding or commenting, positively or negatively, on the charges that Adams had made against Jefferson, charges that hung in the air around the topic like a dark and heavy cloud. It didn't have to be this way, however. After all, Adams could have just as well concluded that the similarity in certain phrases between the national Declaration and the Mecklenburg Declaration was a historical coincidence. It was widely known and accepted that the themes and indeed language of the national Declaration were taken from a variety of sources, as Jefferson himself freely admitted and modern scholars have shown.

Adams could also have concluded that perhaps Jefferson had seen or heard of the Mecklenburg Declaration in some innocent context, even in passing, without leaping to the conclusion that Jefferson had plagiarized from it. After all, contrary to common myth, Jefferson was not the sole "author" of the Declaration of Independence. The draft originally written by Lee, then edited by Jefferson, had been reviewed, edited and commented on by others in committee; perhaps Lee or some other member of the committee had seen the Mecklenburg Declaration and—deliberately or through happenstance—mirrored some of its phrases.

An objective observer could have reached any number of different and less charged conclusions that were neither sinister nor conspiratorial about the similarities between the two documents. But Adams was not an objective observer. The wounds that Jefferson had inflicted on Adams were too deep. Adams' visceral antipathy to and distrust of Jefferson, which waxed and waned over many years but never entirely faded—could not fade, given their life histories—forced Adams to the most extreme and negative conclusion when he first read the Mecklenburg Declaration of Independence: Jefferson was a sham and a crook. If Adams could prove this, Adams' fall from political grace and Jefferson's victory would be reversed. The Mecklenburg Declaration was the secret weapon that Adams believed could undo the political defeats that he had suffered at Jefferson's hands, correct the historical record, and undo past wrongs.

Thanks to Adams, from the moment the Mecklenburg Declaration of Independence became a topic of national discussion and debate, the subject was irretrievably intertwined with a distracting and explosive accusation: that Thomas Jefferson was a plagiarist and his 1776 national declaration a fraud. After all, President Adams himself had said so.

13

"I believe it spurious"
Thomas Jefferson, Original
Mecklenburg Declaration Skeptic

If the name McKnitt be real, and not a part of the fabrication, it needs a vindication by the production of such proof. For the present, I must be an unbeliever in the apocryphal gospel.

— Letter from Thomas Jefferson to John Adams, July 9, 1819

Adams' letter to Jefferson of June 22, 1819, enclosing the text of the Mecklenburg Declaration of Independence arrived at Monticello, Jefferson's home in the foothills of Virginia outside Charlottesville, about July 4 — the forty-third anniversary of the national Declaration of Independence.

It was a time of great celebration, with visitors and notes of congratulations received and toasts drunk. Jefferson was then seventy-six years old, and had been living "temperately," he wrote to Dr. Vine Utley on March 21, 1819, "eating little animal food, and that not as an ailment, so much as a condiment for the vegetables, which constitute my principal diet. I double, however, the Doctor's glass and a half of wine, and even treble it with a friend; but halve its effect by drinking the weak wines only. The ardent wines I cannot drink, nor do I use ardent spirits in any form."[1]

Jefferson's right wrist was stiff, "the consequence of an early dislocation, [which] makes writing both slow and painful." He slept irregularly, often only five hours and not more than eight a night. He rose with the sun and bathed his feet in cold water, a practice he carried on for sixty years. His hearing, although "distinct in particular conversation," was "confused when several voices cross each other, which unfits me for the society of the table." Overall he was in good health given his age, although "too feeble, indeed, to walk much, but riding without fatigue six or eight miles a day, and sometimes thirty or forty."[2]

Although his health was good, the summer of 1819 was a difficult and stressful time for Jefferson, as he was heavily in debt. In 1815 he sold his personal library to the U.S. government for $23,950, but this accounted for less than half his indebtedness; by 1819, his obligations exceeded $40,000. Only his name and reputation kept his creditors from seizing Monticello.

The same year of Adams' letter — 1819 — the University of Virginia was chartered, a cherished project of Jefferson's. It was all consuming, with Jefferson himself serving as architect, project manager and chief financial officer. Jefferson was "involved in every aspect, organizing the curriculum, choosing the site, and designing the buildings. Once construction was under way, he kept watch from his mountaintop by telescope."[3] It was to be his noblest accomplishment, and indeed at his request "Father of the University of Virginia" was inscribed upon his tombstone. The Declaration of Independence, by contrast, was not mentioned.

On July 2, 1819, perhaps the very day that Adams' letter was received, Jefferson wrote a friend, Arthur Spicer Brockenbrough:

> [O]ur two Italian Sculptors arrived at Charlottesville the evening before last and we have to make immediate provision to reimburse to Mr Hollins of Baltimore the sums he has been called on for on their arrival.... [T]he whole sum to be paid him amounts to 840 D ... the proceeds of which should be remitted to Mr Hollins without any delay, as he is one of those who has suffered by the difficulties of the times, and mentions that his situation does not permit him to be in advance.[4]

Money was scarce, and Jefferson did not have cash on hand to repay his friends who had assisted in bringing the Italians over, a fact he found "very embarrassing." Brockenbrough was needed, and needed urgently, to supervise the sculptors. Until he arrived, Jefferson would have to oversee their work, in addition to all his other responsibilities. "I think your presence here immediately is indispensably necessary," he wrote "These men are to be lodged, boarded & set to work. This requires the Quarriers to get to work for raising the stone, common stonecutters to prepare the blocks and other arrangements to get them under way.... In the present unsettled state of things I cannot think of leaving the place for Bedford until your arrival here, and the delay is very distressing to me."[5]

In addition to his personal financial difficulties, his age and health issues, and his massive project of creating the University of Virginia, there was an overwhelming volume of correspondence — personal, professional and administrative — to digest and respond to. When Jefferson received Adams' letter of June 22, it was the third letter from Adams that he had received in little more than a month. He had not yet replied to the earlier letters, but this one would warrant a response.

We do not know what Jefferson thought when he read Adams' letter of June 22 but it must have irritated him greatly. Perhaps he brooded for a few days, but in any event his reply came five days later. It was a point by point critique on the background and legitimacy of this so-called Mecklenburg Declaration. Jefferson was not only irritated by Adams' insinuations, but anxious to reply in full, as evidenced by the length of his reply and the eagerness of the response. In a letter dated July 9 from Monticello he began as follows:

> Dear Sir,
>   I am in debt to you for your letters of May the 21st, 27th, and June the 22d....[6]
>   But what has attracted my peculiar notice, is the paper from Mecklenburg county, of North Carolina, published in the *Essex Register*, which you were so kind as to enclose in your last, of June the 22d. And you seem to think it genuine. I believe it spurious.

In 1812 a volcano was reported to have erupted in Warm Spring, North Carolina. Although widely reported, it turned out to be a hoax. Analogizing from this, Jefferson laid the intellectual foundation for the claim that the Mecklenburg Declaration was a fraud, perhaps one perpetuated by his political enemies. This alleged Mecklenburg Declaration, wrote Jefferson, was like "a very unjustifiable quiz, like that of the volcano, so minutely related to us as having broken out in North Carolina, some half a dozen years ago, in that part of the country, and perhaps in that very county of Mecklenburg, for I do not remember its precise locality."

Jefferson first questioned whether this declaration had even been printed in the *Raleigh Register* at all:

> If this paper be really taken from the Raleigh *Register*, as quoted, I wonder it should have escaped Ritchie [an editor in Richmond], who culls what is good from every paper, as the bee from every flower; and the *National Intelligencer*, too, which is edited by a North Carolinian; and that the fire should blaze out all at once in Essex, one thousand miles from where the spark is said to have fallen.
>
> But if really taken from the Raleigh *Register*, who is the narrator, and is the name subscribed real, or is it as fictitious as the paper itself?
>
> It appeals, too, to an original book, which is burnt, to Mr. [John McKnitt] Alexander, who is dead, to a joint letter from Caswell, Hughes, and Hooper, all dead, to a copy sent to the dead Caswell [here Jefferson must have meant General Davie, to whom Dr. Alexander's postscript indicated a copy had been sent], and another sent to Doctor Williamson, now probably dead, whose memory did not recollect, in the history he has written of North Carolina, this gigantic step of its county of Mecklenburg.

It was all too convenient, Jefferson was saying. Warming to this theme, he continued.

> [The historian] Horry, too, is silent in his history of Marion, whose scene of action was the country bordering on Mecklenburg. Ramsay, Marshall, Jones, Girardin, Wirt, historians of the adjacent States, all silent. When Mr. Henry's resolutions, far short of independence, flew like lightning through every paper, and kindled both sides of the Atlantic, this flaming declaration of the same date, of the independence of Mecklenburg county, of North Carolina, absolving it from the British allegiance, and abjuring all political connection with that nation, although sent to Congress too, is never heard of. It is not known even a twelvemonth after, when a similar proposition is first made in that body.

And if it *had* been sent to Congress, why had no one ever heard of it?

> Armed with this bold example, would not you have addressed our timid brethren in peals of thunder, on their tardy fears? Would not every advocate of independence have rung the glories of Mecklenburg county, in North Carolina, in the ears of the doubting Dickinson and others, who hung so heavily on us? Yet the example of independent Mecklenburg county, in North Carolina, was never once quoted.

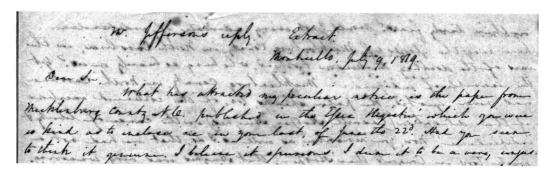

"And you seem to think it genuine," Jefferson wrote Adams on July 9, 1819, upon reading the Mecklenburg Declaration. **"I believe it spurious."** The battle lines were set (Mecklenburg Declaration of Independence, 1775, Accession #2723-m, Albert and Shirley Small Special Collections Library, University of Virginia, Charlottesville, Virginia).

Next, Jefferson turned to the missing links in the story: the three North Carolina delegates, who, as the story went, had received the Mecklenburg Declaration from James Jack:

> The paper speaks, too, of the continued exertions of their delegation (Caswell, Hooper, Hughes) "in the cause of liberty and independence." Now you remember as well as I do, that we had not a greater Tory in Congress than Hooper; that Hughes was very wavering, sometimes firm, sometimes feeble, according as the day was clear or cloudy; that Caswell, indeed was a good whig, and kept these gentlemen to the notch, while he was present; but that he left us soon, and their line of conduct became then uncertain until Penn came, who fixed Hughes, and the vote of the State.

These were explosive charges, especially the one against Hooper ("not a greater Tory in Congress"), and, in a classically Jeffersonian exercise of attack and then retreat, he then walked them back: "I must not be understood as suggesting any doubtfulness in the State of North Carolina. No State was more fixed or forward."

Jefferson, although calling the Declaration "spurious" earlier in the letter, now walked this back as well. "Nor do I affirm, positively, that this paper is a fabrication; because the proof of a negative can only be presumptive. But I shall believe it such until positive and solemn proof of its authenticity shall be produced." The key to whether the story was true or not, as Jefferson immediately recognized, was the keeper of the records and principal eyewitness, John McKnitt Alexander. "If the name McKnitt be real, and not a part of the fabrication, it needs a vindication by the production of such proof," concluded Jefferson. "For the present, I must be an unbeliever in the apocryphal gospel."[7]

Given the insinuations and snide tenor of Adams' letter of June 22, Jefferson's response was in many respects a model of fairness and restraint. Jefferson raised a series of reasonable and logical questions as to the veracity of the *Raleigh Register* account. Jefferson's first contention — that the *Raleigh Register* had never published such an article and the entire episode was a hoax, like the fictitious volcano — was easily answerable. But as Jefferson correctly pointed out, the main actors were now deceased: Alexander himself, Caswell, Hooper and Hughes and the historian Williamson, "now probably dead." Furthermore, Jefferson asked, why had no one heard of this Mecklenburg Declaration? The historians "Ramsay, Marshall, Jones, Girardin, Wirt, historians of the adjacent States, all silent."

These were all legitimate questions, if not unanswerable ones. And indeed Jefferson went out of his way to assert that the Mecklenburg Declaration might, in fact, be true. "Nor do I affirm, positively, that this paper is a fabrication," he concluded. But he would not be convinced otherwise "until positive and solemn proof of its authenticity" was found. Jefferson, in sum, wanted additional evidence. Jefferson was no doubt insulted by Adams' gratuitous attack on Jefferson's friend (and Adams' bitter enemy) Thomas Paine. But Jefferson didn't fall for the bait. He ignored Adams' comments on Paine entirely, and instead focused with relentless logic on the Mecklenburg Declaration, which Adams had used, perhaps subconsciously, as a stalking horse to disparage Paine, and by definition Jefferson himself.

One wonders what Adams must have thought upon reading Jefferson's response. Had he expected Jefferson to confess to having plagiarized the Mecklenburg Declaration? Perhaps he thought Jefferson would hem and haw, and inadvertently disclose the fact that he had, in fact, seen the Mecklenburg document before. Most likely Adams realized that he had overplayed his hand when he saw the logic of Jefferson's objections. In any event, Adams' response to Jefferson, written on July 21, almost immediately after he received Jefferson's letter, is shocking in its disingenuousness, given what we know about his private views:

I am greatly obliged to you -for your Letter of the 9th[8]:

It has entirely convinced me that the Mecklengburg [*sic*] Resolutions are a fiction, when I first read them in the *Essex Register*, I was struck with astonishment. It appeared to me utterly incredible that they should be genuine. [This was false. Nowhere in his original letter had Adams indicated that he believed the Mecklenburg Declaration was false. In fact, what he had concluded, and written to Bentley, was that not only were they genuine, but they also proved that Jefferson was a thief.] I thought it my duty to take measures for the detection of the imposture — for this purpose I instantly inclosed the *Essex Register* to you; knowing that if you had either seen, or heard of these resolutions you would have informed me of it. As they were unknown to you they must have been unknown to all mankind.[9]

In his first letter of June 22 Adams did not inquire of Jefferson whether he had seen them before (he assumed, even implied that Jefferson had) nor ask him whether he believed the Mecklenburg Declaration to be authentic. On the contrary, his entire letter assumed that they were authentic ("What a poor, ignorant, malicious, short-sighted, crapulous mass is Tom Paine's 'Common Sense,' in comparison with this paper!") and not once did he suggest he believed otherwise. Adams did not believe the Mecklenburg Declaration was a fabrication; even Jefferson pointed this out to him, noting, "you seem to think them genuine." Nor had Jefferson irrefutably concluded that they were untrue. Indeed, Jefferson had rather gamely left open the prospect that additional evidence might convince him of their validity. So Adams' total and unilateral surrender does not seem either convincing or, frankly, necessary.

Six days earlier Adams had privately written to Bentley that the Mecklenburg Declaration "must be more universally made known to the present and future generation." Now, less than a week later, he appeared to completely backtrack, obsequiously writing to Jefferson: "[W]ho can be the Demon to invent such a machine after five and forty years, and what could be his Motive — was it to bring a Charge of Plagiarism against the Congress, in [17]76, or against you; the undoubted acknowledged draughtsmen of the Declaration of Independence?"[10]

The person who had raised the "Charge of Plagiarism," of course, was *Adams himself*, both implying it to Jefferson and expressly charging it in letters to others.[11] And here again, after agreeing with Jefferson that the Mecklenburg Declaration must be a fiction, Adams continues in rapturous terms about how exceptional and important they are, and how powerful their impact would have been had they been published. "Had such [Mecklenburg] Resolutions appeared in June 1775 they would have flown through the Universe like wild fire; they would have Elevated the heads of the inhabitants of Boston — and of all New-England above the Stars — and they would have rung a peal in Congress to the utter Confusion of Tory'ism and timidity, for a full year before they were discomforted."[12]

If Adams now believed they were not genuine, why would he continue in this vein? Had he really changed his mind? Was he, as he wrote Jefferson, now "entirely convinced" that the Mecklenburg Declaration was "a fiction?" Of course not. Despite what he wrote to Jefferson, Adams had not abandoned his theory of Jefferson's intellectual piracy. He was still searching for more evidence.

One of the leading proponents of the authenticity of the Mecklenburg Declaration was Senator Nathaniel Macon of North Carolina. Macon had served in the Revolutionary War and had been elected in 1785 to the Continental Congress but had declined to serve. Following the Revolution, he had served as a member of Congress (March 4, 1791–December 13, 1815), including as speaker of the House. He was elected as a Democratic Republican to the U.S. Senate on December 5, 1815, later serving as speaker pro tem. When Adams learned that the truth of the Mecklenburg Declaration was vouched for by Macon (who had submitted the article from Dr. Alexander to the *Raleigh Register*), Adams was impressed. Maybe he was on to something.

"The plot thickens," Adams wrote again to Bentley on August 21, 1819, a month after his backtracking letter to Jefferson.[13] "The name of the Cato of North Carolina, the honest, hoary-headed, stern, determined republican, Macon, strikes me with great force," Adams wrote.[14] If Macon believed in the authenticity of the Mecklenburg Declaration, his word could not easily be discounted. To Adams, Macon's word was easily worth that of the two-faced Jefferson.

Macon's vouching for the Mecklenburg Declaration was powerful. Yet, there remained many unanswered questions. The similarity of the Mecklenburg Declaration of Independence to Jefferson's Declaration, its sudden publication, and its mysterious concealment were "an accumulation of miracles," Adams wrote Bentley. Sketching a theory of the case, as he had as a young attorney, Adams laid out the key facts:

1. The [Mecklenburg] resolutions are such as every county in the thirteen colonies ought to have taken at that moment.
2. The Suffolk resolves, taken about the same time, were sufficiently famous, and adopted by Congress.
3. I was on social, friendly terms with Caswell, Hooper, and Hewes, every moment of their existence in Congress; with Hooper, a Bostonian, and a son of Harvard, intimate and familiar. Yet, from neither of the three did the slightest hint of these Mecklenburg resolutions ever escape.
4. Is it possible that such resolutions should have escaped the vigilant attention of the scrutinizing, penetrating minds of Patrick Henry, R.H. Lee, Mr. Jefferson, Mr. Gadsden, Mr. Rutledge, Mr. Jay, Mr. Sherman, Mr. Samuel Adams? *Haud credo*. I cannot believe that they were known to one member of Congress on the fourth of July, 1776.
5. Either these resolutions are a plagiarism from Mr. Jefferson's Declaration of Independence, or Mr. Jefferson's Declaration of Independence is a plagiarism from those resolutions. I could as soon believe that the dozen flowers of the Hydrangea, now before my eyes, were the work of chance, as that the Mecklenburg resolutions and Mr. Jefferson's Declaration were not derived the one from the other.
6. The declaration of one of the most respectable of the inhabitants of this city, Raleigh, ought to be produced.
7. The papers of Dr. Hugh Williamson ought to be searched for the copy sent to him, and the copy sent to General W.R. Davie.[15]

Adams, in sum, had not abandoned the case. Although there were unanswered questions, he continued to believe — subject to additional evidence — that the Mecklenburg Declaration was real. "That this fiction is ancient and not modern, seems to be ascertained," he concluded. "It is of so much more importance that it should be thoroughly investigated."[16]

For reasons best understood in the context of his passive-aggressive relationship with Jefferson, the mystery of the Mecklenburg Declaration continued to obsess Adams. "I know not whether I have written the tenth part of the reflections that have occurred to me," he wrote, "but I have written more than my eyes and nerves can well bear."[17] The Adams-Jefferson correspondence regarding the Mecklenburg Declaration was not publicly known until the publication of Jefferson's letters in 1829, and other than the above letters, neither is known to have written further on the issue. Publication of the correspondence in 1829 had several immediate effects. First, it propelled the historical controversy onto the national stage. What was, and would likely have remained, an interesting if obscure side note to early nineteenth century history became, for many years, a national obsession. Proving the existence of the Mecklenburg Declaration became the holy grail of many American historians of the time. Without the spark provided by the letters of Jefferson and Adams, this would not have happened.

Second, as a result of the Adams-Jefferson letters, the Mecklenburg Declaration was transformed from an obscure historical debate into a hotly charged political controversy. Whether one believed in the Mecklenburg Declaration of Independence became driven by political considerations — whether one was a Democrat or Republican; a Yankee or Southerner; a Virginian or North Carolinian; a partisan of Jefferson or Adams. The historic facts and circumstances of May 1775 became secondary, mere debating points used to discredit one side or the other. All future discussions over the historical veracity of the Mecklenburg Declaration of Independence should be viewed through this prism.

Finally, and most important, Adams had introduced a new and emotional element into the discussion, the issue of plagiarism. Either Jefferson was a plagiarist, he argued, or whoever had written the Mecklenburg Declaration had plagiarized from Jefferson. As Adams framed the argument, no middle ground was permitted. Arguments over the Mecklenburg Declaration of Independence were a zero sum game.

Adams and Jefferson had made the opening arguments, for and against, the Mecklenburg Declaration. The national debate, what became known as the "Mecklenburg Controversy," would shortly begin.

PART IV. THE MECKLENBURG CONTROVERSY (1829–2012)

14

"Solemn proof"
John McKnitt Alexander's
Version of the Story

The reasons, upon which Mr. Jefferson doubts the Mecklenburg Declaration, are shallow, and the language, with which he chooses to express his suspicions, are indicative of a jealous and malignant spirit.
— Joseph Seawell Jones, "A Defense of the Revolutionary History of the State of North Carolina from the Aspersions of Mr. Jefferson," 1834

Monday, July 5, 1824, was a sweltering summer day in the Carolinas. In Hopewell Presbyterian Church in northern Mecklenburg County parishioners gathered for a special sermon to celebrate the forty-eighth anniversary of American independence. Hopewell was the church that John McKnitt Alexander had helped to found over a half century before. Now he and his wife lay buried in the Scottish-style cemetery out front. That morning, another Alexander of Mecklenburg — the Reverend Doctor M. Winslow Alexander, no doubt distantly related to McKnitt himself— prepared to speak. Following a "very appropriate and eloquent discourse" delivered by the Reverend John Williamson, the pastor at Hopewell, the Rev. Dr. Alexander began a long sermon on the national Declaration of Independence.

"I have this day the honor of being appointed to read to you the Declaration of Independence, made by Congress on the Fourth of July, 1776," he began. "I hope it will not be considered irrelevant to the business of the day, nor repugnant to the true feelings of patriotism, if we, the citizens of Mecklenburg County, should claim a *more* than equal honor in that transaction."[1] The story of Captain Jack and the Mecklenburg Declaration of Independence was intimately known to everyone sitting in the pews that day. It was a story they had grown up hearing; a story that was bred into them; a story they celebrated each May as avidly — indeed more so — than they celebrated the 4th of July. "These are transactions with which you, together with the citizens of this and the adjoining counties, have long been familiar," the Rev. Dr. Alexander concluded. "These have been the frequent topics of conversation amongst us for nearly fifty years — these were the proceedings of our fathers, of our relatives, of our fellow citizens; every individual of whom has descended to the silent tomb."[2]

The old cemetery at Hopewell Presbyterian, where John McKnitt Alexander, Richard Barry and other local patriots are buried. McKnitt's grave is marked with a small flag for Veterans Day 2012 (photograph by the author).

To the churchgoers sitting in the high wooden pews or looking down from the second story balcony at Hopewell that hot July day, the story of the Mecklenburg Declaration was their shared heritage. The great man, John McKnitt Alexander, lay buried not more than a hundred feet away along with three other Mecklenburg Declaration signers; Richard Barry, Matthew McClure and William Graham. "These are their living deeds of patriotism, which misfortune cannot now tarnish, and which the malignant breath of envy durst not now assail to blast."

"Who would not glory in such ancestors?" the minister asked. "Who would not emulate such virtue — Who would not sanction such principles?" Little did the audience that day, or the preacher himself, anticipate the controversy which would bring Mecklenburg and its declaration to national prominence in five short years when Jefferson's papers were posthumously published. The "malignant breath of envy" would soon blast hotter in their direction when the late president Thomas Jefferson emerged as the leading skeptic of their local history.

The publication of Jefferson's disparaging remarks to Adams about the Mecklenburg Declaration of Independence in 1829 was perceived by many in Mecklenburg as an unprovoked assault on their collective memory. It was, in the words of Dr. Joseph McKnitt Alexander, "Mr. Jefferson's denial of this our birthright."[3] Jefferson's casual dismissal of the Mecklenburg Declaration ("spurious"), his disparaging remarks about North Carolina's congressional delegation ("no greater Tory than Hooper") and his generally snide attitude ("this flaming declaration ... never heard of") was to cause "some feeling" in the state, the North Carolina historian Wheeler would write privately.[4]

And in fact, throughout North Carolina animosity towards Jefferson exploded. "Mr. Jefferson," wrote one outraged citizen named Joseph Seawell Jones in 1834, "contributed to smother this public spirit of North Carolina" and deserved "the execration of every native citizen of the State."[5] The title of Seawell's book said it all: *A Defense of the Revolutionary History of the State of North Carolina from the Aspersions of Mr. Jefferson.*

Nicknamed "Shocco" after a small creek near where he grew up, Jones was a true Southern character: hot-tempered, charming and eccentric. He claimed to have killed at least one man in a duel and was fond of what were then called "pranks," but what today we might regard as "financial fraud." After flunking out of the University of North Carolina, Jones attended Harvard Law School, where, after dropping out three times, he finally received a degree in 1839.[6] Jones had more than a passing interest in the Mecklenburg Controversy, however. His mother was the niece of the politician Nathaniel Macon, the same Macon who had sent Dr. Alexander's account on to the *Raleigh Register* in the first place. Jones decided to apply his antebellum polemical skills to a full-throated defense of his native state.

"Whilst the Sage of Monticello was pondering on the various projects of reconciliation with the mother country," Seawell wrote, "while Virginia and even Massachusetts were continually avowing allegiance to the Throne ... the people of Mecklenburg ... dissolved for ever the unhallowed Union of British domination and American allegiance."[7] But Seawell didn't stop there. He attacked Jefferson personally. Jefferson, he wrote, was a "zealous idolator," a "radical autocrat" and a "heathen god."[8] Jefferson's skepticism of the Mecklenburg Declaration, Seawell wrote, "deserves no lighter reproach, than to be denounced a base and unprincipled falsehood, unsupported by any evidence in the range of human inquiry. A more flagrant instance of violation of truth cannot be found in the annals of cabalistic literature."[9] "The reasons, upon which Mr. Jefferson doubts the Mecklenburg Declaration," Seawell concluded, "are shallow, and the language, with which he chooses to express his suspicions, are indicative of a jealous and malignant spirit."[10]

Seawell was not the only one incensed in North Carolina. Outraged patriots damned Jefferson and the arrogant outsiders (especially Virginians and New Englanders) who denied the glorious history of Mecklenburg. Only "liars and slanderers" denied that there was a convention on May 20, 1775, Joseph Wallis wrote in the *National Intelligencer* on August 13, 1857. Wallis, a grandson of John McKnitt Alexander, vividly recalled as a child watching his own father, a Southern minister, throwing a copy of Williamson's *History of North Carolina* to the ground and stamping on it, because, he said, "it did not contain a carefully prepared account of the Declaration." Denying or insulting the Mecklenburg Declaration constituted fightin' words in the Carolinas. Wallis announced that he was prepared to offer "personal satisfaction" to any other doubters brave enough to confront him face to face.[11]

McKnitt's son, Dr. Joseph Alexander, took a more charitable view towards Jefferson. "If Mr. Jefferson were living, I should feel bound to investigate his letter, with that reprehension which it appears to merit; but as he is now in the silent tomb — calm be his repose." Dr. Alexander felt "no disposition to disturb the sanctuary of the grave." "To err," he wrote of Jefferson, "is human frailty."[12]

Jefferson be damned. The Mecklenburgers had no doubts. "We, as a State and particularly as a County, were the pioneers of American independence," announced an editorial in the *Catawba Journal*. The "dignified and independent State of North Carolina" had been "*foremost* in bursting the chains of British oppression and proclaiming our Independence." The editorial was signed, "20th May, 1775." From their perspective, the subject was not open to further debate. "Mecklenburg Declaration of Independence: The Question Settled," announced the *Southern Literary Messenger* of June 1839.[13]

To Virginians, Mecklenburg's claim was as galling to them as Jefferson's words were insulting to the North Carolinians. Virginians fired back. "As the claim of Virginia to the honor of having first declared independence, has been recently disputed," argued one proud Virginian, "it is our duty ... to defend her fair fame from any unjust pretension, come it from any quarter it may."[14] "[I]t has been urged that the people of the county of Mecklenburg in our sister State of North Carolina, made a regular declaration of independence on the twentieth of May [1775], thus anticipating the action of Virginia by a twelve month.... [I argue] it is not only not true that a formal declaration of independence was made ... but that it is impossible to be true."[15]

Virginians were not the only ones who found the story of the Mecklenburg Declaration of Independence fishy. As one article put it, "We are aware, that when publicity was first given to the Declaration in 1819 ... its authenticity was doubted by some, and openly denied by others."[16] *Openly denied* was putting it mildly. In fact, many skeptics found the entire story preposterous. The Mecklenburg Declaration, in passages so similar to Jefferson's national Declaration of Independence, was to many a cheap and transparent forgery. Newspapers printed dozens of angry letters "calling in question the authenticity of the document, as being neither a true paper, nor a paper of a true convention."[17] Jefferson's snide dismissal of "independent Mecklenburg county ... never once quoted" summed up the case for the nonbelievers.

And so the battle lines of the Mecklenburg Controversy were set: Jefferson vs. Adams; North Carolina vs. Virginia; Mecklenburg vs. the World. The more the Yankees and outsiders doubted their history and derided the people of North Carolina, the more staunch and vehement became North Carolina's defense of the Mecklenburg Declaration. As before, these prickly, stubborn Scots-Irish citizens — themselves the descendants of prickly, stubborn Scots-Irish settlers — defended themselves against a hostile, impertinent world. Either one stood with the Alexanders of Mecklenburg or with Jefferson and the Virginians. There was no middle ground.

But if one believed that Jefferson was correct, that the Mecklenburg Declaration did not exist, it meant that either John McKnitt Alexander or his son, Dr. Joseph Alexander — or both of them — had lied.[18] As evidence that McKnitt had lied it was pointed out that in the *Raleigh Register* article he had signed his name as "J. McKnitt," deliberately omitting his last name to cover up the fact that he and John McKnitt were related. To those who knew the Alexanders, this was a terrible libel. John McKnitt Alexander himself often omitted his Alexander name, signing his name "J. McKnitt" in honor of his revered McKnitt ancestors. In a county full of Alexanders, it was common for them to use their first or middle names to distinguish between them. Moreover McKnitt had been a patriot during the Revolutionary War. He was friends with such famous leaders as General William Lee Davidson and William R. Davie, the latter of whom he had provided a copy of the Mecklenburg Declaration for safekeeping. When General Nathanael Greene passed through the region he named one of his encampments "Camp McKnitt Alexander." Surely all this was sufficient to prove that McKnitt was not a liar? The Alexanders, according to their defenders, were the victims of a monstrous miscarriage of historical justice. But not only was the Alexander family honor at stake, so also was the honor of the whole county.

In a lengthy article in the *Yadkin and Catawba Journal* on November 9, 1830, Dr. Alexander set forth the frustration of all of the people in Mecklenburg:

> To every ingenious mind, the difficulty is at once obvious of establishing by *positive* proof, such a transaction, 55 years after its occurrence: when no record of the transaction could *officially* be kept; when a long revolutionary war supervened; the place of its occurrence for a season being in the occupation of the enemy; when all the delegates are in the silent grave, and when the *validity* of the transaction has *never* been called in question until Mr. Jefferson, in a letter of his recently published, pronounced it "a spurious and unjustifiable quiz."

Nevertheless, Dr. Alexander concluded, despite the problems of establishing by positive proof some half century later, and as "difficult as the task may appear, we dread not to meet the closest scrutiny." Jefferson had asked for "positive and solemn proof," and Dr. Alexander was prepared to deliver it, for he believed he had that proof. "There is now a paper in my possession, written and signed by J.M. Alexander," he announced, which "purports to be 'extracted from the old minutes.'" "I hold these papers, certificates, &c., subject to the inspection of any one desirous to examine them."[19]

The paper in Dr. Alexander's possession was, as he put it, a "sheet and torn half sheet" containing handwritten notes of his father. These two pages, extensively analyzed by newspaper writer V.V. McNitt in his book *Chain of Error*, are described as "a leaf, or half of a foolscap sheet, torn at the margins, containing rough notes the senior Alexander [John McKnitt] had written for his own use sometime in the past." The writer concluded they were written sometime prior to 1800.[20] They came to be known as the "rough notes" of John McKnitt Alexander.[21] They are written front and back on a single sheet of paper, 7½ inches wide, and 12½ inches long, are in many places illegible, and contain only a brief sketch of the five resolutions printed in the *Raleigh Register*. Here is what the "rough notes" say:

> On the 19th May 1776 [1775] Pursuant to the Order of Col.º ~~Adam Alexander~~ Thoˢ. Polk to each Captain of Militia in his regiment of Mecklenburg County, to elect nominate and appoint 2 persons of their militia company, clothed ʷⁱth ample powers to devise ways & means to extricate themselves and ward off the dreadfull impending storm bursting on them by the British Nation &c&c.
>
> Therefore on Sᵈ. 19th May the Sᵈ. Committee met in Charlotte Town (2 men from each company) vested with all powers their or their constituents had or conceived they had &c.
>
> After a short conference about their suffering brethren besieged and suffering every hardship in Boston and the American Blood running in Lexington &c the *Electrical fire* flew into every breast — and to preserve order chose Abraham Alexander Chairman & Secretary JMᶜ Alexander.
>
> After a few hours free discussion in order to give relief to suffering America and protect our just & natural right —
> 1ˢᵗ. We (the County) by a *solemn* and *awfull* vote, Dissolved (abjured) our allegiance to King George and the British Nation.

Opposite: The "rough notes" of John McKnitt Alexander. They are indeed in rough shape, although perfectly legible. Note the mark-throughs in the first line and what appears to be the date "1800" crossed out just below the first tear on the right (courtesy Southern Historical Collection, Wilson Library, University of North Carolina at Chapel Hill).

On the 19th May 1775 Pursuant to the Order of Col. Thos. Polk &c to each Captain of Militia in his regiment of Mecklenburg County, to elect nominate and appoint 2 persons of their militia company, closethed with ample powers to devise ways & means to extricate themselves and ward off the dreadfull impending storm brusting on them by the British Nation &c&c

Therefore on ye 19th May the P. Committee met in Charlotte Town 2 men from each company, vested with all powers their Constituents had, &c. After a short conference about their suffering brethren besieged and suffering every hardship in Boston and the American Blood running in Lexington &c the Electrical fire flew into every breast and to preserve order — Chose Abraham Alexander Chairman & J. McKnitt Secretary — in order to give relief to suffering America and protect our just & natural rights

1st. We the County, by a solemn and awfull vote, Dissolved our allegiance to King George & the British Nation ————

2d. Declared our selves a free & independent people, having a right and capable to govern our selves as a part of North Carolina,

3d. In order to have laws as a rule of life for our future government We formed a Code of laws; by adopting our former wholesome laws

4th. And as there was then no officers Civil or Military in our County We Decreed that every Militia officer in P. County should hold and occupy his former commission and Grade — And that every member present of this Committee shall henceforth as a Justice of the peace in the Character of a Committee Man hear and determine all Controversies agreeable to P. laws — preserve Union & harmony in P. County — and to spread the Electrical fire of freedom among our selves &c

5th. &c&c many other laws & ordinances were then made after setting up in the Court house all night — neither sleep After reading and maturing every paragraph they all passed Nem-Con about 2 O'clock May 20. 1775

But in a few days after cooling a considerable part of P. Committee Men convened and employed Captn James Jack of Charlotte, to go express to Congress, then in Philadelphia, with a Copy of all P. Laws &c and a letter to our 3 members there. Richd. Caswell Wm. Hooper & Joseph Hughes in order to get Congress to sanction or approve them &c &c

Capt. Jack returned with a long, full, complasent letter from P. 3 members; recommending our Zeal, perseverance order & forbearance &c all were premature, Congress never had our P. laws on their Table for discussion, though P. Copy was left with them by Capt. Jack

NB. about 1708 Doctor Hugh Williamson then of New York but formerly was member of Congress from this State, applied above by Col. Wm. Polk who was then compiling a in order to prove that the American people in the Revolution — and that Congress were Com

NB. allowing the 19th May to be a cash Act effects in binding all the middle & west firm Whigs — no toreys but not fully represented in the first

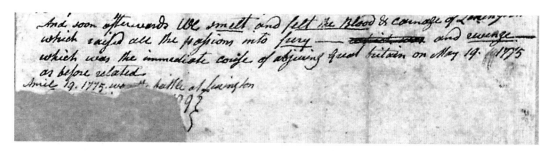

The date is torn at the end of the "rough notes." Is this an 8 or a 9? McKnitt's son stated the pamphlet in which they were found "may have been unrolled since 1788" (courtesy Southern Historical Collection, Wilson Library, University of North Carolina at Chapel Hill).

2ᵈ. Declared ourselves a free & independent people, having a *right* and *capable* to govern ourselves (as a part of North Carolina).

3ᵈ. In order to have laws as a rule of life for our future Government we formed a Code of laws; by adopting our former wholesome laws.

4ᵗʰ. And as there was then no officers Civil or Military in our County we Decreed that every Militia offer in sᵈ. County should hold and occupy his former commission and grade. And that every member present of this Committee shall henceforth [act] as a Justice of the peace, in the character of a Committee Man [to] hear and determine all controversies agreeable to sᵈ. laws [margin torn] peace, union & harmony in sᵈ. County — and to use every [margin torn] spread the Electrical fire of freedom among ourselves & [margin torn, words missing].

5ᵗʰ &c&c Many other laws and ordinances were then ma[de]."²²

Following this skeletal description of the Mecklenburg Declaration, the notes continue: "After sitting up in the Court house all night — neither [torn]. After reading and mastering every paragraph ... All passed Nem-Con [latin for "unanimously"] about 12 O'clock May 20, 1775." The second page describes the ride of Captain Jack and his return, and summarizes historical events during and following the Revolution. At the bottom is written, the "foregoing extracted from the old minutes &c. [Signed] By J.Mᶜ. Alexander."

The handwriting is perfectly clear and legible, and unmistakably in the penmanship of John McKnitt Alexander. But the "rough notes" are admittedly pretty rough. There are strikeouts and corrections in dark pen in several places, notably the deletion of Adam Alexander's name in the first sentence, and the replacement with Thomas Polk. The year "1776" also appears to be corrected to read "1775." Someone — probably McKnitt himself, but possibly someone else at a later time — corrected and recorrected the text, striking out errors and crossing out names.

The "rough notes" are in summary form and clearly not intended as a literal record, but indeed simply as sketches, or as McKnitt's son described them, an "abstract." They are also torn and missing key sections. Specifically, the facing page is torn in the very center of the right margin, a gash one and a half inches deep. The bottom right corner is also missing. This latter torn section cuts clearly through what appears to be McKnitt's concluding signature — and, more important, the date he made the notes.

To the defenders of the Mecklenburg Declaration, here was firsthand, fully corroborating written evidence. Although in summary form, the "rough notes" confirm the story — and the text of the Mecklenburg Declaration — in virtually all respects. Even the terminology between the two versions is the same: "dissolve/abjure" (second resolution); "free and independent" (third resolution); "a Justice of the peace, in the character of a Committee Man [to] hear and determine all controversies" (fourth resolution); and adopting former laws (fifth resolution). The date was missing, it was true, but there was no question as to the authorship or authenticity. The notes provided supporting evidence of the story and clearly validated the text of the five resolutions. To skeptics, however, the "rough notes" were worthless. They were torn in places, illegible and extensively revised. It unclear whether or not McKnitt had copied them from an original record, or even if he really had done so at all. He could have simply written them from whole cloth, as some argued.

Whether or not the "rough notes" were of genuine historical value came down to a single issue: *when were they written?* If they were written prior to the burning of the original papers in April 1800, the "rough notes" could be considered as a copy or extract from the original minutes. If that were true, although the text might not (indeed surely would not) correspond literally to the text of the original Mecklenburg Declaration, the "rough notes" could be considered as a sketch or copy of the original—and thus evidence that the Mecklenburg Declaration as set out in the *Raleigh Register* was correct.

The skeptic's main criticism of the papers was that due to their condition, it was not clear when McKnitt had written them. On the final page the date was torn in half. The final number in a date is visible, but torn in half. The torn number could be either an "8" or a "9" (meaning it was dated either 1789 or 1799—or for that matter, almost any year ending in 9, even 1809). A number of answers were possible. Based on a comparison of other numbers written by McKnitt elsewhere in the document, to this author the torn number looks slightly more like an "8" than a "9," implying they were written in 1788 or 1798. But it simply isn't clear.

Circumstantial evidence suggested the notes predated 1800. Dr. Alexander claimed that he found the notes "after the death of [John] McNitt Alexander in his old mansion house in the centre of a roll of old pamphlets" which were dated between 1774 and 1788. The roll of pamphlets was found among McKnitt's old surveying papers and other old papers, and "may have been unrolled since 1788."[23] Also found amongst McKnitt's papers were written instructions to the Mecklenburg delegates to the State Constitutional Convention in April 1776, probably in the handwriting of Ephraim Brevard. The fact that the notes were bundled in with other papers that were dated around 1778 suggested that the torn date could be 1789. If that were true, the notes predate the fire of 1800 and the Mecklenburg Controversy. They corroborate the text, structure and general spirit of the Mecklenburg Declaration of Independence. They prove that the story is true. Case closed.

And yet, and yet ... The very first line of the "rough notes" reads, "On the 19th May 1776." This was then scratched out and written in as "*1775.*" *1776?* Surely not? What does this error—if indeed it was an error—mean? Another and more telling mistake occurs later in the passage where McKnitt describes the passage of the Mecklenburg Declaration "Nem-Con" ("unanimously") on "May 20, 1775." Before the "1775" the year "1800" appears to have been written in, and then scratched out, in three vertical lines. A similar error occurs later.

Some argued that with this Freudian error, McKnitt clearly wrote the "rough notes" in 1800—that is, the same year the original records were lost in a fire. If that were true, the argument goes, McKnitt was writing the "rough notes" from memory and not from any original record. If that were true, their historical value is seriously diminished. Taking that argument further, it is possible that McKnitt, who was then sixty-seven years old, could have confused certain passages with the national Declaration of Independence, which would explain their similarity to Jefferson's document. Another argument is that if McKnitt had written the notes prior to 1800, he would have simply copied from the Mecklenburg Declaration verbatim and would have had no reason to make "rough notes" at all. But this was more speculation.

To Dr. Alexander, however, the "rough notes" were conclusive, direct evidence that the story was true. Whether written in 1789, 1799 or 1809, and whether regarded as a private diary, a sketch of original records, or a summary for a future historian, the "rough notes" are clear testimony by a key eyewitness. Taken at their face value, the "rough notes" are a copy of the original Mecklenburg Declaration, a copy made some time after the fact but a copy nevertheless. After all, at the conclusion McKnitt clearly writes that the foregoing was copied — "extracted" is the word he uses — "from the old minutes."[24] Unless we believe McKnitt was lying or delusional when he wrote them, they are contemporaneous evidence that the story is true.

"From the preceding," concluded Dr. Alexander, "[i]t appears most probable that there was drawn up by a select committee, a declaration of grievances and a formal Declaration of Independence, which, if so, was the paper sent on by Capt. Jack to Congress; the original of which is lost to us through the death, shortly afterwards [1781] of Doct. Ephraim Brevard, the Chairman of that Committee, and by the occupation of Charlotte by Cornwallis, where the Doctor [Brevard] lived, and where his papers probably were."[25]

Yet despite McKnitt's offer to make these papers "subject to the inspection of any one desirous to examine them," no one took him up on his offer. While copies of a number of documents relating to the Mecklenburg Declaration were published widely by the State of North Carolina in 1831, the "rough notes" were not. Other than McKnitt's summary of their content in his 1832 article, which was not widely circulated outside the county, the "rough notes" were forgotten. For several decades following the Civil War they disappeared entirely among various papers at the University of North Carolina and were presumed lost.[26]

The "rough notes" certainly buttressed the argument that the Mecklenburg Declaration was real. However, the condition of the document, its deletions, and, of most importance, the missing date, meant that the Mecklenburg Controversy could not be conclusively resolved. The search for the "solemn proof" that Jefferson had demanded would continue.

15

"Independence lang before any body else"
Eyewitnesses and Local Legends

More satisfactory evidence, drawn from more reputable sources, Mr. Jefferson, if alive, could not, and would not require. It is not hazarding too much to say, that there is no one event of the Revolution which has been, or can be more fully or clearly authenticated.
— North Carolina Governor Montford Stokes, Governor's Report, 1831

To the frustration of Dr. Joseph Alexander and his supporters, the discovery and public announcement that his father's "rough notes" had been found did not conclusively settle the debate. To many, the surviving papers were ambiguous. Most important, it was not clear when they had been written. The torn final page, with only the number *9,* taunted the reader to guess their date. In the end, McKnitt's "rough notes" were not the smoking gun that the believers had hoped. More evidence had to be found.

In 1829, the North Carolina General Assembly created a select committee with the express intention of settling the Mecklenburg Controversy once and for all. To that end, a committee of five was tasked to "examine, collate and arrange in proper order" all the documents accessible to them "as relate to the Declaration of Independence made by the patriotic men of Mecklenburg in May, 1775."[1] The committee reached out to witnesses in Mecklenburg and surrounding counties and as far afield as Georgia and Tennessee for any surviving participants or observers from the meetings in May 1775 such as Captain James Jack, General Joseph Graham and Major John Davidson.

They also asked Alexander family members to produce any surviving papers of McKnitt, such as the copy of the Mecklenburg Declaration that he had made for General William R. Davie. After more than a year of work, the committee produced a thirty-two-page report, which was published by authority of the North Carolina General Assembly in 1831. The intention was to eliminate all doubt that the story was true. The report announced the following: "The committee are aware that this assertion [of the Mecklenburg Declaration] has elsewhere been received with doubt, and at times met with denial; and it is, therefore, believed to be more strongly incumbent upon the House to usher to the world the Mecklenburg Declaration, accompanied with such testimonials of its genuineness, as shall silence incredulity ... [and] forever secure it from being forgotten."[2]

To stamp a definitive imprimatur of authority and veracity on the committee's report, North Carolina governor Montford Stokes was authorized by the general assembly to review the committee's findings and to write the preface. Governor Stokes was a Revolutionary War veteran and would later serve as a United States senator. He was familiar with many of the participants and the writers of the period. Moreover, Governor Stokes was an actual eyewitness to the story, for he had claimed to have seen with his own eyes an original copy of the Mecklenburg Declaration.

According to McKnitt, sometime prior to April 1800 (when his house burned down and the original papers were lost), he sent "a full copy of said records, at the request of Doctor Hugh Williamson, then of New York: but formerly a representative of Congress from this State."[3] Williamson was writing a history of North Carolina, and McKnitt wanted him to have a copy of the Mecklenburg Declaration so that "those early transactions might fill their proper place in a history of this State."[4] This may have occurred as early as 1787. This paper became known as the "Williamson Copy" of the Mecklenburg Declaration of Independence.[5]

If McKnitt had sent Williamson a copy as early as 1787, it would be the oldest surviving record of the Mecklenburg Declaration. Its presence would erase any conjecture that McKnitt later wrote the text of the Mecklenburg Declaration from memory, as was being claimed.

However, Williamson's published history only went as far as the year 1770 and made no mention of the Mecklenburg Declaration. It is thought that all of Williamson's original papers had been lost in a fire, but for whatever reason, no trace of the Williamson Copy of the Mecklenburg Declaration of Independence has ever been found.

Governor Stokes knew Williamson personally and had seen the Williamson Copy. In a footnote in the preface to the report he wrote, "This copy the writer well recollects to have seen in the possession of Doct. Williamson, in the year 1793, in Fayetteville, together with a letter to him from John McKnitt Alexander, and to have conversed with [Williamson] on the subject."[6] This was proof that one highly credible eyewitness — the governor himself — had seen a copy of the Mecklenburg Declaration in 1793, seven years before the fire at Alexandriana destroyed the original papers.

Stokes was an important eyewitness, but he was not the only one. All in all the committee took the testimony of fourteen witnesses (one was rejected as being unreliable), and their affidavits or testimonies were compiled in the report. Here, surely, was the "positive and solemn proof" that Jefferson had demanded. Some of the testimony was very short. For example, Samuel Wilson's testimony was only three sentences: "I do hereby certify, that in May, 1775, a committee or delegation from the different militia companies in this county, met in Charlotte; and after consulting together, they publicly declared their independence on [sic] Great Britain, and on her Government. This was done before a large collection of people, who highly approved of it. I was then and there present, and heard it read from the Court House door."[7]

Other testimony, such as that of General Joseph Graham or the Rev. Humphrey Hunter, ran several pages in length. But more important than the length of the testimony was the character of the witnesses. Many were decorated veterans of the American Revolution. Two of them were ordained Presbyterian ministers. All were pillars of their community, business and political leaders, whose credibility was above reproach. For men of their social standing at this time, their honor truly was held sacred and to bear false witness for any reason whatsoever was to throw away your life both in this world and in the next.

For example, one principal witness (although not cited by the committee directly) was

William Polk, the son of Colonel Thomas Polk. William was a distinguished veteran of the Revolutionary War, with a national reputation. Though only seventeen at the time, he volunteered as a second lieutenant in the South Carolina militia to fight the British and was wounded at the Battle of Canebrake on December 22, 1775. Upon recovery he joined the Continental Army and was commissioned as a major in the Ninth North Carolina Regiment under General Washington. Polk fought at the battles of Brandywine (September 11, 1777) and Germantown (October 4, 1777), where his jaw was smashed by a musket ball that hit him in the cheek. Polk recovered at Valley Forge in the winter of 1777 before returning to service in the Carolinas.[8]

After the War, Polk served in a number of prominent public offices, including numerous terms in the North Carolina House of Commons, where, according to the *Dictionary of North Carolina Biography*, "he was one of the leading Federalists in the state," and was nominated as a candidate for governor in 1802. At the time of Governor Stokes' report, Polk was "Raleigh's most illustrious citizen."[9] The old Revolutionary veteran was "a venerable remnant of the revolutionary stock, has passed the common boundary of human life, and [is] in a green old age," noted the governor, but was "in the full possession of his faculties."[10] Polk, wrote Governor Stokes, "was present, heard his father proclaim the Declaration to the assembled multitude; and need it be inquired, in any portion of this Union, if *he* will be believed?"[11]

Militia commanded by Joseph Graham and William Davie firing from the courthouse to repel the British advance into Charlotte on September 26, 1780. Graham left a detailed account of the meeting on May 20, 1775, and Davie was given a copy of the Mecklenburg Declaration by McKnitt (courtesy Dan Nance).

Another nationally known witness and friend of Governor Stokes was General Joseph Graham, previously mentioned. Graham, wrote Stokes, was "another surviving officer of the Revolution, a citizen and a soldier worthy of the best days of the Republic," whose testimony "will be read with pleasure and perfect confidence."[12] Graham's written testimony about the events of May 1775 ran nearly two pages and was quite detailed. And given his reputation and accomplishments it was not easily dismissed.

In May 1775, Graham was a fifteen-year-old student at Queen's College and heard the declaration read from the courthouse steps. He enlisted as a private in May 1778 and served in the Fourth Regiment, North Carolina line. During Graham's service he fought at the battles of Stono, Rocky Mount and Hanging Rock, as well as a half a dozen other skirmishes.[13]

But it was the Battle of Charlotte on September 25, 1780, that made Graham a bona fide hero.[14] That month, the local militia received word that Lord Cornwallis' army was on the march from Camden, South Carolina, towards Charlotte. Graham was sent to join General William R. Davie and gather as many men as they could in the town common to contest Cornwallis' advance. Fifty-six militiamen joined Davie's cavalry and took up positions in and around the courthouse in Charlotte. Cornwallis' men advanced from the south, their skirmishers flanking either side of the Salisbury Road which led into town. Cavalry led the way, wearing the pine green jackets of Tarleton's British Legion. (Despite its name, the British Legion was not in fact composed of British men, but rather of loyalists from New York, New Jersey and Pennsylvania.)

As the British advanced into town, Graham's men shot at them from behind trees and buildings and from the protection of the stone wall under the courthouse. Graham was nearly killed when the musket of a man beside him exploded, scattering splinters and hot metal in all directions. Three successful volleys stopped the British dragoons in their tracks. Yet the British greatly outnumbered the militia, and eventually their superior numbers began to push the Carolinians back. As they were driven from Charlotte, Graham and his men turned and fought several delaying actions along the wooded creeks that crossed the Salisbury Road. The British cavalry chased Graham and his men for several miles north. They caught a number of militia, including one young private, sixteen-year-old George Locke, who they hacked to death.

Graham and his men were pursued as far as the grounds of Sugar Creek Presbyterian Church, Craighead's old stomping grounds, where they turned and fought. The militia and British dragoons fired pistols at one another at short range, and then closed to engage in hand-to-hand combat with sabers and short swords:

> As Captain Graham was engaged in a hand-to-hand fight, his horse backed under a limb of a tree which knocked him off. He received three bullets in the thigh, one saber thrust in the side, one cut on the back of the neck and four upon the forehead. And from one of these some of his brains exuded. The cut on the back of the neck must have been given as he fell or fought on foot. It cut a heavy silver buckle which he wore on his stock entirely in two; but for the buckle it would have severed his head from his body.[15]

Graham was left near death, broken and bleeding on the grass, while his men scattered and fled. The British cavalry regrouped around the church, gathered their wounded and prepared to return into town. As they passed Graham's body upon the ground, bleeding from nine wounds, one British soldier aimed a pistol at him, intending to finish Graham off. The commanding British officer, Major Hanger, advised, "Put up your pistol; save your ammunition; he has had enough."[16]

The British rode off. Graham crawled to a nearby spring where he waited to die. That night a young woman named Susan Alexander found him as she came to fetch water. With the aid of her mother they carried Graham back to their house. His clothes were caked with blood, and he was badly cut up, but he was alive. The Alexanders hung flax sacks around the bed so no prying eyes could see that a wounded patriot officer was there. They kept watch over him for several nights. Graham was so quiet that more than once they thought he had died. A few days later British foragers arrived near their farm, looking for milk. It was not safe for Graham to stay. Despite his condition, he had to be moved further into the countryside to another safe house. The Alexanders helped mount Graham on a horse, and he was spirited to a friendly home to recover. It would take him over two months to do so.

Over fifty years later, in October 1832, Graham testified in court in Lincoln County as to his war service, in order to qualify for his pension. The nine scars Graham received in the Battle of Charlotte, "this Court [can] testify are visible at this time."[17] Mrs. Alexander, who saved his life, was granted a pension in 1851 for her services to Graham following the Battle of Charlotte.[18] Following the Revolutionary War, Graham purchased an iron smelter in Lincoln (formerly Tryon) County, across the Catawba River from Mecklenburg along the main stagecoach road from Spartanburg to Salisbury. Nearby, Graham built a plantation home for his growing family and named it "Vesuvius Furnace" after Mount Vesuvius, the volcano just outside Naples, Italy. The iron business made Graham very wealthy, and his family was well known and successful. His son, William A. Graham, would become a North Carolina governor, a U.S. senator and a nominee for vice president. (A noted descendent is the Reverend Billy Graham).

On the strength of testimony from such luminaries as Graham, and Polk, the committee believed it was game-set-match. The truth of the Mecklenburg Declaration would be settled once and for all. "By the publication of these papers," stated the report, "it will be fully verified, that as early as the month of May, 1775, a portion of the people of North Carolina ... did, by a public and solemn act, declare the dissolution of the ties which bound them to the crown and people of Great Britain, and did establish an independent, though temporary government for their own control and direction."[19]

The overall testimony of the thirteen witnesses was compelling and broadly consistent. For example, numerous witnesses recalled that Thomas Polk had summoned two delegates from each militia company to attend a meeting at the county courthouse. All agreed that the meeting had been held in late May, and the majority of the accounts fixed the date as May 19 or 20. Examples follow:

- [T]wo men, selected from each corps, should meet at the Court-House on the 19th of May, 1775 [Rev. Humphrey Hunter].[20]
- [T]he meeting took place in the Court-House, about 12 o'clock on the said 19th day of May, 1775 [George Graham, William Hutchinson, Jonas Clark and Robert Robinson].[21]
- [T]he Declaration took place [o]n the twentieth day of May, seventeen hundred and seventy-five, by the citizens of Mecklenburg. [Alphonsa Alexander, Amos Alexander and Joseph McKnitt Alexander].[22]
- I will give you the details of the Mecklenburg Declaration of Independence on the 20th of May, 1775 [Joseph Graham].[23]

The testimony was generally consistent in its account of the "principal characters" involved as well. In all but the account of James Jack, Abraham Alexander was listed as the chairman of the convention. Jack's account named Hezekiah Alexander as chairman, rather than Abraham Alexander. Hardly a material error and fairly explicable given that Abraham and Hezekiah were related, but a discrepancy nonetheless.

According to Jack's account attendees included "Hezekiah Alexander, who generally acted as Chairman, John M'Knitt Alexander, as Secretary, Abraham Alexander, Adam Alexander, Maj. John Davidson, Maj. (afterwards) Gen. Wm. Davidson, Col. Thomas Polk, Ezekiel Polk, Dr. Ephraim Brevard, Samuel Martin, Duncan Ochletree, William Wilson, [and] Robert Irvin."[24] Others wrote:

- In this business the leading characters were, the Rev. Hezekiah James Balch, a graduate of Princeton College, an elegant scholar, Waightstill Avery, Esq. Attorney at Law; Hezekiah and John M'Knitt Alexander, Esqrs. [and] Col. Thomas Polk. [Francis Cummings].[25]
- The Committee were organized in the court house by appointing Abraham Alexander, Esq. Chairman, and John M'Nnitt Alexander, Esq. Clerk or Secretary to the meeting. [Joseph Graham].[26]
- We are not, at this late period, able to give the names of all the Delegation who formed the Declaration of Independence; but can safely declare as to the following persons being of the number, viz. Thomas Polk, Abraham Alexander, John M'Knitt Alexander, Adam Alexander, Ephraim Brevard, John Phifer, Hezekiah James Balsh, Benjamin Patton, Hezekiah Alexander, Richard Barry, William Graham, Matthew M'Clure, Robert Irwin, Zachias Wilson, Neil Morrison, John Flenniken, John Queary, [and] Ezra Alexander. [George Graham, William Hutchinson, Jonas Clark and Robert Robinson].[27]

Most important, the testimony was consistent about the outcome of the meeting summoned by Col. Polk — that Mecklenburg County had declared independence from Great Britain:

- When the members met, and were perfectly organized for business, a motion was made to declare ourselves independent of the Crown of Great Britain, which was carried by a large majority. [John Davidson].[28]
- [O]n the 20th they again met, with a committee, under the direction of the Delegates, had formed several resolves, which were read, and which went to declare themselves, and the people of Mecklenburg county, Free and Independent of the King and Parliament of Great Britain. [George Graham, William Hutchinson, Jonas Clark and Robert Robinson].[29]
- [T]he aforesaid citizens of Mecklenburg renounced their allegiance to the crown of Great Britain, and set up a government for themselves, under the title of The Committee of Safety. [Alphonsa Alexander, Amos Alexander and Joseph McKnitt Alexander].[30]
- [A]fter due consultation, [they] declared themselves absolved from their allegiance to the King of Great Britain, and drew up a Declaration of their Independence, which was unanimously adopted. [Isaac Alexander].[31]
- [A]fter consulting together, they publicly declared their independence [Samuel Wilson].[32]

- Being young, I was not called on to take part ... but one thing I do positively remember, that she (Mecklenburg county) did meet and hold a Convention, declare independence, and sent a man to Philadelphia with the proceedings. [James Johnson].[33]

The thirteen eyewitness accounts were consistent in theme and message. But, not surprisingly perhaps, given the fifty-plus years that had passed, certain specific details were unclear or inconsistent. For example, some witnesses claimed the Mecklenburg Declaration had been approved by a majority vote, while others said it was a unanimous vote. Accounts were not clear as to whether the critical vote occurred on the 19th or the 20th of May. It was not clear whether the delegates signed a declaration or merely "resolved" upon one. Some accounts had Brevard as the secretary of the meeting, others had McKnitt. But these were ancillary details and irrelevant to the gist of the story, at least in the view of the Committee. The key fact, the core of the entire issue, the unmistakable and definitive story upon which they were all agreed, was that the delegates had "absolved themselves from all allegiance to the British crown" and declared themselves "free and independent."

In addition to the overall message, it was the inclusion of small and personal details that lent the testimony an aura of believability. For example, Hunter recalled that "[o]n that memorable day, I was 20 years and 14 days of age, [and] a very deeply interested spectator."[34] Francis Cummings recalled that he heard Thomas Polk proclaim independence "from the head of the court-house stairs.... I was present, and saw and heard it."[35] And Graham recalled the crowd throwing their hats up, with several being stuck on the courthouse roof.

All in all, given the character of the witnesses, the specific and credible accounts that they provided, and the corroborating evidence of the governor, the testimony simply could not be dismissed. The report put down a clear marker that the story of the Mecklenburg Declaration was not going to quietly fade away.

Of course, a skeptic could argue that the witnesses were all lying, or delusional, or mistaken — and later on these arguments were in fact made. But there was no mistaking the fact that the crux of their collective testimony was that a declaration of independence — nothing less — had occurred in Mecklenburg County on May 20, 1775, and thirteen credible eyewitnesses claimed they had witnessed it. The "combined testimony of all these individuals," wrote Governor Stokes, "prove the existence of the Mecklenburg Declaration, and all the circumstances connected with it, as fully and clearly as any fact can be shewn by human testimony."[36] "More satisfactory evidence, drawn from more respectable sources, Mr. Jefferson, if alive, could not, and would not require. It is not hazarding too much to say, that there is no one event of the Revolution which has been, or can be more fully or clearly authenticated."

The *Governor's Report* was intended as a direct rebuttal to Jefferson's theory that the whole story was a hoax. And in that it was successful. After all, if the story were a hoax, it meant all the eyewitnesses — even Governor Stokes himself — were lying. While some of the most passionate critics may have believed this, most reasonable and rational people did not. To dismiss all of them as liars was impossible.

In addition, the witnesses were all telling the same story. They all said a meeting had taken place, at the same place (the county courthouse) and the same time (May 19–20). They all claimed, again with some minor and immaterial variations, that the same individuals had been involved: Polk, McKnitt Alexander, Brevard, etc. They all claimed the same thing had occurred: a declaration of independence. They all agreed on what happened next: a rider, James Jack, had been appointed to ride to Philadelphia to deliver the resolutions to their congressional delegates. The overall story, its actors, actions and major themes, was the same in every case. If all thirteen witnesses were lying — and each telling the same lie — it led to a related, inescapable conclusion: There must have been a conspiracy among the witnesses.

To any reasonable observer this was stretching the bounds of reality. First of all, leaving aside the irreproachable character of the witnesses, many of them now lived in different states (Jack lived in rural Georgia, for example) and communicating among them would be difficult. Second, who stood to gain from a conspiracy? There was no money involved. Other than John Davidson, none of the witnesses claimed they *themselves* had been delegates, and therefore there was no personal glory or historical fame to be gained. Other than as a spectator, none of the other witnesses (Davidson and Jack excepted, and Jack was only as a messenger, not a leading actor) claimed to have taken any active role in the events of May 1775. There was no motive for the witnesses to lie. And they were all old men; they had nothing to gain and everything to lose by lying. And if they were lying, surely someone in the community would have pointed it out?

There was, of course, family and local fame and glory of a kind that could be claimed, and without question, this played a role in the desire of later generations to preserve the story. Mecklenburg County, of no national prominence or reputation, would arguably achieve considerable renown if the "first" declaration of independence had been announced there. But was this sufficient motive for them all to engage in a conspiracy? The conspiracy theory didn't make any sense. The evidence produced in the *Governor's Report*, whatever its failings, precluded the theory that the entire story was a hoax.

In the years that followed publication of the report, other local eyewitnesses came forward with testimony to corroborate the story. One such witness was Dr. Charles Caldwell. Caldwell did not claim to have taken part in the May convention but did have an interesting story that involved the Mecklenburg Declaration. As a young officer at the Salisbury military academy, Caldwell had escorted President George Washington into Mecklenburg County in the spring of 1791 when the president visited Charlotte as part of a tour of the Southern states.[37]

"As I approached the President," Caldwell wrote, "an awe came over me, such I had never before experienced ... as deeply mortifying, as it was unprecedented." He was, he said, "unmanned." His heart raced, his mind went cloudy, his vision blurred and, "though unsurpassed as a rider," he felt "unsteady in my seat, and almost ready to fall from my horse." He forgot his "oft-repeated" welcome address and became so terrified that he "became positively unable to articulate a word." "Quick to perceive my embarrassment, and equally inclined and prompt to relieve it, Washington returned my salute with marked courtesy, and, speaking kindly, paused for a moment, and then desired that we might proceed."

As Caldwell escorted Washington towards Charlotte, the president asked him, "Pray sir, have you lived long in this part of the country?" "Ever since my childhood, sir," Caldwell replied. "You are then, I presume, pretty well acquainted with it," Washington said. "Perfectly, sir," replied Caldwell. "I am familiar with every hill, and stream, and celebrated spot it contains." "During the late war, if my information be correct, the inhabitants were true to the cause of their country, and brave in its defense," the president continued.

"Your information *is* correct, sir," Caldwell replied. "They were, almost to a man, true-hearted Whigs and patriots, and as gallant soldiers as ever drew swords or pointed rifles in behalf of freedom. In Mecklenburg County, where we now are, and in Rowan, which lies before us, a Tory did not dare to show his face — if he were known to be a Tory. It was in a small town, through which we shall pass, that Lord Cornwallis lay encamped, when he swore that he had never before been in such a [damned] nest of Whigs — for that he could not, in the surrounding country, procure a chicken or a pig for his table, or a gallon of oats for his horse, but by purchasing it with the blood of his soldiers, who went in quest of it."

"Pray, what is the name of that town?" asked Washington. "Charlotte, sir, the county town of Mecklenburg, and the place where independence was declared about a year before its declaration by Congress; and *my father* was one of the Whigs who were concerned in the glorious transaction." Washington "was evidently pleased" with Caldwell's narrative and "at length inquired of me whether he might expect to meet at Charlotte any of the leading members of the convention which prepared and passed the Mecklenburg Declaration of Independence, and especially whether my father would be there."

Caldwell said, "I replied that my father was dead, and that Dr. Brevard, the author of the Declaration was also dead; that, of the members of the convention still living, I knew personally but two — Adam Alexander, who had been president of the body, and John McKnitt Alexander, his brother [*sic*], who had been its Secretary; that they were far advanced in life, and lived at some distance from Charlotte, but that I felt confident their ever-green spirit of patriotism, united to their strong desire to see him, would bring them there, should they be able to travel."[38]

Caldwell was not the only witness to leave behind a personal memoir corroborating the Mecklenburg Declaration story. A second was Robert Henry. Henry was a boy of ten in May 1775, but claimed throughout his life to have been present at the meeting in the courthouse and present at the debates that occurred. A friend of his, Colonel Davidson, later recalled of Henry:

> He was an old man when I first knew him, say fifty years ago [~1841]; he had then retired from the profession of the law which he had practiced many years.... He had been a fine lawyer, and remarkable in criminal cases. He could recite his experiences of cases in most minute detail.... He had a grand history in our struggle for independence; was at Charlotte when the [Mecklenburg] Declaration of Independence was made; but, being a boy at this time, he did not understand the character of the resolutions; but said he heard the crowd shout and declared themselves freed from the British government. He afterwards fought at the battle of Kings Mountain and was severely wounded in the hand and thigh, by a bayonet in the charge of Ferguson's men.[39]

According to a biography, Henry "had just passed his tenth birthday when the father [Thomas] went one day to Charlotte in Mecklenburg county, North Carolina, ten or twelve miles distant, carrying Robert along":

> It was May 19, 1775. When on that day they reached Charlotte the town was full of people. Robert had never seen so many before and the impression made upon his mind by the unusual concourse never left him while he lived. They went to the courthouse in that town and found assembled in the courtroom many men earnestly discussing some question of exciting nature. The deliberations and speeches continued through the day and into the night. In these deliberations Thomas Henry became an active participant. That night Robert Henry slept on his father's great coat behind the door just inside the courtroom where the assembly was in session.

Robert's curiosity was aroused. He asked what these men were doing and was told in reply that they were "declaring for liberty" and "passing resolutions of freedom" and that what they were doing "would bring on war."[40]

Caldwell's and Henry's memoirs were interesting, but more interesting were the unverifiable, but nevertheless persistent, local legends that existed in Mecklenburg County about the Mecklenburg Declaration. This local lore was chronicled by Dr. George Graham, of Charlotte, who was an avid defender of the story.[41]

Graham had an amateur's passion for the subject and built an entire case on the corroborating evidence. On June 21, 1895, Graham delivered the results of his research in a speech before the Scotch-Irish Society of America at a meeting in Lexington, Virginia. The monograph on which the speech was based was thereafter revised and enlarged and published as a pamphlet, running several editions. Graham's evidence was entirely circumstantial, but its novelty was compelling.

The first piece of evidence Graham cited was a poem called "The Mecklenburg Censor" believed to have been written by Adam Brevard, the brother of Ephraim Brevard.[42] In an extant copy, the poem's fifteenth through seventeenth lines read as follows:

> First to withdraw from British trust
> In Congress, they the very first,
> Their Independence did declare.[43]

Most important, the poem was dated March 18, 1777, less than two years following the date of the Mecklenburg Declaration. If accurate, the poem was contemporaneous evidence by a person with direct knowledge of the event. Graham argued that the poem was of "unquestionable authenticity": "Here Adam Brevard, who witnessed the proceedings of the delegates, testifies over his own signature, less than two years after the meeting [on May 20, 1775], that those delegates did 'withdraw from British trust' earlier than the Continental Congress in Philadelphia [on July 4, 1776]."[44]

A second piece of evidence Graham found was a valedictory address delivered by James Wallis, a pupil at Sugar Creek Academy, located three miles from Charlotte, on June 1, 1809.[45] Wallis' remarks read in part:

> On the 19th of May 1775, a day sacredly exulting to every Mecklenburg bosom, two delegates duly authorized from every militia company in this county met in Charlotte — After a cool and deliberate investigation of the causes and extent of our differences with G. Britain, and taking a view of the probable result; pledging their all in support of their rights and liberties; they solemnly entered into and published a full and determined declaration of independence, renouncing forever all allegiance, dependence on or connection with Great Britain; dissolved all judicial and military establishments emanating from the British crown; established others on principles correspondent with their declaration, which went into [immediate] operation; All which were transmitted to Congress by express, and probably expedited the general declaration of independence. May we ever act worthy of such predecessors.[46]

"Where did Wallis get his facts?" Graham asked. "In 1809 neither Martin's 'History' nor 'Anecdotes of the American Revolution' had been printed [both of which contained copies of the Mecklenburg Declaration], and the Davie copy was not published until 1819, ten years subsequent to that date. His only resource then was spectators and delegates to the convention, several of whom were then still living in the county."[47]

Graham also pointed to ancient real property deeds from the Mecklenburg County archives. Unseen for over a century, many of these deeds dated the "independence" of Mecklenburg County to 1775. Graham found eighteen deeds in all, each dated sometime between 1780 and 1792. For example, one read: "This indenture made in the year of our Lord, 1789, and in the 18th day of April and *being the 14th year of the Independence of the State of North Carolina* [emphasis added]." Another read: "This indenture made the nineteenth day of January, the year of our Lord one thousand seven hundred and eighty and *the fifth year of our independence* [emphasis added]."[48] In each case, the deed pinpointed the date of "independence" as 1775 — *not 1776*. "As these deeds were executed and filed thirty and forty years prior to the Mecklenburg controversy," Graham argued, "their testimony is incontrovertible."[49]

In addition, Graham cited certain oral traditions passed down from the Revolutionary period. The first was the nickname of the third son of Major John Davidson, the last surviving participant of the convention. Major Davidson had three sons, the youngest, Benjamin Wilson Davidson, was born on May 20, 1787. "[I]n honor of the Mecklenburg Declaration Benjamin was called by his father 'My Independence Boy,' and to distinguish his identity in a county abounding with 'Davidsons,' was known among the neighbors as 'Independence Ben.'" Another interesting piece of evidence, not cited by Graham, was a toast delivered on the Fourth of July 1808, part of which stated: "The Patriots of Mecklenburg: the first to declare Independence — May their sons be the last to acknowledge themselves slaves." If true, this showed the local legend alive long before it came to the attention of Adams and Jefferson or anyone called it into question.[50]

Then there was the tombstone of the Rev. Hunter in the Steele Creek Presbyterian Church cemetery, which reads:

> SACRED
> to the memory of the
> Rev. HUMPHREY HUNTER,
> who departed this life August 21st,
> 1827, in the 73d year of his age.
> He was a native of Ireland, and
> Emigrated to America at an early
> period of his life. He was one of those
> who early promoted the cause of
> freedom in Mecklenburg county,
> May 20th, 1775, and subsequently
> bore an active part in securing
> the Independence of his country.[51]

If the story of Mecklenburg Declaration were a hoax, surely a well-known and devout Presbyterian like the Rev. Hunter would never have allowed it to be placed on his tombstone?

The sheer durability of the tradition in Mecklenburg County could not easily be discounted. A short anecdote in the *Governor's Report* summed up the local legend. "An aged man near me," wrote John Simeson, "on being asked if he knew any thing of this affair, replied, '*Och, aye, Tam Polk declared Independence lang before any body else.*' This old man is 81."[52] Whatever the skeptics or critics said, it was quite clear that the people of Mecklenburg believed the story. They discussed it openly and were willing to be associated with it publicly. As late as 1833, an obituary in the *Miners' and Farmers' Journal* recorded:

Another Revolutionary Patriot gone. Died, in this county, on the 19th inst., at his residence ten miles west of Charlotte, Mr. Alexander Porter, in the 94th year of his age. He was actively engaged during our Revolutionary Struggle, and was among those who met in Charlotte on the 20th May, 1775, to proclaim independence. He was long a useful and intelligent citizen, a kind and indulgent parent, and died, we believe, in full exercise of the Christian faith.[53]

Similarly, an obituary for Dr. Cyrus Alexander, aged 83, in the *Charlotte Democrat* of 1881 began by explaining that the deceased "was a grandson of Abram Alexander, whose name is made immortal as the chairman of the famous Mecklenburg Declaration of Independence Convention 20th of May 1775."[54]

Descendants of the Polks and Alexanders valiantly kept the local legend alive. When Dr. J.G.M. Ramsey, McKnitt's maternal grandson, returned to Charlotte from his home in

The grave of the Rev. Humphrey Hunter, who left a detailed account of the meeting on May 20, 1775. One line on his grave reads in part, "He was one of those who early promoted the cause of freedom in Mecklenburg county, May 20th 1775" (photograph by the author).

Tennessee in May 1857 for the anniversary, he was treated as a returning hero. The *Western Democrat* for the morning of Tuesday, May 5, 1857, anticipated "a large attendance" of both citizens and strangers "from all parts of the country," and exhorted its readers that "such a reception should be extended to them as will sustain the reputation of the people of this section for hospitality and generous impulses."[55]

A decade following publication of the *Governor's Report*, the Mecklenburg Controversy appeared to have been largely settled. Jefferson's "hoax" theory had been comprehensively disproven by the eyewitness testimony, at least in the view of the people of Mecklenburg county. It was no surprise, then, that the citizens of North Carolina undertook to celebrate the Fourth of July 1839 with "unusual ardour," as the *North-Carolina Gazette* reported.[56] After all, they had contributed a great deal to it, and in their own view, more than most. "It is gratifying to perceive from the Toasts drank in this State," reported the *Raleigh Register* of July 20, 1839, "that but one sentiment pervades our citizens from the mountains to the sea-board, with regard to the authenticity of the Mecklenburg Declaration of Independence — and that sentiment is 'uncompromising hostility' to all attempts to tear this chaplet from the brows of our Revolutionary Patriots."[57]

In Charlotte on a warm summer's evening in July 1839, Colonel J.G. Bynum was called upon to make a toast. After some "spirited remarks," during which he "vindicated the authenticity of the Mecklenburg Declaration of Independence," the colonel raised his glass before him and offered a toast. "North Carolina," he said, as the room full of men rose to their feet with a clatter of silverware and sliding chairs, each raising their crystal wine glass. "Her citizens first declared their Independence at Mecklenburg, and her provincial Congress first recommended a National Declaration of Independence."[58] The room burst forth with a chorus of "hear hear" as glasses were raised.

But just as the Mecklenburg Declaration supporters were celebrating victory, the story was about to take a strange twist. At virtually the same time as Bynum's speech in Charlotte, a letter appeared in the *Southern Literary Messenger* doubting the validity of the Mecklenburg Declaration. In response, one agitated citizen wrote to the *Charlotte Journal* to complain. "The June number of the *Southern Literary Messenger*, contains an article regarding the Mecklenburg Declaration of Independence, the direct object of which is to deny the authenticity of that instrument as *published,* and, in its tendency is insidiously calculated to impeach the motives and injure the character of those venerable patriots who have given their solemn testimony in its favor."[59] "And upon what does this grave denial, this reckless disregard of well-authenticated facts depend?" asked the outraged citizen. "Upon an old newspaper, discovered by Peter Force, Esq., of Washington City, containing certain patriotic resolutions passed by a committee in Charlotte, May 31st, 1775." These "patriotic resolutions," the writer complained, had been wrongly "proclaimed to the world as the *original* Mecklenburg Declaration of Independence! Alas! To what extremities will prejudices carry mankind!"

What on earth was he talking about? What resolutions was he referring to?

16

"All former laws are now wholly suspended"
The Mecklenburg
Resolves Confuse Everyone

I have met with another set of resolutions adopted by Mecklenburg county in May, 1775.... They are expressed in somewhat different terms, and are besides of a much wider scope than those heretofore published; being in fact a general Declaration of the Independence of all the Colonies.

> — Peter Force, announcing the discovery of the
> Mecklenburg (or May 31) Resolves,
> *Daily National Intelligencer*, December 18, 1838

By 1835, a great deal of evidence had been discovered proving — at least in the eyes of its supporters — that there had been a Mecklenburg Declaration of Independence. First there were the "rough notes" of John McKnitt Alexander. Then there was the direct testimony of thirteen witnesses, two of whom were direct participants in the story (John Davidson and James Jack). Corroborating British accounts describing the "horrid and treasonable" resolves of a committee in Mecklenburg had also been found. All in all, a strong body of evidence had been put on the historical record in support of the story. But the evidence remained circumstantial. No one could point to a single piece of paper containing the text of the Mecklenburg Declaration that did not suffer from some evidentiary problem. There was no smoking gun.

And legitimate questions remained. Why was there no mention of the Mecklenburg Declaration in the papers of Congressmen Caswell, Hooper or Hughes? Why did the records of the Continental Congress not mention Captain Jack? Why did the language in the Mecklenburg Declaration strongly resemble Jefferson's Declaration of Independence? Was that a coincidence or something else?

Despite these open questions, to an unbiased observer the preponderance of evidence was clearly in favor of the story. There was no gainsaying the thirteen eyewitnesses, and even British governor Josiah Martin was on record denouncing the "horrid and treasonable" resolves of Mecklenburg County. Questions there were, but the overall evidence was compelling. In fact, if no additional evidence had come to light after the *Governor's Report* of 1831, it seems likely that the tide of popular opinion would have grown in favor of the story and the remaining doubts would have gradually faded away. There was, after all, no counterargument to dispute the eyewitness testimony. But all that would change dramatically and unpredictably in 1838 when a historian named Peter Force made an unexpected discovery.

Peter Force was born near Passaic Falls, New Jersey, on November 26, 1790. As a youth, he was apprenticed as a printer in New York City, and at the age of twenty-two he enlisted in the army in the War of 1812. Following his military service, from 1823 to 1831 he founded and published the *National Journal*, first a semiweekly and then daily newspaper of national events. Force would later enter politics, serving on the Washington, D.C., city council, and twice as mayor (1836–1840).[1] But his real talent and passion lay in researching, collecting and editing historical memorabilia, such as old papers and other curiosities, which he neatly organized, categorized, and published. His most famous work, the *American Archives*, was published from 1837 to 1853 and consisted of nine comprehensive folio volumes of early historical material from 1774, 1775 and 1776.[2]

Force purchased yellowing papers from the families of Revolutionary War veterans and combed through library collections. He acquired old letters, journals, government memos, proclamations and minutes. During one of these quiet hours handling old papers, Force made a discovery that would add to his fame and would propel the Mecklenburg Controversy in an entirely new direction. In a copy of the *Massachusetts Spy or American Oracle of Liberty*

Charlotte-Town, Mecklenburg County, May 31, 1775.
This day the Committee of this county met, and passed the following Resolves:

WHEREAS by an Address presented to his Majesty by both Houses of Parliament, in February last, the American colonies are declared to be in a state of actual rebellion, we conceive, that all laws and commissions confirmed by, or derived from the authority of the King or Parliament, are annulled and vacated, and the former civil constitution of these colonies, for the present, wholly suspended. To provide, in some degree, for the exigencies of this county, in the present alarming period, we deem it proper and necessary to pass the following Resolves, viz.

I. That all commissions, civil and military, heretofore granted by the Crown, to be exercised in these colonies, are null and void, and the constitution of each particular colony wholly suspended.

II. That the Provincial Congress of each province, under the direction of the great Continental Congress, is invested with all legislative and executive powers

Peter Force's discovery of the Mecklenburg Resolves in the **South Carolina Gazette and Country Journal** of June 13, 1775, turned the debate on its head. Supporters saw them as confirmation of the story, while opponents believed this must be the "true" version of the Mecklenburg Declaration (Charleston Library Society, Charleston, SC).

XVII. That any perfon refufing to yield obedience to the above Refolves, fhall be confidered equally criminal, and liable to the fame punifhment, as the offenders above laft mentioned.

XVIII. That thefe Refolves be in full force and virtue, until inftructions from the Provincial Congrefs, regulating the jurifprudence of the province, fhall provide otherwife, or the legiflative body of Great-Britain, refign its unjuft and arbitrary pretentions with refpect to America.

XIX. That the eight militia companies in the county, provide themfelves with proper arms and accoutrements, and hold themfelves in readinefs to execute the commands and directions of the General Congrefs of this province and this Committee.

XX. That the Committee appoint Colonel Thomas Polk, and Doctor Jofeph Kenedy, to purchafe 300 lb. of powder, 600 lb. of lead, 1000 flints, for the ufe of the militia of this county, and depofit the fame in fuch place as the Committee may hereafter direct.   *Signed by order of the Committee,*
            EPH. BREVARD, Clerk of the Committee.

The final paragraph of the Mecklenburg Resolves appointing Thomas Polk and Joseph Kennedy to procure "300 lb. of powder, 600 lb. of lead, and 1,000 flint." None of the witnesses mentions Kennedy even in passing, leading some to conclude there must have been separate meetings on May 20 and May 31 (Charleston Library Society, Charleston, South Carolina).

dated July 12, 1775, Force saw something unusual. They were written resolutions (or "resolves" as they were called) of a committee in "Charlotte-Town, Mecklenburg County."[3]

The preamble of the resolves read as follows:

> Whereas by an Address presented to His Majesty by both Houses of Parliament, in February last, the American colonies are declared to be in a state of actual rebellion, we conceive, that all laws and commissions confirmed by, or derived from the authority of the King or Parliament, are annulled and vacated, and the former civil constitution of these colonies, for the present, wholly suspended. To provide, in some degree, for the exigencies of this county, in the present alarming period, we deem it proper and necessary to pass the following Resolves.[4]

Four resolutions followed. The first announced that "all commissions, civil and military, heretofore granted by the Crown" were "null and void" and "the constitution of each particular colony wholly suspended." The second delegated, or "invested," "all legislative and executive powers" to the "Provincial Congress of each Province," and declared "no other legislative or executive does or can exist, at this time, in any of these colonies." Put differently, the resolves vacated the power of Parliament throughout the American colonies. "As all former laws are now wholly suspended in this province," continued the resolves, "and the [Continental] Congress have not yet provided others, we judge it necessary, for the better preservation of good order, to form certain rules and regulations for the internal government of this county, until laws shall be provided for us by the Congress."[5]

The chain of logic set forth in the preamble clause and the first three resolutions was direct, legalistic and sequential. The British Parliament had declared the colonies in "actual rebellion" in February 1775. That being the case, all "laws and commissions confirmed by or derived from the authority of the King or Parliament" were, by definition, "annulled and vacated." Because the Second Continental Congress, then meeting in Philadelphia, had not yet provided new laws to fill this void, the committee in Mecklenburg had decided to do it themselves.

The fourth resolution called upon the "inhabitants of this county" to meet and organize themselves into nine companies, eight for the county of Mecklenburg and one for the town of Charlotte. The militia were instructed to "choose a Colonel, and other military officers" to lead them. These officers, democratically chosen and elected, were to "exercise their several powers by virtue of this choice, and independent of the Crown of Great Britain, and former Constitution of this Province."[6] The resolutions were unsigned and had, as Force later wrote, "no accompanying editorial remarks."[7]

Curiously, they were dated May 31, 1775 — eleven days after the eyewitnesses claimed that the Mecklenburg Declaration had been adopted in Charlotte. When Force found them, moldering in a sixty-three-year-old newspaper, the resolutions had no title, no context, and no explanation. What they were, who wrote them, and what they meant were all complete mysteries. Whatever they were, they were exciting and they had the potential to rewrite history, especially if they could be seen as corroborating the story of the Mecklenburg Declaration of Independence. As an antiquarian, Force immediately understood the importance of what he had found.

Force took his discovery public by publishing his find in the *Daily National Intelligencer* of December 18, 1838.[8] "The Resolutions of Mecklenburg county, North Carolina, of May 20, 1775, dissolving all political connexion between the 'citizens' of that county and Great Britain" Force wrote, "have excited more attention the last eight years than any other occurrence of the Revolution. The authenticity of these resolutions has been questioned, yet no others have been produced; and it could not be denied that they, or others of a like character, were passed...."[9]

> In the course of my examinations into the popular proceedings of that period of our history, I have met with another set of resolutions adopted by Mecklenburg county in May, 1775, which answer very well to the description given by Governor Martin. They are expressed in somewhat different terms, and are besides of a much wider scope than those heretofore published; being in fact a general Declaration of the Independence of all the Colonies.[10]

A second reprinting of the four resolves was found in the *New York Journal, or the General Advisor* of June 29, 1775.[11] This proved that the Mecklenburg Resolves Force had discovered had circulated more widely than originally believed. Force's discovery electrified not only the historical community but also the public at large. "Never was a time when the interest of the Country was so awakened to historical and antiquarian researches," the historian George Bancroft wrote breathlessly to Force in March 1842.[12]

Spurred on by Force's discovery, other historians searched for evidence of these so-called Mecklenburg Resolves. In 1847, Dr. Joseph Johnson found an extended version of the resolutions in the Charleston Library Society, in an aged copy of the *South-Carolina Gazette and Country Journal* dated June 13, 1775.[13] (These were subsequently reprinted in the *Raleigh Register* of February 14, 1847.[14]) A year later, in the summer of 1848,

George Bancroft found another version in the British State Paper Office in London.[15] For over sixty years no written records corroborating the rebellion in Mecklenburg County had been located. Suddenly, they were popping up all over the place. The version that Dr. Johnson found in Charleston was longer — by five times — than the four resolutions Force had discovered; twenty resolutions in all. Not only were resolutions popping up everywhere, but they were growing in length. The original four resolutions Force had discovered, and which Dr. Johnson and others later found in an expanded version, would become known as the "Mecklenburg Resolves," or sometimes the "May 31st Resolves," to differentiate them from the Mecklenburg Declaration.[16]

What were they? And more important, did they corroborate the story that had been printed in the *Raleigh Register*? After all, they were clearly different in tone, date and character from the story that McKnitt had told the world. The Mecklenburg Resolves were extremely detailed, technical and dry. After the first resolutions, they largely dealt with administrative issues and legal process. For example, Clauses VI–XV dealt with setting the court calendar, the election of constables and the issuance of warrants. Clause XVI provided that anyone who accepted a "commission from the Crown ... shall be deemed an enemy to his country" and subject to apprehension.[17] The next clause provided that "any person refusing to yield obedience to the above Resolves, shall be considered equally criminal, and liable to the same punishment." Clauses XVIII and XIX provided as follows:

> XVIII. That these Resolves be in full force and virtue, until instructions from the Provincial Congress, regulating the jurisprudence of the province, shall provide otherwise, or the legislative body of Great-Britain, resign its unjust and arbitrary pretensions with respect to America.

> XIX. That the eight militia companies in the county, provide themselves with proper arms and accoutrements, and hold themselves in readiness to execute the commands and directions of the General Congress of this province, and this Committee.

The twentieth and final clause instructed "Colonel *Thomas Polk*, and Doctor *Joseph Kenedy*, to purchase 300 lb. of powder, 600 lb. of lead, 1000 flints, for the use of the militia of this county, and deposit the same in such place as the Committee may hereafter direct" [emphasis in the original]. The resolves were signed by Ephraim Brevard, clerk of the committee.

It was obvious, and conceded by all, that the Mecklenburg Resolves were not the same as the Mecklenburg Declaration. First, the Mecklenburg Resolves seemed more "governmental" in their nature, as one observer pointed out.[18] Unlike the five resolutions of the Mecklenburg Declaration, which were short, memorable and punchy, the twenty clauses of the Mecklenburg Resolves were dry and bureaucratic. They contained none of the soaring language of the Mecklenburg Declaration. These new resolves read like a company charter, not a rallying cry for independence. As Force put it, the two documents "are expressed in somewhat different terms."[19]

Second, the dates were different. The Mecklenburg Resolves were dated May 31, when by all accounts the Mecklenburg Declaration had occurred on May 20, eleven days earlier. Finally, the Mecklenburg Resolves were signed by Ephraim Brevard. The vast majority of the witnesses had said John McKnitt Alexander had acted as secretary of the convention. In addition, the Mecklenburg Resolves mention an individual named Joseph Kennedy. Not a single witness mentions Kennedy in the *Governor's Report*, even in passing. His name first arises in the context of the Mecklenburg Resolves. How to account for this?

The explanation, argued supporters of the Mecklenburg Declaration, was that the

Mecklenburg Resolves were corroborating evidence of the revolutionary actions of the committee of safety following the Mecklenburg Declaration of Independence. This explained the two dates. The delegates had met on May 19–20 and declared independence. After that, a committee of safety had drafted the Mecklenburg Resolves to provide for governance of the county. The two papers — the Mecklenburg Declaration and the Mecklenburg Resolves — were not contradictory. They were complementary.

According to this theory, this explained why the two documents were different in form and content, as well as why Abraham Alexander was remembered as the chairman of the convention, while Ephraim Brevard's name appeared as a clerk on the Mecklenburg Resolves. It also explains why Joseph Kennedy is not remembered by any of the witnesses, even though his name features prominently in the Mecklenburg Resolves. Kennedy was present at a different, later meeting.

Some evidence to this effect was contained in the Mecklenburg Declaration itself. In the *Raleigh Register* account, for example, the final resolution noted that, "a *number of bye laws were also added*, merely to protect the association from confusion, and to regulate their general conduct as citizens [emphasis added]." McKnitt's "rough notes" also state that following adoption of the Mecklenburg Declaration, "many other laws and ordinances were then ma[de]." The "rough notes" also note that Captain Jack was sent "express to Congress (then in Philadelphia) with a copy of all S^d. resolutions and laws &c.," implying that more than one document had been drafted in May 1775 in Charlotte.

Similarly, the testimony of John Simeson, who was a young militiaman in May 1775, read, "I was under arms near the head of the line, near Col. Polk, and heard him distinctly read *a long string of Grievances, the [Mecklenburg] Declaration and Military Order above* [emphasis added]. I likewise heard Col. Polk have two warm disputes with two men of the county, who said the measures were rash and unnecessary. He was applauded and they silenced."[20] While it's not clear what documents Polk read, Simeson's testimony implied there was more than one document. Could the Mecklenburg Resolves be the "Military Order" Simeson had heard?

By this logic, the Mecklenburg Resolves were excellent corroborating evidence of the meetings that followed independence. Further support for this argument was provided by the fact that the Mecklenburg Resolves read like a draft constitution for the county. If the county had declared itself "free and independent" from Great Britain on May 20, it was appropriate for the committee of safety to provide for temporary government. Logically, a constitution follows a declaration of independence, not the other way around.

While discovery of the Mecklenburg Resolves had a galvanizing effect on supporters of the Mecklenburg Declaration, paradoxically it had the same effect on the skeptics. Prior to discovery of the Mecklenburg Resolves the tide of events was with the Mecklenburg supporters. Given the eyewitness evidence, doubters were forced into one of two unsatisfactory and largely unconvincing positions. The first theory, propounded by Jefferson, was that the story was simply a hoax. This theory could not and did not survive the eyewitness evidence that had emerged. The second explanation was that the witnesses were all wrong. To this skeptics could point to the discrepancies in the testimony, as well as the fact that by 1830 most of the witnesses were very old.

Supporters retorted that minor irregularities in the facts did not disprove the entire story. After all, did it really matter if Brevard, rather than McKnitt, was secretary of the convention? Or if certain individuals — such as Ezekiel Polk, William Wilson or Duncan Ochiltree — were or were not present? Or whether twenty-six delegates attended or twenty-eight or thirty-two? To the advocates, these details were ancillary to the overall story and the fact that some recollections were at odds did not discount the accuracy of the episode.

But for some people, the facts were secondary. The story of the Mecklenburg Declaration, with Polk heroically declaring the county "free and independent" and Captain Jack riding to Philadelphia, was simply too good to be true. No proof would ever win over these doubters. As Jefferson's biographer Tucker put it in 1837, "the idea of *independence* being seriously attempted, even by a single state, much less a single county in a single state, could not have been entertained by any rational being."[21] The story simply *couldn't* be true.

The skeptics had a serious problem, however: How to account for the testimony of thirteen sworn witnesses and McKnitt's "rough notes"? Facts, as Churchill said, are stubborn things. And like it or not, the supporters of the Mecklenburg Declaration had certain facts in their favor, facts that could not be easily dismissed, facts that had to be explained. Prior to discovery of the Mecklenburg Resolves, critics had no theory that could incorporate the facts and dismiss the story as untrue. One either believed the story as told by the witnesses or one did not. All of that changed with the discovery of the Mecklenburg Resolves. To the skeptics, discovery of the Mecklenburg Resolves would be a blow from which the cause of the Mecklenburg Declaration has yet to recover.

Discovery of the Mecklenburg Resolves made possible a third conclusion, other than that the story was a hoax or the witnesses were all wrong: the truth lay somewhere in the middle. In other words, the Mecklenburg Controversy was a case of mistaken identity.

This third theory went as follows. The witnesses were not lying. There was no hoax and no conspiracy. But the recollections of the witnesses were flawed, the product of "fallible human recollection," as a later critic put it.[22] The events and resolutions the witnesses recalled, so the theory went, was the passage of the Mecklenburg Resolves. There had never been a Mecklenburg Declaration of Independence. It was a figment of the imagination. "The facts shown by the resolutions of May 31, 1775, and other authentic records preclude the possibility of any such action having been taken on May 20, 1775," in this view.[23] Others agreed. Professor George Tucker, of the University of Virginia, who wrote a two-volume *Life of Thomas Jefferson*, wrote to Force on March 12, 1839, in excitement that Force's discovery "must be the genuine one."[24] Historian George Bancroft felt the same, writing to Force on March 15, 1842, that he believed the resolutions Force had found "to be the true ones."[25]

There was some support for this argument. First, all of the witnesses were admittedly old when their testimony was given: James Jack was 88; George Graham was nearly 62; William Hutchinson 68; and John Davidson, the only surviving delegate, 95. The events they were recollecting had occurred over fifty years earlier. For example, Graham admitted that his testimony was "as well as I can recollect after a lapse of fifty-five years."[26] Another witness, Simeson, wrote that in his "precarious, feeble old age" he was "too blind to write fair, and too old to write much sense."[27] In the same letter to William Polk, Simeson admitted that Polk himself "cannot state much from recollection" despite having been there himself when the Mecklenburg Declaration was proclaimed. Given their age and the passage of years, how accurate could their testimony really be?

Skeptics pointed out that the evidence was equally consistent with the Mecklenburg

Resolves being the only "true" document produced. Governor Martin had written, "The Resolves of the Committee of Mecklenburgh, which your Lordship will find in the enclosed Newspaper, surpass all the horrid and treasonable publications that the inflammatory spirits of this Continent have yet produced." Even so, this could equally describe the Mecklenburg *Resolves*, rather than the Mecklenburg *Declaration*. Similarly, in a letter dated June 18, 1775, from Richard Cogdell to North Carolina congressman Richard Caswell, Cogdell wrote, "[Y]ou'l Observe the Mecklenburg resolves, exceed all other Committees, or the Congress itself."[28] Which "resolves" was Cogdell referring to? It wasn't clear.

The mistaken identity theory also permitted the skeptics to dismiss the significance of the Mecklenburg Resolves as an issue of no historical importance. After all, unlike the Mecklenburg Declaration, the Mecklenburg Resolves never used the phrase "free and independent." Therefore, they argued, the Mecklenburg Resolves were only limited or "qualified" in their scope, and thus were nothing of significance — and certainly far short of a "declaration of independence." And for that matter, there were a number of other documents in the colonies that predated May 20, 1775, that could be argued were equally rebellious as the Mecklenburg Resolves.

"Bold as these resolutions were," sniffed one later doubter, "they did not declare the 'entire dissolution of the Laws Government and Constitution of this country' as Governor Martin in his haste supposed but merely provided for 'the better preservation of good order' in the county during the suspension of the laws under the declaration of the British Parliament and the British civil officer."[29] Jefferson's biographer, a skeptic, also pooh-poohed the significance of the resolves noting, "Mecklenburg being then a frontier county of the state, and bordering on the mountainous region, the act was far less bold and hazardous than if it had taken place in the middle or lower part of the state."[30] By this argument, what had transpired in Mecklenburg was far less than supporters of the Mecklenburg Declaration had claimed.

Force, who had found the resolves, believed in the mistaken identity theory. He viewed the Mecklenburg Resolves as the "true" Mecklenburg resolutions, although in a sense, he didn't understand what the fuss was all about. "The genuineness of the document commonly known as the Mecklenburg Declaration is a point upon which the people of North Carolina are (needlessly, we think) extremely sensitive." After this reasonable and sensitive beginning, Force then expressed the presumptuous and dismissive logic that drove North Carolinians blind with rage: "Needlessly — because the means by which its spuriousness is established prove, beyond possibility of doubt, that a series of resolutions indicative of great patriotism and energy was adopted by the citizens of Mecklenburg County in the Spring of 1775."[31]

Other than muddying the historical waters, discovery and publication of the Mecklenburg Resolves changed no one's position. The believers argued that the Mecklenburg Resolves were bylaws drawn up by the committee, an action which was consistent with the entire story. Skeptics, on the other hand, had a new line of attack. Namely, that the Mecklenburg Resolves were the only "true" document that had been adopted in Charlotte, and one that fell short of the claims of its supporters.

But there was one major problem with the mistaken identity theory. McKnitt had claimed many times that he had made copies of the Mecklenburg Declaration from the original records. And these copies read nothing like the text of the Mecklenburg Resolves. How to explain the discrepancy? The explanation, argued the critics, was that McKnitt had not copied the text of the Mecklenburg Declaration from original records, but instead he must have written it from memory. Perhaps he even cribbed from Jefferson's work, or perhaps they got confused in McKnitt's aged mind. This would explain the similarities between the Mecklenburg Declaration and Jefferson's draft of 1776. If this could be proven, it might be the final nail in the coffin of the story of the Mecklenburg Declaration of Independence. Of course, there was no evidence to this effect. But that was not going to stop an obscure professor from the University of North Carolina named Dr. Charles Phillips.

17

Tampering with the Evidence
Charles Phillips and the Davie Copy

It may be worthy of notice here, to observe that the foregoing statement, tho fundamentally correct; yet may not literally correspond with the original records of the transactions of said ~~delegation &~~ court of Enquiry; as all those records and papers were burnt (with the house) on April 6, 1800.
— John McKnitt Alexander, Davie Copy, 1800

Following Peter Force's discovery in 1838 of the Mecklenburg Resolves in an old newspaper, the search for other corroborating evidence of the Mecklenburg Declaration intensified. Many hoped that an original copy could be found somewhere. But where? The final sentence of the *Raleigh Register* article dropped two tantalizing clues.

The first clue was the statement that "a copy of the proceedings was sent to Hugh Williamson, in New York, then writing a History of North Carolina." The second clue was that "a copy was sent to Gen. W.R. Davie." If either of these copies could be found they would provide proof positive of the existence of the declaration. "The papers of Dr. Hugh Williamson ought to be searched for the copy sent to him, and the copy sent to General W.R. Davie," President Adams wrote in haste to William Bentley on August 21, 1819.[1] Adams' suggestion was not immediately followed up on, however, and when it was it was too late.

Williamson died on May 22, 1819, in New York City. His papers were stored in a warehouse in Pearl Street. In December 1835, what became known as the "Great Fire" of New York destroyed large sections of the city, including the warehouse in which the Williamson papers were kept. Whatever papers regarding the Mecklenburg Declaration Williamson may have had were irretrievably lost.[2] The search of the papers of William R. Davie was more productive. McKnitt and Davie were friends and worked together as militia officers during the Revolution. Dr. Joseph Alexander, McKnitt's son, made inquiries with General Davie's son, William. The copy McKnitt claimed he had sent Davie was found amidst the deceased General's old papers.

The clerk of the Superior Court of Mecklenburg County, Samuel Henderson, retrieved the copy from the Davie family and Dr. Alexander asked him to sign an affidavit describing the circumstances of finding the paper:

I, Samuel Henderson, do hereby certify, that the paper annexed was obtained by me from Maj. William Davie in its present situation, soon after the death of his father, Gen. William R. Davie, and given to Doct. Joseph M'Knitt by me. In searching for some particular paper, I came across this, and, knowing the hand writing of John M'Knitt Alexander, took it up, and examined it. Maj. Davie said to me (when asked how it became torn) his sisters had torn it, not knowing what it was.[3]

The paper came to be called the "Davie Copy" of the Mecklenburg Declaration. In 1830, the year it was found, it was in pretty rough shape. In fact, all that remained were a few pages; in each case, the bottom half of a torn sheet, plus a final third (or perhaps fourth) page, remained fully intact. Although torn, these remaining sections of the Davie Copy were entirely legible, written in the clear and flowing hand of McKnitt, and twice attested to and signed by him.

The first section of the Davie Copy begins thus: "and to them unrepresented [TORN] might impose; or support their brethren who were doomed to sustain the first shock of that power, which if successful thereon; would overwhelm all in the common calamity."[4] The first full sentence, then begins: "Conformable to these principles Col.° ~~Adam Alexander~~ Thos Polk through Solicitations issued an order to each Captains Militia Company in the County of Mecklenburg (then comprising the present County of Cabarrus) directing each Militia company to elect two persons & delegate to them ample powers to divise ways & means to aid and assist their suffering brethren in Boston."

The second torn half page begins with the fourth resolution of the Mecklenburg Declaration as shown in the *Raleigh Register* version of 1819. Two things are of interest in the fragmentary first two pages. In the first page the name Adam Alexander is deleted and the name Thomas Polk inserted as the man responsible for summoning the meeting. The exact same deletion and correction occurs in the "copy in an unknown Hand." The strike-through of Alexander's name was probably made later by someone other than McKnitt, but it's not clear by whom or when.

The text on the second page is exactly as in the "copy in an unknown hand" and the *Raleigh Register* article. The final page of the Davie Copy has two strikeouts, more minor corrections, and is written in a less free-flowing manner than at the beginning. There are also more interrupting dashes between thoughts. Clearly, at this point McKnitt was no longer copying from an existing record but freely narrating on his own. Except for the concluding narrative paragraphs, the Davie Copy is a verbatim copy of the "copy in an unknown hand." Either the Davie Copy was copied from the "copy in an unknown hand" or both were taken from another missing record. There is no other explanation. They are identical.[5]

But we do not have to infer this. McKnitt wrote this in clear, unambiguous language, a declaration no one could miss. At the end of McKnitt's narrative summary (which concludes with Captain Jack's return from the Second Continental Congress) McKnitt began a new paragraph. But before he did, he wrote the following sentence: "*Thus far from the Journals & records of Sd. Committee.*"

This sentence was underlined, possibly by McKnitt himself, possibly by his son. Either way, it was intended to illustrate its importance and added as a breakpoint. The meaning of the sentence is clear: the narrative summary, including presumably the five resolutions comprising the Mecklenburg Declaration — in other words, everything prior *to this point* ("thus far")—had been copied by McKnitt from the surviving "journals and records" of the convention. It is copied from original source material, but exactly what source material we do not know. We do know, because he said so, that it came from the journals and records. We just do not have those journals and records and so do not know what else was in them.

To drive this point home, McKnitt's son drew the symbol of a hand, pointing with one finger at the line and written below it: "here the copy of the record ends," meaning the narrative that followed was *not* copied verbatim from the surviving records. To underscore the point even further, lest anyone have any doubt, in the left margin Dr. Alexander wrote, "this is from recollection & as to Dunn & Booth is incorrect as to time." Dr. Alexander then signed his name, as he customarily did to differentiate himself from his father's signature, as "J. McKnitt."

Following McKnitt's conclusory line, "*Thus far from the Journals & records of Sd. Committee*," he began a narrative of actions regarding the committee of safety and court of enquiry in Mecklenburg County during the Revolution. Finally, in the last paragraph of the Davie Copy, McKnitt made a refreshing and candid admission before certifying and attesting his name:

> It may be worthy of notice here, to observe that the foregoing statement, tho fundamentally correct; yet may not literally correspond with the original records of the transactions of said ~~delegation &~~ court of Enquiry; as all those records and papers were burnt (with the house) on April 6, 1800.[6]

The words "delegation &" were clearly and deliberately crossed out by McKnitt presumably at the time of writing. The deletion is in the same color pen and consistent with some of his other corrections. In other words, he wrote the wrong words and then deleted them to insert the correct ones. In the other surviving pages of the Davie Copy, the only other correction of this sort is the deletion of "Adam Alexander" and his replacement with "Thomas Polk" noted above. The same correction is made in the "copy in an unknown hand," indicating that someone (possibly McKnitt, but possibly someone unknown) corrected both copies contemporaneously, perhaps upon someone's recommendation. Adam Alexander was McKnitt's cousin and had been the colonel commanding the Mecklenburg Militia, so putting in his cousin as issuing the order was a natural mistake. The error may have been pointed out to him by some third party, or on reflection he may have realized his mistake.

Why would McKnitt delete the words "delegation &"? What did it mean? There was no clear explanation, but a similar deletion on the page sheds light on his intention. Earlier, McKnitt deleted the word "arrested" and replaced it with the word "charged" in the following passage:

> From this S[d]. delegation, originated the Court of Enquiry, who constituted & held their first court soon after Lord Cornwallis removed from Charlotte (that Hornet's nest, as he called it) in 1780. This Court was held in Charlotte, at Col. James Harris [and] at Col. Martin Fifers, alternately, one week at each place. It was a Civil Court, founded on military process—before this judicature all suspicious persons were made to appear—formally tried and banished—or continued under guard—its jurisdiction was as unlimited as Toryism—and its Decrees as final as the confidence and patriotism of the County. Several were ~~arrested~~ *charged* and brought before them from Lincoln, Rowan and Anson Counties. Messrs. Booth and Dunn were brought from Salisbury—tried—and sent off under guard—and never returned [emphasis added]."[7]

Why the change? One explanation may lie in the context of when McKnitt wrote the Davie Copy. The Revolutionary War had ended little more than a decade before. Particularly in the southern colonies it had been a civil war. Neighbors had fought, even murdered, one another; friendships were broken, many forever. Many individuals, some probably innocent, had been brought before military tribunals, imprisoned or sent away and their property confiscated.

Setting forth the historical record, McKnitt wanted to be as precise as possible. To record, for all time, that an individual had been "arrested" by the council of safety was to forever brand that individual with a charge of treason. A "charge," on the other hand, was a suspicion, a belief that had to be proven in court. Charges during the war were common, and many were dismissed upon further review. McKnitt was a scrupulous man, and in setting out the facts for posterity, he moderated his language so as not to confuse a mere allegation or "charge" with an actual "arrest" or conviction.

As he wrote the first section of the Davie Copy, McKnitt had before him some existing records. This is clear from the fact that the paper is a copy of something, not free writing. However, when McKnitt wrote the second section he did not have in front of him the original records of the court of enquiry. These, he stated unambiguously, had been burnt in April 1800. McKnitt wanted to make this distinction clear, so he chose his words carefully. By the words "~~delegation &~~ court of Enquiry" he was making clear that he did *not* have in his possession the papers of the court of enquiry. He was writing these verdicts from recollection. It was a useful and scrupulous admission.

But there was a problem. After the first part, McKnitt clearly writes that he was copying from the actual surviving "journals and records" of the convention. But these had been lost in the fire of 1800, so what "journals and records" was he referring to? Possibly he simply meant the "copy in an unknown hand," or possibly some other records now lost. Or possibly he copied from the "journals and records" before the fire and then wrote the second part after the fire. The fire destroyed only one home at Alexandriana, so other papers (such as the "copy in an unknown hand") kept in another part of the property did survive. But the mystery of what "journals and records" McKnitt had in front of him is unresolved.

No good deed goes unpunished. While discovery of the Davie Copy should have been a definitive, nearly clinching, piece of evidence in the search for proof of the Mecklenburg Declaration, it turned out to be its undoing.

Charles Phillips, mathematics professor and polemicist extraordinaire who passionately detested the story of the Mecklenburg Declaration of Independence. His article "May, 1775" became the definitive "anti" account (courtesy North Carolina Collection, University of North Carolina at Chapel Hill Library).

The deletion of the words "delegation &," in fact the entire paragraph, threw a shadow of doubt over the accuracy of his testimony. Part of this was McKnitt's own fault. After all, it could be argued, why had he written the words *delegation &* in the first place, and why was it necessary to delete them? Could he have had other motives that were not so pure? His deletions created ambiguity, of that there is no question. In any event, his final paragraph in the Davie Copy, with or without the deletions, would become a bludgeon to beat the entire history of the Mecklenburg Declaration of Independence nearly to death.

The 1831 state report published Henderson's affidavit, in which he described how he obtained the Davie Copy, but it didn't publish the text of the Davie Copy itself. The reason is likely because the Davie Copy only reiterated the same text that had been published in the *Raleigh Register*, so why bother? Perhaps it was thought unnecessary. Perhaps its incomplete and fragmentary character made it look suspect. Nor was a copy otherwise made available to the public. The Davie Copy remained hidden from public view in the private papers of Dr. Alexander for many years, and then after his death was held in the private collection of the chancellor of the University of North Carolina, Dr. David Swain. Other than perhaps the chancellor himself, for decades no one saw the Davie Copy or knew exactly what it said. No one, that is, but a hitherto obscure professor of mathematics named Dr. Charles Phillips. In 1853, Phillips was teaching mathematics and engineering at the University of North Carolina at Chapel Hill.

Phillips had been raised in an academic family and, as a boy, he was called "Old Fatty," on account of his "tendency to corpulency."[8] His upbringing seems to have been rigorous, stern and joyless. Phillips' father was known as "John Bull" or "Old Johnnie" due to his affection for the British Empire. As Phillips put it, his father had "remained an Englishman all his days and bequeathed many characteristics of his nationality to his children."[9] As a result, Phillips was an Anglophile all his life. He used English spellings for words ("parlours" and "vapours") instead of the American equivalents and cultivated an air of culture and superiority.

As a teacher, he was rigid and doctrinaire. "He was a man of very strong convictions and inflexible will," said one writer, "and when he began a crusade he stayed with it."[10] His sister described him as "not a little inclined to be overbearing" and lacking "deference, amiability, insight."[11] His brother-in-law, the president of the University of North Carolina, recalled that "[i]n social conversation in those days [the 1850s] he often appeared to be impatient of contradiction, or even of difference of opinion from him on the part of his intimates."[12] If this was how his friends and relatives described him, we can only imagine what his enemies thought of him.

Perhaps it was his sentimental attachment to Great Britain. Perhaps, as a transplanted Yankee living in the rural South, he felt himself an outsider. Or perhaps it was his mathematical training and strict Presbyterian upbringing. Whatever the clinical diagnosis, Phillips developed a particular obsession: he detested the story of the Mecklenburg Declaration of Independence. "The idea of a movement in 1775 for complete and final independence," as one writer put it, "was distasteful to him."[13] As the same observer concluded, Phillips was "the most persistent disbeliever in the Mecklenburg Declaration."[14]

His aversion to the story was obvious in his private writings. He described himself as an "unbeliever in the prevalent myth" and called the story a "Charlotte falsehood."[15] "No 'true men'" could have wanted to secede from English governance in 1775, he wrote. "Presbyterians raised on the Shorter Catechism in the backwoods of N.C. were not apt to blow off steam about *the inherent and inalienable rights of man*. Jefferson brought that stuff from Paris."[16] Independence in 1775 was "a cutting off the fingers — not below, but above — the knuckles," as Phillips put it.[17]

Not only did he find the story unbelievable but Phillips had no respect for the eyewitnesses. He alleged that Revolutionary War hero William Polk was untrustworthy as a witness: "All he cared for was to establish the prominence of his father, whatever was done in Charlotte, and whenever it was done." Polk, Phillips wrote, "did not care a bawbee" about the true story.[18] He mocked the other "venerable witnesses" such as James Jack.[19] Phillips' personal and private obsessions would have remained of no larger importance but for the fact that by being on the faculty of the University of North Carolina he had access to the one document that few others had ever seen: the Davie Copy.

In May 1853 Phillips published an article in the *North Carolina University Magazine* entitled "May, 1775." This was to become the standard "anti" account of the Mecklenburg Declaration among historians for the next century. Phillips himself would be called upon by numerous historians, including Lyman Draper and William Hoyt, as a character witness to attest that the story was untrue. Even today, Phillips' article is cited as evidence that the story of the Mecklenburg Declaration is "spurious." "May, 1775" runs approximately ten pages in length, of which just over three — almost one-third of the entire article — are filled with reprinting of the Mecklenburg Declaration and Mecklenburg Resolves in their entirety. Prior to this point, for nearly the first two pages of the article, Phillips engages in a meandering narrative, one worth quoting at length, especially as this paper is still widely regarded as the definitive account for the skeptic's case:

> The revolutionary history of North Carolina is a noble history — one in which its citizens may properly be very complacent. Among the first in the field of battle, North Carolina never left it. South Carolina and Georgia at one time were conquered Provinces. North Carolina, although at one time reduced to great extremity, never was conquered, the enemy himself being witness. Jefferson has declared that "no State was more fixed or forward," and the researches that are now making into our history gradually reveal the entire truthfulness of his assertion. To this research we have willingly lent the pages of our Magazine, and every true lover of his State should be gratified at the result. The present season of the year is full of associations connected with the spring of 1775. Every May comforts us for the chills and pains of the winter now past — it is delightful with its own peculiar treasures, and it exhilarates us with bright promises of the future.[20]

Warming to his seasonal theme, he continues:

> The soul of man has its seasons as well as his soil. There has been a winter of deadness, whose storms disturbed only a desolation. This was succeeded by the time of sowing the seeds of truth and righteousness. Now seems to be the month of May, wherein what has been sown is promising abundant harvests, and what is yet needed may still find time for development and maturity. There will be a season of repose wherein all trees and plants are steadily growing for the harvest — and then the end shall come — when the great white throne shall be set, the angels be sent forth to separate the tares from the wheat, and all, according to their works, shall receive unerring praise or blame. In the physical world it is well to observe the various relations of the seasons...."[21]

And on and on and on, almost ad infinitum. Phillips writes roughly three hundred words before he even gets to the word *Mecklenburg*. Not until after nearly page three does Phillips get to the theme of his article, which is to "impartially" weigh the arguments for and against the veracity of the Mecklenburg Declaration. He then proceeds with a turgid and unexceptional rehashing of the existing evidence, with no real thesis and no conclusion.

In short, what was true in his article "May, 1775" was not new, and what was new was not true. Phillips' article would have been consigned to a deserved oblivion but for one novel and astonishing observation that he made regarding the Davie Copy. He wrote:

> The oldest edition of the "Davie copy" was furnished by John McN. Alexander to Gen. Davie, then a resident of South Carolina. The age and the degree of reverence to be given to its contents are unanswerably fixed by this conclusion to the manuscript: "It may be worthy of notice here to observe that the foregoing statement though fundamentally correct, yet may not literally correspond with the original record of the transactions of *said delegation and* court of enquiry, as all those records and papers were burnt, with the house, on April 6th, 1800 [emphasis added]."[22]

Subtly but deliberately, Phillips misquoted the Davie Copy by reinserting the words that McKnitt had deleted: *delegation &*. Arguably, this gave the passage a meaning entirely different than what a fair reading would intend. Nor did Phillips mention that the words had been struck through in the original. Phillips then concluded: "From this certificate it is clear that Mr. Alexander never intended to set forth the 'Davie copy' as containing any more than the *substance* of what was resolved in Charlotte, in May, 1775 [emphasis added]."[23] In other words, Phillips alleged that McKnitt had not copied the Davie Copy from an original record, but rather had written it from memory. That this was not an innocent or inadvertent error on Phillips' part was apparent with his other omission. Phillips also failed to mention the sentence at the top of the page: "*Thus far from the Journals & records of Sd. Committee.*"

In short, in his article "May, 1775" Phillips gave a grossly misleading account of what the Davie Copy actually said. "A conscientious writer of history would have reported observing the line 'Thus far from the journals and records,' and would have given his reason for restoring words deleted by their author," writes one student of the episode. Instead, "Phillips was silent on both points, and offered no explanation as to why he published a copy that differed totally in effect from the author's statements."[24]

The historical value and meaning of the Davie Copy were open to debate. And regardless of whether one was a Jeffersonian doubter or an Adams believer, a reasonable person could make a number of different arguments as to what the deletion of the word *delegation* implied for the meaning of the final passage of the Davie Copy. A skeptic could conclude that McKnitt had originally meant to include the word *delegation* and then had second thoughts and deleted it. This could be said to show that McKnitt was not copying from an original record. A believer could conclude that by striking the word *delegation* McKnitt was simply clarifying the historical account. But, in all fairness, the deletion of the word was ambiguous. McKnitt's deletions—and the final paragraph as a whole—were subject to interpretation. The deletions in the Davie Copy raised legitimate interpretive questions and reasonable minds could disagree, but by failing to accurately report what the document said, Phillips crossed the line from objective historical testimony. He had tampered with the evidence. That Phillips was plainly aware of what he was doing can be inferred from another circumstantial fact: he published the article anonymously.

Phillips' "revelation" was a bombshell. For the skeptics of the Mecklenburg Declaration, McKnitt's "confession" was the final proof that the story was not true. The argument that

Thus far from the Journals & records of S. Committee

...... here the copy of the records ends; The delinquent harmony, unanimity & exertion in the cause of Liberty & independence evidently resulting from these regulations and the continued exertion of said delegation apparently tranquilized this section of the State & met with the approbation of the Council of Safety who held their sessions alternately at Newbern & Wilmington — and who confirmed or approved the official Acts of Delegation

The phrase "Thus far from the Journals & records of S[aid] Committee" indicated McKnitt had copied the preceding passage from some existing records. Phillips ignored this sentence in his article "May, 1775" (Courtesy Southern Historical Collection, Wilson Library, University of North Carolina at Chapel Hill).

the Mecklenburg Declaration had been entirely written from McKnitt's memory and not copied from any original records became the standard skeptic talking point ever after. One history puts it this way:

> Phillips' action in thus changing this key statement to make it say exactly opposite to what Alexander did say must remain a mystery of North Carolina history. Certainly it is indefensible if he did it in order to further his contention; if innocently he overlooked the fact that the words had been eliminated by their author, he demonstrated himself to have been in that research careless and unreliable. But in any event and whatever the explanation, his gross error has done more to rally the myth-contenders than any one other contribution.[25]

The powerful impact of Phillips' article is all the more mystifying given how vapid, shallow, and unoriginal it is. Nor was it grounded in any original research. In fact, the only documents Phillips appeared to have in his possession, and on which the article was based, were a copy of the Mecklenburg Resolves, the state's report of 1831, and, critically, the as-yet-unpublished Davie Copy. Nonetheless, Phillips gave an intellectual foundation to what would become a cult of denial. And just as with other similar cults, countervailing evidence, logic or argumentation became beside the point. The eyewitness testimony? All wrong. The "rough notes" of McKnitt? Forgeries. The circumstantial evidence? Untrue.

And like other denial cults — moon landings, 9/11 "truthers" or Obama "birthers" — Phillips had a slightly loopy, highly conspiratorial theory to explain away all the evidence that conflicted with his worldview — namely, that the only copy of the Mecklenburg Declaration that had ever existed was the Davie Copy: "I have always believed that in dealing with (handling) what I had in 1853, I was in possession of the only originals then in existence — all that were ever known at any time."[26] Ignoring the other evidence available to him — the "rough notes" that Dr. Alexander had announced in 1830 which were open to "the inspection of any one desirous to examine them" and the "copy in an unknown hand" — Phillips was convinced that "there never has been more than one *original,* viz., that which Dr. Sam Henderson found mutilated [i.e., the Davie Copy]."[27]

This statement implies, or rather asserts, that the other copies, and in particular the version found in the *Raleigh Register,* had to have been copied from the Davie Copy. This was hard to explain on the existing facts, especially given that the Davie Copy was torn in several key places. It also didn't make sense given that McKnitt had pointed the world to the existence of the Davie Copy in the first place. Be that as it may, Phillips believed that

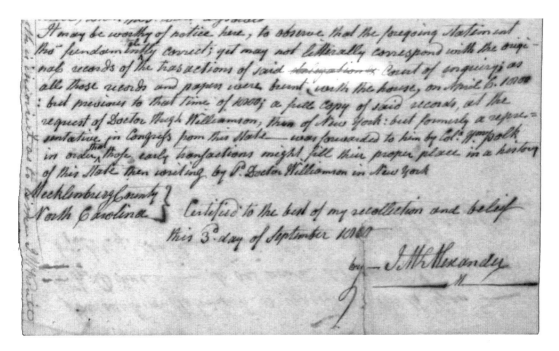

The final paragraph of the Davie Copy and the deleted words ("delegation &"), which Phillips rein-serted in his article without telling anyone. It was argued this fundamentally changed the meaning of what McKnitt had written (courtesy Southern Historical Collection, Wilson Library, University of North Carolina at Chapel Hill).

Dr. Joseph Alexander "got and used the Davie copy for his publication in 1819 & then returned it to the Davies."[28] Later, "when a fuss was kicked up ... this copy was sent for (either by a Polkite or an Alexanderite) & then found to be mutilated." Phillips admitted he wasn't able "to cite chapter and verse" for this theory, but that was his explanation.[29]

It became impossible to gainsay Phillips' findings because following the Civil War, the Davie Copy was lost. This left Phillips as the sole witness, the only source, the single "authority" on the Davie Copy. As he put it, "the existence of that famous Jno. McK. Alexander certificate rests now on my veracity."[30] An article by James Welling in the *Magazine of American History* in March 1889 noted that the Davie Copy "is now reported to be lost or mislaid, but the authenticity of the certificate, as transcribed and published by Prof. Phillips, *has never been questioned* [emphasis added]. I have private letters from him in which he confirms the textual accuracy of the certificate as given above in its integrity. His high personal character is a sufficient guarantee for his loyalty to truth in this matter."[31]

In fact, not until 1917, was the Davie Copy located, by Dr. J.G. de Roulhac Hamilton, history professor at the University of North Carolina. He found it among the papers of Dr. Battle, a nephew by marriage of Phillips. And even then it remained hidden for another twenty years, almost (as some suggested) as if on purpose. "Ever since my student days I have heard that the 'Davie Copy' was somewhere in our archives," wrote the author Archibald Henderson in July 1939. "I made repeated searches through the historical papers and doc-uments preserved in the locked vault in the University Library." Henderson noted that the leading writer on the subject, William Hoyt, had also searched in the UNC library for the

Davie Copy but "could not find the elusive document. Again and again I have been importuned to unearth the 'Davie Copy,' and reveal its salient features to the public. Of course it was here all the time. But it was of no service to anybody, since it was not, until recently, accessible to investigators."[32]

An amazing thing had happened. An obscure professor of *mathematics* had been loaned a valuable, original historical document, one with no known copies. This document held several clues to one of the greatest controversies in American history. Based on his sole possession of this historical document, this professor then wrote a bombshell article that made a profound impact on historians' views on the Revolutionary period. And then the original historical copy disappeared, leaving Phillips as the sole authority on what it said.

All this raises a question: Did Phillips deliberately hide the Davie Copy? He was, after all, the last person to see it. As the world's foremost expert, one might logically conclude that he had a vested interest in ensuring that the Davie Copy survived. One might even conclude that Phillips would have made and kept a copy for himself. But he did neither of these things. In fact, in later years when other historians were looking for the Davie Copy, Phillips was entirely unhelpful. The historian Lyman Draper was collecting historical material for a book on the Mecklenburg Controversy he was writing (never published). Draper asked Phillips where he might find the Davie Copy, to which Phillips blandly responded, "That paper I understand cannot be found either among Gov. Swain's papers or among those of the Hist. Society." He even suggested the document might no longer exist, pointing out that the "papers of the Davie family were burned during Genl. Sherman's progress through South Carolina."[33]

In the book *Chain of Error*, the writer V.V. McNitt makes the case that Phillips knew he had acted in bad faith and was anxious to divert attention from himself regarding his misquoting of the Davie Copy. According to McNitt, "It is clear from the context of certain letters to [historian] Dr. Draper that Dr. Phillips was somewhat nervous about the Davie Copy, which he possibly might hope might never appear again; that he sought to induce [University of North Carolina president] Dr. Swain to accept joint responsibility for his judgment of the Mecklenburg Declaration as stated in his 1853 article, which he called 'our article,' and that he was anxious for a concurring verdict from Dr. Draper."[34] He also sought corroborating witnesses to his version of the story. Phillips tried to enlist other allies to his aide. "Our President here Dr. Battle is, with you, an unbeliever in the prevalent myth about Mecklenburg," Phillips wrote to Draper in June 1885. "But it is worth of examination if only to dispel popular faith in such traditions."[35]

As his fame grew, Phillips acted as if he were a man trying to hide something. In a letter dated June 8, 1875, to Draper he wrote, "I shall thank you to let my name appear as seldom as possible. I have enough to bear in the matter of the Jno. McK. Alexander certificate. It seems that I am the only eye-witness to its existence, and my testimony is, to say the least, at present, *inconvenient*."[36] In another he asked that Draper "be discreet in making use of what I tell you. I do not want to [be] regarded as trying to degrade some of the worthiest people in N.C."[37]

He need not have been so worried. Phillips had tapped into a strong and deep current of disbelief about the Mecklenburg Declaration. His explanation satisfied a school of thought that simply felt the story could not be true but that had difficulty explaining the existence of the surviving papers, such as the Davie Copy. His contention that McKnitt had written the text of the Mecklenburg Declaration purely from memory, and not from any source material, would influence generations of historians, including Draper, William Hoyt and A.S. Salley, Jr., all of whom would expressly rely on Phillips' interpretation of the Davie Copy. Phillips' misquoting of the Davie Copy would not be discovered until the early twentieth century, by which time Phillips' theory had become settled conventional wisdom. It was Jefferson's ultimate revenge.[38]

18

Death by a Thousand Cuts
The Case Against the Mecklenburg
Declaration of Independence

The folly of the "Twenty-Seven Signers" is so absurd that I will make this offer. I will pay ten dollars for every name which any one can prove was signed to either the so-called Declaration of May 20th or to the Resolves of May 31st, apart from those of the Chairman and the Secretary.
— Charles Van Noppen, *"The Supineness of the North Carolina Historical Association and the Ignorance of the North Carolina Society of Colonial Dames,"* 1912

Charles Phillips was not a serious writer or critic and his case against the Mecklenburg Declaration of Independence rested largely on misinterpreting and, what was more serious, tampering with the evidence. The same could not be said of several later historians who, taking their lead from Phillips' theory that McKnitt had written the entire story from memory, began a more systematic and effective assault on the Mecklenburg Declaration of Independence.

The seminal "anti" work was published in 1907 by a historian named William Henry Hoyt. His work, in part entitled *The Alleged Early Declaration of Independence by Mecklenburg County ... Is Spurious* began: "Since it was first brought to the attention of the general public in the year 1819 the declaration of independence which is alleged to have been issued on May 20, 1775, by a convention held in Charlotte ... has been the subject of the most mooted question and acrimonious controversy of the history of the American Revolution."[1] Hoyt's book was a sustained attack upon every piece of evidence that had been put forward in favor of the story. His writing style was balanced and seemingly objective, unlike some of the more shrill May 20 declaration opponents. Indeed, Hoyt claimed to have begun his research hoping to write a defense of the document, "but the irresistible logic of facts drove me to my present position."[2]

Hoyt marshaled an impressive and seemingly comprehensive array of counterarguments, theories and criticisms against the witnesses. He argued forcefully that it was inconceivable that any colonists would have desired independence in the summer of 1775. He pointed out that no one nationally, regionally, or even, it appeared, locally had heard of the fabled declaration at the time, which indicated that there could not truly have been a declaration of independence in the area. Then Hoyt examined all of the existing documents and was the first to point out that McKnitt's "rough notes" could have been (indeed, likely were) written in or sometime after the year 1800. Hoyt then stated that the evidence was generally consistent with the Mecklenburg Resolves of May 31 and concluded this was the only true paper and the controversy was just a case of mistaken identity:

> [W]e may reasonably presume that after July 4, 1776, the May 31st resolves were loosely called a declaration of independence by many persons, and that in the course of time, as their phraseology and terms were forgotten, and the number of their surviving authors diminished, they were looked back upon in Mecklenburg county generally, and to some extent in the surrounding section of country, as a formal declaration of independence. In the light of our study of the records of 1775 ... this supposition becomes a certainty.[3]

Hoyt's work remains the definitive skeptics' version of the story of the Mecklenburg Declaration. Indeed, many historians still today believe it is the final word on the entire episode.

Hoyt's theory that the story of the Mecklenburg Declaration of May 20 was simply a case of "mistaken identity" with the Mecklenburg Resolves of May 31 was plausible, but to some it remained unsatisfying. Could this theory explain why Joseph Graham or William Polk, both credible witnesses, gave the date as May 20 and not May 31? Was it reasonable that all of the witnesses had been mistaken on the date? And what were people to make of Governor Stokes' comment that he had "seen" a copy of the declaration in the possession of the historian Williamson? These questions hung in the air, unresolved.

Moreover, many of Hoyt's arguments, such as the idea that "no one" was prepared to contemplate independence from Great Britain in May 1775, could equally be made against the existence of the Mecklenburg Resolves. Like the lawyers' infamous defense at the 1997 murder trial of O.J. Simpson, Hoyt had dozens of clever, very specific criticisms of the evidence, but ultimately none of it added up to a coherent explanation. To those disinclined to believe in the existence of the declaration, Hoyt gave a deeply gratifying explanation, but he had not "proved" the story was false any more than Graham or the other "pro–MecDec" partisans had "proved" it was true. His was a theory — a good theory, a plausible theory, but nothing more.

Yet in the popular mind Hoyt's arguments were largely successful. As in the O.J. trial, most people didn't follow the details too closely and easily missed the forest for the trees. The length and complexity of Hoyt's arguments were impressive, as was his relentless confidence that the story was, as Jefferson had said, "spurious." To many, his relentless criticism was proof enough. So in the end, while Hoyt failed to provide a smoking gun, his "death by a thousand cuts" approach was successful.

Other historians took their cue from Hoyt's work and piled on. The most aggressive was a colleague of Hoyt's named A.S. Salley, Jr. Salley was secretary of the South Carolina Historical Commission and a proud South Carolina patriot. As such, the idea that North Carolina might claim preeminence in igniting the American Revolution was vile to him. Using Hoyt's work as a point of departure, Salley wrote a blistering article in 1908 in the *American Historical Review* in which he concluded that "the facts shown by the resolutions of May 31, 1775, and other authentic records preclude the possibility of any such action having been taken on May 20, 1775."[4]

Where Hoyt was nuanced and analytical, however, Salley was a historical sledgehammer. Although Salley's arguments were not new, the decisiveness of his approach was. He maintained that all of the evidence that the proponents of the Mecklenburg Declaration had collated, including the eyewitness accounts and the existing papers, was simply false. For example, where Hoyt had argued that the various eyewitnesses cited in the state report of 1831 may have suffered from faulty memories, Salley took it a step further. He made the astonishing claim that their testimony was not simply in error, but had been coached. To him it was clear that witnesses such as James Jack "had before them the printed version of the alleged 'Declaration'" when they gave their accounts.[5]

Salley pointed out niggling inconsistencies in the testimony as proof that the stories were faked. For example, some witnesses remembered that Adam Alexander had called the meeting (as the documents seemed to indicate), while others said it was Thomas Polk. To Salley, irregularities like this (which others might argue were minor) discredited the entire story. Similarly, he pointed out that Captain Jack claimed that when he passed through Salisbury in June 1775 "the General Court was sitting." Due to the fact that this must have been the first week of June, "it is evident that Jack carried the resolutions of May 31" and not the Mecklenburg Declaration.[6]

One by one Salley attempted to discredit the various individuals associated with the story. Certain of the "alleged" signers — including Richard Harris, Abraham Alexander, and Robert Irwin — had continued to serve as magistrates through July 1776, he noted, "in the name of the King." He also noted that William Kennon, "another alleged signer, practiced before the King's court at Salisbury on the second of June, 1775" while Waightstill Avery was appointed attorney for the Crown at Salisbury on August 2, 1775.[7] Salley argued that these actions were incompatible with the same men having engaged in a declaration of independence in the previous months. This argument ignored the fact that many of the same delegates to the state Constitutional Convention in 1775 also made public affirmations of their "allegiance" to the Crown. Such public avowals of allegiance were routine for public office holders even after war with Great Britain began, and in many cases up to the moment of independence.

In addition to these ad hominem attacks, Salley took great glee in punching holes in the local legends in Mecklenburg County which Graham and others cited as "definitive proof." First there was the son of William Davidson, born on May 20 and thus known (according to family tradition) as "Independence Ben." According to Salley, "It appears to be debatable whether 'My Independence Boy' was not born on the 4th of July rather than the 20th of May."[8] This was a rather unsporting conclusion (and for that matter, incorrect). But Salley was on safer ground in concluding that family legends were not particularly strong evidence in any event.

Salley systematically crushed each piece of evidence in the same fashion, using a sledgehammer to kill a gnat. The valedictory address delivered at Sugar Creek Academy on June 1, 1809, which read in part, "on the 19th of May 1775, a day sacredly exulting to every Mecklenburg bosom, two delegates duly authorized from every militia company in this county met in Charlotte," was a fake and "evidently prepared by a person of mature years," he wrote. Similarly, the real property deeds which appeared to cite the year 1775 as the first year of local independence, rather than 1776, were the result of common error. The people of the region were widely illiterate, mistakes were common, and often they didn't even know what year it was. To Salley, these old deeds proved nothing.

Proof or myth? The grave of Benjamin Wilson Davidson in Hopewell. Davidson was born on May 20, 1787, and, according to family lore, was nicknamed "Independence Ben" (photograph by the author).

Finally, there was the case of the anonymous 1777 poem "The Mecklenburg Censor," which was said to include these lines:

> First to withdraw from British trust
> In Congress they the very first,
> Their Independence did declare.

If the poem were real, it constituted pretty good corroborative evidence. The only problem was that the three lines cited above (which Graham had quoted in his book) were not actually in the poem. "There is a complete copy of 'A Modern Poem' in the Charleston Library," asserted Salley with devastating finality, "it bears annotations by a citizen of Charlotte in 1777, *and does not contain the three lines quoted* [emphasis added]."[9] *What?* The historian Wheeler and presumably Graham, who cited it, had all asserted to the world that the lines in question—*their independence did declare*—were in the poem. Even the historian Draper, who was a skeptic, had stated that those lines were in the poem. Had they all gotten it wrong?

In a fascinating twist to this subplot, there were, in fact, two versions of the same poem. The first, quoted by Graham, was entitled "The Mecklenburg Censor," had no stated author, was dated March 18, 1777, and contained the three lines regarding Mecklenburg's Declaration of Independence. The second version, cited by Salley, was entitled "A Modern Poem," was written by "The Mecklenburg Censor," and dated March 30, 1777. The version *without* the three important lines, was, as Salley stated, in the Charleston Library. The version *containing* the three lines, was in the Francis Lister Hawks Papers in the Southern

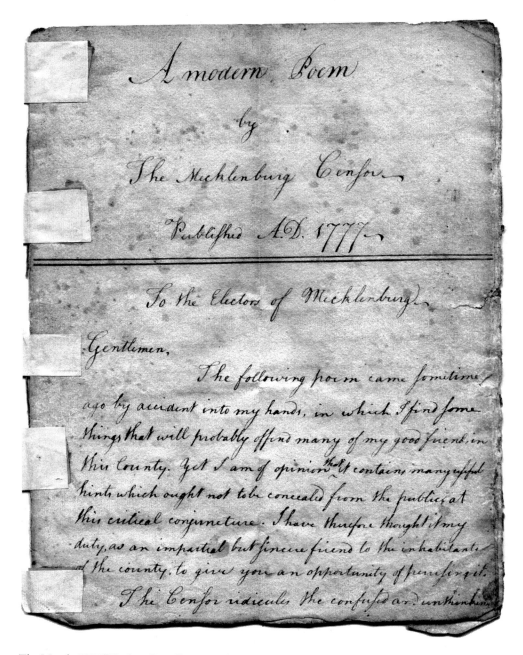

The March 1777 "Modern Poem" was cited as evidence both for and against the Mecklenburg Declaration. One version contained three lines that seemed to corroborate the story, while in this version those lines are missing (Charleston Library Society, Charleston, South Carolina).

Historical Collection at the University of North Carolina. However, this latter version was a copy made in the 1850s by Edward Constantine Davidson, a Charlotte lawyer and member of the North Carolina House of Commons.[10] It was not clear from what original Davidson made the copy, although some experts believe it was from an earlier version of the poem.

The two versions were substantially the same, although the Charleston version included two important sections not found in the University of North Carolina version, and vice versa. Most important, the Charleston version does not contain the eight lines regarding Mecklenburg's independence.[11] In short, it was not clear that the "Mecklenburg Censor" proved anything, and in any event it simply created more confusion. In a way, "The Mecklenburg Censor" was the entire Mecklenburg Controversy in a nutshell. There were two versions of the same document and their authors were unknown. The two papers had different dates. And one version that seemed to confirm the story just two years after the event was actually a copy made 75 years after the fact.

To the critics, the "Mecklenburg Censor" was also a good example of the underhanded lengths to which loyal supporters of the Mecklenburg Declaration had gone to win the argument. Time and again, supporters would claim that the case had been "proven" or "settled" by newly discovered evidence, when on further review the new evidence was seen to be suspect. Like the boy who cried wolf, the supporters of the Mecklenburg Declaration wore out any goodwill by repeated claims to have won the argument.

Other local legends, such as the testimony of Caldwell, also crumbled under closer scrutiny. Caldwell was the young military cadet who wrote a detailed account of discussing the Mecklenburg Declaration of Independence with President Washington during the president's visit in May 1791. In Caldwell's case it was not clear that his story was untrue, but there were concerns that the story might have been embellished after the fact. First, he wrote the story at least fifty years later (probably in the late 1840s or early 1850s). By this time, the Mecklenburg Controversy was well under way and Caldwell would have had reason to remember something that had not happened, or had not happened the way he remembered it.

Then there was Caldwell himself. While he was an accomplished physician, he was also, well, *strange*. According to the editor of *Washington's Southern Tour*, Caldwell was "vain and eccentric," full of "egotism" and "evidently regarded the whole occasion as one deserving elaborate description."[12] Caldwell's account of his conversation with Washington was stilted and highly artificial in places. All of which raised a fair question: did Caldwell make the story up? Or, to put it more charitably, did he consciously or unconsciously merge a true story (his meeting with Washington) with an invented version of what they discussed? It was not clear. At a minimum, Caldwell's account suffered the same evidentiary flaws as some of the other eyewitness testimony.

Historians pointed out that many of the local legends that had arisen about the Mecklenburg Declaration, such as Caldwell's story, were simply unsupported by the facts. For example, it was commonly believed (and still is) that the Mecklenburg Declaration was *signed* by all men present. But who said so? Only one of the witnesses claimed this. The rest said the resolutions had been *adopted*. Even McKnitt's grandson conceded that there was no evidence that the Mecklenburg Declaration had been signed, only that it had been adopted.[13] For what it is worth, a parallel national myth grew up around the "signing" of the Declaration of Independence on July 4, which in point of fact did not happen until many days, and in some cases months, later.

Similarly, the list of delegates who adopted the Mecklenburg Declaration was not recalled with consistency and seemed to grow over time. The governor's commission in 1831 arrived at a total of twenty-six names. According to the Mecklenburg Resolves, there were nine companies in Mecklenburg at the time (eight for the county and one for Charlotte), which would have resulted in eighteen attendees. To confuse things further, the 1831 list of twenty-six names did not include John Davidson, who testified in the *Governor's Report* that he was a delegate — and if you included Davidson, the number of delegates was twenty-seven.[14] In the historian Ramsey's list compiled in the mid–nineteenth century the number of signers grew to thirty-two. If you were a skeptic of the story, such irregularities made for easy sport. "The folly of the 'Twenty-Seven Signers' is so absurd that I will make this offer," wrote one critic, Charles Van Noppen. "I will pay ten dollars for every name which any one can prove was signed to either the so-called Declaration of May 20th or to the Resolves of May 31st, apart from those of the Chairman and the Secretary."[15]

According to other local stories, some Catawba Indians had ridden into Charlotte on May 20 to support the settlers in their claim for independence. Others alleged that British general Cornwallis burned down Captain Jack's home in 1780 in revenge for his role in carrying the Mecklenburg Declaration to Philadelphia. Some said that the fire at McKnitt's house in 1800 was caused by arson set by loyalists. And so forth. If that weren't enough, in 1875 a purported witness named Jimmie Belk came forward to claim he had witnessed the meetings one hundred years earlier.

You could dismiss these stories as harmless urban legends, mere barnacles of untruth that had grown over time on the historical ship, just as the myth of the "signing" of the national Declaration of Independence on July 4 had developed over the years. Local legends were hardly unique to Mecklenburg or the story of the Mecklenburg Declaration but can be found across the original thirteen colonies. Using them as "proof" to deny the declaration would be like using the story of George Washington cutting down the cherry tree or throwing a dollar across the Potomac to deny that he had ever been either general or president. Nonetheless, if you wanted to punch holes in the entire story, these small errors added up. Moreover, these fuzzy details gave weight to Hoyt's "mistaken identity" theory that all of the eyewitnesses had confused a real document (the Mecklenburg Resolves) with a mythical one (the Mecklenburg Declaration).

Finally, regional bias against the South played a role in the case against the Mecklenburg Declaration, particularly in the period of Reconstruction following the end of the Civil War. Anti-southern animus was high. Former Confederate general Joseph E. Johnson was the chief marshal at the 1875 centenary commemoration in Charlotte, which was later seen as proof of "the purely sectional nature of this attempt to rob from the whole American people a portion of its priceless, united and legal inheritance." It was all "the Latest Tar-Heel Humbug." A Northern paper called the Mecklenburg Declaration "a Great Rebel Fraud" and nothing more than an "attempt of the South to steal the glory of the nation."[16]

According to the skeptics, the entire story has been entirely disproved, fact by fact, piece by piece, until the whole rotten structure collapsed of its own weight. "Mr. Hoyt has conclusively shown that the alleged 'Declaration' is spurious," triumphantly concluded Salley.[17] And of course, the fact that the original was nowhere to be found seemed to clinch their case. "Mec Dec Is Around Here Somewhere," sneered the *Charlotte News* on May 21, 1957.[18] "We're terribly sorry the Declaration has been mislaid temporarily," mocked the article, "but it's around here somewhere alright."

The skeptics had an evidentiary problem of their own, however. Hoyt and Salley were adept at attacking each piece of evidence piecemeal. The eyewitness testimony could be picked apart. Dates or facts could be shown to be in contradiction. Key documents were undated, torn, or illegible. All of that was true. But in the end, there remained one key piece of evidence that had to be accounted for, that had to be explained, or demolished. That was the document found in McKnitt's papers — the anonymous, and mysterious "copy in an unknown hand." Even if every other piece of evidence had been accounted for, the "copy in an unknown hand" still stood like a rock. It was perfectly legible. It was the foundation of the entire story. The story set forth in it was generally confirmed by the testimony of the witnesses and confirmed McKnitt's "rough notes" in every way.

Someone, at some point, had written this account, whether from memory, copied from an original record, or invented from whole cloth. To the believers, the conclusion was obvious: it was an authentic record of the transactions, copied by someone after 1792. It was anonymous and undated, to be sure, but so what? As Dr. Alexander had written of these quibbles, "it matters not." The witnesses, the circumstantial evidence, even the British accounts of the time, could all be explained away, but not this. This document was the sun around which every other planet of the story revolved. But if you followed the irresistible logic of the skeptics, the "copy in an unknown hand" *could not be* true. And if it were not true, someone had to have invented it. But who?

It was not John McKnitt Alexander. Even a cursory comparison of his handwriting showed that he was not the author. There was another suspect, however: his son, Dr. Joseph Alexander, the same Dr. Alexander who had started the whole controversy when he presented the paper to the *Raleigh Register*. If Dr. Alexander had forged the "copy in an unknown hand" the entire story was false. In a widely read article in the *American Historical Review* in 1908, Salley made this claim. According to Salley, Dr. Alexander had forged the "copy in an unknown hand," passed it off as an anonymous paper and fabricated a cover story as to how he had found it. "[T]he evidence appears to be convincing," Salley wrote, "that Dr. Joseph McKnitt Alexander was himself the author of that spurious 'Declaration.'"[19]

Salley argued that Dr. Alexander carefully avoided giving his real name in the *Raleigh Register* version, signing instead simply as "J. McKnitt," and failed to disclose that the "John M'Knitt Alexander dec'd" who gave him the papers was in fact his own father. In addition, Dr. Alexander conceded that no "official" records of the May convention were ever kept, while noting that the papers in his possession said they were "extracted from the old minutes." If the originals were lost in a fire at his home, as he claimed, how was it that other records such as the "copy in an unknown hand" had survived? There were too many internal contradictions and too much backtracking in Dr. Alexander's testimony, according to Salley. It was all fishy. To Salley, it was obvious that the inconsistencies in this testimony proved that Dr. Alexander was "evidently leaving loop-holes to escape in the event that he was 'cornered.'"[20]

According to Salley, the "copy in an unknown hand" was written — or "roughly constructed," in Salley's words — from the "rough notes" of his father, John McKnitt Alexander. Dr. Alexander had changed the wording somewhat in an attempt to disguise the fact that the same author was at work. In fact, the strike-throughs and corrections in the documents were not true corrections made by another writer after the fact, but rather falsifications, fake errors made to look like corrections. It was all part of this deception. "As a matter of fact," Salley concluded, the Alexanders "never did have a single original record" regarding the Mecklenburg Declaration. Nothing, he concluded, "came from original sources."[21]

Behind the scenes, Phillips continued to poison the waters. In a private letter to Salley,

Phillips told him, "The condition of the originals in our possession here [at UNC], the diversity of handwriting, the frequent interlineation, erasures, etc., show that the younger Alexander [Dr. Joseph] tried to set forth a poem in Alexandrian measure."[22] In his cryptic way, Phillips placed the thought into Salley's mind that Dr. Alexander had forged the "copy in an unknown hand."

Relying on Phillips, Salley made the following conclusion, which became the gospel truth for the "anti" camp for decades to come: "It was now perfectly clear that the document given to [Congressman William] Davidson by Dr. Alexander and subsequently published in the *Raleigh Register was a fabrication*; that Dr. Joseph McKnitt Alexander gave it to the world as a genuine copy of the original, although, by his subsequent admission, he did not know its origin; and that when he himself discovered evidence to show that it was not a copy of an original he continued to deceive the public into believing that it was."[23] Salley argued that a "charge of forgery against Dr. Alexander could not be directly proven, but we submit that the circumstantial evidence against him is very strong; strong enough to convict any man of fewer champions."[24] Jefferson's hoax theory had come full circle, with one important variation. The author of the hoax was no longer John McKnitt Alexander, as Jefferson had first believed, but his son, Dr. Joseph Alexander.

To paraphrase Gladstone, Salley's argument was a mixture of bold assertion, persistent exaggeration, constant misconstruction, and copious, arbitrary and baseless prophecy. Whatever one's view on the Mecklenburg Controversy as a whole, an objective examination of the documents would seem to clear Dr. Alexander of the charge of authorship of the "copy in an unknown hand."[25] Nor did the circumstantial facts support this theory. After all, if he *had* written the paper, that fact could easily be shown by a comparison of the handwriting. Why would Dr. Alexander expose himself in such an obvious forgery? In addition, Dr. Alexander seemed as confused by the meaning and origin of the "copy in an unknown hand" as anyone else. Surely if he were intending to commit fraud he would have been much more assertive in his statements and definitive in his explanations. Finally the Alexander family was widely considered by those that knew them to be honest and scrupulous. All in all the evidence did not support Salley's theory that Dr. Alexander was guilty of fraud. His charge of forgery was as reckless as Adams' earlier charge against Jefferson.

Nonetheless, this and other attacks did not stop Hoyt and Salley from declaring total victory in their war against Graham and other supporters of the Mecklenburg Declaration of Independence. Hoyt and the skeptics, Salley triumphed, had "completely refuted, every item of evidence Graham has presented in behalf of his 'Declaration,' and [Hoyt's] arguments have over-shadowed those of Dr. Graham in logical conclusions at every point."[26] Hoyt had "destroyed the entire foundation of this false structure — has not left even a prop to hold it up — and has hurled it into the slough of historical myths where it is to be hoped the truth-loving world will let it remain."[27]

These relentless attacks took their toll on the morale of the story's supporters. Although there was no single piece of evidence which could be said to have disproven the story, it seemed to be dying the death of a thousand cuts. Yet ultimately it was not Hoyt or any other skeptic's work that undermined the story. A changing world decided it just didn't care much anymore. The Mecklenburg Controversy was to end not with a bang but with a whimper.

19

"The faithful disperse"
The Controversy Fizzles Out

It is only the local patriotism of North Carolinians that has kept the legend alive.
—*Manchester Guardian*, May 21, 1909

The first known public commemoration of the Mecklenburg Declaration of Independence occurred fifty years after the fact in Charlotte on May 20, 1825. Festivities began at 11:00 a.m. with a cavalry and artillery procession, followed by "a band of revolutionary veterans, 60 or 70 in number, wearing badges with the figures '75 stamped on them."[1] At First Presbyterian Church, the Reverend Humphrey Hunter led a prayer then recited the Mecklenburg Declaration. This was followed by a patriotic oration that caused "tears to trickle down the furrowed cheeks of numbers of the war-worn and hoary-headed veterans."[2] The ceremonies concluded with music and cannon fire interspersed with much drinking. Similar commemorations occurred throughout the following decades, usually involving musketry, drinking and passionate recitations of the five famous resolutions. In 1835, for example, Governor Swain and U.S. Senator Willie Mangum attended.

But the high-water mark of the Mecklenburg Declaration commemorations was on May 20, 1875, the 100th anniversary of the event. Charlotte's business and civic leaders were determined to put the city on the map by hosting a gala unparalleled in the state's history. In late March 1875, a meeting was held in the editorial rooms of the *Charlotte Observer* "to discuss measures relative to the proper celebration of the 100th Anniversary of the 20th of May, Mecklenburg Declaration of Independence."[3] Befitting the purpose of the meeting, speeches were first made — more than ten, in fact — and, felicitously, resolutions of the planning committee were moved and, of course, "unanimously adopted." They resolved to appoint a subcommittee to petition the general assembly, "asking that the 20th of May be constituted a LEGAL HOLIDAY in the State of North Carolina, as a mark of recognition by the State, of the authenticity of the immortal Declaration which has cast lasting luster on the names of North Carolinians."[4] Although the effort went nowhere, subsequent projects to institutionalize MecDec would bear fruit.

The committee resolved to take measures to "arouse public interest in the Centennial, and to invite the ladies of every locality to hold concerts, entertainments, &c. for the purpose of raising funds in aid of the measure." The ladies were encouraged to "accept this resolution as a special invitation for them to be present on the occasion."[5] Committees and subcommittees were organized, speakers approached, and calendars cleared. An advertisement in the *Southern Home* (published weekly by ex-general D.H. Hill) on March 22, 1875, two months prior to the commemoration celebrations, announced in all capital letters the impending "Mecklenburg Centennial Celebration."[6] It was civic boosterism at its finest.

A centennial map of Charlotte ("May 20th 1775/May 20th 1875") was sponsored by more than a dozen local businesses, including Richard Moore ("Dealer in Stoves, Tinware and Hardware"), Mecklenburg Iron Works ("BRASS WORKS of all Kinds"), Wilson & Black ("Best Stomach Bitters"), J.K. Purefoy ("Dealer in Books & Stationery, Notions, Fancy Goods, Toys, Confectioneries, Pipes & Cigars") and, appropriately for the financial center that Charlotte would later become, Commercial National Bank ("Capital: $200,000").

A solicitation was made to all descendants of participants in the May convention, or "signers," as they were called locally. "I saw in the *Southern Home* your suggestion to get a list of the grandchildren now living of the patriotic Mecklenburg Declaration of Independence," James Morrison wrote in a letter to the *Southern Home* on March 22, 1875. "I am near 83 years old; have been an invalid for three years past, confined to the house most of the time with asthma. I am the only grandson now living of Neal Morrison, who was one of the signers of the Mecklenburg Declaration."[7]

The planning paid off. According to a special dispatch to the *New York Times*, more than 25,000 people attended the ceremonies in Charlotte. The *Times* correspondent was awakened at dawn on May 20 by a "fierce cannonading and the clangor of bells." The reporter concluded with what the citizens of Mecklenburg would doubtless consider Yankee arrogance; "A hasty walk about Charlotte reveals the fact that, although a city, it is but a small one." In fairness the *Times* correspondent did favorably report that the city had a "sylvan character," with such "trees, shrubbery and flowers, all in full foliage and blossom, must make it delightful as a place of quiet residence."[8]

Skeptics mocked and ridiculed the declaration and the celebrations in Charlotte. "If contemporaneous testimony makes its existence historically incredible," complained one writer in the *North American Review*, "the subsequent acts and declarations of its reputed authors and supporters make its existence morally impossible."[9] Even Dr. Phillips got involved, writing an anonymous nastygram in the *New York Evening Post*:

> The Alleged Declaration of Independence — The
> Imaginary Meeting May 20 and the Real One
> May 31— Thomas Jefferson Not a Plagiarist.

Phillips began by citing himself (again, anonymously) as the "authority" that had proven "beyond peradventure that what is known as the declaration of May 20, 1775, originated in a patriotic effort of Mr. John McKnitt Alexander, in whose house the original records were burnt, to rescue from oblivion the deeds of his compatriots" by writing from memory the "alleged" Mecklenburg Declaration.[10] Still nursing his personal vendetta, Phillips concluded: "So, Messrs. Editors, your readers will understand that one of the declarations to be centennialized on the 20th is the production of a patriotic memory in 1800 ... and they will have good grounds for concluding that Jefferson was not a plagiarist."[11]

Despite the protests of the deniers, momentum was with the "MecDec" supporters, at least within the state, and they moved to capitalize on their success. The date May 20, 1775, was already on the North Carolina state flag, so advocates took steps in the years following the 1875 commemoration to add it to the state seal. By act of the general assembly the great seal of the State of North Carolina was required by law to be two and one-quarter inches in diameter and would picture Liberty and Plenty.[12] *Liberty? Plenty?* This was pretty innocuous stuff for a great seal. The design was not terribly imaginative or representative of the state itself: the iconography — a horn of plenty, sheaves of wheat — could represent any state in the union. (And since when was North Carolina a major wheat-producing state anyway?) The seal was bland and unoriginal. Critics argued that it didn't personify anything specific to North Carolina. Where were the sand dunes of the Outer Banks, the Blue Ridge Mountains, or anything distinctive to North Carolina?

Finally, where was the state motto? Massachusetts had *Ense Petit Placidam, Sub Libertate Quietem* ("By the Sword We Seek Peace, but Peace Only Under Liberty") and Virginia *Sic Semper Tyrannis* ("Thus Always to Tyrants"). North Carolina was the only state without a motto among the original thirteen colonies.

In 1893, Jacob Battle, a member of the general assembly, set out to remedy this. "Contrary to the usage of nearly all the states of the American union," Battle's bill of February 21, 1893, began, "the coat-of-arms and the great seal of this state bear no motto."[13] A "suitable motto," was called for, he suggested, one "expressive of some noble sentiment and indicative of some leading trait of our people, [which] will be instructive as well as ornamental, and the state should also keep in perpetual remembrance the immortal declaration of independence made at Charlotte."[14] The new motto Representative Battle proposed was *Esse Quam Videri* ("To Be, Rather Than to Seem To Be"). Also, "on the coat-of-arms, in addition to the motto, and [at] the bottom, there shall be inscribed at the top the words, 'May the 20th, 1775.'" The date of the Mecklenburg Declaration of Independence was now engraved on the official Great Seal of the State of North Carolina. Not "May 31st," not "Mecklenburg Resolves," but "May the 20th."

It was a metaphorical middle finger to the skeptics, doubters and adversaries of the Mecklenburg Declaration of Independence. Others may question our history, Battle was stating, but we do not. Others may disbelieve in the Mecklenburg Declaration, but we do not. Others may mock us, but we don't care. We know the truth. *Esse Quam Videri.* To *be* rather than to *seem* to be. The MecDec supporters followed up on this success by establishing monuments in Charlotte. In May 1898, they erected a monument to the signers in front of the county courthouse in downtown Charlotte. Thousands of visitors came to Charlotte for the unveiling. Former vice president Adlai Stevenson of Illinois (grandfather of a future U.S. presidential candidate) gave the commemoration address on a wooden platform on the grassy lawn of First Presbyterian Church, a block from where the original log courthouse had once stood. The parade was "more than a mile long," and "perhaps the longest ever held in North Carolina." (Dr. Phillips, of course, weighed in against "the foolishness now agitated of erecting a Monument at Charlotte."[15])

Just over a decade later, a presidential visit — the first of four in connection with the May 20 commemorations — was organized. In an age when travel was still difficult, such an event made international headlines. "President Taft was the principal figure yesterday in the extensive celebrations at Charlotte, North Carolina, of the 134th anniversary of the Declaration of Independence by the Mecklenburg Convention in 1775," reported the English newspaper *Manchester Guardian* in May 1909.[16]

Local businesses seized on the MecDec celebrations. F.C. Abbott & Company, a local real estate company, promised that visitors during the "Great Mecklenburg Celebration" would have their railroad fare repaid "from any point in this state or from upper South Carolina if you buy one of our choice properties."[17] If that weren't enough enticement, the celebrations featured a series of events in nearby Latta Park: J.H. Shield's Great Southern Show (a circus including "The Statue Turning to Life" and "Lunette, the Flying Lady"), twenty-five comedians, a brass band, Dr. D.B. Boyd's "Arabian Freak Horse," Dare Devil Doherty (making a flying leap on a bicycle), and a Queen City Drum Corps exhibition. Firing drills were also to be given daily at 5:30 by the Charlotte Artillery Troop.[18]

Fifty thousand smiling citizens greeted President Taft enthusiastically as he spoke "in eulogy of Anglo-Saxon progress," which, he said, had been carried on "because of Anglo-Saxon reliance on deeds rather than a proneness to empty boasting." President Taft was joined onstage by Charlotte's most famous citizen, Anna Morrison Jackson, the widow of Confederate general Stonewall Jackson. President Taft's size was so great — he weighed over 400 pounds — that a specially built chair had to be constructed for him to sit in onstage. As the president spoke, "a remarkable thunderstorm burst over Charlotte, and drenched both the President and his hearers. It lasted for so long and was so severe that the subsequent parade had to be abandoned."[19] Nature was not the only one throwing cold water over MecDec that year. The *Manchester Guardian* found it "rather surprising that Mr. Taft should have gone South the other day to take part in celebrating the anniversary of the Mecklenburg Declaration of Independence," as, it snottily opined, "[t]here is absolutely no contemporary evidence for the Mecklenburg document" and the fact that it was a forgery "has practically been confirmed by recent historical scholarship." "It is only the local patriotism of North Carolinians," the paper concluded, "that has kept the legend alive."[20]

While local boosters continued to support the declaration, a few other North Carolinians were equally enthusiastic in fighting *against* recognizing May 20. In the same year that President Taft visited, Charles L. Van Noppen, a publisher from Greensboro, organized a protest effort in the pages of his newspaper. His focus was the proposal to place a memorial plaque in the rotunda in the state capitol building in Raleigh commemorating the Mecklenburg Declaration. "It is a well-known fact that every unbiased investigator of the question in the past twenty years has repudiated the so-called Declaration of May 20th, but on the other hand emphasized that the Resolves of May 31st, which practically constituted a Declaration of Independence and were generally known as such, is the only document that can be proven," he asserted in a one of several pamphlets he wrote and published on the subject.[21] "The placing of this tablet will be a monument to the Supineness of the Historical Commission and to the Ignorance and Prejudice of the North Carolina Society of Colonial Dames, and a constant testimony to the State's stupidity."[22]

Van Noppen did more than simply complain, however. He took it upon himself to write a short screed, which, like most canonical works in the MecDec oeuvre, gave away its theme in the title: *The Mecklenburg Declaration of Independence Written in 1800.* "Is the State of North Carolina so lacking in moral fiber that she will sit calmly by and let this fraud be perpetrated under the name of patriotism?" Van Noppen asked. "I have often wondered why the manhood and womanhood of Charlotte did not assert itself and find out what they are worshipping.... If Charlotte wants May 20 as a day to celebrate and advertise herself, why let her have that day or April fool's day or any other day, but the great State of North Carolina should refuse to longer reverence that day as a historical date when every well-informed person on North Carolina history knows that that date is an *Error*."[23]

The Controversy inevitably became involved in North Carolina politics. In 1909, the North Carolina General Assembly passed a bill authorizing county school boards to purchase copies of Captain Samuel A. Ashe's *History of North Carolina* for rural school libraries. Ashe had originally been a proponent of the Mecklenburg Declaration story but for reasons known only to himself had changed his mind. In his *History,* he seized the skeptic's argument that there was no Mecklenburg Declaration of May 20th, just mass confusion with the Mecklenburg Resolves. Ashe did not adduce any additional evidence to support his findings, but no matter. The various witnesses who had given evidence of the state in 1830 ("thirty other old men," as Ashe described them) were all wrong; the surviving records were "written from memory," as Dr. Phillips had earlier shown. "That some [witnesses] erroneously mentioned the date as May the 20th was doubtless a mere inadvertence.... They all had in mind the same occasion"—May 31, the date of the Mecklenburg Resolves.[24]

For Mecklenburgers these were fighting words, but worse was to come. To further prime an already incendiary mix, volume one of Ashe's *History* had been published in 1908 by Charles Van Noppen, the same Van Noppen who had earlier denounced the elderly matrons of the Colonial Dames for their "stupidity." This was political dynamite. Parents were outraged. Being outraged, they wrote or visited their elected officials and let their outrage be known. As it happened, the speaker of the house at the time was A.W. Graham, the son of former governor William A. Graham, who had been the principal speaker at the massive 1875 anniversary commemoration and was a direct descendent of both Major John Davidson and General Joseph Graham, principal witnesses to the MecDec, and Mecklenburg heroes. So when W.C. Dowd, state representative from Mecklenburg and publisher of the *Charlotte News*, moved that the act permitting the purchase and dissemination of Ashe's *History* be recalled and reconsidered by the general assembly, his motion quickly passed 56 to 39. The MecDecers had won the day.[25]

Time had not yet been called in the Ashe vs. Graham round, however. In a pamphlet directed at Graham in response to the general assembly vote, Ashe claimed that Graham's father, the ex-governor, had changed his mind and become a MecDec skeptic just before his death. This was a blood libel in the Graham family. Speaker Graham responded that his father had "never changed his views, [and] that he died in the full faith and assurance that the patriots of Mecklenburg did make a Declaration of Independence on May 20, 1775." Graham objected to ongoing proposals to remove the date from the state flag, which he described as a "mutilation," and intimated darkly that corporate interests were behind the publication of Ashe's *History*.[26] Meanwhile, May 20 commemorations flourished in Charlotte.

"GREATEST MAY TWENTIETH IN CHARLOTTE HISTORY" predicted the *Charlotte Observer* in all uppercase letters in a banner headline on Sunday, May 14, 1916: "Program for Three Days Includes Events That Will Eclipse All Former Celebrations; BEST WILL COME LAST; Address of President Wilson, His Reception and Pageantry of Parade All on Last Day."[27]

Just before ten o'clock on a warm Saturday morning, on May 20, 1916, Charlotte mayor T.L. Kirkpatrick and a handful of other dignitaries waited anxiously at the Southern Railroad station in Charlotte. Ties were adjusted and readjusted, handwritten greeting notes read and reread, sweaty hands wrung over and over. A line of cavalrymen sat on horseback nearby,

The *Charlotte Observer* proclaimed President Wilson's visit on May 20, 1916, "the greatest event in North Carolina history." Four sitting presidents would attend the Mecklenburg Declaration ceremonies in Charlotte (Taft, Wilson, Eisenhower, and Ford) (courtesy of the Robinson-Spangler Carolina Room, Charlotte-Mecklenburg Public Library).

their backs rigid, staring straight ahead under the hot mid-morning Carolina sun, waiting to escort the president and his party to the reviewing stand on College Street.

By the morning of Wilson's arrival, the Mecklenburg Declaration celebrations had been going on for two days, beginning Thursday at nine in the morning with three separate brass bands playing in downtown Charlotte. An hour later, Lakewood Park opened for visitors, boasting a "well stocked zoo" with "wild animals," as well as "boating, dancing and numerous other attractions." For the more sporting minded, a morning baseball game between Asheville and the Horner Military School was scheduled, then more band concerts, more mid–afternoon baseball (Greensboro vs. Charlotte at Wearn Field), a final nighttime band, and finally, at nine o'clock that evening, "Payne's spectacular fireworks." And this was just day one.[28]

If the Charlotte crowds were worn out by the combination of boating, baseball, bands and fireworks, it was not apparent, for two days later they began gathering along Tryon Street in downtown to catch a glimpse of the main attraction — the president himself. President Wilson's arrival, it was reported, was met with "pageantry without parallel in the history of Southern celebrations," as evidenced by a "mammoth parade five miles long," winding its way past the president's reviewing stand. Brass bands, bagpipes, fifes and drums "in volume and quality like none ever heard here before" filled the air "with melody and patriotic sentiment."[29] Waiting to receive them were the governors of South Carolina and Virginia; various prominent Mecklenburg citizens, including Heriot Clarkson, a local Charlotte lawyer acting as master of ceremonies; and the Revered A.A. McGeachy, pastor of Second Presbyterian Church, there to deliver the invocation. North Carolina governor Locke Craig, who with his staff had arrived the day before to a seventeen-gun salute, was given the honor of introducing President Wilson. After pleasantries and handshakes were exchanged with the tall, aloof and aristocratic president, himself a fellow Presbyterian and Southerner, Wilson was given the keys to the city by Mayor Kirkpatrick.

For an hour and a half, these spectators waved cheerfully, or nodded solemnly, as marching bands, schoolchildren, boy scouts and army troops paraded by in an ongoing spectacle. The British *Manchester Guardian* reported a "huge assemblage" for the presidents' speech.[30] It was, reported the local paper, "easily the greatest event ever held in North Carolina." This was exaggerated boosterism, perhaps, but who would argue with it? The second presidential visit to Charlotte — a city of only a few thousand people — in ten years was pretty impressive and demonstrated the resolve (so to speak) of the pro–MecDec crowd.

These forces clearly had the momentum, at least locally, and while they did, they searched high and low for the key that could unlock the riddle: the missing document itself. "Declaration Reported Unearthed in London," announced the *Charlotte Observer* on January 29, 1917. A solider in the U.S. Army in France had written his parents that he had found a "true copy" of the Mecklenburg Declaration of Independence in London. The soldier promised to "find out more" about the document, and additional details were "awaited with interest." The article ended with a note of caution, however: "The document, drafted May 20, 1775, has been several times reported to have been found, and because the reports each time turned out to be false, a complete investigation will have to be made before too much credence is now attached to any report."[31] This, too, proved to be another false alarm. Nothing came of this lead; like so many others, it proved to be a dead-end.

The searchers were undeterred, and more "definitive proof" continued to be found. "Mecklenburg Declaration: Official Recognition of it Discovered in Two Ancient Law Licenses in 1828 and 1829," noted one article.[32] "Proof of Mecklenburg Declaration Is Found in Old Law Book, Attested by Old Citizens," reported the *Charlotte Observer* on May 31, 1939.[33] Another article in February 28, 1950, announced that someone "Digs Up Proof in Two Books."[34] "Those Doubting Thomases who disbelieve the story of the Mecklenburg Declaration of Independence need to harken to W.C. Allen," began the article. Allen, then ninety years old, "claims he has discovered proof of the signing of the Mecklenburg Declaration May 20, 1775 ... after a seven year hunt." Allen *did* have proof, but his "discoveries" were references to the Mecklenburg Declaration in Lossing's *Pictorial Fieldnotes of the American Revolution* published in 1850; this was nothing new and certainly nothing definitive.

When the leads dried up, the Mecklenburg advocates fell back on bald assertion, attempting to bludgeon the skeptics into submission. "Mecklenburg Declaration Opponents 'Put on Spot,'" reported the *Charlotte Observer* on May 7, 1939: "Discovery of Long Lost 'Davie Copy' Stirs Widespread Discussion — Supporters Jubilant; Opponents Unconvinced — Many Questions Answered."[35] Other headlines promised breakthroughs in the controversy: "Strong Evidence Favors Meck Dec"[36]; "Witnesses Would Swear Meck Dec Is Real"[37]; "Mecklenburg Declaration Now Declared Authentic."[38]

In each case, the evidence proved to be less than definitive upon closer examination. While the search for the missing declaration went on, the commemorations continued. In 1953, President Eisenhower became the third president to visit Charlotte for the celebrations. Lady Bird Johnson, the wife of President Lyndon Johnson, attended in 1968, and President Gerald Ford in 1975. Despite the star-power, however, the May 20 commemorations began to lose steam. "Battles Over Mecklenburg Declaration Are Nothing New," one paper blasély reported in May 1955[39]: "Public discussion of the May 20, 1775, Declaration has been dormant for so long that most people had forgotten the subject's explosive potential." "Few besides those with a hankering for historic detail had any reason to remember the long record of 'the great controversy,' admitted alike by ardent advocates and seasoned skeptics to be 'the most mooted question' in the history of the American Revolution." What the article didn't say, but what was becoming increasingly apparent, was that few cared about the subject anymore. Quietly, the Mecklenburg Controversy began to fade from popular view.

The world had moved on. Issues of states' rights — and bragging rights over one state's relative prominence in the American Revolution, which ultimately was the crux of the emotional resonance of the controversy — were quaint, anachronistic and outdated. The civil rights struggle of the 1960s — some important battles of which, such as forced busing, were fought in Charlotte itself— led to reevaluations of early American history, not only of the Civil War era, but of the Revolutionary period as well. For many, May 20, being a Southern celebration, had negative associations with the Confederacy, Jim Crow, and segregated water fountains. After all, North Carolina had seceded from the Union on May 20, 1861, and the date May 20, 1775, had appeared on many Civil War Confederate battle flags and was on the state flag itself. Many of the actors in the May Convention were slave owners, including Polk and McKnitt. The Mecklenburg Declaration was no longer in tune with the times.

This was certainly political correctness but with some justification. Historical commemorations — especially of the Civil War — became suspect, even hijacked in many cases by extreme conservative or racist movements. Phrases such as "heritage" were perceived as racist code words. Historical symbols, in particular the display of the Confederate battle flag, whether at public buildings or old cemeteries, had turned into divisive political issues. True, the Mecklenburg Declaration had little to do with any of this, but it was a *symbol* and one endowed with other historical associations, not all of them appealing. Fairly or not, the MecDec became collateral damage in the wholesale devaluation and dismissal of Southern history.

By the 1980s, the May 20 commemorations had become unfashionable, even embarrassing. The ideal of Charlotte as a "New South" city was in vogue. Old buildings were torn down with zeal. Financial-services-driven prosperity, tall shiny skyscrapers, and looping highways were the future. Local history was backwards-looking, provincial, déclassé. Added to this was the fact that the entire subject — its arguments, counterarguments, rebuttals and proofs — had simply grown too byzantine and arcane for most observers to follow.

What was the difference between the Mecklenburg Declaration and the Mecklenburg Resolves? Why were there two dates? Who were all these Alexanders and Davidsons, with weird names like Hezekiah and Ephraim? Who could keep track of all this, and why would someone want to? It was all too much to digest. As the years passed, the various elements of the story mixed together into a fact puddle. A natural tendency developed to simply discount the entire story as a hoax.

For two hundred years the controversy had in part continued to exist because of the ongoing public commemoration of May 20 as a public holiday in Mecklenburg County. But with waning interest in the subject, time was running out for May 20. Efforts to remove the date from the state flag and seal were attempted but were beaten back. (In March 1971, "enraged" members of the Mecklenburg house delegation defeated a bill in the general assembly to remove the date from the state seal.[40])

But, in the new political environment of the 1980s and 1990s, with the desire to add Martin Luther King Jr. Day as a new holiday, May 20 was jettisoned. On Monday, February 1, 1982, in a contentious three to two vote, the Mecklenburg County Board of Commissioners voted to remove May 20 as an official Mecklenburg County holiday. Elimination of the public commemoration validated in many minds a basic belief: It had been a myth all along.

Although flagging, the story would not die. It was kept alive by the historical memory of a handful of citizens, many of them direct descendants of Thomas Polk, Hezekiah Alexander, John Davidson and Joseph Graham and others with no personal connection to Mecklenburg but a deep respect and affection for local history. To the descendants, the story was not only a matter of family pride but a personal, and deeply emotional, matter. Their forebears had been the first to declare independence from Great Britain. They were, as the families said, the descendants of *signers* (nearly 1,500 such descendants, as of 2013).

They attended Hopewell, Sugaw Creek or Steele Creek Presbyterian churches, where they passed the graves of their ancestors every Sunday. They walked the fields of Alexandriana, McKnitt's old plantation, where as recently as the mid–1960s there remained an old slave cabin, tilted, weathered, silent, and fading into an anonymous pile of wooden ruin, like so many abandoned tobacco barns or old cabins on narrow two-lane roads in the countryside. They drove up Tryon Street past Sugaw Creek Presbyterian Church, where Craighead once preached in the open fields, or down Old Steele Creek Road where General Robert Irwin and Humphrey Hunter lay buried. Each May 20 the great-great-great grandchildren, grandnephews or grandnieces of the Polks, Craigheads and Alexanders would stand in what was now called Independence Square in the busy center of Charlotte beneath the shadow of the Bank of America headquarters. There, surrounded by reenactors in Revolutionary-era attire, someone dressed as Thomas Polk would read the five stanzas of the Mecklenburg Declaration (*not* the Mecklenburg Resolves) while the sound of fifes and drums accompanied the crash of muskets and cannon and the shouts of "Huzzah!" in commemoration of the event. But the crowds grew smaller every year. "Traditional County Holiday Dying Out," reported the *Charlotte News* in 1973.[41] By the late 1990s, young investment bankers and lawyers, many of them transplanted New Yorkers or Ohioans, rushed past the old men in strange attire. They didn't know or care what the noon commemoration was all about.

"Every May 20th a small group of dedicated citizens from the Mecklenburg Historical Association, the local historic society, gathers at the monument that was erected in 1898 in Uptown Charlotte by the defenders of the document," observed local historian Dan Morrill. "It is a poignant scene. Most Charlotteans drive by in their sleek automobiles and take no notice of what is transpiring. Someone reads the 'Meck. Dec.,' and a wreath is laid.... Then the faithful disperse and resume the routine of daily living, only to return for another brief ceremony 365 days later."[42] By 2000, the Mecklenburg Controversy was effectively over. Except for a handful of die-hards, the advocates of the Mecklenburg Declaration of Independence had surrendered, unconditionally. The Mecklenburg Controversy had fizzled out.

PART V. CLUES AND EXPLANATIONS

20

Red Herrings
Fraud, Forgery and the
Case Against Jefferson

Every one must be persuaded, at least all who have been minute observers of style,
that one of these papers has borrowed from the other, for they are identical, not in
one instance, but in several, and not in single words only, but in phrases composed of
many.

— George Tucker, *Life of Thomas Jefferson*, 1837

From the beginning of the Mecklenburg Controversy, a central theme was the striking similarity of certain phrases it contained to those found in the Declaration of Independence of July 4, 1776. The historian George Tucker, in his two-volume *Life of Thomas Jefferson*, pointed in particular to the second clause ("dissolve the political bands") and the third clause ("our lives, our fortunes and our most sacred honor") of the Mecklenburg Declaration as being so similar to the Declaration of Independence that "we cannot suppose it to be the result of accident."[1]

John Adams agreed that this was no "accident," and was blunt in his conclusion of what these similarities implied. "Either these resolutions are a plagiarism from Mr. Jefferson's Declaration of Independence," John Adams argued, "or Mr. Jefferson's Declaration of Independence is a plagiarism from those resolutions." Jefferson "must have seen" the Mecklenburg Declaration, Adams wrote, "for he has copied the spirit, the sense, and the expressions of it verbatim, into his Declaration of the 4th of July, 1776."[2] There was no other plausible explanation of the facts.

Later writers agreed with Adams. "This remarkable document, as will be readily recognized by all readers, is too close a paraphrase of the immortal Declaration of Independence of July 4, 1776, to admit of any other conclusion than that one of them was borrowed from the other," one editorialist wrote. "Which is the borrower and which the borrowed is the question to be settled."[3]

Supporters of the Mecklenburg Declaration alleged that Jefferson was the guilty party, as Adams had suggested. This ignited a series of responses from Jefferson defenders, as well as the deniers, the most notorious of whom was Charles Phillips, discussed in detail earlier. This group contended that it was clear that the "spurious" text had been cobbled together

190

by John McKnitt Alexander, or perhaps his son, Dr. Joseph McKnitt Alexander. The Alexanders' motives in writing the document were either benign or nefarious, depending on your point of view. Some believed McKnitt was an old man who in a fit of patriotic nostalgia "misremembered" the text and confused it with the national declaration. Others, such as Salley (egged on by Phillips), saw a sinister and deliberate hoax by Joseph Alexander. Either way, the skeptics were united in their belief that the Mecklenburg Declaration, as Phillips put it, was a "suspicious paper on its very face."[4]

If the issue was whether Thomas Jefferson or one of the Alexanders had stolen from the other, to many the better argument was clearly with the Jeffersonians. Jefferson was a founder of the country, a former president and an icon, revered throughout the world. Certainly, to his supporters at least, he was above suspicion (of course Adams, who knew him better, had disagreed). Still, if Jefferson said he had never heard of the Mecklenburg Declaration, it was reasonable to take him at his word. And more to the point, there was absolutely no evidence that linked Jefferson to the Mecklenburg document, making such a charge against Jefferson absurd. Or was there?

The *Cape Fear Mercury* was a newspaper published in Wilmington, North Carolina, during the Revolutionary period. It was one of a handful of newspapers that circulated in the backcountry. Governor Martin had objected to some "treasonable resolves" published in the *Cape Fear Mercury* in the summer of 1775 and had sent a copy to his superiors in London. (Martin had referred to reports in the same newspaper on a number of other occasions.) In a letter of June 30, 1775, to the Earl of Dartmouth, Governor Martin wrote, "The Resolves of the Committee of Mecklenburgh, *which your Lordship will find in the enclosed News Paper* [emphasis added], surpass all the horrid and treasonable publications that the inflammatory spirits of this Continent have yet produced."[5] Martin further mentioned in this letter that the resolves he had seen "were sent off by express to the Congress at Philadelphia as soon as they were passed in the Committee," so it was clear they were important.

This was the smoking gun supporters of the Mecklenburg Declaration were looking for. They seemed to have a contemporary record of the actual declaration. Now all they needed to do was to find that newspaper. If they could get their hands on the "enclosed newspaper" that Martin sent to Dartmouth and it contained a copy of the Mecklenburg Declaration of Independence, the controversy would be settled once and for all. Historians believed that the "enclosed News Paper" was an edition of the *Cape-Fear Mercury* likely published between June 21 and June 30, 1775.[6] As with all official communications, Martin's letter was recorded and preserved by the British government. The letter of June 30, along with the enclosed newspaper with the "treasonable" resolutions of Mecklenburg, was designated Dispatch No. 34 and placed in the British Public Records Office in London.

In the mid–nineteenth century, Dispatch 34 was located. But, although the letter and other enclosures were in the file, the "enclosed News Paper" was missing.[7] On the back of the last page of the letter in the file, there was a pencil notation: "Printed Paper taken out by Mr. Turner for Mr. Stevenson, August 15th, 1837." The newspaper had been removed for Andrew Stevenson, the United States ambassador to Great Britain. Why had Stevenson had Turner search out this newspaper in the Public Records Office for him? The year 1837 was at the height of the Mecklenburg Controversy. Clearly, Stevenson had acted either at his own initiative or on instructions from Washington.

It seems possible that Stevenson could have removed the paper to protect Jefferson's reputation. If the newspaper existed and contained the Mecklenburg Declaration of Independence, that would prove its existence and establish its precise wording. It would rekindle the argument that Jefferson had lifted passages from it. Of course, even it if existed it could be argued that Jefferson had never seen the Mecklenburg Declaration, but it would destroy the case made by the doubters that it was, as Jefferson had said, "spurious." The suggestion that Stevenson, the U.S. ambassador to the Court of St. James, may have hidden or destroyed the newspaper is shocking, but Stevenson's involvement raises certain suspicions. As the writer Graham pointed out in 1898:

> Mr. Stevenson was a contemporary of Thomas Jefferson and no doubt his friend, as he was a citizen of Virginia, born in 1784, belonged to the same political party, and was a prominent member of the legislature and Congress during the last twenty years of the ex-president's life, and minister to England from 1836 to 1841. For what purpose he borrowed the *Cape Fear Mercury* we are not informed, as he never published the contents or told anyone he had seen the paper.[8]

It has been suggested that Stevenson had been asked by someone (possibly even President Van Buren, according to Merrill Peterson in *The Jefferson Image in the American Mind*) to search the British archives for evidence which would clear Jefferson of the charge of plagiarism. However, according to one history, "nothing was ever reported from Stevenson on the subject."[9] This was very strange. If Stevenson had found that the *Cape Fear Mercury* did not contain the Mecklenburg Declaration, but rather contained the Mecklenburg Resolves (or even for that matter something entirely different), that would have settled the matter once and for all. As an advocate of Jefferson, he no doubt would have reported it quickly and widely. But Stevenson never said a word.

Supporters of the Mecklenburg Declaration found it "very remarkable" that, despite the public discussion, "nowhere can we find that Mr. Stevenson participated in the debate, although he had obtained information from the *Cape Fear Mercury* that would completely settle the dispute as to plagiarism on the part of his friend Mr. Jefferson."[10] It was also noted that after his stint in London Stevenson went on to be rector of the University of Virginia, the university founded, of course, by Jefferson. Stevenson died in 1857 but over the course of twenty years he "never broke his silence on this subject."[11] Stevenson had taken the paper for some purpose — but what was it? His involvement and subsequent silence was all very puzzling.

After Ambassador Stevenson's death in 1857, the historian Wheeler wrote to his son, John White Stevenson, himself a prominent politician, inquiring about the mysterious disappearance of this key piece of evidence in the Mecklenburg Controversy. Wheeler was informed that "though the missing copy could not be found, dispatches and other memoranda among the deceased minister's papers indicated that the copy had once been in his possession."[12] Others attempted to find the missing document. A newspaper correspondent for the *New York Herald* visited John White Stevenson (then a senator for the state of Kentucky) at his home in 1875 to inquire about the paper. The following conversation took place:

> "I have my father's papers," he [Stevenson] said, directly [when] the object of my visit was stated.
> "And may I inquire their condition?"
> "Contrarily to what you may have been informed, they have not remained unopened since their return from London."

"They have been examined then?"

"Yes," replied the Senator, "They are all in accurate order, and the contents of every box is known. Indeed, they were all methodically copied out and bound under the directions of my father during his life."

"You say, sir, that the contents of the boxes are known?"

"Yes, sir."

"Can you, then, give me any information of the paper noted at the Colonial Office, as withdrawn by the consent or under the responsibility of your father — the report of the Royal Governor of North Carolina on the transactions of May 31, 1775?"

"That document," said the Senator, "is not among my father's papers. But in its stead is a memorandum which states that though the paper was withdrawn under the sanction of my father it was not withdrawn for his use, but for the use of another person whose name is there given."

"And you remember that name, of course?"

"No; I have forgotten it."[13]

At that point, the trail went cold. The newspaper Stevenson removed from the file, for whom and for what purpose has never been discovered. Skeptics argued that it didn't matter. Salley argued with persuasive logic that the missing paper would have contained the Mecklenburg Resolves anyway, not the Mecklenburg Declaration.

Be that as it may, to any neutral observer the circumstances of the paper's disappearance are suspicious. And to the Mecklenburg Declaration supporters, it was a clear act of bad faith and destruction of evidence. To them it was clear that Stevenson had examined Dispatch No. 34, found that the *Cape Fear Mercury* did in fact contain the Mecklenburg Declaration, and destroyed the evidence. This could not be proven of course, but the surrounding facts were deeply troubling. Whether the newspaper Stevenson removed contained a copy of the Mecklenburg Resolves (as the skeptics claim) or the only extant copy of the Mecklenburg Declaration (as some have argued) may never be known. By the same token, whether Stevenson's loss of the paper was simply carelessness or something more sinister cannot be proven either. But, as with Phillips' suppression of the Davie Copy, to supporters of the story it seemed to show a lack of good faith on the part of the skeptics.

In 1905, the story of the *Cape Fear Mercury* took a bizarre turn. That July, *Collier's* magazine published an article by Dr. S. Millington Miller in which he claimed to have discovered the missing newspaper. According to Miller he had purchased Stevenson's papers a year before. In them he had discovered the missing newspaper. The *Collier's* article included a picture of the lost paper, which clearly showed the text of the Mecklenburg Declaration — not the Mecklenburg Resolves. It appeared that the mystery had been solved, and the existence of the Mecklenburg Declaration proven. The definitive proof that Jefferson had demanded was finally in hand.

The celebration was brief however. There was something fishy about the whole affair. Miller first claimed to have purchased a bulk of papers from Stevenson's estate, but later his story changed. He also "showed a good knowledge of the chemistry of producing blots, old ink-stains, and paper discolorations —*too* good a knowledge," in fact.[14] Finally, to an expert eye, his version of the *Cape Fear Mercury* had material differences in numbering, type style and other important details from newspapers of the era. The historian Salley summarized these inaccuracies in a pamphlet that comprehensively proved Miller's discovery was fake.[15]

Undeterred, Miller contacted some prominent Charlotteans and offered to sell them the newspaper for $5,000. They arranged to meet in a Baltimore hotel to discuss his offer.

In what must have been a tense meeting, they grilled Miller on his paper. Where had he found it? How did he know it was real? And what of Salley's article concluding it was a forgery? Miller evaded and obfuscated but insisted it was genuine. They asked Miller if he would surrender the paper to them temporarily in order for them to have it examined by an independent expert. Miller knew the game was up and agreed, turning over the "missing" copy with an agreement that they would get back to him in a few weeks. Less than a week later, Miller privately met with Worthington Ford, chief of the Manuscripts Division of the Library of Congress with, lo and behold, *another* copy of the lost *Cape Fear Mercury*. Another awkward meeting ensued, and again Miller departed. This time, however, Miller and his forgery disappeared entirely and were never heard from again.

Miller's *Cape Fear Mercury* hoax became a public relations debacle for the supporters of the Mecklenburg Declaration. Although Miller's attempted financial fraud had nothing to do with their support of the Mecklenburg Declaration per se, in the public mind the matter was again associated with the word "hoax." Disbelievers argued that the *Cape Fear Mercury* episode was only the latest attempt to pass off a fake document by advocates of the Mecklenburg Declaration. They pointed out that several earlier efforts had been made to pass off "copies" of the document as originals. For example, Dr. Ramsey (McKnitt's grandson), a well-known writer and public figure, had created a copy called the "Tennessee Copy" of the Mecklenburg Declaration, probably around 1875, complete with Greek columns and modern type-face. Some zealous supporters got carried away, and claimed that the copy had been distributed prior to 1800 and was thus a genuine copy of the document, but this was untrue.[16]

Similarly, in 1906, a well-meaning supporter produced a facsimile of the Mecklenburg Declaration with "signatures" at the bottom. The signatures were copied from actual historical documents, but of course the document was a composite. Unlike Miller's effort, this was not an attempt at fraud but was clearly intended as a commemorative piece and not as proof of anything. However, the outcry from the skeptics was deafening. There the Mecklenburgers go again, they said, manufacturing evidence of the nonexistent document. The bad blood between the two sides was such that every misunderstanding became an excuse to cry fraud or forgery.

The accusations and counter-accusations of lies and deceit—and side issues such as the missing *Cape Fear Mercury*—perpetuated a silly argument that has clouded the issue about the veracity of the Mecklenburg Declaration to this day—namely, that the text of the Mecklenburg Declaration and the National Declaration were so similar, and so unique, that the documents had to have some interrelationship. According to this view, it was impossible for the two documents to have been developed independently of one another. If you believed this, either Jefferson or McKnitt had to have been a villain in the story. Supporters of Jefferson passionately defended him from the charge of plagiarism, and of course supporters did the same for McKnitt. But the trap that both parties fell into was the belief that *someone* must have copied *something* from the other. As one historian in 1874 argued, phrases such as *dissolve the political bands* and *lives, fortune and sacred honor* "were too many in number and peculiar in structure to have been accidental coincidences."[17]

But was this necessarily true? A more plausible explanation was that both documents used language that was common to the period and that neither document needed to have any relationship with the other in order to be genuine. A closer examination shows this

DECLARATION OF INDEPENDENCE

BY THE

Citizens of Mecklenburg County, North Carolina,

MAY 20, 1775.

In conformity to an order issued by the Colonel of Mecklenburg County, in North Carolina, a CONVENTION, vested with unlimited powers, met at Charlotte, in said County, on the Nineteenth day of May, 1775, when ABRAHAM ALEXANDER was chosen Chairman, and JOHN McKNITT ALEXANDER Secretary. After a free and full discussion of the object of the Convention, it was

UNANIMOUSLY RESOLVED,

I. THAT whosoever, directly or indirectly, abetted, or in any way, form or manner, countenanced the unchartered and dangerous invasion of our RIGHTS, as claimed by Great Britain, is an *ENEMY TO THIS COUNTRY*, to *AMERICA* and to the **INHERENT** and **INALIENABLE RIGHTS** of **MAN**

II. RESOLVED, THAT WE, the CITIZENS OF MECKLENBURG COUNTY, do hereby Dissolve the Political Bands which have connected us to the *mother country*, and hereby **ABSOLVE** ourselves from all **ALLEGIANCE** to the British crown, and ABJURE ALL POLITICAL CONNECTION, CONTRACT OR ASSOCIATION, with that nation who have wantonly trampled on our *RIGHTS & LIBERTIES* & inhumanly shed the INNOCENT BLOOD of American Patriots at Lexington.

III. RESOLVED, THAT **WE DO HEREBY DECLARE OURSELVES A FREE & INDEPENDENT PEOPLE**, ARE, and of right OUGHT TO BE, a *sovereign and self-governing association* under the CONTROL of NO POWER other than that of our GOD, and the General Government of Congress; to the maintenance of which *INDEPENDENCE*, we SOLEMNLY PLEDGE to each other, our MUTUAL CO-OPERATION, our LIVES, our FORTUNES and our MOST SACRED HONOR.

ABRAHAM ALEXANDER, Chairman.
J. M. ALEXANDER, Secretary.

Adam Alexander,	Henry Downs,	Duncan Ochletree,
Hezekiah Alexander,	John Flenniken,	John Phifer,
Ezra Alexander,	John Ford,	Thomas Polk,
Charles Alexander,	William Graham,	Ezekiel Polk,
Waitstill Avery,	James Harris,	Benjamin Patton,
Ephraim Brevard,	Robert Irwin,	John Queary,
Hezekiah J. Balch,	William Kennon,	David Reese,
Richard Barry,	Matthew Mc'Clure,	Zacheus Wilson, sen.,
John Davidson,	Neill Morrison,	William Wilson.
William Davidson,	Samuel Martin,	

MAY.   1775.

AERE PERENNIUS.   DIEU ET MONDROIT.

Fac Simile of the oldest publication of the Mecklenburg Declaration of Independence.

COLUMBUS PRINTING WORKS, COLUMBUS, OHIO.

The "Tennessee Copy" of the Mecklenburg Declaration. This commemorative copy led some to believe it was a pre–1800 copy of the document and critics to cry forgery (Wilson Library, University of North Carolina at Chapel Hill).

explanation is entirely plausible. First of all, forgotten today (and even forgotten during the period when the controversy began) is that the use of famous, classical phrases was an expected and routine form of communication among educated men in the Revolutionary period. Higher education was mainly a study of the classics in the original languages as well as in translation. By the time a man had finished Oxford or Harvard or William and Mary, they were intimately familiar with these texts (plus some of the contemporary ones such as Addison's *Cato*) and able to pepper their conversation with them. Educated men of the period, well versed in Latin and Greek, had a common repertoire of ancient phrases and ideas (both classical and biblical) that they used as a sort of linguistic shorthand. What sounds so high-flown to us today was at the time simply the common language of educated men. This point was lost on generations of historians, such as Tucker or Phillips. For example, the first resolution of the Mecklenburg Declaration uses the phrase "inherent and inalienable rights of man." Charles Phillips, arch-priest of the skeptics, mocked this phrase as being entirely inauthentic. "These men did not in 1775 vapour on about 'lives and sacred honour,'" he wrote.[18] Presbyterians, he stated in another letter, "in the backwoods of N.C. were not apt to blow off steam about *the inherent and inalienable rights of man*. Jefferson brought that stuff from Paris."[19]

But Phillips was entirely wrong. Variations of the phrase "inherent and inalienable rights" were common currency during the period. During the Stamp Act protests of 1765 the Massachusetts legislature sent a circular inviting all the colonies to send delegates to a congress at New York. Representatives from nine colonies attended and adopted a "Declaration of Rights and Grievances." The prelude of this declaration noted "it our indispensable duty to make the following declarations, of our humble opinions, respecting the *most essential rights and liberties* of the colonists." The second resolution in this declaration read, "His Majesty's liege subjects in these colonies are entitled to all the *inherent rights and privileges* of his natural born subjects within the kingdom of Great Britain." Note that this phrase appears three times, in different variations, in this document that precedes the Mecklenburg Declaration by a decade.

Nor was this phraseology confined to the towns and cities of New England. The Fairfax, Virginia resolutions of July 1774, referenced the "privileges of a free people and the natural rights of mankind." In a letter of November 1775 from Silas Deane to James Hogg describing the settlement of the Province of Carolina, Deane pointed out the duty of government was "to secure the *general and inalienable rights of man* to the settlers."[20] The Virginia Declaration of Rights of June 1776, which also preceded the national Declaration of Independence by a month, used the phrases "all men are by nature equally *free and independent*, and have certain *inherent rights*, of which, when they enter into a state of society, they cannot, by any compact, deprive or divest their posterity." (Similarly, the phraseology *are, and of right ought to be* may sound unique to our modern ears, but in the period it was boilerplate. To give but one example, the Declaratory Act of March 1766, which followed repeal of the Stamp Act but reasserted Parliament's right to tax the colonies, read in part, "the said colonies and plantations in *America* have been, *are, and of right ought to be,* subordinate unto, and dependent upon the imperial crown and Parliament of *Great Britain.*")

Not only that, but the phrases *inalienable rights* and *free and independent* can both be shown to have been used in Mecklenburg County at this time. In a petition from

Mecklenburg County to Governor Tryon in 1769 asking for repeal of the Marriage and Vestry Acts, the Scots-Irish settlers "declare[d] ourselves entitled to have and enjoy *all the rights and privileges* of his Majesty's subjects in Great Britain" and argued that the Marriage Act "obstructs the *natural and inalienable right* of marriage."[21]

In September 1775 — just four months after the Mecklenburg Declaration and nearly a year before the declaration of July 4, 1776 — instructions (thought to be written by Ephraim Brevard, also believed to be one of the authors of the Mecklenburg Declaration) were given to Mecklenburg's delegates to the First Provincial Congress meeting in Hillsboro. Section one reads, "You are instructed to vote that the late province of North Carolina *is & of right ought to be, a free and independent State.*"[22] Section two provides the following: "You are instructed to vote for the Execution of a civil Government under the Authority of the People for the future security of all the Rights, Privileges & Prerogatives of the State, and *the private, natural & unalienable rights* of the constituting Members therefore, either as men or Christians." (The influence of Alexander Craighead could still be seen in the instructions as well; section fourteen called upon them to "oppose the toleration of popish idolatrous worship.")

Similarly, in neighboring Rowan County, the committee of safety resolved in June 1775 that "by the Constitution of our Government *we are a free People*, not subject to be taxed by any power but that of that happy Constitution which limits both Sovereignty and Allegiance."[23] And not coincidentally, surely, a year later, point one of the "Instructions to the Delegates from Mecklenburg to the Provincial Congress at Halifax, N.C. in November 1776" stated, "you shall consent to and approve the Declaration of the Continental Congress declaring the thirteen United Colonies *free and independent States.*" So much for Phillips' snarky comment about backwoods hicks.

A similar mistaken assumption arises around the second clause of the Mecklenburg Declaration, which states that they "*hereby dissolve the political bands* which have connected us to the Mother Country, and hereby *absolve ourselves from all allegiance to the British Crown.*" Jefferson's biographer Tucker concluded that the "accidental agreement of two minds in thought and expression," by which he meant the similarity in word choice between this and the National Declaration, "can scarcely be conceived."[24] But in fact the similarities are quite easily conceived. The verb "dissolve" was commonly used to describe political relationships in the period, as many historians have since pointed out. In the summer of 1775, the neighboring county of Rowan adopted resolutions resolving, among other things, "a general Association ... ought to be entered into and not *dissolved* till the just Rights of the said Colonies are restored to them." A year earlier, Fairfax County, Virginia, had accused the British government of attempting to "*dissolve* the original compact" between the colonists and Great Britain. *Dissolve* was a common verb in the context of political associations. Intellectual property theft is not necessary to explain its use in the Mecklenburg Declaration. Similarly it was the standard practice (prior to the Revolution) for resolutions to reiterate royal "allegiance" in the first or second paragraph. A resolution rescinding that allegiance would do so in the first or second paragraph, as in the case of the Mecklenburg Declaration. The language is quite expected.[25]

But the phrase that Tucker and others found most extraordinary in the Mecklenburg Declaration was "*our mutual co-operation, our lives, our fortunes, and our most sacred honor.*" It was this expression, he concluded, that must have been the result of "a sort of patriotic forgery."[26] But is forgery a necessary explanation? The historian James Welling, a skeptic of the Mecklenburg Declaration, pointed out, "[A]s between Mr. Jefferson and the author of the Mecklenburg Declaration, the only question that can arise ... relates to the origin of the famous phrase in which they both enunciate the pledge of 'lives, fortune and sacred honor.' And from this phrase we ought to rule out the words, 'our lives and fortunes,' for the pledge of *these* was among the commonplaces of that time. It occurs *passim* in the political literature of 1775 and 1776."[27]

But if the entire Mecklenburg Controversy boiled down to whether or not the phrase "lives, fortune and sacred honor" (or even, for that matter, the phrase "sacred honor") was so original and distinct that it *must* have been plagiarized either from or by Jefferson (depending on your point of view) then there really wasn't much of a controversy at all. Even a cursory review of pro- and anti–British resolutions of the period proves the phrase "lives and fortune" was as common as grass, while "sacred" was routinely used in connection with descriptions of the sovereign, honor or of freedom generally. I will give but a few examples just from the Carolinas (emphasis added in each case):

> [We] are ready and Willing, at *the Expense of Our Lives and Fortunes* to defend, being fully convinced of the Oppressive and Arbitrary Tendency of a late Act of Parliament, imposing Stamp Duties on the Inhabitants of this Province....[28]
> — North Carolina Stamp Act Protest (1762)

> I shall endeavour to probe and to heal if possible by all such lenient applications as may best answer that purpose and be most consistent with the *sacred honor* and dignity of his Majesty's Government....[29]
> — Letter from Governor Josiah Martin to Wills Hill, Marquis of Downshire (April 12, 1772)

> We will bear true and faithful allegiance to His Majesty King George the third, and that we will ever at the *expence of our lives and fortunes*, defend and protect his *sacred person*, and the succession of the Crown to his Royal Issue....[30]
> — Halifax Resolves, North Carolina (August 1774)

> [I]n congress an association was signed by all the members present solemnly engaging their *lives and fortunes*....[31]
> — Circular letter to the inhabitants of South Carolina (June 1775)

> [W]e will go forth and be ready to sacrifice *our lives and fortunes* to secure her freedom and safety....[32]
> — Liberty Point Resolves, Wilmington, North Carolina (June 1775)

> [D]o solemnly engage to take up arms and risk *our lives and our fortunes* in maintaining the freedom of our country ... [and] we will continue in and *hold sacred* 'till a Reconciliation shall take place between Great Britain and America on Constitutional principles which we most ardently desire....[33]
> — Tryon Resolves, North Carolina (August 1775)

> Resolved, that we will at all times, whenever we are called upon for that purpose, maintain and defend at the *Expense of our Lives and Fortunes,* his Majesty's Right and Title to the Crown of Great Britain....[34]
> — Rowan Resolves, North Carolina (August 1775)

His Excellency Governor Martin, hath taken a very active and instrumental share in opposition to the means which have been adopted by this and the other United Colonies for their common safety, as well to disunite this from the rest as to weaken

the Efforts of the Inhabitants of North Carolina *to protect their Lives, Liberties and Properties* against any force which may be exerted to injure them....[35]
— Hillsboro Convention, North Carolina (August 1775)

We are truly invigorated with the warmest Zeal and Attachment to the British Constitution and Laws upon which our *Lives and fortunes* and the welfare of the Province now depend....[36]
— Address of inhabitants of Rowan and Surry Counties, North Carolina (circa 1775)

[G]o forth and be ready to sacrifice *our Lives and Fortunes* to secure Freedom and Safety....[37]
— South Carolina Committee of Safety (June 1775)

And so forth. Nor is it surprising that these phrases should recur in the national declaration. According to historian Pauline Maier, "The observation that Jefferson borrowed ideas from other writers was not original to the twentieth century. Richard Henry Lee, Jefferson recalled, said the Declaration had been 'copied from Locke's treatise on government,' and John Adams, in his 1822 letter to Timothy Pickering, asserted that there was 'not an idea in it, but what had been hackneyed in Congress for two years before.'"[38] Jefferson himself told James Madison in 1823 that he "did not consider it as any part of my charge to invent new ideas altogether, and to offer no sentiment which had ever been expressed before."[39] In other words, no one disputed whether the text of the national declaration was altogether unique or original. In fact, quite the opposite was true.

Admittedly, it could be argued that the incorporation of the phrase "lives and fortunes" with that of "sacred" (as in "sacred honor") was unique in the national declaration. But is the combination of such daily phrases (as shown above) "inconceivable," as Tucker and other historians allege? Of course not. Indeed, in 1775 the inhabitants of Anson County, adjacent to Mecklenburg, had come close to using the exact phrases side by side (but for the word "sacred"):

[I]t is solely upon the wisdom and virtue of that superior legislative might that the safety of our *lives and fortunes*, and the *honour* and welfare of this country, do most principally depend [emphasis added].[40]
— Address of inhabitants of Anson County, North Carolina (circa 1775)

In short, none of the phrases included in the Declaration of Independence was so unusual or uncommon at that time that it was implausible a group of educated men, using political phrases in regular circulation, could have composed something similar. It remains plausible today. The building blocks were there in the popular vocabulary of the age.[41]

Finally, and ironically, Tucker's defense of Jefferson from the charge of plagiarism was entirely redundant, not only because it was unnecessary, but also because Jefferson was not even the author of most of the phrases that led to the charges of plagiarism in the first place. Richard Henry Lee, a colleague of Jefferson and member of the drafting committee, is believed to have been responsible for the use of almost all of the phrases that the skeptics pointed to as evidence of theft.[42] Specifically, Lee is known to have drafted the following resolution on July 2, 1776: "Resolved, that these United Colonies are, and of right ought to be, free and independent States; that they are absolved from all allegiance to the British Crown; and that all political connection between them and the state of Great Britain is, and of right, ought to be, dissolved." It was this clause in particular that caused Adams to charge Jefferson with plagiarism upon reading the Mecklenburg Declaration. But Jefferson wasn't even the principal author of the passage in question. Only Adams' personal animosity and mistrust of Jefferson led him down this dead-end passage and triggered the entire later controversy.

As one critic put it, "those who have sought to find in the Mecklenburg Declaration a 'coigne of vantage' [position of advantage] from which to discharge their arrows at Mr. Jefferson's literary fame, have wasted their strength in an idle contention."[43] But the opposite was also true. The skeptics' contention that McKnitt had stolen passages from the declaration, either because he was old and confused or deliberately as a hoax, was just as speculative as the conspiracy theories involving Jefferson. It's entirely *possible* that the college-educated Presbyterian lawyers and writers of Mecklenburg (particularly Brevard, Balch and Kennon) *could* have written a document using many of the common phrases of the age and period. A theory of plagiarism for or against Jefferson was not necessary to account for these similarities.

In point of fact, neither the authors of the Mecklenburg Declaration nor Jefferson (nor Lee) need to have copied from the other. Without Adams' hysterical accusations, this theory might never have come up and certainly would not have taken on a life of its own. All in all, it was a red herring in the story of the Mecklenburg Declaration of Independence.

21

"Frey u. independent von England"
The Moravian Explanation

Now you remember as well as I do, that we had not a greater Tory in Congress than Hooper; that Hughes was very wavering, sometimes firm, sometimes feeble, according as the day was clear or cloudy.
        —Letter from Thomas Jefferson to John Adams, July 9, 1819

The strongest argument against the existence of the Mecklenburg Declaration is the lack of a single, unambiguous piece of paper that can be clearly dated before 1800. The "copy in an unknown hand" might be this piece of paper, but that can't be proven. McKnitt's "rough notes" might qualify, but they are badly torn, putting the date in question, and in them the year "1800" appears to have been written and then marked through.

This is important because the lack of a single piece of paper dating prior to 1800 — the year the originals were lost in a fire — is cited by skeptics as evidence that McKnitt must have written his account from memory and not from any original record. By the time the controversy commenced in 1831, all of the key participants except Major John Davidson and Captain James Jack were long dead, the surviving eyewitnesses very old, the original documents lost to fire, destroyed or mislaid. The British records — while conclusive about "unnatural rebellion" and "treason" in Mecklenburg County — were ambiguous as to exactly what had occurred. No secondary, impartial, unambiguous evidence existed to validate the later eyewitness accounts. If the skeptics were correct, what had occurred in Mecklenburg was a "conditional" act of rebellion — subject to reconciliation with the king — not a declaration of independence. Some even argued that the whole story was a local myth despite the proven existence of the Mecklenburg Resolves of May 31.

The whole controversy turned on the words "free and independent" alleged to have been used in the third resolution of the Mecklenburg Declaration. These words made the document a true declaration of independence rather than one of dozens of anti–British resolutions passed in the spring and summer of 1775. These words do not appear in the Mecklenburg Resolves, which is why critics argued that the resolves did not constitute a true declaration and thus were of marginal historical importance. Whether the people of the region had truly declared themselves "free and independent" or had done something less dramatic was the crux of the matter.

In September 1904, O.J. Lehman made a curious and possibly explosive discovery.

201

Lehman lived near present-day Winston-Salem. He fought in the Confederate army and after the Civil War formed a partnership with another veteran. Together, they opened two general trading stores, one of which was near the old Moravian settlement of Bethania. In 1879, Lehman and his partner built a steam-powered "new modern tobacco factory" that manufactured plug tobacco. As well as being a major business owner in the area, Lehman had an interest in local history and, because he lived in Bethania, a village in the region the Moravians called "Wachovia," he had unrivalled access to the original records of the German settlers.

In addition to being farmers and early settlers, Moravians were merchants and traders. In the eighteenth century a main "Wagon Road" ran through their settlements of Bethabara, Bethania and Salem, connecting them with the major commercial centers of the time. The Moravians traveled frequently, selling goods in Philadelphia, purchasing supplies in the port city of Charleston, or visiting Hillsboro and New Bern. As businessmen, they were well-informed. Being non–English dissenters, they tried to maintain a policy of neutrality as relations disintegrated between the American colonists and the British government. They kept methodical, detailed and well-written diaries and descriptions of current events in legible *Hochdeutsch*.

What Lehman found in 1904, although he likely did not know its significance, was called by the Moravians a *Beilage*, meaning historical sketch, or fragment. Such fragments included "[m]emoirs, accounts of special Church service, historical sketches" or other special or unique written accounts.[1] These were inserted, loose, between the pages of the diary — often undated and almost never signed.

The *Beilage* Lehman discovered was long — forty handwritten pages of tight German script, running forty-two lines per page. It was undated and unsigned, although in one passage it described an act of the assembly of 1783, suggesting that at least part of it was written after this date. It was written in German, but not entirely; several key words (particularly the word "independent") were in English:

> *Ich kan zu Ende des 1775stᵉⁿ Jahres nicht unangemerkt lassen, dass schon im Sommer selbigen Jahres, das ist im May, Juny, oder July, die County Mecklenburg in Nord Carolina sich für so frey u. independent von England declarirte, u. solche Einrichtung zur Verwaltung der Gesetze unter sich machte, als jamalen der Continental Congress hernach ins Ganze gethan. Dieser Congress aber sahe dieses Verfahren als zu frühzeitig an* [emphasis added].[2]

In English this read as follows:

> I cannot leave unmentioned at the end of the 1775th year that already in the summer of this year, that is in May, June, or July, the County of Mecklenburg in North Carolina declared itself free and independent of England, and made such arrangements for the administration of the laws among themselves, as later the Continental Congress made for all. This Congress, however, considered these proceedings premature.

Lehman's discovery was analyzed in an extended essay by Adelaide Fries, a Moravian scholar. Entitled "The Mecklenburg Declaration of Independence as Mentioned in Records of Wachovia," the essay was first published in the *Wachovia Moravian* in April 1906 and reprinted and widely read the following year in pamphlet form. In her analysis, Fries concluded that the *Beilage* was written by Traugotte Bagge, a well-known and respected Moravian merchant. It was, she concluded, "neither a diary, nor a mechanical compilation from a diary. It is an historical sketch, well written, clear-cut, showing keen insight into the affairs of the State and Nation."[3] The text covered a number of years and various topics, including sailors onboard ships in Charleston harbor throwing their goods overboard in 1775 when they were denied permission to dock; the scarcity of salt and other commodities during that period; and the depreciation of paper money in 1777. The section on Mecklenburg, Fries wrote, "is plainly a part of the original document, and entitled to all the credence that may be given to any part thereof."[4]

According to the *Beilage*, Mecklenburg County had declared itself "*frey u. independent.*" Whoever had written the *Beilage* had even used the English word *independent*, not the German equivalent. Surely this was not an accident. But was it the most literal recitation of the facts? The passage noted that Congress had declared the proceedings "premature," the same word many of the witnesses had used. The account also describes two events. First, a declaration of independence from England ("*von England declarirte*") and the establishment of a new provisional government ("made such arrangements for the administration of the laws among themselves, as later the Continental Congress made for all"). This seemed to powerfully confirm the story of the Mecklenburg Declaration.

Fries' article seemed to throw the case wide open. "The friends of the Mecklenburg Declaration have recovered a striking piece of evidence in support of their case," wrote (skeptical) historian H. Addington Bruce in the *North American Review* of July 1906. "Historians can no longer afford to treat the problem with the superstition of incredulity. They have now to deal, not with nebulous theories nor with hypotheses sustained by little more than the enthusiasm of local pride and patriotism; but with concrete data which must be accepted or explained away."[5] Fries' scholarship and explanation was "clear and convincing," concluded historian Waldo Leland, "and seems to me the final word."[6] Another scholar agreed the Fries article was set out in a "fair and truly scientific spirit of research."[7]

To Mecklenburg supporters, it was game, set, match. Here was the contemporaneous, pre–1800, unbiased, wholly corroborating evidence that the skeptics had long called for. "The discovery of the 'Bagge Manuscript' effectually sets at rest the question of the Mecklenburg Declaration of Independence," one historian confidently if entirely incorrectly concluded, "except perhaps in the minds of those who are unwilling to consider the matter in a fair and unbiased light."[8] Remarkably, "even Mr. Salley," one wrote, "agrees with me that your conclusions are beyond reproach."[9]

On closer examination, the case was not as open and shut as it might seem at first glance. Fries had found excellent corroborating evidence, no doubt, but she still had not found the definitive text of the declaration itself. In addition, if the *Beilage* was written after 1783, it could be argued that the Moravians had remembered the phrase "free and independent" after the fact, when it described the whole country. Who could be sure the Mecklenburgers had really used that phrase at the time, eight years earlier? Nevertheless, it was powerful new circumstantial evidence.

What did Fries think about her discovery? In a letter dated June 20, 1916, to Dr. Weeks, a skeptic, she wrote, "So far as the Mecklenburg Declaration is concerned I would say that I have taken, and expect to take no part in the public controversy."[10] She continued:

[B]ut since you raise the question of the testimony of our Moravian Archives I am quite willing to tell you that I consider them as corroborating the story as told in the J. McKnitt paper [the "rough notes"], and I have never been able to see any difficulty in accepting that as a simple, straightforward, credible, statement of facts.

I can not otherwise account for the use of "Free and Independent" which persists in the tradition, and in our records here, but is not in the Resolves; nor does your theory explain the interval of several days as given by J. McKnitt, nor why men at boiling point of excitement over the news from Lexington, which certainly must have reached Charlotte by the 19th, should have waited eleven days before doing anything.

Warming to her theme, she added the following:

The loss of a minute book by fire does not invalidate it, so I do not consider the J. McKnitt paper as "the first draft of the Declaration," but merely as a clear statement of facts as to what happened, nor can the Revolves of May 31st be the "only official record," if the [manuscript] records were all burned. It would be just as logical, it seems to me, to insist that the Resolves were a forgery because you could not show the original minute book from which they were copied!

All in all, she concluded, "I stand by Traugott Bagge until somebody can *prove* to me that he did not know what he was talking about [emphasis in the original]."

Painting believed to be of Richard Caswell, one of two congressional delegates to whom Captain Jack says he delivered the Mecklenburg Declaration. Caswell's private views on American independence in 1775 "were held in closest confidence, and to this day they are not certainly known" (courtesy of the State Archives of North Carolina).

Despite the publication of the fragment with the words "free and independent," questions remained. Why did the congressional records not mention the Mecklenburg Declaration or even, for that matter, the Resolves? Why did the papers of Caswell, Hooper and Hughes not refer to either of them? Here, the Moravian records held another clue. According to the diaries, on his return ride to Charlotte from Philadelphia in July 1775, Jack was carrying with him a "circular addressed to Mr. Traugott Bagge," the same Bagge that the author Fries identifies as writing the *Beilage*. A circular, or circular letter, was a letter or notice intended for wide circulation — the colonial-era version of a "breaking news" alert. A rider read aloud the news, and the recipient signed his name to indicate that the news had been received. The rider then passed on to the next village, delivered his message, had his circular signed, and passed on down the road.

The "circular" in this case was very special, for, according to the diary account, "it was signed by Hooper, Hewh [*sic*], and Casewell [*sic*], and contained an *Encouragement* to take up arms."[11] The authors of the circular are unmistakable: Hooper, Hughes and Caswell, the three North Carolina delegates to the Second Continental Congress, the delegates Jack was sent to meet. The circular Captain Jack was delivering to Traugotte Bagge was an "Open Letter" addressed to the "Committees of the several Towns and Counties of the Province of North Carolina"[12] and was dated June 19, 1775. The Moravian settlements were not more than a few days' ride from Charlotte. Assuming for the sake of argument that it took Jack ten days to ride from Philadelphia (a reasonable estimate for those times), he must have left Philadelphia sometime before June 27 in order to be in Wachovia by July 7, the day the Moravian journals record a messenger from Mecklenburg passing through. And given that the circular he was carrying with him was dated June 19, Jack must have met with the congressional delegates sometime between June 19 and June 27.

The Open Letter Jack was carrying from the delegates began as a call to arms: "When the liberties of a People are invaded, and Men in authority are laboring to raise a Structure of Arbitrary Power upon the Ruins of a free Constitution, it is natural for us Inhabitants of America ... to be anxious for our approaching Fate and to look up to the Sources which God and the Constitution furnish to ward off or alleviate the impending Calamity." The news of Lexington had shaken the colonies to the core and seemed to portend that any one of them could be next. "Think not that his Schemes are to end here," the letter read. "No, if success should strengthen his hands the Inhabitants of the Southern Colonies would soon feel the Weight of his Vengeance."

In New York, Massachusetts and Delaware, the people had formed themselves into local militias and began to store gunpowder in anticipation of impending conflict. North Carolina, however, "alone remains an inactive Spectator of this general defensive Armament. Supine and careless, she seems to forget even the Duty she owes to her own local Circumstances and Situation." The three congressmen called upon the citizens of the state to form themselves into militias: "The Election of the officers and the Arrangement of the men must depend upon yourselves." They implored the men of the province to "study the art of Military with the utmost attention, view it as the Science upon which your future security depends." There was no time to waste. "The Crisis of America," they warned, "is not at a great distance."

But after calling upon the citizens to arm themselves and prepare to resist British aggression, the final sentence of the Open Letter sounded a strange and dissonant note.

[L]ook to the reigning Monarch of Britain as your rightful and lawful sovereign.... [D]are every danger and difficulty in support of his person, crown and dignity and consider every man as a Traitor to his King who infringing the Rights of his American Subjects attempts to invade those glorious Revolution principles which placed him on the Throne and must preserve him there.

Your rightful and lawful sovereign? What did this mean? What this meant was that Caswell, Hooper and Hughes—as was true of the vast majority of the people in the colonies—were not ready or willing to conclude that British rule was the problem, only the current British government. This is what was meant by the phrase "Arbitrary Minister," as opposed to "Arbitrary Monarch." Rather than being a declaration of independence, the delegates' Open Letter was, in the end, a declaration of loyalty.

The argument that protection of American liberties and loyalty to the British Crown were consistent, indeed indistinguishable, sounds confusing today, but at that period it was quite common. English liberties existed by virtue of the Americans' rights as British subjects. The king was the ultimate guarantor of those rights. The Americans might be badly governed, went the argument, but the basis for the redress of their grievances was petition to the Crown. The idea of outright American independence was still an extreme, radical view held by only a very few in the colonies. Most colonists were simply not ready to take this step. They wanted greater liberty under British rule, not freedom from British rule.

When Jack met the North Carolina delegates that June, the Second Continental Congress was split on this very issue. On the one hand were those who believed that outright confrontation with Britain was inevitable and the only solution to America's distress was a clean and final break. John Adams was one of the advocates of this view. On the other hand, a second camp was seeking peaceful reconciliation with the Mother Country. Most were vacillating, like estranged spouses in the middle of a bitter divorce torn from one day to the next by competing emotions and views that could change depending on the news of the day. The Open Letter from the three North Carolina delegates — prepare for war, but also reaffirm your loyalty to the king — vividly illustrates this dichotomy.

The reconciliation party was strong in Congress in the summer of 1775. In July, while Jack was returning to Charlotte, a petition to the king of England, later known as the "Olive Branch Petition," was adopted by the Congress. A first draft of the Olive Branch Petition was written by Thomas Jefferson but was considered too confrontational. A toned-down draft written by John Dickinson of Pennsylvania was adopted by Congress on July 5 and sent to London on July 8.

Addressed to his "Most Gracious Sovereign" from "your Majesty's faithful subjects of the Colonies," the petition pledged the delegates "to use all the means in our power, not incompatible with our safety, for stopping the further effusion of blood, and for averting the impending calamities that threaten the British Empire."[13] Most important, the Olive Branch Petition clearly disavowed any expression of independence from Britain. It read in part as follows:

> Attached to your Majesty's person, family, and Government, with all devotion that principle and affection can inspire, connected with Great-Britain by the strongest ties that can unite societies, and deploring every event that tends in any degree to weaken them, we solemnly assure your Majesty, that we not only most ardently desire the former harmony between her and these Colonies may be restored, but that a concord may be established between them upon so firm a basis as to perpetuate its blessings, uninterrupted by any future dissensions, to succeeding generations in both countries.[14]

Despite what they felt were reasonable grievances and complaints, they continued, "your Majesty will find your faithful subjects on this continent ready and willing at all times, as they ever have been, with their lives and fortunes, to assert and maintain the rights and interests of your Majesty, and of our Mother country."[15] This profession of loyalty to Britain was signed by forty-nine delegates, including Thomas Jefferson, John Adams, Patrick Henry and Benjamin Franklin.

And that brings us back to Captain Jack. When he arrived in Philadelphia that June, Congress was debating the Olive Branch Petition. The outrage of Lexington had cooled since April, and the prospect of a hundred more Lexingtons fought all over the colonies gave the delegates a sobering sense of dread. While Congress was preparing an address to the king pledging renewed loyalty, provocative acts by radical factions within the colonies were considered unwelcome. A public discussion of independence undercut the entire attempt at reconciliation with the Mother Country. If word got out among the delegates that some portion of their constituents were in favor of outright independence, it might have had unforeseen consequences. Without question, such a spontaneous act would have rallied the more extreme radical elements of the Congress, who could have pointed to it as an example of the will of the people. Jack's message, therefore, declaring Mecklenburg "free and independent" in late June 1775 could not have been more poorly timed. North Carolina's delegates would have been particularly unreceptive to such a message. Consider the two delegates to whom Jack says he delivered the Mecklenburg Declaration: Richard Caswell and William Hooper.

Caswell had been a member of the Colonial Assembly from 1754 to 1776 and speaker of the North Carolina house during the Regulator uprising of 1771. In fact, Caswell himself as a militia officer had commanded the right wing of Governor Tryon's army when it defeated the ill-organized Regulators at the Battle of Alamance. Caswell had seen firsthand the violence and devastation that civil conflict had brought upon North Carolina. He had himself enforced the drastic consequences of rebellion against British power. Possibly for that reason, or simply by temperament, Caswell was known to keep his political views close to his vest. In 1775, he was seen as a moderate and certainly not associated with the radical Whig factions. In fact, at this time, no one really knew where Caswell stood on the main issue of relations with Britain. According to the *Dictionary of North Carolina Biography*, "The period from 1765 to 1775 was for North Carolina a decade of developing anti–British sentiment, protest activities, and public demonstrations. During this period, Caswell's private views were held in closest confidence, and to this day they are not certainly known."[16] Caswell was a behind-the-scenes player. A public renunciation of British rule, as had occurred in Mecklenburg, was not his style. He would not have championed such a message and would have seen it as dangerous and provocative, even assuming he was sympathetic to it at all.

What about William Hooper, the second delegate Jack mentions? Hooper was classically educated, having graduated from Harvard College with marked distinction in oratory in 1760. He studied law under James Otis, a brilliant New England lawyer and outspoken defender of American rights. Hooper's meteoric political rise began in 1773 when he was named one of nine North Carolina leaders to a "Committee of Correspondence." Hooper was "handsome, well-bred and well-educated, with courtly manners and a pleasing personality," according to the *Dictionary of North Carolina Biography*. He was a rising political star in the summer of 1775.[17] "[Richard Henry] Lee, Patrick Henry and Hooper are the orators of the Congress," wrote John Adams.[18] Hooper was not a radical however. In fact, his political leanings were generally conservative, or as Jefferson caustically put it so many years later, "we had not a greater Tory in Congress than Hooper." As an indication of Hooper's state of mind, in September 1775 at a meeting of the Provincial Congress in Hillsboro, North Carolina, nearly five months after the battles of Lexington and Concord, Hooper said, "We have been told that independence is our object; that we seek to shake off all connection with the parent state. Cruel suggestion! Do not all our professions, all our actions, contradict this?"[19]

What would Caswell and Hooper have thought as they read the Mecklenburg Declaration? Without doubt they would have been cold, even hostile, to it. Neither Caswell nor
Hooper would have wanted to act upon it. Given their temperaments and political views
it is inconceivable that either of them would have brought Jack's message before the general
Congress, especially when sensitive negotiations were ongoing regarding the Olive Branch
Petition. Even giving both of them the greatest benefit of the doubt as to their views and
motives, even assuming they generally supported or sympathized with the views expressed
by their backcountry constituents, it strains credulity that either man would have raised the
Mecklenburg Declaration before the general Congress at that time.

That being said, they may have felt obligated to at least inform the third North Carolina
delegate, Joseph Hughes, and solicit his opinion as to Jack's message. Assuming for the
sake of argument that the two delegates were on the fence as to what to do, there is little
or no doubt that Hughes would have killed off any further discussion of taking the Mecklenburg Declaration further, permitting any publication of it, or even speaking of it to
anyone else. Forty-five years old, Hughes was a merchant and a moderate Whig leader. In
the summer of 1775, he was not advocating the cause of American independence. In fact,
even as the Revolution unfolded over the next several years, Hughes was never fully committed to the cause. Jefferson, in that famous letter of 1819, described Hughes' political

William Hooper, the second delegate with whom Captain Jack said he met. According to Jefferson, "there
not a greater Tory in Congress than Hooper." Did
Hooper and Caswell conspire to suppress the story?
(courtesy of the State Archives of North Carolina).

views as "very wavering, sometimes
firm, sometimes feeble, according as the
day was clear or cloudy."

Adams doubted whether Hughes
really believed in American independ-
ence at all, even as late as July 4, 1776.
In a letter dated March 28, 1813, Adams
wrote, "You enquire ... whether 'every
Member of Congress' did, on the 4th of
July 1776, in fact cordially approve of
the declaration of Independence?'"[20]
The answer, wrote Adams, was no. And
Exhibit A for his argument was a delegate from North Carolina named Joseph
Hughes. "I then believed," wrote
Adams, "and I have not since altered my
Opinion, that there were several who
signed with regret, and several others
with many doubts and much luke-
warmness." The motion for a declaration of independence, Adams continued,
"had been upon the carpet for Months,
and obstinately opposed from day to
day." He explained:

Majorities were constantly against it.
For many days the Majority depended
upon Mr. Hews of North Carolina.

While a member one day was speaking and reading documents from all the Colonies to prove that the Public Opinion, the general sense of all was in favor of the measure, when he came to North Carolina and produced letters and public proceedings which demonstrated that the Majority of that Colony were in favor of it, Mr. Hews who had hitherto constantly voted against it, started suddenly upright, and lifting up both his hands to Heaven as if he had been in a trance, cry'd out "It is done! And I will abide by it." I would give more for a perfect Painting of the terror and horror upon the Faces of the Old Majority at that critical moment than for the best piece of Raphael.[21]

As Adams makes clear, Hughes was just barely capable of embracing American independence in July 1776. The very idea, as Adams put it, caused some members of Congress "terror and horror," and may have produced the same in Hughes himself. So imagine Hughes' feelings if he had received such a message *thirteen months earlier*. Whatever Caswell and Hooper may have thought, there is absolutely no question that Hughes would have been emotionally, irrevocably and passionately opposed to the actions in Mecklenburg. Nor would he have been alone. In the view of historian David McCullough, "if the Mecklenburg document arrived [at the Continental Congress in May 1775], it would have been squelched because they didn't want any talk of independence."[22] Whether Hughes talked the other two out of it or whether they were unanimous that the Mecklenburg Declaration needed to be suppressed is not known.

The most likely scenario is that, as politicians are wont to do in handling troubling constituents, the delegates politely received Jack, smiled, took copies of his papers and resolutions, thanked him for his efforts, and then took no further action. Possibly they destroyed the treasonous papers that Jack brought them. Certainly they would have done nothing to preserve or publicize them. Probably they considered the whole episode not worthy of further comment. Whatever they thought, they sent Jack home and did not speak further about the incident.

Ironically, both Adams and Jefferson alluded to this simple explanation in their letters. Privately, Adams wrote to a friend on July 15, 1819: "Its total concealment from me is a mystery, which can be unriddled only by the timidity of the delegates in Congress from North Carolina."[23] Jefferson's response to Adams corroborates this suspicion: "You remember as well as I do," Jefferson had written Adams, "that we had not a greater Tory in Congress than Hooper" and "that Hughes was very wavering, sometimes firm, sometimes feeble, according as the day was clear or cloudy."[24] Thus Adams' statement that "I cannot believe that they [the Mecklenburg Declaration] were known to one member of Congress on the fourth of July, 1776," is almost certainly true — with the sole exceptions of the two North Carolina delegates with whom Jack met.[25] If this theory is true, the real villain in the story was not Jefferson (as Adams supposed) nor John McKnitt Alexander (as Jefferson believed). The real culprits were the North Carolina delegates who suppressed the "horrid and treasonable" resolves of their constituents.

22

Occam's Razor
Summing Up the Case for the
Mecklenburg Declaration

Occam's razor: A scientific and philosophic rule ... that the simplest of competing theories be preferred to the more complex.

—Merriam-Webster's Dictionary, 2013

The Moravian writings discovered in the beginning of the twentieth century should have been the "smoking gun" providing independent evidence that the leaders of Mecklenburg County had declared themselves "free and independent" in May 1775, consistent with the story of the eyewitnesses and, more important, using the same language as that in the text of the Mecklenburg Declaration. And yet the Moravian discovery, much like the discovery of the Mecklenburg Resolves a century earlier, did not change anyone's mind. The positions on both sides were too entrenched to admit of any reconsideration, even when new evidence emerged. Even today, it is clear that until and unless an actual copy of the Mecklenburg Declaration of Independence is ever discovered, the controversy will not rest.

But this is not likely to happen. John McKnitt Alexander, the man most familiar with the original records, maintained that the critical papers had been lost in the fire of April 1800. McKnitt had hinted that a few original copies of the Mecklenburg Declaration might still exist, such as the Davie Copy (which was found) and the Williamson Copy (which was not). Then there were McKnitt's "rough notes," which, depending on your point of view, were either an abstract of the true declaration (possibly written in the 1790s but more likely about 1800) or simply the twisted ramblings of McKnitt's imagination. Finally, there was the "copy in an unknown hand," anonymous and undated, which confused things further. In any event, by the twenty-first century all extant papers have been picked apart by scholars and historians without settling the controversy. No further discoveries regarding the Mecklenburg Declaration seem likely. Nevertheless, a few die-hard "MecDec" believers cling to the hope that a missing copy might turn up unexpectedly, perhaps one stored in someone's attic or hidden behind a picture discovered at an antique sale or misplaced among ancient and forgotten papers in the British Museum or the North Carolina archives. These are far-fetched dreams, but none of them are impossible. Notwithstanding McKnitt's testimony, some believers reason there could be more than one original copy in existence, possibly as many as half a dozen.

As evidence of this, it is pointed out that in the "rough notes" McKnitt stated Captain Jack carried with him "a copy of all S[d]. resolutions and laws" and that "[a] copy was left with them [Congress] by Capt[n]. Jack." Some historians argue that there were at least four copies delivered by Jack: one for the Speaker of the House and one copy for each of the three North Carolina delegates.[1] This is logical but unproven. Another suggests that a copy was tabled at the provincial congress that met in Hillsboro in August 1775.[2] It is also worth noting Captain Jack himself claimed that "in passing through Salisbury the General Court was then sitting — at the request of the court *I handed a copy of the resolutions to Col. Kennon, an Attorney, and they were read aloud in open court.*"[3] This seems to suggest that Jack carried more than one copy of the Mecklenburg Declaration with him. Where had these copies all gone? And could the original document still exist, perhaps stashed in the papers of Caswell, Hooper, Hughes or Kennon?

There are other leads which suggest that an original, undiscovered copy might still exist. The first is the work of François Xavier Martin, a French historian who wrote a history of North Carolina, published in 1829.[4] Martin's history gives a detailed account of the Mecklenburg Declaration, including text that is very close to the version in the *Raleigh Register*. What is more, the chapter in Martin's work which contains the Mecklenburg Declaration is believed to have been written between 1791 and 1809, well before the controversy arose and before Martin could have seen the version in the *Raleigh Register*.[5] So where did Martin's version of the Mecklenburg Declaration come from, if not from the declaration itself?[6] In support of this theory, it was pointed out that Martin was acquainted with several of the principal witnesses, including Joseph Graham, James Harris and Robert Irwin, and may have heard the story from them or even received a copy of the original records. Martin was said to have told a colleague that he received a copy of the Mecklenburg Declaration "[i]n the Western part of the state [of North Carolina], prior to the year 1800."[7] He further claimed that "it was not obtained from [John McKnitt] Alexander."[8] But from whom Martin received his copy and where it went, no one knows.[9]

In addition to these tantalizing clues, Adam Brevard, brother of Dr. Ephraim Brevard, said that he had seen drafts of the Mecklenburg Declaration among his brother's miscellaneous papers:

> In the Autumn of 1776, the writer [Adam Brevard] being one of the number who composed the College or Academy (Queen's College) lived with a brother, Dr. Ephraim Brevard, into whose possession the letters, orations and other exercises (usual in such institutions) were handed over for wrapping paper and other uses... My curiosity frequently led me to ransack and examine the several contents for aid and assistance in my own task, when I came across a Declaration of Independence by Mecklenburg County. Upon requiring an explanation from the Doctor [Brevard], he informed me that it was the mass or rudiments out of which he had sometime before drawn the aforesaid instrument, which had been dispatched to Congress.[10]

Dr. Brevard's papers were likely destroyed during the British occupation of Charlotte in the autumn of 1780, or at least they have never been located.

Another theory held that one original participant, Duncan Ochiltree, had taken a copy of the Mecklenburg Declaration with him when he fled Charlotte in the autumn of 1780 after collaborating with British troops. Ochiltree was believed to possess a key to the courthouse, where the original documents may have been kept. According to this theory Ochiltree took the originals with him to curry favor with the British. As such, his papers might have ended up in the British archives or the British Museum. It was an interesting theory, but like so many, whether it was true or not could not be proven.

Finally, of course there was the missing *Cape Fear Mercury* of June 1775, the newspaper that Governor Martin said contained "horrid and treasonable resolves" of a committee in Mecklenburg. Did the paper contain the Mecklenburg Declaration (as believers held) or the Mecklenburg Resolves (as the skeptics argued)? The paper has never been found, and therefore the question cannot be answered either way. But the fact that it was "borrowed" from the London archives by a defender of Jefferson, and was never seen again, led to all kinds of conspiracy theories.

The Xavier copy, Brevard's notes, the missing *Cape Fear Mercury*: were these red herrings or possible clues? While some continue to believe that another copy of the Mecklenburg Declaration might exist somewhere, the evidence suggests it is not likely. First of all, McKnitt had accounted for all of the known copies, such as the Davie and Williamson copies. He never suggested that additional copies might exist. And no one had worked harder to find the missing document over the years than the Alexander family, but ultimately without success. In addition, in the nineteenth century, archives in Charleston and London were searched by historians with no additional evidence being unearthed. Barring some unexpected development, the paper chase appears to be at an end.

The doubters conclude that because no original copy of the Mecklenburg Declaration has been found the story is not proven. Believers argue that while the original document is admittedly lost, this does not render the story untrue anymore than the fact that the original copy of the Emancipation Proclamation, many of J.S. Bach's masses and several of Beethoven's piano sonatas were destroyed means they never existed either. In the supporters' view, the question was not whether the document could be located. Admittedly, it could not. The question was whether the preponderance of the evidence proved that the basic story was true. Circumstantial evidence, they argue, is still evidence, and can be quite good evidence at that.

While supporters of the Mecklenburg Declaration make a good case based on circumstantial evidence, they are also guilty of overplaying their hand and attributing an importance to the story that it, even if it is true, simply does not have. It could logically be the case that the story is true, that there was in fact a declaration of independence in the county in the summer of 1775 but that this fact alone left no wider historical ripples. The story could be true and be nothing more than a historical footnote. But that wasn't good enough for many of its supporters. They were determined to prove not only that the story was *true*, but also that the story *mattered*. And those were two different things.

Dr. Joseph Alexander was guilty of this when he wrote that the Mecklenburg Declaration gave "the *primary impulse* to our national Independence ... in producing the Declaration subsequently made by the Legislature of North Carolina & perfected on 4 July 1776 by our National Congress."[11] This was an exaggeration. Even by Alexander's own account, Congress considered the actions in Charlotte premature and took no further action on them. It was absurd to believe that the Mecklenburg Declaration somehow gave any momentum or impetus to any national movement for independence. In fact, the facts showed that if that was its purpose it was stillborn.

Alexander was a partisan witness, of course, and could be excused for exaggerating his case. But other historians equally overstated the importance of the Mecklenburg Declaration of Independence. Alexander Garden, for example, wrote that "the similarity of sentiment expressed [was] so strong" in the Mecklenburg Declaration "as to give conviction that the Mecklenburg resolutions were *constantly in view* when the committee of Congress drew that momentous document which we consider the palladium of our lives and liberties."[12]

Other partisan historians made equally grandiose claims. These hyperbolic statements soured many neutral observers, who believed that the supporters of the Mecklenburg Declaration were wildly exaggerating its importance. Boasts that the Mecklenburg Declaration gave the "primary impulse" to national independence (per Alexander) or that it was "constantly in view" when Congress debated independence (as Garden said) or, for that matter, that Jefferson had borrowed from the text (as many argued) were simply unsustained by any evidence. They gave the event a relevance it simply did not have. This was a different question, of course, than whether it ever existed, but in the minds of many these issues merged.

As of 2013, the Mecklenburg Controversy has clearly been won by the skeptics in the mind of the general public. The prevailing academic view is that the existence of the Mecklenburg Declaration has been comprehensively disproved, and that those who believe in it are sad and naïve holdouts, unwilling to accept the scientifically demonstrated, objective evidence proffered by Hoyt, Salley and others.

An anonymous comment on the *Charlotte Observer* chat page in May 2011 sums up the popular view. "Some historians do not question [the Mecklenburg Declaration's] existence," someone wrote. "All serious historians do.... What snippets of anecdotal storytelling that have been passed down do not meet any standards of historical research. Unless some new evidence has emerged in the many years since I was a history major in college there is nothing to indicate this is any more than the nice 'feel good' local fable it has always been." While it's probably more accurate to say that few historians are interested in the issue at all, a broader question is whether this appeal to authority is still true. Do "all" serious historians question the existence of the Mecklenburg Declaration of Independence?

For many years, the answer was clearly yes. Since the publication of Hoyt's book in 1907, the consensus in academic circles has been that the story is, to use Jefferson's word, "spurious." The major historical works of the last several decades on the subject of North Carolina either ignore the subject altogether or treat as a given that the entire episode is a hoax and unworthy of comment. For example, *North Carolina Illustrated, 1524–1984* (edited by H.G. Jones) mentions the Mecklenburg Declaration of Independence only in passing and puts the phrase in sarcastic quotation marks in the index. William Powell's *North Carolina: A History,* Dan Morrill's *Southern Campaigns of the American Revolution* and Hugh Rankin's *The North Carolina Continentals* ignore the topic altogether, although the latter does mention the Mecklenburg Resolves. Noted historian Pauline Maier summarizes this perspective in her excellent book *American Scripture*:

> Today the predominant opinion of "most sensible" modern historians, as Merrill Peterson, put it, supports Jefferson's position.... When compared to other documents of the time, the "Mecklenburg Declaration of Independence" supposedly adopted on May 20, 1775, is simply incredible. It makes the reaction of North Carolinians to Lexington and Concord more extreme than

that of the Massachusetts people who received the blow. The resolutions of May 31, 1775, of which there is contemporary evidence, were also radical, but remain believable.[13]

"Simply incredible." Maier's words have remained the consensus view for several decades. However, in the last decade, the prevailing (indeed, nearly unanimous) view among historians that the Mecklenburg Declaration of Independence is entirely a myth has begun to change, and change greatly. For example, David McCullough, two-time Pulitzer Prize winner for his biographies of John Adams and Harry Truman, when asked his view on the topic, said, "All my instincts, all my experiences over the years incline me to believe it is true. And well worth exploring, worth commemorating and keeping alive. The evidence is circumstantial, but it's very good circumstantial evidence and there's a good deal of it. And I'm very impressed by the opinions of John Adams, and he took it seriously."[14] Writer and political commentator George Will agrees with McCullough. "What occurred [July 4] in Philadelphia might have been a Declaration of Independence, but the first such occurred on May 20, 1775," he wrote in an article in the *Washington Post*. "Thus did a settlement on the fringe of the British Empire declare war on that Empire."[15]

In recent years, a local historical group called the May 20th Society has brought well-known historians to Charlotte on May 20 and asked for their opinion on the subject. Cokie Roberts, an Emmy Award winning journalist and author of *Founding Mothers* and *Ladies of Liberty*, gave a speech at the dedication of a statue of Captain Jack in Charlotte in May 2010. "There is no question that the Mecklenburg Declaration of Independence happened," she said. "There is not a question in my mind. First of all, there is plenty of evidence but

British historian Andrew Roberts speaking in Charlotte in May 2011. "If twenty-six North Carolinians say that something took place," said Roberts, "my inclination as a historian is to believe them" (courtesy Nancy Pierce/May 20th Society).

secondly when you have folk memory that's *that strong*, it's always right. And often people don't like that, as in Sally Hemmings and Thomas Jefferson. But it turned out to be right.... [T]here is just no question in my mind that this is true."[16]

Similarly in 2011, Andrew Roberts, arguably Britain's most prominent military historian and author of *Masters and Commanders* and *The Storm of War,* gave his take on the controversy:

> I've learned in twenty years of writing history books that because there is no extant, contemporaneous documentary proof of something, it doesn't mean it didn't happen; fires that destroy crucial documents are incredibly common throughout history and that oral history can sometimes be more visceral and honest than written history anyhow.
>
> Of course, the Mecklenburgers of 1819 could not remember, verbatim, precisely what they declared so bravely in 1775, but that doesn't in any way undermine the likelihood of their having called for independence a year earlier than the Revolutionaries in Philadelphia. If twenty-six North Carolinians say that something took place, my inclination as a historian is to believe them.[17]

In short, the uniform view that the story of the Mecklenburg Declaration is a discredited hoax has begun to crumble. There are a number of reasons for this. First, the stakes of the Mecklenburg Controversy no longer matter much to anyone. Nearly two centuries ago people cared deeply about whether Virginia, Massachusetts or North Carolina could claim primacy for starting the American Revolution. Today, the issue is of little relevance to society at large. Second, the belief in what constitutes "history" has undergone a sea change. In the nineteenth century historical scholarship was driven by fixed adherence to documents and their literal interpretation. Secondary sources, in particular local or oral traditions of history, were considered unreliable. If something was not written down, it simply did not rise to the level of credible historical evidence. Today a belief in community tradition is given more credence. Similarly, what is called a "bottom-up" view of history is fashionable. In this theory, lesser known individuals such as McKnitt or Polk are considered to be as legitimate or as important as iconic figures such as Hamilton or Jefferson.

And speaking of Jefferson ... Perhaps most important, disbelief in the Mecklenburg Declaration has weakened as a result of changing views of the character of Thomas Jefferson. The cult of defending his sacred name, which was so important to many of the skeptics, such as Phillips, is now entirely passé. As a result, the motivation of historians to clear Jefferson of the charge of plagiarism no longer exists. In addition, Jefferson's testimony as a character witness against the Mecklenburg Declaration has suffered gravely of late, given that another "local myth" with which he was associated, that of his slave/mistress Sally Hemmings, turned out to be true after all, 230 years later and despite generations of defenders claiming the story was false. Simply put, Jefferson is no longer the last word on the Mecklenburg Declaration.

Because of these considerations, a more balanced view is evolving of the Mecklenburg Declaration, one that does not portray Jefferson as either a hero to be defended against his detractors or a villain who committed plagiarism. An alternative explanation that the Mecklenburg Declaration of Independence may have existed but was not known to the major characters of the time is becoming accepted by many historians. As one local historian, Dan Morrill, himself a skeptic of the entire saga, was forced to conclude, "There's no question that Capt. Jack went to Philadelphia. The question is: What did he have in his saddlebag?

We know he had the Mecklenburg Resolves, which were a remarkable display of defiance. Could he have had the Mecklenburg Declaration of Independence? Maybe."[18] *Maybe* is not an answer that satisfies either the die-hard skeptics or the true believers. But perhaps that is the point. As Morrill said, "Let's make one thing clear. One cannot demonstrate conclusively that the Mecklenburg Declaration of Independence is a fake. The dramatic events of May nineteenth and May twentieth could have happened. Ultimately, it is a matter of faith, not proof. You believe it or you don't believe it."[19]

So what is the truth? Did the Mecklenburg Declaration occur or not? The well-known philosophical principle of "Occam's razor" holds that the simplest theory is usually the most likely. Following this principle, the following summary of the facts is in my view the simplest and most elegant explanation of what actually occurred in the summer of 1775.

On May 19, 1775, Scots-Irish Presbyterians in Charlotte had met for the specific purpose of discussing what could be done to further support their brothers under blockade by the British army in Boston when they received news of the Battle of Lexington. Alarmed and enraged upon receiving this news, the county leaders debated, drafted and adopted a declaration of independence that was announced on May 20, 1775. It was a symbolic act, intended to rally the community behind the leaders and to prepare for the war certainly to come. It was an *action* of the delegates, one that was *resolved upon*, not intended as a literal, written declaration to be widely published, unlike the national declaration of July 4, which was done expressly for that purpose. It was not intended for wider publication, which explains why it was not published in any contemporary accounts.

The exact text of these resolutions can never be known, but they certainly incorporated phrases and ideas common to the times. There is no reason to disbelieve that McKnitt's "rough notes," or for that matter the "copy in an unknown hand," do not substantially convey the actual text. This is true even if one believes that both documents were composed after the year 1800, for that matter, or even if they were written entirely from McKnitt's memory. Beyond a reasonable doubt, the phrase "free and independent" was used in what was resolved upon, as those exact words must have been widely communicated and are corroborated by the Moravian diaries.

Other bylaws and resolutions were then drafted and at least one set, which came to be called the Mecklenburg Resolves, was published. The gap in time is quite easily explained in that the patriot leaders were establishing a new government for the county and discussing what to do next. This is also consistent with the letter and spirit of the resolves, which state that the dissolution of British government in North Carolina was already a foregone conclusion. As many have pointed out, a declaration of independence precedes a constitution, not the other way around.

The actions on May 19 and 20 were controversial ("rash"), so before making them widely known the county leaders sent an emissary to the North Carolina congressional delegates in Philadelphia for their "sanction or approval." Lacking the consent of the delegates, they did not widely disseminate their actions, except through the Mecklenburg Resolves, which covered up their actions under the guise of legalism. In this explanation, the Mecklenburg Resolves are a logical next step and a coherent part of the story, not the "true document" existing in a vacuum and in contradiction to what the witnesses say took place. We know that the congressional delegates from North Carolina were political conservatives ("no greater Tory"), and even if they hadn't been, the timing for such an action was terrible, since the Olive Branch Petition was then in discussion in Congress. For these reasons, the actions in Mecklenburg were deemed "premature" and never acted upon.

The above explanation is not only possible but entirely logical and consistent with all of the evidence. It accepts the written evidence with all its faults and ambiguities. It does not require conspiracy theories involving Jefferson or the Alexanders. It does not suppose bad faith in any of the actors involved, nor does it presume that more than a dozen witnesses mixed up the dates in the same exact way, as one has to believe if one discounts the story. It also accounts for the durability of the local legend, in particular the phrase "free and independent," which recurs verbatim in the Moravian diaries, and of importance, a phrase that does not occur in the Mecklenburg Resolves. In sum, one can conclude that the story of the Mecklenburg Declaration of Independence is true while also concluding that it was (and remains) of no broader national significance or importance beyond being a point of local pride.

Belief in the Mecklenburg Declaration of Independence in Charlotte, its hometown, has long undergone ebbs and flows. At times it has been the most important event in the city, and at others it has been almost entirely forgotten. In the last decade the story has regained a new lease on life, arising nearly Phoenix-like from historical oblivion. In May 2012, a local artist named Will Puckett completed a year-long project to paint the scenes from the Mecklenburg Declaration of Independence on an underpass called the Matheson Street Bridge on North Davidson Street, in the northern Davidson area of Charlotte. The

The legend of Captain James Jack has had a revival in Charlotte in recent years. Here Jerry Linker as Captain Jack is leading the 2010 Thanksgiving Day parade (photograph by the author).

The legend lives on. In May 2010 this one-and-a-half–life-size statue of Captain Jack by artist Chas Fagan was unveiled near uptown Charlotte (courtesy Chas Fagan/Nancy Pierce).

Matheson Street Bridge mural is over 14,000 square feet in total and includes six large murals, each 60 by 100 feet, on the sloping area under the bridge as well as eight columns, each painted with a central character from the MecDec story. In bright, theatrical scenes reminiscent of the work of Mexican artist Diego Rivera, Puckett brought the main themes to life: the arrival of the news of Lexington, the revocation of the charter of Queen's College, the signing of the Mecklenburg Declaration, and the arrest of Booth and Dunn. On one side, McKnitt's home, Alexandriana, is seen burning as a copy of the Mecklenburg Declaration of Independence flies out the window. On the opposite side of the street, 27 militia leaders sign the document, while James Jack prepares to ride north. Alexander Craighead, Queen Charlotte, James Jack — even Dunn's dog named Tory — are all pictured.

Also in May 2012, a five-ton stone memorializing the Mecklenburg Declaration of Independence was placed on Tryon Street in downtown Charlotte, very near where the old courthouse once stood. It is part of the Charlotte Liberty Walk, a Revolutionary War walking tour that includes sites such as Brevard's and Polk's homes, the site of Queen's College and the Battle of Charlotte. Red granite paving stones bearing a silhouette of Captain James Jack on horseback were installed by the City of Charlotte in a three-quarter mile route linking the sites together. Local artist Dan Nance painted images for each site and created an interactive Web site and mobile application.[20]

Captain James Jack, in particular, seems to have benefited most from the resurgent interest in the story. Not only is his image engraved in paver stones in uptown Charlotte, but each year a figure dressed in period costume leads the Charlotte Thanksgiving Day parade as Captain Jack, returned from the grave. In May 2010 over 2,000 people stood under a blistering Carolina sun on the campus of Central Piedmont Community College, one mile from uptown Charlotte, to witness the unveiling of the *Spirit of Mecklenburg,* an equestrian statue of Captain Jack by artist Chas Fagan. Fagan's other works include statues of Ronald Reagan, one in the rotunda of the nation's Capitol in Washington and a second in front of the U.S. embassy in London, as well as an official portrait of First Lady Barbara Bush that hangs in the White House. In attendance that day were two dozen descendants of Captain Jack, some of whom had traveled from as far away as California to attend. "Don't Tread on Me" flags waved in the crowd. A local farrier named Jerry Linker (who in 1975 reenacted Captain Jack's entire 500 plus-mile ride to Philadelphia) rode on horseback dressed as Captain Jack.

Just after noon, a handful of schoolchildren pushed a button releasing a curtain held in place by scaffolding to reveal the one-and-half–life-size statue. In Fagan's work, Captain Jack's horse is at a full gallop. Jack leans forward, his face set against the wind. A haversack is slung over his right shoulder in which is contained the Mecklenburg Declaration of Independence. Jack is turning the horse north, heading along the Wagon Road to Philadelphia, riding to meet Caswell, Hooper and Hughes. Costing just over half a million dollars, the statue was entirely funded through private donations, proving that notwithstanding the pooh-poohing of academic historians, pride in the local legend still lives in Charlotte.

Historians will continue to quibble over the veracity of the story of the Mecklenburg Declaration of Independence, but on that hot day in Charlotte the people of Mecklenburg cast their verdict in 3,000 pounds of sandy-gray bronze. Two hundred thirty-five years after the fact, and despite generations of doubters and skeptics, the spirit of Mecklenburg, the spirit of "freedom and independence" personified by John McKnitt Alexander, Thomas Polk, James Jack and others, continues to burn brightly — whatever the documents may, or may not, say.

Chapter Notes

In citing works in the notes, short titles have exclusively been used except with respect to magazines, newspapers or periodicals. Long titles may be found in the Bibliography. Works frequently cited have been identified by the following abbreviations:

CR   *The Colonial and State Records of North Carolina.* Reference is first made to the volume number and the corresponding pages as shown in the digital edition maintained online by the University of North Carolina at Chapel Hill. Where possible I have included the title of the work and the date. These are found in the online category either by searching a quote within the text or the reference itself. A hard copy of the *CR* can also be found at the Carolina Room of the CML (see below).

CML   The Charlotte-Mecklenburg Public Library in uptown Charlotte, North Carolina, contains a wealth of information concerning the Mecklenburg Declaration of Independence, and in particular the lives of the signers, in its Carolina Room. Old newspapers, such as the *South Carolina and American General Gazette* from the Revolutionary War period as well as the *Catawba Journal* from the 1830s and 1840s, were provided by the CML and can be accessed there.

Draper   Papers in the Lyman Draper collection, University of Wisconsin, regarding the Mecklen-
MSS   burg Declaration of Independence (microfilm collection in the Carolina Room of the CML).

Governor's   *The Declaration of Independence by the Citizens of Mecklenburg County, published by the*
Report   *Governor Under the Authority and Direction of the General Assembly of the State of North Carolina* (Raleigh: Lawrence & Lemay, 1831). An online version is maintained by the Charlotte Mecklenburg Public Library at www.cmstory.org in document index in "All About the Declaration" section. Page references in the notes refer to the copy in the online version.

SHC   Mecklenburg Declaration of Independence Papers in the Southern Historical Collection at the Wilson Library, University of North Carolina, Chapel Hill. The SHC includes the original papers of John McKnitt Alexander, including the "rough notes" and the Davie Copy. It also includes the "copy in an unknown hand," as well as the original certificates and papers cited in the *Governor's Report*. Original letters and papers of Dr. Joseph Alexander are also contained in the SHC.

Prologue

1. The Collet map is from the collection of Tryon Palace Historic Sites and Gardens, New Bern, North Carolina, North Carolina Department of Cultural Resources, Division of Archives and History: "A map of the most inhabited part of Virginia containing the whole province of Maryland with part of Pennsylvania, New Jersey and North Carolina" (Joshua Fry and Peter Jefferson, 1751; also available online). The Catawbas lived near the confluence of the Catawba River and a smaller creek originally called *Soogaw* (or *Sugoree*), meaning "group of huts." Over many years, *Suga* or *Sugaw* was Anglicized by the European settlers to *Sugar*, until the brown creek became known as *Sugar*

Creek and its origins (and the Sugaw tribe) disappeared (Blythe and Brockmann, *Hornets' Nest*, 435). "This creek undoubtedly takes its name from the Sugeree Indians (John Lawson's spelling) or Sugaree Indians (Douglas L. Rights' spelling).... The predominant version in records of the Presbyterian Church, Colonial Records of North Carolina, and in old deeds is 'Sugar,' although such variations as 'Suger,' 'Shugar,' 'Sugercreek,' and 'Suga,' have been found in various records. In 1924 the pastor of Sugar Creek Presbyterian Church, evidently influenced by Foote's pronunciation, had the Mecklenburg Presbytery officially change the spelling of the name of the church to 'Sugaw.' This action seems never to have been rescinded, notwithstanding that all historical evidence available tends to prove that the original name of 'Sugar' should apply to both church and creek" (Blythe and Brockmann, *Hornets' Nest*, 435). The Catawbas' name in their own language is usually given as Iswa, Esaw or sometimes Yap Ye Esaw (pronounced 'yeh is-WAH h'reh') which translates loosely to "people of the river" (*Catawba River Companion*, 17). The Catawba (or "Catawban") Nation was a catchall term for what was in reality a dozen or more loosely aligned native American tribes (primarily the Sugarees, Shuterees, Esaws, Waxhaws and others in addition to the Catawbas) who lived thirty or so miles south of the border of Mecklenburg County. (One Indian leader observed in 1717 that "there were many Nations under that [Catawba] name" and as late as the 1740s there were more than 20 languages spoken by the federated tribes on the river) (Merrell, *Indians' New World*, 110).

2. Smith, *Journal*, 74.

3. See generally Rouse, *Great Wagon Road*.

4. Smith, *Journal*, 74.

5. *The Colonial and State Records of North Carolina* (hereafter *CR*), Carolina Room, Charlotte-Mecklenburg Public Library, "Letter from William Legge, Earl of Dartmouth to Josiah Martin," May 3, 1775, pp. 1240–1242.

6. Ramsay, *History*, 102.

7. Anonymous, "Copy in an Unknown Hand," Southern Historical Collection (hereafter SHC), University of North Carolina, Chapel Hill.

8. Ramsay, *History*, 113.

9. 9 *CR*, "Resolutions by Inhabitants of Rowan County Concerning Resistance to Parliamentary Taxation and the Provincial Congress of North Carolina," August 8, 1774, pp. 1024–1026.

10. Anonymous, "Copy in an Unknown Hand," SHC.

11. Alexander, *Rough Notes,* SHC.

12. 23 *CR*, "Acts of the North Carolina General Assembly," November 7, 1768-December 5, 1768, pp. 759–783.

13. Stuart Jeffries, "Was This Britain's First Black Queen?" *Guardian* (UK) (online edition), March 11, 2009.

14. McNitt, *Chain of Error*, 23.

15. 23 *CR*, "Acts of the North Carolina General Assembly," March 2, 1774-March 25, 1774, pp. 931–976.

16. Tarleton, *History*, 159–160

17. Smith, *Journal*, 74.

18. Washington, *Diary*, 197.

19. Collet, see note 1.

20. *Adams-Jefferson Letters*, 542.

21. *Governor's Report*, 14.

22. *Adams-Jefferson Letters*, 542.

23. Adams, *Works*, 383.

24. *Adams-Jefferson Letters*, 542.

Chapter 1

1. Wheeler, *Sketches*, 63.

2. 7 *CR*, "Minutes of the Lower House of the North Carolina General Assembly," October 30, 1766-December 2, 1766, p. 354.

3. Powell, *North Carolina*, 23.

4. Horne, *Narratives,* 71.

5. Ibid., 72. See also excerpts from Horne at http ://www.learnnc.org/lp/editions/nchist-colonial/2043.

6. Lawson, *A New Voyage*, 86.

7. Ibid., 87.

8. Horne, *Narratives*, 73.

9. Samuel Wilson, "An Account of the Province of Carolina," in Salley, *Narratives*, 170.

10. Horne, *Narratives*, 68.

11. Quoted in Landrum, *History of Upper South Carolina*, 1.

12. Ibid.

13. Ibid.

14. Ibid., 2.

15. Ibid., 1.

16. Ibid.

17. Quoted in Learn NC, "The Arrival of Swiss Immigrants," http://www.learnnc.org/lp/editions/nchist-colonial/2049.

18. Powell, *North Carolina*, 27.

19. 7 *CR*, "Report by Patrick Gordon Concerning Government in North Carolina," June 29, 1767, pp. 472–491.

20. Woodmason, *Carolina Backcountry*, 80–81.

21. Wheeler, *Sketches*, 31.

22. Ibid., 35.

23. Ibid., 40.

24. 6 *CR*, William Saunders, Preface to vol. 6, iii-iv.

25. Ibid., iii.

26. Ibid.

27. 10 *CR*, "Petition from Inhabitants of Mecklenburg County concerning North Carolina Church Laws," 1015–1017.

28. 6 *CR*, William Saunders, preface to vol. 6, iv.

29. Ibid.

30. Ibid.

31. Quoted in Digges, Connor, et al., *History*, 238.

32. 6 *CR*, "Letter from Arthur Dobbs to the Board of Trade," August 3, 1760, pp. 279–280.

Chapter 2

1. For an excellent summary of the Scots-Irish immigration see Blethen and Wood, *From Ulster to Carolina*, 22.

2. Woodmason, *Carolina Backcountry*, 50.

3. Ibid., 60.

4. Ibid., 52.

5. In Blethen and Wood, *From Ulster to Carolina*, introduction.

6. Ibid., 5–9.

7. Ibid., 7.

8. Ibid., 13.

9. Ibid., 19.

10. Ibid., 20.

11. Ibid., 19.

12. Ibid., 17–18.

13. Ibid., 23.

14. Ibid., 23–24.

15. Tompkins, *History of Mecklenburg*, 18.

16. In Blethen and Wood, *From Ulster to Carolina*, 30.

17. Woodmason, *Carolina Backcountry*, 14.

18. Washington, *Diary*, 196–198.

19. Powell, *History*, 9.

20. Camp, *Influence of Geography*, 8.

21. *Catawba River Companion*, 16.

22. Tompkins, *History of Mecklenburg*, 16.

23. 5 *CR*, "Letter from Arthur Dobbs to the Board of Trade of Great Britain," August 24, 1755, p. 355.

24. Kratt, *Spirit of the New South*, 16.

25. 7 *CR*, "List of Taxables in North Carolina for the Year 1765," p. 145–146. The list was broken down county by county and each county broken down between "white men, taxable" and "black and mulattoes, male and female." Mecklenburg, for whatever reason, was not broken down in those categories but only gave a total figure.

26. 7 *CR*, "List of Taxables in North Carolina for the Year 1767 and Report on Church of England Parishes," pp. 540–541.

27. 6 *CR*, "Minutes of the North Carolina Governor's Council," December 4, 1762-December 31, 1762, pp. 794–795.

28. A third, the *North Carolina Gazette,* had been published in Wilmington from 1763 to1767: "With the mail facilities of those days, those little sheets (for they were of the very smallest size) had but little circulation anywhere, and none at all, it may be said, in the interior" (8 *CR*, preface, v).

29. Camp, *Influence of Geography*, 23.

30. Alexander, *History of Mecklenburg*, 6.

31. Tompkins, *History of Mecklenburg*, 22–23.

32. Schaper, *Sectionalism and Representation*, 294.

33. Woodmason, *Carolina Backcountry*, 33.

34. Dan Morrill, *A History of Charlotte and Mecklenburg County,* online edition, chapter 1.

35. *Mecklenburg County Court Minutes*, 16.

36. Ibid., 116.

Chapter 3

1. Woodmason, *Carolina Backcountry*, 55.

2. Al, *The Covenants*, 244.

3. Great Britain, *Report of the Royal Commission*, 147–148.

4. Howie, *Faithful Contendings Displayed*, 303.

5. Craighead, *Craighead Family,* 39. For the details and descriptions of Craighead's life in this chapter I am greatly indebted to an excellent master's degree paper by Lila McGeachy Ray, "Alexander Craighead: With Drawn Sword," Pittsburgh Theological Seminary, 2001.

6. Bolton, *Scotch Irish Pioneers*, 87.

7. Ray, *Craighead*, 25.

8. Ibid., 3.

9. Ibid., 2.

10. Original copies of Craighead's writings are difficult to find. Excerpts from his writings (if not taken from Ray, see note 5) have been taken entirely from an online source for the *Renewal of the Covenants*, http://www.truecovenanter.com/kirkgovt/creaghead_reasons_of_receding_1743.html.

11. Ibid., preface.

12. Ford, *Scotch-Irish in America*, 397.

13. Smylie, *History*, 49.

14. Baldwin, *Sowers of Sedition*, 52–53.

15. Ibid., 52.

16. Gallay, *Voices*, 190.

17. Benjamin F. Owen, "Letters of Rev. Richard Locke and Rev. George Craig," *Pennsylvania Magazine of History and Biography* 24 (Philadelphia: Historical Society, 1900), 474.

18. *Renewal of the Covenants,* editor's introduction, http://www.truecovenanter.com/kirkgovt/creaghead_reasons_of_receding_1743.html.

19. Maclaren, *Original Secession Magazine*, 246.

20. McClintock, *Cyclopaedia of Biblical*, 525.

21. Hanna, *Scotch-Irish*, 41.

22. Ray, *Craighead*, 3.

23. Ibid., 56.

24. McGeachy, *History of the Sugaw Creek*, 22.

25. Hodge, *Constitutional History*, 171.

26. Ray, "Craighead," 57.

27. Ibid.; Sedgwick, *Bowels of Tender*, 403.

28. Ray, "Craighead," 59.

29. Ibid., 59–60.

30. Presbyterian Church, *Records of the Presbyterian Church*, 163.

31. Ray, "Craighead," 67.

32. *Renewal of the Covenants,* editor's introduction, http://www.truecovenanter.com/kirkgovt/creaghead_reasons_of_receding_1743.html.

33. Ray, "Craighead," 67. The "Renewal of the Covenant" was "a vivid anticipation of that more famous renewal of a covenant which was the American Revolution" (Clark, *Language*, 264).

34. Armstrong, *Presbyterian Enterprise*, 59.

35. Baldwin, *Sowers of Sedition*, 66.

36. Ibid.

37. Ibid., 67.

38. Ward, *Britain and the American South*, 17.

39. McGeachy, *History of the Sugaw*, 13–14.

40. Ibid., 30.

41. Foote, *Sketches*, 187.

42. Woodmason, *Carolina Backcountry*, 55.

43. 7 *CR*, "Letter from Andrew Morton," pp. 252–253.

44. Ibid.

45. 10 *CR*, "Petition from Inhabitants of Mecklenburg County Concerning North Carolina Church Laws," 1769, p. 1017.

46. Hanna, *Scotch-Irish*, 15.

47. 10 *CR,* "Petition from Inhabitants," 1769, p. 1016.

48. Ibid.

49. Hodge, *Constitutional History,* 484.

50. Drymon, *Scotch Irish,* 43.

51. McGeachy, *History of the Sugaw*, 38. "The immediate successor of Mr. Craighead was Joseph Alexander, a connexion of the McKnitt branch of Alexanders, a man of education and talents, of small stature, and exceedingly animated in his pulpit exercises" (5 *CR*, William Foote, "History of the Presbyterians in North Carolina," 1846, p. 1224).

52. Hanna, *Scotch-Irish*, 40.

53. Morrill, *History of Charlotte*, 9.

Chapter 4

1. Walpole, *Letters,* 223.
2. Woodmason, *Carolina Backcountry,* 43.
3. Ibid., 16–17.
4. Ibid., 45.
5. Ibid., 57.
6. Ibid., 30.
7. Ibid., 45.
8. Ibid.
9. Kars, *Breaking Loose Together,* 31.
10. Ibid.
11. Ibid., 37.
12. For an excellent summary of the Sugar Creek episode see James Williams, "The Sugar Creek War," a private paper prepared in connection with the Mecklenburg Historical Association. A copy may be obtained by contacting the MHA.
13. Powell, *North Carolina,* 24.
14. 5 *CR,* William Saunders, preface, xxxiii.
15. Ibid.
16. Ibid., xxxiv.
17. Ibid.
18. Except where otherwise noted, the account of McCulloh's confrontation with Polk in Mecklenburg and quotes throughout this chapter are taken from 7 *CR,* "Minutes of the North Carolina Governor's Council," May 7, 1765-May 9, 1765, pp. 10–31.
19. Kars, *Breaking Loose Together,* 36.
20. William Mecklenburg Polk, *Leonidas Polk: Bishop and General,* n.d., 17.
21. Kars, *Breaking Loose Together,* 43.
22. Ibid., 44.
23. 7 *CR,* "Minutes of North Carolina Council," April 3, 1765-April 8, 1765, pp. 4–7.
24. 7 *CR,* "Minutes of North Carolina Council," 37–39.
25. 7 *CR,* "Letter from Henry Eustace McCulloh," May 9, 1765, pp. 32–34.
26. Ibid.
27. Ibid.
28. Ibid.
29. 7 *CR,* "Minutes of North Carolina Council," 37–39.
30. Kars, *Breaking Loose Together,* 46–47
31. Ibid., 52.
32. Norton, *Spirit of Charlotte,* 15.
33. 7 *CR,* "Minutes of North Carolina Council," 10–31.
34. 7 *CR,* "Letter from Henry Eustace McCulloh," May 9, 1765, pp. 32–34.

Chapter 5

1. *Meck. Co. Court Minutes,* 1779, pp. 289–290.
2. 23 *CR,* "Acts of the North Carolina General Assembly," 1774, March 2, 1774-March 25, 1774, p. 966.
3. McNitt, *Chain of Error,* 20.
4. 7 *CR,* "Report by Patrick Gordon Concerning Government in North Carolina," June 29, 1767, p. 480.
5. Ibid., 481.
6. *Meck. Co. Court Minutes,* April 1775, pp. 178–179.
7. Ibid., 49.
8. For a detailed description of the local power of magistrates in this period, see 7 *CR,* "Report by Patrick Gordon Concerning Government in North Carolina," June 29, 1767, pp. 480–481.
9. 7 *CR,* "Report by Patrick Gordon Concerning Government in North Carolina," June 29, 1767, pp. 479–480. In October 1774, John Johnston was taken into custody for "swearing profusely" and fined fifteen shillings. He was then kept in jail for three months to answer a charge of "assaulting and beating Cornellus Quigly" (*Meck. Co. Court Minutes,* 21). In July 1777, George Grier was fined £10 for "contempt of authority" when he "armed a prisoner by delivering him a sword while in Custody of the Sheriff" (*Meck. Co. Court Minutes,* 115).
10. 9 *CR,* "Letter from Josiah Martin to William Legge, Earl of Dartmouth," July 13, 1774, pp. 1009–1014.
11. See summary of this episode from *North Carolina History: A Digital Textbook,* an online source published by UNC-Chapel Hill, http://www.learnnc.org/lp/editions/nchist-revolution/4258. The episode is taken from Harry McKown, "November 1765: The Stamp Act Crisis in North Carolina," *This Month in North Carolina History,* November 2006.
12. Powell, *North Carolina,* 49.
13. Ibid.
14. Kars, *Breaking Loose Together,* 155.
15. Ibid., 126.
16. Ibid.
17. Ibid.
18. 25 *CR,* "Acts of the North Carolina General Assembly," 1770–1771, pp. 519d, 519f.
19. Ibid., 519e.
20. Ibid.
21. 8 *CR,* "Letter from William Tryon to Wills Hill, Marquis of Downshire," March 12, 1771, p. 526.
22. Ibid.
23. Ibid., 527.
24. 8 *CR,* "Minutes of the North Carolina Governor's Council," January 19, 1771-January 28, 1771, p. 490.
25. 8 *CR,* "Letter from John Frohock and Alexander Martin to William Tryon," March 18, 1771, p. 533.
26. Ibid., 535.
27. 8 *CR,* "Deposition of Waightstill Avery Concerning the Actions of the Regulators," March 1771, p. 519.
28. Ibid., 519–521.
29. Barefoot, *Revolutionary War Sites,* 404.
30. 9 *CR,* "Memorandum from the Board of Trade of Great Britain to George III," February 26, 1772, p. 248.
31. Ibid.
32. Ibid., 250.
33. Ibid.
34. Ibid.
35. 9 *CR,* "Order of the Privy Council of Great Britain Concerning Acts of the North Carolina General Assembly," April 22, 1772, p. 285.
36. 9 *CR,* "Proclamation by Josiah Martin Concerning an Act of the North Carolina General Assembly Concerning Queen's College," June 28, 1773, p. 665.

37. See for an example of reporting in the Southern colonies in the *South Carolina and American General Gazette*, April 28-May 5, 1775.

38. "Circular Letter to the Committees in South Carolina, April 27, 1775," in The *South Carolina and American General Gazette*, April 28-May 5, 1775 (emphasis in the original).

39. *South Carolina and American General Gazette*, June 23–30, 1775.

40. Ibid., April 28-May 5, 1775.

41. Alexander, *Rough Notes*, SHC.

42. 9 *CR*, "Letter from William Legge, Earl of Dartmouth to Josiah Martin Dartmouth," May 3, 1775, 1241.

43. Alexander, *Rough Notes*, SHC.

44. Ibid.

Chapter 6

1. Ramsey, *Autobiography*, 5. Dr. Ramsey, McKnitt's grandson, who lived in Tennessee on an estate he named "Mecklenburg," was as accomplished, if not more so, as his grandfather. Not only was he a doctor, writer and historian of Tennessee, but, in the words of his biographer, he was "a man of exceptional versatility whose varied activities extended from the practice of medicine to the financing of railroads. He was a canal commissioner and a school commissioner, the president of banks and a farmer, a Presbyterian elder and a poet, a register of deeds, a contributor to magazines, a Confederate treasury agent, a postmaster, an operator of a ferry, a trustee of colleges, and a philosopher who thought deeply upon the problems of the South and the nature of Southern people" (preface to Ramsey, *Autobiography*, xxix.

2. McNitt, *Chain of Error*, 67.

3. Ramsey, *Autobiography*, 320.

4. Information on the life of John McKnitt Alexander comes courtesy of the Carolina Room at the Charlotte-Mecklenburg Public Library (hereafter CML), in particular Alvah Stafford, *Alexander Notebooks* (Charlotte, NC: CML, 1985) and *Hezekiah Alexander Information* (Charlotte, NC: CML, n.d.). In addition, Mrs. Mary Boyer kindly provided a wealth of genealogical and primary source materials on Alexander, including copies of his originals records she collected from the Department of Archives and History in Raleigh, North Carolina, and other sources (she is *the* resource for all things Alexander). For additional information on his life see also Ramsey, *Autobiography* 1–5, and Graham, *Mecklenburg Declaration and Life of Signers*, 111–114.

5. Ramsey, *Autobiography*, 5.

6. Ibid.

7. McNitt, *Chain of Error*, 67.

8. Ibid.

9. Preface to Ramsey, *Autobiography*, xxix.

10. At the top of her tombstone in Hopewell cemetery is the coat of arms of the State of Pennsylvania, her birthplace. It shows two rearing horses facing one another before a shield, on which is perched an eagle. Behind each horse is a stalk of corn, and on the shield itself are three symbols: a ship, a plough, and sheaves of wheat. Beneath is written *Virtue, Liberty and Independence*—the state motto of Pennsylvania. A six-stanza poem follows that reads in part, "as a faithful and agreeable friend, a wife, a Mother, a Mistress and an Economist she merited the imitation of all her female acquaintance and reflected honour on her sex." At the bottom in all capitals is the epitaph: "Ab Hoc Momento Pendet Aeternitas" (On this Moment Hangs Eternity), an epitaph commonly found in Scotland and Ireland in the mid-1750s.

11. 9 *CR*, "Resolutions by Inhabitants of Rowan County Concerning Resistance to Parliamentary Taxation," August 8, 1774, p. 1026.

12. 8 *CR*, "Act of the North Carolina General Assembly concerning Queen's College," January 15, 1771, p. 487.

13. They were not universally liked, the Alexanders. An anonymous piece of rhyming doggerel verse dated March 30, 1777, parodies McKnitt as manipulative, arrogant and rapacious, while his brother Hezekiah (here named "Squire Subtle," implying that he is crafty or devious) is portrayed as a Machiavellian aristocrat, manipulating the citizens for his own personal ends. In one passage, Subtle (Hezekiah) "harangues the crown" like a presumptuous aristocrat:

> *My countrymen, poor senseless throng,*
> *O'er whom I've watch'd with care so long,*
> *Although I move in higher spheres,*
> *Nor feel your little hopes and fears,*
> *My godlike mind can deign to bend,*
> *And sometimes to your needs attend.*

14. For example, one attendee gave the "leading characters" as "the Rev. Hezekiah James Balch, a graduate of Princeton College, an elegant scholar, Waightstill Avery, Esq., Attorney at Law; Hezekiah and John M'Knitt Alexander, Esqrs., Col. Thomas Polk, andc andc." Almost all other accounts are similar (*Governor's Report*, 18).

15. Colonel Abraham Alexander was an elder at Sugar Creek and David Reese an elder at Poplar Tent and at Rocky River. Adam Alexander, Robert Queary and James Harris were also elders at Rocky River; John Flennekin at Providence Presbyterian; and General Robert Irwin at Steele Creek. McKnitt was an elder at Hopewell, as were Matthew McClure and William Graham, the latter said to be so devout that he refused to do any labor, even preparing meals, on the Sabbath.

16. As a side note, Ochiltree collaborated with the British during Lord Cornwallis' two-week occupation of Charlotte in September 1780. When the British left he was told by McKnitt to leave upon pain of death and never to return to Mecklenburg. As a result, some have later speculated that Ochiltree had been a delegate but his fellow citizens later struck his name from the list as a result of his collaborating with the British.

Chapter 7

1. 9 *CR*, "Letters Concerning News of the Battle of Lexington in Massachusetts," April 20, 1775-May 9, 1775, p. 1229.

2. Ibid., 1238.

3. Ibid.

4. Charleston newspaper (fragments), courtesy of CML, May 12–19, 1775, likely the *South Carolina and American General Gazette*.

5. *South Carolina and American General Gazette*, June 23–30, 1775.

6. Ibid.

7. "Circular Letter to the Committees of South Carolina, April 27, 1775," *South Carolina and American General Gazette*, April 28–May 5, 1775.

8. *South Carolina and American General Gazette*, June 2–9, 1775.

9. Ibid.

10. Ibid., April 28–May 5, 1775.

11. 9 *CR*, "Letter from William Bull to William Legge, Earl of Dartmouth," May 15, 1775, p. 1260.

12. N.C. Historical Comm., *Records of the Moravians*, 873.

13. *Governor's Report*, 18.

14. Ibid., 19.

15. Ibid., 20.

16. Ibid., 19–20.

17. Ibid., 22, 20.

18. Ibid., 19.

19. Alexander, *Rough Notes*, SHC.

20. *Governor's Report*, 21.

21. Ibid., 19.

22. Ibid., 21. It seems difficult to believe that an agitated group animated by "fury and revenge" would engage in a "dispassionate discussion." But of course Hunter was not a participant, merely, as he states, an observer. It is also unclear why a young boy would be permitted into a specially convened meeting of elected delegates of only adults. In addition, it is reasonable to suppose that the delegates would want to have made the deliberations secret and logically would have excluded random bystanders. On the other hand, Hunter's account was intended to be more than simply eyewitness testimony. It was taken from the historical manuscript he was writing on the Revolutionary War in the South. Therefore, his account was probably based not only on what he himself observed, but incorporated historical information of the time, as well as facts with which he may have been familiar.

23. Alexander, *Rough Notes*, SHC.

24. *Governor's Report*, 21.

25. Ibid., 19.

26. Ibid., 26.

27. Ibid., 27.

28. Ibid., 23–24.

29. This is according to the later text in the *Raleigh Register*. See *Governor's Report*, 13–14.

30. Ibid., 14.

31. Alexander, *Rough Notes*, SHC (emphasis in the original).

32. *Governor's Report*, 21.

33. Ibid., 24.

34. Ibid., 26.

35. Ibid., 19–20.

36. Ibid., 21.

37. Ibid., 16.

Chapter 8

1. Blackstone, *Commentaries,* vol. 2, book 4, pp. 4–5 [6].

2. Statute of Treasons, 25 Edw. 3, stat. 5, c. 2 (1351).

3. Blackstone, *Commentaries,* vol. 2, book 4, p. 58 [81]; see also Bradley Chapin, "Colonial and Revolutionary Origins of the American Law of Treason," *William and Mary Quarterly* 17, no. 1, 3rd series (January 1960), 4–21.

4. Blackstone, *Commentaries,* vol. 2, book 4, p. 58 [82].

5. Ibid. Blackstone noted one exception, however. There were "cases of national oppression [in which] the nation has very justifiably risen as one man, to vindicate the original contract subsisting between the king and his people."

6. 8 *CR, Boston Gazette,* July 22, 1771, 642.

7. See Alexander, *Rough Notes,* SHC.

8. *Governor's Report,* 24.

9. Ibid., 25.

10. Alexander, *Rough Notes,* SHC.

11. *Governor's Report,* 27, original in the SHC.

12. N.C. Historical Comm., *Records of the Moravians,* 875–876.

13. The account of the arrest of Booth and Dunn from this chapter is taken largely from 10 *CR,* "Memorandum from John Ross Dunn Concerning His Imprisonment," July 27, 1776, pp. 673–678.

14. 10 *CR,* "Minutes of the Provincial Congress of South Carolina," November 6–7, 1775, pp. 305–306.

15. 10 *CR,* Dunn Memo, 675.

16. Ibid.

17. 13 *CR,* "Letter from Thomas Polk to George Washington," June 26, 1778, p. 451.

18. James Collins, "Autobiography of a Revolutionary War Solider," *Southern Voices,* 75–76.

19. 10 *CR,* "Letter from Josiah Martin to William Legge, Earl of Dartmouth," p. 231.

20. *Governor's Report,* 25.

21. Alexander, *Rough Notes,* SHC.

22. See discussion in McNitt, *Chain of Error,* 46.

23. 10 *CR,* "Letter from the Rowan County Committee of Safety to the Mecklenburg County Committee of Safety," June 1775, p. 11.

24. Ibid.

25. 10 *CR,* "Address from the Rowan County Committee of Safety to the County Militias Rowan County (N.C.)," June 1775, 10–11.

26. Alexander, *Rough Notes,* SHC.

Chapter 9

1. Alexander, *Rough Notes,* SHC.

2. Ibid.

3. Hunter, *Sketches,* 61–62.

4. Ibid., 64.

5. *Governor's Report,* 16.

6. Ibid., 24.

7. Ibid., 16.

8. N.C. Historical Comm., *Records of the Moravians,* 874–875.

9. Hunter, *Sketches*, 67.

10. James Collins, "Autobiography of a Revolutionary War Solider," *Southern Voices*, 74–75.

11. Ibid., 75.

12. 10 *CR*, "Letter from Josiah Martin to William Legge, Earl of Dartmouth," p. 231.

13. Ibid. Martin noted that the only messenger to reach him was "from a considerable Body of Germans, settled in the County of Mecklenburg, who brought me a loyal declaration against the Very extraordinary and traiterous [*sic*] resolves of the Committee of that County."

14. 10 *CR*, "Letter from Josiah Martin to William Legge, Earl of Dartmouth," June 30, 1775, p. 48.

15. *Governor's Report*, 16.

16. Ibid., 17.

17. Ibid., 16.

18. Alexander, *Rough Notes*, SHC.

19. Hunter, *Sketches*, 68–69.

20. The governing executive board of the worldwide Moravian Church was called the Unity Elder's Conference or UEC, also seen written in German as *Unitäs Aeltesten Conferenz* or *UAC*. Headquartered at Berthelsdorf near Herrnhut in Germany, the UEC was responsible for supervision of the spiritual affairs of the church, as well as being the "supreme authority" over all decisions made by other committees within the church (such as decisions made by the settlers in the Carolina piedmont).

21. N.C. Historical Comm., *Records of the Moravians*, 874.

22. Ibid., 875 (emphasis in the original).

23. Ibid., 876 (emphasis in the original)

24. Ibid., 876, fn 13.

25. Alexander, *Rough Notes*, SHC (emphasis in the original).

26. Ibid.

Chapter 10

1. Ashe, *History*, 459.

2. 10 *CR*, "Minutes of the Bladen, Brunswick, Duplin, and Wilmington-New Hanover County Committees of Safety," May 20, 1775-May 21, p. 1775, 26.

3. Ibid., 27.

4. The following discussions of Martin's life are from Stumpf, *Martin*. This paragraph is from Stumpf, *Martin*, 6–8.

5. Ibid., 3–5.

6. Ibid., 11.

7. Ibid.

8. Ibid., 13, 15.

9. Ibid., 20.

10. Ibid., 22.

11. Ibid., 28.

12. Ibid., 35.

13. Ibid., 44.

14. "Circular Letter to the Committees in South Carolina, April 27, 1775," in the *South Carolina and American General Gazette*, April 28-May 5, 1775 (emphasis in the original).

15. Stumpf, *Martin*, 18.

16. Ibid., 67.

17. 9 *CR*, "Minutes of the North Carolina Governor's Council," March 6, 1775, p. 1146.

18. Following account of the meeting from the official minutes in 10 *CR*, "Minutes of the North Carolina Governor's Council," June 25, 1775, pp. 38–40.

19. Ibid., 38.

20. This and the quotes from Martin which follow are in 10 *CR*, "Letter from Governor Martin to the Earl of Dartmouth," June 30, 1775, beginning at 41.

21. Ibid., 47–48.

22. Ibid., 49.

23. The following account of the meeting is from the official minutes in 10 *CR*, "Minutes of the North Carolina Governor's Council," July 18, 1775, pp. 106–107.

24. 10 *CR*, "Proclamation by Josiah Martin Concerning the Election of Delegates to the Provincial Congress of North Carolina and Militia Officers and Loyalty to Great Britain," August 15, 1775, pp. 141–151.

25. 10 *CR*, "Minutes of the Provincial Congress of North Carolina," August 20, 1775-September 10, 1775, p. 180.

26. 10 *CR*, "Letter from Josiah Martin to William Legge, Earl of Dartmouth," August 28, 1775, p. 232.

27. Stumpf, *Martin*, 92.

28. Tarleton, *History*, 168.

29. Ibid., 159–160.

30. Ibid., 160.

31. Ibid.

Chapter 11

1. One hundred years after Phifer's death the writer C.L. Hunter reported that a "decaying headstone, scarcely legible, marks the last resting-place of this true patriot" at his estate, called Red Hill, on the Salisbury Road. It was said that to show their contempt for Phifer British soldiers lit a fire on his grave when encamped there in the cold spring of 1781 following the crossing of the Catawba River and the Battle of Cowan's Ford (Hunter, *Sketches*, 54).

2. The Rocky Springs Cemetery is located in a one-acre plot of woods in Mint Hill, North Carolina, five hundred feet off Brief Road near mailbox 8730. Although there are many graves, only twenty-four are marked with headstones with names. Three others sites are marked with initials carved on fieldstones, and more than one hundred graves are marked with fieldstones showing no initials or dates. The site is overgrown and largely forgotten except for the diligence of church members who volunteer to maintain it.

3. See Boyte, *Houses of Charlotte*, 12–14.

4. Hunter, *Sketches*, 48.

5. I am greatly indebted to Mrs. Mary Boyer of Charlotte, who has diligently collected and kindly shared articles, original source material and transcriptions of information related to Ephraim Brevard (as well as other signers). Information on Brevard's life is inconsistent in some details. Some articles say he was imprisoned in Charleston, others in Florida. There are varying accounts of his service as a surgeon (or assistant surgeon) as well as where he may be buried. In any

event, good (if inconsistent) accounts can be found in the *Mecklenburg Gazette*, February 4, 1976, p. 5; Graham, *Mecklenburg Declaration and Lives of Its Signers*, 103–107; and Hunter, *Sketches*, 47–48.

6. Will of Ephraim Brevard, in the private papers of Mrs. Mary Boyer. Original in the North Carolina state archives.

7. Ibid.

8. Queen's College (also called Queen's Museum) was renamed Liberty Hall in 1777. In 1784 the school was relocated to Salisbury and the building in Charlotte fell into disrepair. In 1897, while excavating for a new county courthouse, a human femur bone was unearthed, presumably from one of the bodies of Revolutionary patriots — or British soldiers — buried on the grounds. For that matter, it could in theory have been the bones of Ephraim Brevard. The original location of Queen's College has long been paved over and today is surrounded by skyscrapers, although a DAR marker and bronze plaque (giving an incorrect date as to the year its charter was revoked — 1772, not 1782) mark the approximate site. In May 2012 a plaque to Brevard was placed in downtown Charlotte on the corner of College and Trade streets as part of the Charlotte Liberty Walk, an uptown historical walking tour.

9. Ashe, Weeks, and Van Noppen, *Biographical History*, 3.

10. Foote, *Sketches*, 206.

11. In a bill of sale from the period, McKnitt wrote "that on the 6th of April" the "said note, Bill of Sale, and said accounts, with nearly all his Bonds, Notes, Deeds, books, papers ... were consumed by fire in and with the house of his son Joseph Alexander." However, not everything was lost in the fire, McKnitt noted. Some records survived. In the same affidavit he notes that "his surveying book" was "not burned."

12. Alexander, Davie Copy, SHC.

13. Foote, *Sketches*, 206.

14. Ibid.

15. Ibid., 205.

16. Wirt, *Patrick Henry*, v.

17. Ibid., ix-x.

18. Ibid. Wirt would become the subject of another more bizarre controversy in 2005 when it was discovered that the Wirt family crypt in Washington's Congressional Cemetery had been robbed and his skull stolen. An eccentric collector of JFK memorabilia kept the skull until his death in October 2003, after which it was given to District of Columbia councilman Jim Graham to return it to its proper resting place. As Graham was unable to get the cemetery to confirm that it was, in fact, Wirt's skull, it sat in Graham's office in an old metal box painted with gold block letters reading "Hon. Wm. Wirt" for nearly two years before the Smithsonian could confirm its identity and return it to its proper place (Peter Carlson, "Tale from the Crypt," *Washington Post*, October 20, 2005.

19. Wirt, *Patrick Henry*, 416.

20. Ibid.

21. Ibid., 417.

22. Ibid., 80.

23. Ibid., 66.

24. Ibid., 417.

25. *Raleigh Register*, April 30, 1819, reprinted in *Governor's Report*, 13–15.

26. Ibid.

27. In copying a new draft, Dr. Alexander (or perhaps the editors of the *Raleigh Register*) had made some minor and essentially immaterial changes: the old English "thro" had been changed to "through"; "awfull" to "awful"; "desolve" to "dissolve"; "S^d." to "said"; and so forth. In addition, the word "*Resolved*" was added before each of the five resolutions; in the first clause, the phrase "Great Britain is an enemy to this County" became "to this *Country*"; in the second clause, the word "innocent" was not included before the clause "blood of American patriots"; the words "civil and religious" were dropped from clause three, which read in the original "independence *civil and religious*"; and one concluding sentence dealing with procedural matters ("a selection from the members present shall constitute a Committee of public safety for sd. County") was not included at all. Other than this handful of changes, however, none of which substantively affected the text, narrative or structure, the text in the *Raleigh Register* was indeed a "true copy" (see McNitt, *Chain of Error*, 39–40). The original draft that was sent to the *Raleigh Register* no longer exists, but given that the "copy in an unknown hand" and the version as printed were essentially identical is an indication that Dr. Alexander had copied from that draft.

28. McNitt, *Chain of Error*, 33 (also referred to sometimes as the "copy in an unknown handwrite").

29. Ibid.

30. Ibid.

31. SHC. McNitt tentatively dates the copy in an unknown hand as 1794 (McNitt, *Chain of Error*, 34). Also see Hoyt, *Mecklenburg Declaration*, 135–136.

Chapter 12

1. McCullough, *Adams*, 113.

2. Ibid., 380.

3. Ibid., 448.

4. Ibid.

5. Ellis, *Passionate Sage*, 115.

6. Ibid., 117.

7. McCullough, *Adams*, 594.

8. Ellis, *Passionate Sage*, 115.

9. Ibid., 116.

10. McCullough, *Adams*, 602–603.

11. Jefferson, *Works*, 174.

12. Ibid.

13. McCullough, *Adams*, 607.

14. Ibid., 605.

15. The Adams letter that follows is from *Adams-Jefferson Letters*, 542.

16. Ibid.

17. Adams letter to William Bentley, dated July 15, 1819, in Adams, *Works*, 381.

18. Ibid.

19. Ibid.

20. Ibid.

21. Adams letter to William Bentley, August 21, 1819, in Adams, *Works*, 383.

Chapter 13

1. Letter from Thomas Jefferson to Dr. Vine Utley, March 21, 1819, in Jefferson, *Writing*, 313.
2. Ibid.
3. McCullough, *Adams*, 634.
4. Thomas Jefferson to Arthur Spicer Brockenbrough, July 2, 1819. This can be found at the UVA Electronic Text Center, UVA Library, http://etext .lib.virginia.edu/toc/modeng/public/Jef3Gri.html.
5. Ibid.
6. Jefferson's letter to Adams dated July 9, 1819, quoted throughout can be found in Jefferson, *Writings*, beginning 314 (also in *Adams-Jefferson Letters*, 543–544).
7. The foregoing quotes are from *Adams-Jefferson Letters*, 543–544.
8. *Adams-Jefferson Letters*, 545.
9. Ibid.
10. Ibid.
11. McNitt also makes this point in *Chain of Error*: "It was *Adams himself* who had first cried plagiarism" (71 (emphasis added)).
12. *Adams-Jefferson Letters*, 545.
13. Adams, *Works*, 383.
14. Ibid.
15. Ibid.
16. Ibid., 383–384.
17. Ibid., 384.

Chapter 14

1. Address of Dr. Winslow Alexander in Hopewell Church, July 5, 1824, *Catawba Journal*, October 19, 1824, SHC.
2. Ibid.
3. Dr. Joseph McKnitt Alexander, "Declaration of Independence by the Citizens of Mecklenburg County," *Yadkin and Catawba Journal*, November 9, 1830 (courtesy of the CML).
4. Force, *Calendar*, 28.
5. Jones, *Defense*, vii.
6. Biography of "Shocco" Jones by Thomas Kevin Cherry, "A North Carolina Charlatan," *North Carolina Libraries* (Summer 2003), 8–9. According to Cherry, Jones spent his final years living in a cabin in the woods.
7. Ibid., 295.
8. Ibid., vi, 310, 330.
9. Ibid., 329.
10. Ibid., 15.
11. "Historical Literature of North Carolina," in *Harvard University Bulletin* 7, no. 53 (ed. Justin Winsor) (January, 1894), 326.
12. Dr. Joseph McKnitt Alexander, "Declaration of Independence by the Citizens of Mecklenburg County," *Yadkin and Catawba Journal*, November 9, 1830.
13. *Historical Literature of N.C.*, 325.
14. Grigsby, *Virginia Convention*, 20.
15. Ibid., 20, 25.
16. *Historical Literature of N.C.*, 325.
17. Foote, *Sketches*, 207.
18. Ironically, Dr. Joseph Alexander shared many traits with Jefferson. They both came from prominent southern families active in the Revolution. Like Jefferson, Dr. Joseph Alexander was well educated for his time, attending Princeton to study theology and enter the ministry. Like Jefferson, Dr. Joseph Alexander read widely in his youth the French enlightenment philosophers — Montesquieu, Voltaire, Diderot, D'Alemhert, Buffon, and Rousseau — and, like Jefferson, he was extraordinarily influenced by them, so much so he seems to have dropped (or at least questioned) his religious faith in favor of Enlightenment rationalism. In the recollections of a friend who knew him, his immersion in the secular, rational writings of the philosophes "may for a time have diverted his attention from spiritual things." Instead of becoming a Presbyterian minister — as his father had anticipated — he returned to Mecklenburg as a physician. Like Jefferson he believed in studying and examining the natural world. He wrote extensively and articulately on a variety of matters historical and scientific, collected historical documents and manuscripts, and corresponded with the major civic leaders of his age — the governor, William Polk (son of Thomas Polk), and other Revolutionary descendants. A friend recalled of him that he "early developed indications of not only genius and talents, but the highest attributes of intellect, sound judgment and profound thinking." Later in his life, perhaps drawn by the deep historical roots of Hopewell Church and the Presbyterians in the region, he returned to the church of his father and became a professor of religion. And, recalled another friend, he "continued through life, until the infirmities of old age prevented, to be active in the promotion of its interests, in alleviating and ameliorating the condition of men" (Foote, *Sketches*, 209–10).
19. Dr. Joseph McKnitt Alexander, "Declaration of Independence by the Citizens of Mecklenburg County," *Yadkin and Catawba Journal*, November 9, 1830.
20. McNitt, *Chain of Error*, 36, 32.
21. See McNitt, *Chain of Error*, 36–38, for a good summary of the rough notes. The originals are in the SHC.
22. In a letter from Dr. Joseph Alexander to Governor Stokes, dated April 5, 1831, he wrote as follows: "All the papers in my possession, together with such certificates authenticating the same as I could hastily procure, I forwarded at the request of Colonel Fisher to him, and I understand they are left for your selection.... You will find two or 3 original papers referred to as left by John McKnitt Alexander — one merely an abstract of the proceedings of 20 May 1775 [e.g., the rough notes] — one a full statement of the proceedings (hand write unknown) [e.g., the copy in an unknown hand] — and the third paper — the one deposited with General Davie and after his death found amongst his papers by Doctr. Sam Henderson, and restored to us [the Davie Copy] — this paper you will find to be an exact transcript of the second mentioned paper, as far as it is untorn — *the inference is that they were exact copies of the original proceedings* [emphasis added].... I do not know that I have any other papers on the subject that would aid you in the publication" (Letter

from Dr. Joseph McKnitt Alexander to Governor M. Stokes, April 5, 1831, SHC).

23. Certificate of Dr. Joseph Alexander, SHC.

24. Alexander, *Rough Notes*, SHC.

25. Dr. Joseph McKnitt Alexander, "Declaration of Independence by the Citizens of Mecklenburg County," *Yadkin and Catawba Journal*, November 9, 1830.

26. Today, what is arguably the only surviving sketch of what might be America's first declaration of independence lies in a manila file folder in a blue-gray box (both acid-free) in the Southern Historical Collection at Wilson Library at the University of North Carolina at Chapel Hill. It is little examined and barely remembered.

Chapter 15

1. *Governor's Report*, 9.

2. Ibid., 10.

3. Alexander, Davie Copy, SHC ("previous to that time of 1800; a full copy of S^d. records, at the request of Doctor Hugh Williamson, then of New York; but formerly a representative in Congress from this State — was forwarded to him by Col. Wm. Polk in order that those early transactions might fill their proper place in a history of this State them compiling by S^d. Doctor Williamson in New York").

4. Ibid.

5. See Alexander, *Rough Notes*, SHC "About 1787 Doctor Hugh Williamson (then of New York: but formerly was member of Congress from this State) applied [torn] [sic] above by Col$^{o.}$ Wm Polk, who was then compiling a [torn] [sic] in order to prove that the American people [torn] [sic] in the Revolution — and that Congress were *Com* [torn] [sic]."

6. *Governor's Report*, 5.

7. Ibid., 26.

8. Powell, *Dictionary*, 114.

9. Ibid.

10. *Governor's Report*, 6.

11. Ibid.

12. Ibid.

13. See Graham, *Papers*.

14. Ibid.

15. Graham, *Papers*, 64.

16. Ibid.

17. Ibid., 49.

18. "Susan Alexander is said to have saved the life of Joseph Graham, N.C. Partisan Rangers. The said Joseph Graham was severely wounded at Charlotte September 26, 1780. He was found by Susan Alexander, who took him to her house, washed and dressed his wounds and cared for him until he recovered" ("Widow's Revolutionary Pension #20568," in Graham Papers, 66).

19. *Governor's Report*, 9.

20. Ibid., 20.

21. Ibid., 23.

22. Ibid., 17.

23. Ibid., 18.

24. Ibid., 16.

25. Ibid., 18.

26. Ibid., 19. According to Hunter, "the following were selected, and styled Delegates, and are here given, according to my best recollection, as they were placed on roll: Abram Alexander, sen'r, Thomas Polk, Rich'd Harris, sen'r, Adam Alexander, Richard Barry, John M'Knit Alexander, Neil Morison, Hezekiah Alexander, Hezekiah J. Balch, Zacheus Wilson, John Phifer, James Harris, William Kennon, John Ford, Henry Downs, Ezra Alexander, William Graham, John Queary, Chas. Alexander, Waitstill Avery, Ephraim Brevard, Benjamin Patton, Matthew M'Clure, Robert Irwin, John Flenniken, and David Reese. Abram Alexander was nominated, and unanimously voted to the Chair. John M'Nnit Alexander and Ephraim Brevard were chosen Secretaries" (20–21).

27. Ibid., 24.

28. Ibid., 27.

29. Ibid., 23–24.

30. Ibid., 17.

31. Ibid., 26.

32. Ibid.

33. Ibid., 28.

34. Ibid., 22.

35. Ibid., 18.

36. Ibid., 6.

37. Caldwell's account that follows is from Henderson, *Washington's Southern Tour*, 278 — 287.

38. The foregoing Caldwell testimony is in Henderson, *Washington's Southern Tour*, beginning at 278. Caldwell appears at first glance to be a credible witness. Following his graduation from the Salisbury Military College he was appointed professor of natural history at the University of Pennsylvania and later, in 1819, he served as head of the medical department of Transylvania University in Lexington, Kentucky. In 1837 Dr. Caldwell founded the Louisville Medical Institute, holding the chairs of the Institutes of Medicine, Medical Jurisprudence and Chemical Medicine departments. He was an eminent and respected physician and teacher, "a man of distinction," as Henderson put it, "widely acquainted with eminent scientists and distinguished public characters in England and Europe as well as in the United States" (Henderson, *Washington's Southern Tour*, 278, fn 1).

39. In Arthur, *Western North Carolina*, 381.

40. From F.A. Sondley, "Buncombe's First School Master," *Asheville Citizen*, March 4, 1928. Like Graham, Henry was also a credible witness. In October 1780, while still a schoolboy, Henry had fought at the Battle of Kings Mountain, where he was badly wounded in the hand and thigh by a bayonet. In February 1781, he fought at the battle of Cowan's Ford, where troops under William Lee Davidson attempted to slow the crossing of the Catawba River by Lord Cornwallis's army. Following the Revolution, Henry moved to the mountains and was the first lawyer and teacher in the area. On January 6, 1863, he died at the age of 98 years, the oldest veteran of the Battle of Kings Mountain (Arthur, *Western North Carolina*, 381).

41. Graham, *Mecklenburg Declaration*.

42. Ibid., 30–31.

43. Ibid.

44. Ibid., 31.

45. Ibid., 33. Wallis' remarks were printed in the

Raleigh Minerva of August 10, 1809, and copied in part into the *Catawba Journal* of July 11, 1826. See also Mc-Nitt, *Chain of Error*, 85.

46. In Graham, *Mecklenburg Declaration*, 33.

47. Ibid., 34.

48. And a third: "This indenture made the twenty ninth day [of] April in the year of our Lord one thousand seven hundred and eighty and in the *Fifth Year of American Independence*" (emphasis added).

49. Graham, *Mecklenburg Declaration*, 32.

50. H. Addington Bruce, "New Light on the Mecklenburg Declaration of Independence," *Magazine of History with Notes and Queries* 4 (New York, William Abbatt, July-December 1906), 264.

51. In Foote, *Sketches*, 421.

52. *Governor's Report*, 26.

53. *Miners' and Farmers' Journal*, October 26, 1833.

54. *Charlotte Democrat*, April 29, 1881, 5.

55. *Western Democrat,* May 5, 1857.

56. Letter from C.M.W., in *North-Carolina Gazette*, July 1839.

57. *Raleigh Register*, July 20, 1839.

58. Ibid.

59. Article by "C.L.H.," *Charlotte Journal*, September 5, 1839, SHC.

Chapter 16

1. Force, *Calendar,* preface.

2. Ibid. See also McNitt, *Chain of Error*, 86–87.

3. McNitt, *Chain of Error*, 86. This paper is also referred to as the *Massachusetts Spy or American Oracle of Liberty* of July 12, 1775 (Hoyt, *Mecklenburg Declaration*, 18).

4. The preamble plus four resolves were from the *Daily National Intelligencer* (Washington, DC), December 18, 1838, p. 2. The text of the Mecklenburg Resolves is widely available from a variety of sources, including Salley, *Mecklenburg Declaration*, 16–19. The text of the resolves quoted in this chapter is from the original version of the *South-Carolina Gazette and Country Journal* of June 13, 1775 (no. 498) held in the collection of the Charleston Library Society, Charleston, South Carolina.

5. *Washington* (DC) *Daily National Intelligencer*, December 18, 1838.

6. Ibid.

7. Letter from Peter Force to C.L. Hunter, July 3, 1839, in Force, *Calendar*, 10.

8. McNitt, *Chain of Error*, 86 (the article is dated December 17, 1838, but appears in the December 18 edition); "Historical Literature of North Carolina," *Harvard University Bulletin*, no. 57; it can also be found in vol. 7, no. 5 (ed. Justin Winsor)(January 1894), 325.

9. *Washington* (DC) *Daily National Intelligencer*, December 18, 1838; Hoyt, *Mecklenburg Declaration*, 18.

10. *Washington* (DC) *Daily National Intelligencer*, December 18, 1838.

11. Ibid., 86.

12. Letter from George Bancroft to Peter Force, March 15, 1842, in Force, *Calendar*, 15.

13. McNitt, *Chain of Error*, 86. Also see Hoyt, *Mecklenburg Declaration*, 18–19. Text of the resolves

are from the original version of the *South-Carolina Gazette and Country Journal* of June 13, 1775 (see note 4 of this chapter).

14. "Historical Literature of North Carolina," *Harvard University Bulletin*, no. 57, or vol. 7, no. 5 (ed. Justin Winsor) (January, 1894), 325.

15. Hoyt gives the year of Bancroft's discovery as 1847 (Hoyt, *Mecklenburg Declaration*, 18–19). However, see letter from George Bancroft to Governor David Swain dated July 4, 1848, where Bancroft notifies Swain of the discovery, suggesting the year is in fact 1848 (Force, *Calendar*, 15). In addition to the sources mentioned in the text, the resolves were found in several contemporary newspapers, including the Charleston *South-Carolina Gazette and Country Journal* of June 13, 1775, and reprinted in abbreviated form in the *New York Journal* of June 29, 1775, and *Massachusetts Spy* of July 12, 1775. In both instances the original source was credited to Charleston. They were also printed in the *New Bern North-Carolina Gazette* on June 16, 1775, and the *Wilmington Cape-Fear Mercury* on June 23, 1775. See Salley, *Mecklenburg Declaration*, 16, and McNitt, *Chain of Error*, 86.

16. For discussion and full text of the Mecklenburg Resolves, see Graham, *Mecklenburg Declaration*, 38–43.

17. This and the text that follows is from the *South-Carolina Gazette and Country Journal* of June 13, 1775, no. 498, held in the collection of the Charleston Library Society, Charleston, South Carolina.

18. Letter from C.L. Hunter to Peter Force, June 22, 1839, in Force, *Calendar*, 10.

19. Peter Force, *Daily National Intelligencer,* December 18, 1838; in Force, *Calendar*, 8.

20. *Governor's Report*, 25.

21. Tucker, *Life of Jefferson*, 471.

22. Salley, "The Mecklenburg Declaration: The Present Status of the Question," 24.

23. Ibid., 29.

24. Letter from George Tucker to Peter Force, March 12, 1839, in Force, *Calendar*, 9–10.

25. Ibid. Not everyone agreed. C.L. Hunter, a North Carolina newspaper correspondent, wrote to Force on June 22, 1839, that while some believed the Mecklenburg Resolves to be the same as those of May 20, 1775, "he did not" (Letter from C.L. Hunter to Peter Force, June 22, 1839, in Force, *Calendar*, 10).

26. *Governor's Report*, 18.

27. Ibid., 25.

28. In Salley, "The Mecklenburg Declaration: The Present Status of the Question," 19.

29. Ibid., 24.

30. Tucker, *Jefferson, Volume II*, 471–472.

31. Letter from Peter Force to Lyman Draper, August 13, 1875, in Force, *Calendar*, 29.

Chapter 17

1. Adams, *Works*, 383.

2. Draper, Mecklenburg Declaration, 37–38.

3. *Governor's Report*, 15; Alexander, Davie Copy, SHC.

4. Passages that follow from Alexander, Davie Copy, SHC.

5. The fact that the Davie Copy and the "copy in an unknown hand" are identical is proven decisively by even a cursory review of the two documents. Had McKnitt been simply drafting freehand, rather than copying from a written record, there would inevitably have been discrepancies, plus any deletions that had occurred, corrections, and strike-throughs. And in fact, in the final four paragraphs of the Davie Copy (in which McKnitt summarizes the court of enquiry and the committee of safety of the Revolutionary period), a narrative section not contained in the "copy in an unknown hand," there are four amendments and two deletions, which prove he is writing rather than simply transcribing.

6. He then noted that prior to 1800 "a full copy of S^d. records, at the request of Doctor Hugh Williamson, then of New York; but formerly a representative in Congress from this State — was forwarded to him by Col. Wm. Polk in order that those early transactions might fill their proper place in a history of this State then compiling by S^d. Doctor Williamson in New York."

7. As his son's comment shows ("as to Dunn and Booth is incorrect as to time"), this paragraph is also significant in that, in it, McKnitt says the trials of Tories, conducted in 1775, took place in 1780–81. This throws a shadow on the accuracy of the entire paper and shines a light on the mental state of McKnitt as he wrote 25 years or so after the events in question.

8. For the life of Phillips see Richard Battle, "Memoir of Rev. Charles Phillips, D.D., LL.D.," *North Carolina University Magazine*, no. 1 (Chapel Hill: Students of University of North Carolina, 1890).

9. "As for myself, my father was an Englishman, my Mother was of an old New Jersey Dutch Reformed family," Phillips wrote to Lyman Draper in a letter dated October 28, 1881 (Draper Papers, Wisconsin Historical Society).

10. McNitt, *Chain of Error*, 89. In 1966, V.V. Mc-Nitt, a New England newspaper editor educated in Michigan (no relation to any of the North Carolina McKnitts), wrote a succinct and cogent argument regarding the Davie Copy and the errors made by Phillips in *Chain of Error*. This book and the arguments it puts forth has informed my investigation to a large extent.

11. McNitt, *Chain of Error*, 111.

12. Battle, "Memoir of Phillips," 19 (see note 8 above).

13. McNitt, *Chain of Error*, 104.

14. Ibid., 88.

15. Letters from Charles Phillips to Lyman Draper, June 13, 1885 and October 28, 1881, Draper Papers, Wisconsin Historical Society.

16. McNitt, *Chain of Error*, 89.

17. Ibid., 89.

18. Ibid., 104.

19. Ibid., 104–105.

20. This and passages that follow are from Charles Phillips, "May, 1775," *North Carolina University Magazine* (1853), 168.

21. Ibid., 168–169.

22. Ibid., 175.

23. Ibid.

24. McNitt, *Chain of Error*, 96.

25. Blythe and Brockmann, *Hornets' Nest*, 61.

26. McNitt, *Chain of Error*, 89.

27. Ibid.

28. Ibid., 90.

29. Ibid.

30. Ibid., 105–106.

31. Welling, "Mecklenburg Declaration of Independence," 224.

32. Archibald Henderson, "The Davie Copy," reprint from the *Alumni Review*, University of North Carolina, Chapel Hill, July, 1939.

33. McNitt, *Chain of Error*, 105.

34. Ibid., 106.

35. Letter from Charles Phillips to Lyman Draper, June 13, 1885, Draper Papers, Wisconsin Historical Society.

36. McNitt, *Chain of Error*, 105.

37. Ibid., 109.

38. The supporters of the Mecklenburg Declaration of Independence have not forgotten Phillips' perfidy. As recently as September 2011 former judge Chase B. Saunders made a presentation in Charlotte to the Mecklenburg Historical Association in which he sought a "trial of UNC Professor Charles Phillips for academic misconduct in his 1853 publication, defaming the drafters and declaring the episode a fraud, for wanton negligence in conducting his research and thereby failing to meet generally accepted standards of academic research and materially deviated from said standards."

Chapter 18

1. Hoyt, *Mecklenburg Declaration*, iii.

2. Ibid.

3. Ibid., 112.

4. Salley, "Present Status of the Question," 29.

5. Ibid., 30.

6. Ibid.

7. Ibid., 31.

8. Salley, "Present Status of the Question," 36. Recent research has been unable to prove whether or not Benjamin Wilson was in fact known as "Independence" Ben at all. Beyond family tradition there is no written evidence to this effect. A recent paper on the Davidson family by Jim and Ann Williams notes that historian Chalmers Davidson states that local people did not take much note of the date May 20 until the Mecklenburg Controversy began in 1819 and "therefore doubts that [the nickname] 'Independence Ben' was attached to the boy in childhood. There is also some doubt as to whether he was called 'Ben' at all," they conclude (James Williams and Ann Williams, "The Davidsons of Rural Hill: The First Three Generations," paper prepared for Rural Hill, August 31, 2012, p. 29).

9. Salley, "Present Status of the Question," 35 (emphasis added).

10. See E. Thomson Shields, Jr., "'A Modern Poem,' by the Mecklenburg Censor: Politics and Satire in Revolutionary North Carolina," *Early American Literature* 29, no. 3 (1994), 206. Shields' article gives a thorough discussion of the two versions of the poem.

11. Ibid., 213–214: "Little is known about the provenance of either the Charleston Library Society

or the Southern Historical Collection manuscripts. How the one manuscript ended up in Charleston is unknown. It may be speculated that because river transportation was more reliable than overland routes, the people of Mecklenburg County traded with Charleston as much or more than they did with cities in the eastern part of North Carolina. Therefore, it would have made as much sense for the author or editor to try and publish the work in Charleston as in a North Carolina city, as seen by the fact that the Mecklenburg Resolves were published in Charleston three days before they were published in New Bern" (226, fn. 3). Finally, to confuse the thin and perishable facts regarding the poem further, "the only specific information known" about the poem cited by Wheeler and Graham "is that it was placed in its folder among the Hawks Papers [at UNC] in 1947" (226–227, fn. 3). Predictably, "the original manuscript of the Southern Historical Collection text"— the version that Davidson had copied for Hawks —"has not been located and is probably no longer extant" (206). It is worth pointing out that Graham had relied on the poem as evidence against the better advice of North Carolina governor David L. Swain, who had seen the manuscript and believed that it was little more than "a series of doggerel verses ... of questionable authenticity" (206). Governor Swain's view on the poem seems to be unclear; Graham attested that he spoke of its "unquestionable authenticity." Graham noted that "the genuineness of this poem if vouched for by Hon. Lyman Draper ... Wheeler's History of N.C., Vol. II ... and by Governor Swain, in whose possession the poem was at the time of his death, in 1868" (Graham and Graham, *Why North Carolinians Believe,* 20). There was a final, unstated implication in this complicated saga: the lawyer Davidson who made the copy deliberately altered the text to include the reference to Mecklenburg's independence. Given that the Hawks Collection text omitted an introduction by the "editor," as well as some explanatory notes at the end, both of which the Charleston text included, this was plausible. Today, the facts are too tangled to even begin to unravel the accuracy or veracity of the "Mecklenburg Censor."

12. Henderson, *Washington's Southern Tour,* 278. For an example, consider how Caldwell describes his first seeing Washington riding towards him: "In the midst of this landscape, already abundantly attractive and exciting, just as I had advanced about half-way up the hill, the President turned its summit, and began to descend. The steps of his charger were measured and proud, as if the noble animal was conscious of the character and standing of his rider.... [I]t reminded me of Brahma's descent from the skies" (Henderson, *Washington's Southern Tour,* 281–282).

13. See Ramsey, *Autobiography,* 283. In a letter to Draper dated May 23, 1875, Ramsey noted that "as to the *names* of the *delegates* (for there were no signers) the list given was the result of various combined recollections and thus varied a little.... [John Hill] Wheeler [in *Reminiscences*] has the list *correct.*"

14. The list of Humphrey Hunter is the same as the *Governor's Report,* or 26 in total. However, the testimony of James Jack identified John Davidson as a

signer, bringing the number to 27. This list (27) is cited by the historian F.X. Martin and used on a monument raised in Charlotte in 1898. Ramsey adds five other names to the list: William Davidson, Samuel Martin, Duncan Ochiltree, Ezekiel Polk and William Wilson (32).

15. Charles L. Van Noppen, "The Supineness of the North Carolina Historical Association and the Ignorance of the North Carolina Society of Colonial Dames" (Greensboro, 1912).

16. "Mecklenburg: A Great Rebel Fraud," *National Intelligencer,* May 20, 1893, in Draper.

17. Salley, "Present Status of the Question," 36–37.

18. "Mec Dec Is Around Here Somewhere," *Charlotte News,* May 21, 1957

19. Salley, "Present Status of the Question," 37.

20. Ibid.

21. Ibid., 38. Similarly, the Davie "copy," he wrote, was a work of fiction from beginning to end, liberally plagiarized from the Declaration of Independence. After all, he wrote, "the Davie 'copy'" (here he was almost orally snickering with his sarcastic use of quote marks) "was examined at Chapel Hill by Professor Charles Phillips, of the university faculty, who contributed an admirable paper on the subject of the 'Declaration' to the issue of the *North Carolina University Magazine* for May, 1853" (42). "It is very doubtful," wrote Salley, erroneously relying on the unreliable Phillips, "if the original Davie 'copy' was 'perfectly the same' as the paper in the unknown hand." What's more, "Professor Phillips, who compared the two original papers, says that the two resolutions differ in the two documents in perhaps one important particular." None of this was true — but no matter.

22. Ibid.

23. Ibid., 42–43.

24. Ibid., 43.

25. Extended comparison tends, in the view of this author, to clear Dr. Alexander of having written the "copy in an unknown hand." While it must be admitted that the penmanship is similar in many respects, it is also sufficiently different in key aspects. It is demonstrably *not* in the penmanship of John McKnitt Alexander. Moreover, it makes no sense for Dr. Alexander to have made annotations in the margins, as he did, or to have forwarded the document on to others if he had written it himself. The "copy in an unknown hand" is clearly not in the same handwriting as any of the other witnesses quoted in the *Governor's Report.* Nor, in this author's view, is the handwriting that of William Polk, as McNitt speculates in *Chain of Error.* As of now, the author remains unknown and may never be known.

26. Salley, "Present Status of the Question," 36.

27. Ibid.

Chapter 19

1. *Raleigh Register,* June 7, 1825.

2. *Catawba Journal,* May 31, 1825. For an excellent summary of the Mec Dec commemorations throughout the years, see a paper by Jeff Forret, "The Mecklenburg Declaration of Independence, May 20, 1775:

The Significance of Its Commemoration in Nineteenth-Century North Carolina History," April 1997
(courtesy of CML).

3. *Southern Home*, March 22, 1875.

4. Ibid.

5. Ibid.

6. Ibid.

7. Ibid.

8. "Mecklenburg: The Centennial Celebration,"
New York Times, May 20, 1875.

9. James Welling, "The Mecklenburg Declaration
of Independence, May 20, 1775," *North American Review* (Boston: Osgood, April 1874), 288.

10. McNitt, *Chain of Error*, 107.

11. Ibid., 107–108.

12. Grimes, *History of the Great Seal*, 24. From the
Civil War until 1885 the North Carolina state flag had
carried the twin dates May 20, 1775 (for the Mecklenburg Declaration), and May 20, 1861 (the date of
its secession from the Union). The latter date was
dropped in 1885 and replaced with the date April 12,
1776, the date that the state resolved on independence
from Great Britain and approved what became known
as the "Halifax Resolves."

13. *Public Laws and Resolutions of the State of North
Carolina Passed by the General Assembly at Its Session,
1893,* chapter 145. See Grimes, *History of the Great
Seal*, 40.

14. Ibid.

15. Letter from Charles Phillips to Lyman Draper,
October 28, 1881, Draper Papers, Wisconsin Historical
Society: "Colonel Wheeler told me in my own house
that he had no authority save the talk of modern times
for saying that there was any *signing* at Charlotte" (emphasis in the original).

16. "American Independence," *Manchester Guardian*,
May 21, 1909.

17. *Charlotte Daily Observer*, May 20, 1906, 15.

18. Ibid.

19. "American Independence," *Manchester Guardian*,
May 21, 1909. The "Taft Chair" still exists and is kept
at Johnson C. Smith University in Charlotte.

20. Ibid.

21. Charles L. Van Noppen, "The Supineness of the
North Carolina Historical Association and the Igno-
rance of the North Carolina Society of Colonial
Dames" (Greensboro: N.p., 1912).

22. Blackburn Johnson, "Battles Over Mecklenburg Declaration Are Nothing New," *News and Observer,
Raleigh*, May 15, 1955.

23. Charles L. Van Noppen, *The Mecklenburg Declaration of Independence Written in 1800* (Lynchburg,
VA: Brown-Morrison, 1912).

24. S.A. Ashe, "The Mecklenburg Declaration: More
About the Exact Date of the Resolves," *Uncle Remus'
Home Magazine*, 18–19 (n.d.). As an interesting side-
bar, Ashe himself had been a living witness to history
and later in life wrote a moving memoir of the dying
days of the Confederacy, which he had witnessed firsthand as a young man in Charlotte in April 1865. One
observer noted, "Though he writes from memory, he
tells the story of those eventful and sorrowful days, now
forty-five years ago, with unquestionable accuracy." But

forty-five years was a long time, and Ashe was by now
just "another old man" himself. If Ashe could "clearly
recall events" that had taken place forty-five years earlier, one writer asked with keen irony, "why should he
disbelieve Mecklenburg Declaration eyewitnesses?"

25. Blackburn Johnson, "Battles Over Mecklenburg Declaration Are Nothing New," *News and Observer, Raleigh*, May 15, 1955.

26. Ibid.

27. "Greatest May Twentieth in Charlotte History,"
Charlotte Observer, May 14, 1916.

28. Ibid.

29. Ibid.

30. "President Wilson and Peace," *Manchester
Guardian*, May 23, 1916. The *Guardian* reported that
"Germany propagandists here are making remarkable
attempts to appeal to neutral sympathy. Since Germany abandoned her illegal submarine warfare and
Ambassador Bernstorff called off his packs of dyna-
miters and torchbearers, the Germans are being represented as wearing haloes."

31. "Declaration Reported Unearthed in London,"
Charlotte Observer, January 29, 1917.

32. Source Unknown, probably *Charlotte Observer*,
circa 1903.

33. "Proof of Mecklenburg Declaration Is Found
in Old Law Book, Attested by Old Citizens," *Charlotte
Observer*, May 31, 1939.

34. "Digs Up Proof in Two Books," *Charlotte Observer*, February 28, 1950.

35. R.W. Madry, "Mecklenburg Declaration Opponents 'Put on Spot,'" *Charlotte Observer*, May 7, 1939.

36. *Charlotte Observer*, June 5, 1974.

37. Francis Clarkson, "Witnesses Would Swear
Meck Dec Is Real," *Charlotte Observer*, March 13,
1974.

38. Olivia Rhodes, "Mecklenburg Declaration
Now Declared Authentic," source unknown, probably
the *Charlotte Observer* (n.d.).

39. Blackburn Johnson, "Battles Over Mecklenburg Declaration Are Nothing New," *Raleigh News
and Observer*, May 15, 1955.

40. "'Meck Dec' Survives Big Test," *Charlotte Observer*, March 20, 1971.

41. Emery Wister, "Independence: Traditional
County Holiday Dying Out," *Charlotte News*, May
21, 1973.

42. See Morrill, *Historic Charlotte,* online edition,
chapter 2, for additional views on the Mecklenburg
Controversy.

Chapter 20

1. Tucker, *Jefferson*, vol. 2, p. 464.

2. Adams letter to William Bentley, dated July 15,
1819, in Adams, *Works*, 381.

3. *Weekly Commercial*, April 21, 1875, in Draper.

4. Phillips, "May, 1775," 174.

5. 10 *CR*, "Letter from Governor Martin to the
Earl of Dartmouth," June 30, 1775, p. 48.

6. Salley, "Present Status of the Question," 21. According to Salley, the paper "could only have been one
issued between June 21 and June 30, and was undoubt-

edly *The Cape-Fear Mercury* of Wilmington, of Friday, June 23, 1775." Per Salley, "it was necessarily the Wilmington paper of that date [Friday, June 23, 1775] or the New Bern paper of the same date, as all other papers were too far off to have permitted of the news of the 21st going and the printed paper coming back between the 21st and the 30th." Salley argued that the paper printed the Mecklenburg Resolves of May 31, not the Mecklenburg Declaration, which he believed did not exist. If Salley were correct, where did the *Cape Fear Mercury* obtain a copy of the Mecklenburg Resolves? Salley suggested they had "probably copied the Mecklenburg resolutions of May 31 from the *North-Carolina Gazette* of the 16th, though it is possible that a third copy of the [Mecklenburg] resolution was sent to *The Cape-Fear Mercu*ry and arrived too late for use in the issue of the 16th." But unless the paper is found, this is all guesswork.

7. See discussion in Salley, "Present Status of the Question," 22.

8. Graham and Graham, *Why North Carolinians Believe*, 40–41.

9. Peterson, *Jefferson Image*, 143: "The Mecklenburg enthusiasm left no lasting scars on the Jefferson image" (144).

10. Graham and Graham, *Why North Carolinians Believe*, 40.

11. Ibid.

12. Ibid., 41.

13. In Draper.

14. Salley and Ford, "S. Millington Miller," 556–557.

15. Ibid.

16. See the Draper manuscript, which is the copy Wheeler uses in *Reminisces.*

17. Welling, "The Mecklenburg Declaration of Independence," 261.

18. McNitt, *Chain of Error*, 106.

19. Ibid., 89.

20. 10 *CR*, "Letter from Silas Deane to James Hogg," November 2, 1775, 301.

21. 10 *CR*, "Petition from Inhabitants of Mecklenburg County Concerning North Carolina Church Laws, 1769, p. 1017.

22. "Instructions to the Delegates of Mecklenburg County," September 1, 1775, SHC (emphasis added).

23. 10 *CR*, "Address from the Rowan County Committee of Safety to the County Militias," June 1775, p. 11.

24. Tucker, *Jefferson,* vol. 2, p. 464.

25. For example, the first resolution of the Chestertown Resolves of May 1774 announces "we acknowledge his majesty George III, King of Great Britain, France and Ireland, to be our rightful and lawful sovereign to whom we owe and promise all dutiful *allegiance* and submission." The Suffolk, Massachusetts, Resolves of September 1774 do the same, as do the Tryon Resolves of October 1775 ("We the subscribers professing our *allegiance* to the King"). Tryon County was adjacent to Mecklenburg.

26. Tucker, *Jefferson,* vol. 2, p. 468.

27. Welling, "The Mecklenburg Declaration of Independence," 262.

28. 7 *CR*, "Association by Some Inhabitants of North Carolina Concerning the Stamp Act," February 18, 1766, p. 182.

29. 9 *CR*, "Letter from Josiah Martin to Wills Hill, Marquis of Downshire," April 12, 1772, p. 279.

30. 9 *CR*, "Resolutions by Inhabitants of Halifax (Town) Concerning Resistance to Parliamentary Taxation," August 22, 1774, p. 1038.

31. 10 *CR*, "Circular Letter to the Inhabitants of South Carolina," June 30, 1775, p. 53.

32. Jones, *Defense*, 179.

33. 10 *CR*, "Minutes of the Tryon County Committee of Safety," August 14, 1775, p. 162.

34. 9 *CR*, "Resolutions by Inhabitants of Rowan County Concerning Resistance to Parliamentary Taxation," August 8, 1774, p. 1024.

35. 10 *CR*, "Minutes of the Provincial Congress of North Carolina," August 20, 1775-September 10, 1775, p. 186.

36. 9 *CR*, "Address of Inhabitants of Rowan and Surry Counties to Josiah Martin Concerning Loyalty to Great Britain" (n.d., circa 1775), 1160.

37. *South Carolina and American General Gazette*, June 2–9, 1775.

38. Maier, *American Scripture*, 124.

39. Ibid.

40. 9 *CR*, "Address of Inhabitants of Anson County to Josiah Martin Concerning Loyalty to Great Britain" (n.d., circa 1775), p. 1162.

41. Going outside the Carolinas, even more examples could be given. I will give but two: the Fairfax (Virginia) Resolves (July 1774) stated, "[S]hould the town of Boston be forced to submit to the late cruel and oppressive measures of Government, that we shall not hold the same to be binding upon us, but will, notwithstanding, religiously maintain, and inviolably adhere to, such measures as shall be concerted by the general Congress, for the preservation *of our lives, liberties, and fortunes*"; the Bush River (Maryland) Resolutions (March 1775) held in part, "We do most solemnly pledge ourselves to each other, and to our country, and engage ourselves by every tie held sacred among mankind, to perform the same *at the risk of our lives and fortunes.*"

42. Welling, "The Mecklenburg Declaration of Independence," 262.

43. Ibid.

Chapter 21

1. Fries, *Mecklenburg Declaration in Records of Wachovia,* 4.

2. Ibid., 3.

3. Ibid., 5.

4. Ibid.

5. H. Addington Bruce in the *North American Review* in July 1906; also in Fries, *Mecklenburg Declaration in Records of Wachovia,* 11.

6. Fries, *Mecklenburg Declaration in Records of Wachovia,* 11.

7. Ibid., 10.

8. Ibid.

9. Ibid., 11.

10. Letter from Adelaide Fries to Dr. Weeks, June 20, 1916, from the Adelaide L. Fries Papers, 1907–1939, Manuscript Collection Special Collections, Atkins Library, University of North Carolina-Charlotte.

11. N.C. Historical Comm., *Records of the Moravians*, 876 (emphasis in the original).

12. 10 *CR*, "Circular Letter from William Hooper, Joseph Hewes, and Richard Caswell to the Inhabitants of North Carolina," June 19, 1775, pp. 20–23. Quotes that follow are from this source.

13. Congress, *Journals of the American Congress*, 104.

14. Ibid., 105.

15. Ibid., 106.

16. Powell, *Dictionary of North Carolina Biography*, vol. 1, p. 343.

17. Ibid., vol. 3, p. 200.

18. Ibid., 200.

19. 10 *CR*, "Minutes of the Provincial Congress of North Carolina," August 20, 1775-September 10, 1775, p. 202.

20. John Adams to William Plumer, March 28, 1813, in Burnett, *Letters*, 537; and Adams, *Works,* vol. 10, p. 762.

21. Ibid.

22. Leigh Dyer, "Mec Dec Finds Famous backer: Historian McCullough Declares He's a Believer," *Charlotte Observer*, May 17, 2007, p. 1B.

23. Adams letter to William Bentley, dated July 15, 1819, in Adams, *Works*, 381.

24. *Adams-Jefferson Letters*, 543 — 544.

25. Adams, *Works*, 383.

Chapter 22

1. Graham, *Mecklenburg Declaration*, 18: "[T]here is abundant evidence to prove that at least seven authentic copies of those resolutions were in existence before the proceedings of the conventions were burned in 1800." Graham argues that in addition to the above four copies, a fifth was printed in the *Cape Fear Mercury*, a sixth was sent to the historian Williamson, and the historian Martin had a seventh.

2. Foote claims that a copy was sent to the moderator of the first Provincial Congress that met in Hillsboro in August 1775 "and was laid before the committee of business, but not particularly acted upon, as the majority of the body were still hoping for reconciliation on honorable terms" (*Sketches*, 40). There is no indication in the colonial records that a copy of the Mecklenburg Declaration was produced at the Hillsboro Convention, nor is it clear what led Foote to make this claim.

3. *Governor's Report,* 16 (emphasis added).

4. Francois-Xavier Martin, *History*, 372–376.

5. See Graham, *Mecklenburg Declaration*, 19–25; also see McNitt, *Chain of Error*, 75.

6. Or from a later version published by Judge Murphey. This is the explanation McNitt gives in *Chain of Error*, 75–76.

7. In Graham, *Mecklenburg Declaration*, 25.

8. Ibid. A version also appeared in Alexander Garden's *Anecdotes of the American Revolution*, which — some argued — independently corroborated the general story. This was named the "Garden" version of the Mecklenburg Declaration. See Graham, *Mecklenburg Declaration*, 26–30 and McNitt, *Chain or Error*, 75. The writer Washington Irving also believed in the Mecklenburg Declaration of Independence. In his life of Washington he writes, "Above all, it should never be forgotten, that at Mecklenburg, in the heart of North Carolina, was fulminated the first declaration of independence of the British crown, upwards of a year before a like declaration by congress" (Washington Irving, *The Life and Times of Washington* (New York: Putnam and Sons, 1876), 524).

9. In McNitt, *Chain of Error,* 74. In August 1819, William Polk sent Judge Archibald D. Murphey a copy of the narrative and resolutions that had been published in the *Raleigh Register.* Murphy was compiling documents for a history he was writing on the state. In a cover note, Polk wrote to Murphey, "I cannot vouch for their being in the words of the Committee who framed them, but they are essentially so." Murphey had them published in the *Hillsboro Recorder* of March, 1821 (copy no longer exists), which McNitt concludes is the origin of the "Martin" and "Garden" versions of the text (75).

10. "An Important Historical Document," *Charlotte Democrat*, December 25, 1891, p. 2; see also the *Southern Home*, July 5, 1875.

11. Dr. Joseph Alexander, Unpublished Manuscript, SHC (emphasis added).

12. Garden, *Anecdotes,* 9 (emphasis added).

13. Maier, *American Scripture*, 173–174. Of course, whether the Mecklenburg Resolves are "believable" or not is quite beside the point; they demonstrably exist.

14. Leigh Dyer, "Mec Dec Finds Famous Backer: Historian McCullough Declares He's a Believer," *Charlotte Observer*, May 17, 2007, p. 1B. In the interests of full disclosure, McCullough was the guest of the May 20th Society, a nonprofit organization based in Charlotte, when he made the above remarks. Andrew and Cokie Roberts were as well.

15. George Will, "America's Self-Validating Tradition," *Charlotte Observer*, July 3, 2008.

16. Speech in Charlotte, May 19, 2010. Video courtesy of the May 20th Society.

17. Speech by Andrew Roberts given in Charlotte, May 19, 2011. See www.may20thsociety.org/events/past-mecdec-events/?q=841. Roberts based his conclusion on the fact that many of the Mecklenburgers were Scots-Irish: "You can take it from an Englishman that there are no worse trouble makers in history than the Scots-Irish.... Indeed half of the reason for setting up the British Empire in the first place was to give the Scots-Irish something to do very far away."

18. "Statue Salutes 'Meck Dec,' Its Mystery," *Charlotte Observer*, May 16, 2010.

19. Morrill, *Historic Charlotte*, online edition, chapter 2.

20. In the interests of full disclosure this author was involved as an advisor to both the Matheson Street mural and the Charlotte Liberty Walk projects.

Bibliography

Abbatt, William, ed. "The Mecklenburg Declaration of Independence May 20, 1775." *Magazine of History with Notes and Queries* 3 (1905), 291–321.

_____. "New Light on the Mecklenburg Declaration of Independence." *Magazine of History with Notes and Queries* 4 (1906), 230–237.

Adams, John. *The Works of John Adams.* Vol. 10. Boston: Little Brown, 1856.

Alexander, J.B. *The History of Mecklenburg County from 1740 to 1900.* Charlotte: Observer Printing House, 1902.

Alexander, Julia McGehee. *Charlotte in Picture and Prose.* New York: Blanchard Press, 1906.

Allen, William Cicero. *North Carolina History Stories.* Book 3. Richmond: B.F. Johnson, 1901.

_____. *The Story of Our State, North Carolina.* Raleigh: Dixie Press, 1942.

Armstrong, Maurice Whitman. *The Presbyterian Enterprise: Sources of American Presbyterian History.* Philadelphia: Westminster Press, 1956.

Arnett, Alex Mathews. *The Story of North Carolina.* Chapel Hill: University of North Carolina Press, 1933.

Arthur, John Preston. *Western North Carolina: A History (From 1730–1913).* Asheville: Edward Buncombe Chapter of the Daughters of the American Revolution, 1914.

Ashe, Samuel A'Court. *History of North Carolina from 1584 to 1783.* Vol. 1. Greensboro: Van Noppen, 1908.

Ashe, Samuel A., Stephen B. Weeks, Charles L. Van Noppen, eds. *Biographical History of North Carolina from Colonial Times to the Present.* Vol. 7. Greensboro: Charles L. Van Noppen, 1908.

Balch, Thomas Willing. *Balch Genealogica.* Philadelphia: Allen, Lane and Scott, 1907.

Baldwin, Alice M. *The New England Clergy and the American Revolution.* New York: F. Ungar, 1958.

_____. "Sowers of Sedition: The Political Theories of Some of the New Light Presbyterian Clergy of Virginia and North Carolina." *William and Mary Quarterly* 5, no. 1. 3rd series (1948): 52–76.

Barefoot, Daniel. *Touring North Carolina's Revolutionary War Sites.* Winston-Salem, NC: John F. Blair, 1998.

Battle, Richard H. "Memoir of Rev. Charles Phillips, DD, LLD." *North Carolina University Magazine* 10, no. 1 (June 20, 1891).

Blackstone, Sir William. *Commentaries on the Laws of England in Four Books.* Philadelphia: Geo. T. Bisel, 1922.

Blethen, H. Tyler, and Curtis W. Wood, Jr. *From Ulster to Carolina: The Migration of the Scotch-Irish to Southwestern North Carolina.* Raleigh: North Carolina Division of Archives and History, 2005.

Blythe, LeGette, and Charles R. Brockman. *Hornets' Nest: The Story of Charlotte and Mecklenburg County.* Charlotte: McNally, 1961.

Bolton, Charles Knowles. *Scotch Irish Pioneers in Ulster and America.* Boston: Bacon & Brown, 1910.

Borden, Pat. "Marker's Removal Heralds New Mall." *Charlotte News,* December 30, 1983.

Boyte, Jack Orr. *Houses of Charlotte and Mecklenburg County.* Charlotte: N.p., 1992.

Bradley Chapin, "Colonial and Revolutionary Origins of the American Law of Treason." *William and Mary Quarterly* 17, no. 1. 3rd series (1960): 4–21.

Bright, John M., Hon. "Oration Delivered at the Centennial Celebration of the Mecklenburg Declaration of Independence, at Charlotte, N.C., May 20, 1875, by Hon. John M. Bright of Tennessee." Nashville: Oration, 1875.

Burnett, Edmund Cody. *Letters of Members of the Continental Congress.* Vol. 10. Washington: Carnegie Institution, 1921.

Camp, Cordelia. *The Influence of Geography Upon Early North Carolina.* Raleigh: Carolina Charter Tercentenary Commission Box 1881, 1963.

Cappon, Lester J., ed. *The Adams-Jefferson Letters: The Complete Correspondence Between Thomas Jefferson and Abigail and John Adams.* Chapel Hill: University of North Carolina Press, 1988.

Caruthers, Eli Washington. *A Sketch of the Life and Character of the Rev. David Caldwell, D.D.* Greensboro, NC: Swaim and Sherwood, 1842.

Clark, J.C.D. *The Language of Liberty, 1660–1832.* Cambridge: Cambridge University Press, 1994.

Connor, R.D.W. *History of North Carolina.* Vol. 1. Chicago: Lewis, 1919.

Craighead, Alexander. *Reasons of Receding from Present*

Judicatures and Constitution. Philadelphia: B. Franklin, n.d.

_____. *Renewal of the Covenants.* Globe, 1748.

Craighead, James Geddes. *The Craighead Family: A Genealogical Memoir of the Descendants of Rev. Thomas and Margaret Craighead, 1658–1876.* Philadelphia: Sherman, 1876.

Davidson, Chalmers G. "Celebrating May 20 for 200 Years." *State* (April 1975).

Davidson, Chalmers. "'Yes' Forces Believe References Back Claim." *Mecklenburg Neighbors,* May 18, 1988.

Draper, Lyman C., and Craig L. Heath, eds. *The Mecklenburg Declaration: Its Origin, History and Actors with a Bibliography of Its Literature, and Explanatory Documents.* Westminster, MD: Heritage Books, 2004.

Drymon, M.M. *Scotch-Irish Foodways in America.* N.p.: Wythe Avenue Press, 2009.

Ellis, Joseph J. *Passionate Sage.* New York: W.W. Norton, 2001.

Foote, William Henry. *Sketches of North Carolina.* New York: Robert Carter, 1846.

Ford, Henry Jones. *The Scotch-Irish in America.* Princeton University Press, 1915.

Fries, Adelaide L. *The Mecklenburg Declaration of Independence as Mentioned in Records of Wachovia (1907).* Raleigh: Edwards & Broughton, 1907.

Fryar, Jack E., Jr., ed. *Benson J. Lossing's Pictorial Field-Book of the Revolution in the Carolinas and Georgia.* Wilmington: Dram Tree Books, 2005.

Gallay, Alan, ed. *Voices of the Old South: Eyewitness Accounts, 1528–1861.* Athens: University of Georgia Press, 1994.

Garden, Alexander. *Anecdotes of the American Revolution.* Charleston: A.E. Miller, 1828.

Graham, George W., MD. *The Mecklenburg Declaration of Independence, May 20, 1775, and Lives of Its Signers.* New York: Neale, 1905.

Graham, George W., MD, and Alexander Graham, AM. *Why North Carolinians Believe in the Mecklenburg Declaration of Independence of May 20th, 1775.* 2nd ed. Charlotte: Queen City, 1895.

Graham, William Alexander. *General Joseph Graham and His Papers on North Carolina Revolutionary History: With Appendix, an epitome of North Carolina's Military Services in the Revolutionary War and of the Laws Enacted for Raising Troops.* Raleigh: Edwards & Broughton, 1904.

Great Britain Royal Commission on Historical Manuscripts. *Report of the Royal Commission on Historical Manuscripts.* H.M. Stationery Office, 1897.

Grigsby, Hugh Blair, and J.W. Randolph, eds. "The Virginia Convention of 1776: A Disclosure Delivered Before the Virginia Alpha of the Phi Beta Kappa Society, in the Chapel of William and Mary College, in the City of Williamsburg, on the Afternoon of July 3rd, 1855 by Hugh Blair Grigsby." Richmond: J.W. Randolph, 1855.

Grimes, J. Bryan. *The History of the Great Seal of the State of North Carolina.* Raleigh: Department of Archives, 1966.

Haag, Richard. "Celebrations Ranged from Bands to Brawls." *Mecklenburg Neighbor,* May 18, 1988.

Hamilton, J.G. De Roulhac, and Henry McGilbert Wagstaff. *The North Carolina Constitution of 1776 and Its Makers: The German Settlers in Lincoln County and Western North Carolina.* Chapel Hill: University of North Carolina Press, 1912.

Hanna, Charles Augustus. *The Scotch-Irish; or, The Scot in North Britain, North Ireland, and North America.* New York: G.P. Putnam's Sons, 1902.

Henderson, Archibald. *Cradle of Liberty: Historical Essays Concerning the Mecklenburg Declaration of Independence.* Mecklenburg Historical Association, 1955.

_____. "The Significance of the Transylvania Company in American History." Delivered at the Transylvania Memorial Celebration, Boonesborough, Ky., Oct. 12, 1935.

_____. *Washington's Southern Tour, 1791.* Boston: Houghton Mifflin, 1923.

Hodge, Charles. *The Constitutional History of the Presbyterian Church in the United States of America.* Philadelphia: W.S. Martien, 1839.

Horne, Robert. "A Brief Description of the Province of Carolina (1666)." In A.S. Salley, Jr., *Narratives of Early Carolina, 1650–1708.* New York: Charles Scribner's Sons, 1911.

Howie, John. *Faithful Contendings Displayed.* John Bryce, 1780.

Hoyt, William Henry, AM. *The Mecklenburg Declaration of Independence: A Study of Evidence Showing That the Alleged Early Declaration of Independence by Mecklenburg County, North Carolina, on May 20th, 1775, Is Spurious.* New York: G.P. Putnam's Sons, 1907.

Hunter, C.L. *Sketches of Western North Carolina.* Raleigh: Raleigh News Stream, 1877.

Hurt, Melissa Dearing Jack. *Alabama Bound: Family Sketches of a Long Line of Storytellers, the Jacks, Morgans, Wymans, Boyntons, Martins, Hunters and Dearings.* Lakemont, GA: Copple House Books, 1988.

Jefferson, Thomas. *The Works of Thomas Jefferson.* Vol. 11. New York: Cosimo, 2009.

_____. *The Writings of Thomas Jefferson.* Vol. 4. Charlottesville: F. Carr, 1829.

Jones, H.G. *North Carolina Illustrated, 1524–1984.* Chapel Hill: University of North Carolina Press, 1983.

Jones, Joseph Seawell. *A Defense of the Revolutionary History of the State of North Carolina from the Aspersions of Mr. Jefferson.* Boston: Charles Bowen, 1834.

Kars, Marjoleine. *Breaking Loose Together: The Regulator Rebellion in Pre-Revolutionary North Carolina.* Chapel Hill: University of North Carolina Press, 2002.

Kerr, James, et al. *The Covenants and the Covenanters: Covenants, Sermons, and Documents of the Covenanted Reformation.* Middlesex, UK: Echo Library, 2008.

Kratt, Mary Norton. *Charlotte: Spirit of the New South.* Winston-Salem, NC: John F. Blair, 1992.

Lamb, Martha J., ed. "Mecklenburg Declaration of Independence May 20, 1775." *Magazine of American History with Notes and Queries* 12 (1889), 31–45.

Landrum, John. *Colonial and Revolutionary History of Upper South Carolina.* Greenville, SC: Shannon, 1897.

Lawson, John, and Hugh Talmage Lefler, eds. *A New Voyage to Carolina.* Chapel Hill: University of North Carolina Press, 1967.

Maier, Pauline. *American Scripture: Making the Declaration of Independence.* New York: Vintage, 1998.

Martin, Francois-Xavier. *The History of North Carolina from the Earliest Period.* Vol. 2. New Orleans: A.T. Penniman, 1829.

McClintock, John, and James Strong. *Cyclopaedia of Biblical, Theological, and Ecclesiastical Literature.* Harper, 1894.

McCulloh, Henry Eustace. *Letter from Henry Eustace McCulloh to Edmund Fanning.* Vol. 7. *Colonial and State Records of North Carolina.* 1765.

McCullough, David. *John Adams.* New York: Simon & Schuster, 2001.

McCullough, Gary L. *The Hezekiah Alexander Homesite and Related History of Charlotte and Mecklenburg County.* 2003.

McGeachy, Neill Roderick. *A History of the Sugaw Creek Presbyterian Church.* Rock Hill, SC: Record Printing Co., 1954.

McNitt, V.V. *Chain of Error and the Mecklenburg Declaration of Independence.* Palmer, MA: Hampden Hills Press, 1960.

Mecklenburg County, North Carolina, Court Minutes Docket Book 1, 1774–1780. Greenville, SC. Southern Historical Press, 1996.

Merrell, James H. *The Indians' New World: Catawbas and Their Neighbors from European Contact Through the Era of Removal.* New York: W.W. Norton, 1989.

Meyer, Duane. *The Highland Scots of North Carolina, 1732–1776.* Chapel Hill: University of North Carolina Press, 1961.

Milks, Diane, Yon Lambert and Louise Pettus. *The Catawba River Companion.* Spartanburg, SC: Palmetto Conservation Foundation Press, 2003.

Miller, S. Millington, MD. "The True Cradle of American Liberty; Independence Bell Rang a Year Earlier in Charlotte than in Philadelphia." *Collier's National Weekly,* July 1, 1905.

Moore, James Hall. *Defense of the Mecklenburg Declaration of Independence: An Exhaustive Review of and Answer to All Attacks on the Declaration.* Raleigh: Edwards Broughton, 1908.

Morrill, Dan L. *Historic Charlotte: An Illustrated History of Charlotte and Mecklenburg County.* San Antonio: Historical Publishing Network, 2009.

Nevin, Alfred. *Men of Mark of Cumberland Valley, Pa., 1776–1876.* Fulton, 1876.

Peterson, Merrill. *The Jefferson Image in the American Mind.* Charlottesville: University of Virginia Press, 1998.

Polk, William Mecklenburg. *Leonidas Polk: Bishop and General.* New York: Longmans, Green, 1893.

Powell, William S., ed. *Dictionary of North Carolina Biography.* Chapel Hill: University of North Carolina Press, 1996.

Powell, William S. *North Carolina: A History.* Chapel Hill: University of North Carolina Press, 1977.

Presbyterian Church in the United States. *Records of the Presbyterian Church in the United States of America: Embracing the Minutes of the Presbytery of Philadelphia, 1706 to 1716; the Synod, 1717 to 1758; the Synod of New York, 1745 to 1758; the Synod of Philadelphia and New York, 1758 to 1788.* 1841.

Preyer, Norris W. *Hezekiah Alexander and the Revolution in the Backcountry.* Charlotte: Heritage, 1987.

Publications of the North Carolina Historical Commission. *Records of the Moravians in North Carolina (1752–1775).* Vol. 2. Raleigh: Edwards & Broughton, 1925.

Ragosta, John A. *Wellspring of Liberty.* Oxford University Press, 2010.

Ramsay, David. *The History of the American Revolution.* 2 vols. Indianapolis: Liberty Fund, 1990.

Ramsey, Dr. J.G.M., and William B. Hesseltine, eds. *Dr. J.G.M. Ramsey Autobiography and Letters.* Knoxville: University of Tennessee Press, 2002.

Ray, Lila McGeachy. "Alexander Craighead: With Drawn Sword." Master's thesis, Pittsburgh Theological Seminary, 2001.

Ray, Worth S. *The Mecklenburg Signers and Their Neighbors.* Austin: Worth S. Ray, 1946.

Romine, Dannye. *Mecklenburg: A Bicentennial Story.* Charlotte: Independence Square, 1975.

Rouse, Parke, Jr. *The Great Wagon Road.* Richmond: Dietz Press, 2004.

Salley, A.S., Jr. "The Mecklenburg Declaration: The Present Status of the Question." *American Historical Review* 13, no. 1 (1908): 16–43.

Salley, A.S., Jr., and Worthington Ford. "S. Millington Miller and the Mecklenburg Declaration." *American Historical Review* 11, no. 3 (1906).

Schaper, William. *Sectionalism and Representation in South Carolina.* Washington, DC: Government Printing Office, 1901.

Scotch-Irish Society of America. *The Scotch-Irish in America: Proceedings and Addresses of the Seventh Congress at Lexington, VA., June 20–23, 1895.* Nashville: Barbee & Smith, 1895.

Sedgwick, Obadiah. *The Bowels of Tender Mercy Sealed in the Everlasting Covenant.* 1661.

Shields, E. Thomson, Jr. "'A Modern Poem,' by the Mecklenburg Censor Politics and Satire in Revolutionary North Carolina." *Early American Literature* 29, no. 3 (1994): 205–232.

Smylie, James Hutchinson. *A Brief History of the Presbyterians.* Louisville, KY: Geneva Press, 1996.

Smyth, Thomas Rev., DD. *The True Origin and Source of the Mecklenburg and National Declaration of Independence.* Columbia, SC: I.C. Morgan, 1847.

Southern, Ed, ed. *Voices of the American Revolution in the Carolinas.* Winston-Salem: John F. Blair, 2009.

Sproull, John W., Thomas Sproull, David Burt Willson, and James McLeod Willson. *The Reformed Presbyterian and Covenanter.* Myers, Shinkle, 1888.

Stumpf, Vernon O. *Josiah Martin: The Last Royal Governor of North Carolina.* Durham, NC: Carolina Academic Press, 1986.

Swope, Gilbert Ernest. *History of the Big Spring Presbyterian Church, Newville, Pa., 1737–1898.* Newville, PA: Times Stream, 1898.

Tarleton, Lieut. Col. Banastre. *A History of the Campaigns of 1780 and 1781 in the Southern Provinces of North America*. North Stratford, NH: Ayer, 2007.

Tompkins, D.A. *History of Mecklenburg County and the City of Charlotte*. Vol. 1. Charlotte: Observer Printing House, 1903.

Tucker, George. *The Life of Thomas Jefferson, Third President of the United States*. Part Two. London, 1837.

United States Continental Congress, *Journals of the American Congress*. Vol. 1. Washington, DC: Way and Gideon, 1823.

Van Noppen, Charles Leonard. *The Mecklenburg Declaration of Independence Written in 1800*. Booked Ventures, 2010 (reprint). First published by Brown-Morrison, 1912.

Virginia Magazine of History and Biography. Book Reviews. July 1896.

Waddell, Joseph Addison. *Annals of Augusta County, Virginia: With Reminiscences Illustrative of the Vicissitudes of Its Pioneer Settlers; Biographical Sketches of Citizens Locally Prominent, and of Those Who Have Founded Families in the Southern and Western States; a Diary of the War, 1861-'5, and a Chapter on Reconstruction*. Richmond: Wm. Ellis Jones, 1886.

Walpole, Horace. *The Letters of Horace Walpole*. Vol. 9. Oxford: Clarendon Press, 1904.

Ward, Joseph P. *Britain and the American South: From Colonialism to Rock and Roll*. Jackson: University Press of Mississippi, 2009.

Washington, George. *The Diary of George Washington, from 1789 to 1791*. New York: Charles Richardson, 1860.

Weeks, Stephen Beauregard. *Truth and Justice for the History of North Carolina: The Mecklenburg Resolves of May 31, 1775 vs. "The Mecklenburg Declaration of May 20, 1775."* Greensboro: Charles L. Van Noppen, 1908.

Welling, James. "The Mecklenburg Declaration." *Magazine of American History with Notes and Queries* 21 (1889).

_____. "The Mecklenburg Declaration of Independence, May 20, 1775." *North American Review* (1874).

Wheeler, John Hill. *Historical Sketches of North Carolina*. Vol. 1. Elibron Classics, 2007.

_____. *Reminiscences and Memoirs of North Carolina and Eminent North Carolinians*. Washington: Henkle, 1885.

White, Henry Alexander. *Southern Presbyterian Leaders*. New York: Neale, 1911.

Williams, James. "The Sugar Creek War." Unpublished manuscript. Courtesy of the Mecklenburg Historical Association, Mecklenburg, North Carolina.

Wilson, Samuel. "An Account of the Province of Carolina." In A.S, Salley, *Narratives of Early Carolina*. New York: Charles Scribner's Sons, 1911.

Winsor, Justin, ed. *Harvard University Bulletin* 7, no. 4 (October, 1893).

Wirt, William. *Sketches of the Life and Character of Patrick Henry*. Philadelphia: James Webster, 1817.

Woodmason, Charles. *The Carolina Backcountry on the Eve of the Revolution: The Journal and Other Writings of Charles Woodmason, Anglican Itinerant*. Edited by Richard J. Hooker. Chapel Hill: University of North Carolina Press, 1953.

Index

Numbers in *bold italics* indicate pages with photographs.

241